PRISON JOURNAL

GEORGE CARDINAL PELL

PRISON JOURNAL

Volume 1

The Cardinal Makes His Appeal

27 February–13 July 2019

With an introduction by George Weigel

IGNATIUS PRESS   SAN FRANCISCO

Quotations from George Cardinal Pell's breviary are from *The Divine Office*, 3 volumes (Sydney: EJ Dwyer, 1974).

Cover photograph courtesy of George Cardinal Pell

Cover design byRoxanne Mei Lum

© 2020 by Ignatius Press, San Francisco
All rights reserved
ISBN 978-1-62164-448-4 (PB)
ISBN 978-1-64229-142-1 (eBook)
Library of Congress Control Number 2020945860
Printed in the United States of America ∞

CONTENTS

Introduction by George Weigel 7

Chronology 13

Week 1: Remanded in Custody 15

Week 2: Ash Wednesday in Solitary 24

Week 3: Sentencing 40

Week 4: Sublime Company 58

Week 5: Spiritual Mediocrity 77

Week 6: Eroding Social Capital 94

Week 7: Perfection through Suffering 110

Week 8: Holy Week 126

Week 9: Easter Week 143

Week 10: Divine Mercy 160

Week 11: Hostile Operations 178

Week 12: Questions without Answers 196

Week 13: Daughter of Time 215

Week 14: Looking Ahead 232

Week 15: Appealing the Conviction 249

Week 16: Descent of the Holy Spirit 266

Week 17: Mystery of the Trinity 285

Week 18: Real Presence 303

Week 19: Web of Deceit 320

Week 20: Hopes and Dreams 334

INTRODUCTION

by George Weigel

This prison journal should never have been written.

That it was written is a testament to the capacity of God's grace to inspire insight, magnanimity, and goodness amidst wickedness, evil, and injustice. That it was written so beautifully bears witness to the Christian character that divine grace formed in its author, George Cardinal Pell.

How and why the author found himself in prison for over thirteen months for crimes he did not commit, and indeed could not have committed, is another story, far less edifying. A brief telling of this tawdry tale will, however, set the necessary context for what you are about to read, even as it underscores just how remarkable this journal is.

On April 7, 2020, the High Court of Australia issued a unanimous decision that quashed a guilty verdict and entered a verdict of "acquitted" in the case of *Pell vs. The Queen*. That decision reversed both the incomprehensible trial conviction of Cardinal Pell on a charge of "historic sexual abuse" and the equally baffling decision to uphold that false verdict by two of the three members of an appellate court in the state of Victoria in August 2019. The High Court's decision freed an innocent man from the unjust imprisonment to which he had been subjected, restored him to his family and friends, and enabled him to resume his important work in and for the Catholic Church.

Close students of *Pell vs. The Queen* knew that the case ought never have been brought to trial. The police investigation leading to allegations against the cardinal was a sleazy trolling expedition. The magistrate at the committal hearing (the equivalent of a grand

---

The original version of this essay, "Justice, Finally", appeared in *Catholic World Report*, 6 April 2020.

jury proceeding) was under intense pressure to bring to trial a set of charges she knew were very weak. When the case was tried, the Crown prosecutors produced no evidence that the alleged crime had ever been committed, basing their argument solely on the testimony of the complainant—testimony that was inconsistent over time and that was shown to have been deeply flawed. There was no corroborating physical evidence, and there were no witnesses to corroborate the charges.

To the contrary. Those directly involved in Melbourne's cathedral at the time of the alleged offenses, two decades earlier, insisted under oath and during cross-examination that it was impossible for events to have unfolded as the complainant alleged: neither the time frame used by the prosecution to describe the alleged abuse nor the complainant's description of the layout of the cathedral sacristy (where the crimes were said to have been committed) made sense. This extensive testimony in the cardinal's defense was never seriously dented by the prosecution. Moreover, the sheer impossibility that what was alleged to have happened actually happened was subsequently confirmed by objective observers and commentators, including those who had previously held no brief for Cardinal Pell (and one who was a severe critic).

Pell vs. The Queen was also prosecuted in a way that raised grave doubts about the commitment of the Victoria authorities to such elementary tenets of Anglosphere criminal law as the presumption of innocence and the duty of the state to prove its case "beyond a reasonable doubt". In this regard, Justice Mark Weinberg, the dissenting judge in the August 2019 appellate decision, made a crucial jurisprudential point while eviscerating his colleagues' rationale for upholding Cardinal Pell's conviction: by making the complainant's credibility the crux of the matter, both the prosecution and Weinberg's colleagues on the appellate panel rendered it impossible for *any* defense to be mounted. Under this credibility criterion, no evidence of an actual crime was required, nor was any corroboration of the allegations; what counted was that the complainant seemed sincere. But this was not serious judicial reasoning according to centuries of the common law tradition. It was an exercise in sentiment, even sentimentality, and it had no business being the decisive factor in convicting a man of a vile crime and depriving him of his reputation and his freedom.

As Justice Weinberg's extraordinary, over two-hundred-page dissent was digested by jurists and veteran legal practitioners in Australia, and as the post-appeal lifting of a press blackout on coverage of the Pell trial exposed the thinness of the prosecution's case, a rising tide of concern among thoughtful people, convinced that a grave injustice had been done, could be felt—even at a distance of thousands of miles from Melbourne. That concern may have been reflected in the decision by the High Court, Australia's supreme judicial body, to accept a further appeal (which need not have been granted).

Similar concerns were evident from the bench in the sharp grilling of the Crown's chief prosecutor when the High Court heard the cardinal's appeal in March 2020. That two-day exercise made it plain, again, that the Crown had no case that would meet the standard of guilt beyond a reasonable doubt; that the jury in the cardinal's second trial (held because of a hung jury at his first trial) returned an unsafe and, indeed, insupportable verdict; and that the two judges of the Victoria Supreme Court who upheld that conviction (one of whom had no criminal law experience whatsoever) made grave errors of the sort that their colleague, Justice Weinberg, identified in his dissent.

The High Court's decision to acquit Cardinal Pell and free him was thus both just and welcome. The question of how any of this could have happened to one of Australia's most distinguished citizens remains to be examined.

The vicious public atmosphere surrounding Cardinal Pell, especially in his native state of Victoria, was analogous to the poisonous atmosphere that surrounded the Dreyfus Affair in late-nineteenth-century France. In 1894, raw politics and ancient score-settling, corrupt officials, a rabid media, and gross religious prejudice combined to convict an innocent French army officer of Jewish heritage, Captain Alfred Dreyfus, of treason; Dreyfus was cashiered from the army and condemned to imprisonment in the fetid hell of Devil's Island, off the coast of French Guiana. The Melbourne Assessment Prison and Her Majesty's Prison Barwon, the two facilities in which George Pell was incarcerated, are not Devil's Island, to be sure. But many of the same factors that led to the false conviction of Alfred Dreyfus were at play in the putrid public atmosphere of Victoria during a Pell witch-hunt that extended over several years.

The Victoria police, already under scrutiny for incompetence and corruption, conducted a fishing expedition that sought "evidence" for crimes that no one had previously alleged to have been committed; and, by some accounts, the police saw the persecution of George Pell as a useful way to deflect attention from their own problems. With a few honorable exceptions, the local and national press, abandoning all pretense to journalistic integrity and fair-mindedness, bayed for Cardinal Pell's blood. Someone paid for the professionally printed anti-Pell placards carried by the mob that surrounded the courthouse where the trials were conducted. And the Australian Broadcasting Corporation—a taxpayer-funded public institution—engaged in the crudest anti-Catholic propaganda and broadcast a stream of defamations of Cardinal Pell's character (one of which was aired during the deliberations of the High Court).

To imagine that an unbiased jury could have been empaneled in these fevered circumstances is to imagine a great deal—and perhaps to imagine the impossible. Yet the law in Victoria did not allow the cardinal to request a bench trial by a judge alone. So what might have been imagined to be a sober legal proceeding came to bear the hallmarks of a slow-motion political assassination by judicial means.

It does not strain credulity to imagine that that was, all along, the intention of some of those involved in the persecution of George Pell.

Throughout his ordeal, Cardinal Pell was a model of patience and, indeed, a model of priestly character, as this journal attests. Knowing that he was innocent, he was a free man even when incarcerated. And he put that time to good use—"an extended retreat", as he called it—cheering his many friends throughout the world and intensifying an already-vigorous life of prayer, study, and writing. Now that he is able to celebrate the Mass again—a form of worship he was denied for over four hundred days—I have no doubt that the cardinal is including among his intentions the conversion of his persecutors and the renewal of justice in the country he loves.

As a citizen of Vatican City, Cardinal Pell had no legal obligation to abandon his work in Rome to return to Australia for trial. The thought of relying on his diplomatic immunity never occurred to him, though. He was determined to defend his honor and that of the Australian Church, which he had led in addressing the crimes and sins of sexual abuse (and in many other ways) for years. George Pell placed his bet on the essential fairness of his countrymen.

The High Court vindicated that wager, at the last possible moment.

The Pell prison journal demonstrates that the High Court's decision freed a man who could not be broken: a man whose vibrant Christian faith sustained him under extraordinary pressures. During his doctoral studies at Oxford in the late 1960s, young Fr George Pell had ample opportunity to ponder the faithful witness of Thomas More and John Fisher under grave pressure. He could not have known then that he, too, would suffer calumny, public vilification, and unjust imprisonment. But, like More and Fisher, George Cardinal Pell took his stand on the truth, confident that the truth is liberating in the deepest meaning of human freedom.

The journal you are about to read illustrates that liberation in a luminous way.

George Weigel is Distinguished Senior Fellow of Washington's Ethics and Public Policy Center, where he holds the William E. Simon Chair in Catholic Studies. His twenty-seventh book, The Next Pope: The Office of Peter and a Church in Mission, *was published in July 2020 by Ignatius Press. He and Cardinal Pell have been friends since 1967.*

CHRONOLOGY

16 July 1996	Pope John Paul II names Auxiliary Bishop George Pell the archbishop of Melbourne, Australia.
26 March 2001	George Pell becomes the archbishop of Sydney, Australia.
21 October 2003	Pope John Paul II makes Archbishop Pell a cardinal.
25 February 2014	Pope Francis appoints Cardinal Pell to the newly created position of prefect of the Secretariat for the Economy, which manages the finances of the Holy See and the Vatican.
29 June 2017	Australian police charge Cardinal Pell with multiple historical sexual assault offenses.
5 March 2018	Having denied the charges and voluntarily returned to Australia, Cardinal Pell appears in Melbourne Magistrates' Court for the filing of the charges against him.
1 May 2018	After dismissing several of the charges, a Melbourne magistrate rules that the cardinal will stand trial for the others.
2 May 2018	Cases are divided into two trials: the first will concern charges dating to when Pell was the archbishop of Melbourne in the 1990s; the second will deal with charges dating to when he was a young priest in the 1970s.
20 September 2018	First trial, which began 15 August 2018, ends in a hung jury.
11 December 2018	Retrial, which began 7 November 2018, ends in a guilty verdict.

26 February 2019	Prosecutors drop the second set of charges dating to the 1970s.
27 February 2019	Cardinal Pell is remanded in custody and taken to prison.
13 March 2019	Cardinal Pell is sentenced to six years in prison.
5–6 June 2019	Appeal is made to the Supreme Court of Victoria.
21 August 2019	Appeal is rejected 2-1.
10–11 March 2020	Appeal is made to the High Court of Australia.
7 April 2020	High Court overturns all convictions by 7-0 decision, and Cardinal Pell is released from prison.

WEEK 1

Remanded in Custody

27 February–2 March 2019

Wednesday, 27 February 2019[1]

While I have slept well for the last months, it took me longer to get to sleep last night, and I woke before the 6:00 am alarm. Mass as usual in the McFarlanes' dining room, graced with images of the Duke of Wellington, W. G. Grace,[2] and Victor Trumper,[3] who had probably never attended daily Mass before.

I chose the votive Mass of Our Lady as during the long travail I had placed myself under her protection. It is taking longer than I hoped, but I still feel protected. After everything, all the other spurious charges have been scuttled.[4]

---

[1] This entry was written on Cardinal Pell's first day in jail, after he was remanded in custody ahead of sentencing, following his conviction on 11 December 2018. The outcome of the trial and its proceedings were the subject of a suppression order by the court, because of plans for a further trial of a separate set of charges related to Cardinal Pell's time in Ballarat. These charges were withdrawn by the prosecution for lack of admissible evidence on 26 February 2019, and the suppression order was then lifted.

[2] William Gilbert Grace (1848–1915), great English cricketer during the reign of Queen Victoria.

[3] Victor Trumper (1877–1914), great Australian cricketer in the late nineteenth and early twentieth centuries.

[4] A reference to the prosecutor's decision on 26 February 2019 to withdraw the swimming pool charges that were to form the basis of a second trial and to the other charges withdrawn before and during the committal hearing in March 2018 and dismissed by the magistrate at the conclusion of the committal on 1 May.

Joseph and Susan Santamaria,[5] with daughter Helen just back from London, attended to show support.

Chris Meney[6] came down last night, and after Mass and breakfast, Tim [McFarlane][7] drove us both to the court. Very hostile crowd, especially one poor man, middle-aged, whose face was contorted with rage. I wonder what the Church did to him. However most of the crowd were media.

Waiting beforehand, I recognized Paul [Galbally][8] had bad news, and so he then announced they did not think it would be useful to seek bail in the Court of Appeal this afternoon. I waited for the views of [Robert] Richter[9] and Ruth [Shann],[10] then consented. I would be in jail in the afternoon.

A good deal of the sentence discussion was surreal and Kafkaesque, as the judge listed the many reasons why the attack was implausible and then tried to conjecture my motivation! According to Ruth, even the prosecutor—and we know of the judge's views, too— believed me innocent.

Remanded into custody, I was strip-searched by two Filipino guards, both respectful. One told me he had sat in court for the case and knew I was innocent, while three members of the protection service who had looked after us during the trials wished me well and said they were pleased to know me. Apparently even David Marr[11] conceded to Denis Shanahan[12] and Richter that he did not believe me guilty on this one! I almost forgot to bow to the judge on leaving the court.

Handcuffed for the drive to the assessment centre. On arrival, I went through a series of registrations and a thorough medical quizzing. All courteous, but a series of delays behind locked doors.

---

[5] Joseph and Susan Santamaria. The Hon Joseph Santamaria is Queen's Counsel and a former judge of appeal in the Supreme Court of Victoria. In a Commonwealth country, a Queen's (or King's) Counsel is a lawyer who has been appointed by the British Crown to be "Her (or His) Majesty's Counsel learned in the law".

[6] Chris Meney is the chancellor of the Archdiocese of Sydney, a friend and cousin.

[7] Tim and Anne McFarlane are close personal friends of Cardinal Pell. Tim is a solicitor and mediator.

[8] Paul Galbally is a partner in the law firm of Galbally and O'Bryan and the principal solicitor for Cardinal Pell.

[9] Robert Richter is Queen's Counsel, a leading barrister in committal and trials.

[10] Ruth Shann is the junior barrister to Robert Richter and Bret Walker.

[11] David Marr is a journalist and the author of *The Prince: Faith, Abuse and George Pell*, a hostile biography of Cardinal Pell.

[12] Denis Shanahan is the political editor of *The Australian*.

As I was judged to be at some risk of self-harm, I was under regular observation during the night. Among the other prisoners, whom I will not see, all in their own cells, a woman wept occasionally (or so it seemed), while one or two others cried out with anguish and repetitive profanity. I only scored a couple of honourable mentions.

I was a bit exhausted and slept deeply until woken by the observer. I tried my usual rosary to get back to sleep, but only dozed.

In every way, it is a relief the day is over. I am now at the quiet heart of the storm, while family, friends, and wider Church have to cope with the tornado.

God our Father, give me strength to come through this, and may my suffering be united with your Son Jesus' redemption for the spread of the Kingdom, the healing of all the victims of this scourge of paedophilia, the faith and well-being of our Church, and especially for the wisdom and courage of the bishops, who have to lead us out of the dark shadows into the light of Christ.

Thursday, 28 February 2019

Spoke by phone to David, Judy, and Bec [Pell][13] on Wednesday night. David was very distressed, and I forgot to mention his birthday today.

My second day, my first full day, closed officially with the main 3:30 pm meal. Earlier than a retirement home.

Kartya [Gracer][14] and Paul [Galbally] called. The appeal is set down to be heard on June 11, but the plan is to approach the Court of Appeal for bail soon after the sentencing on Wednesday week (13 March). Three senior judges have been appointed, including [Mark] Weinberg,[15] who is likely to have a crucial role. The team well pleased with the three appointees.

Richter will move to one side, and Bret Walker[16] will lead. Robert believes we might get a good initial view of their estimate of the evidence at the request for bail, and even bail might be a possibility.

---

[13] David Pell is Cardinal Pell's brother; Judy is his wife; Rebecca and Georgie are their daughters.

[14] Kartya Gracer is a senior associate and solicitor assisting Paul Galbally.

[15] Justice Mark Weinberg is a judge of appeal, Supreme Court of Victoria.

[16] Bret Walker is senior counsel, the leading barrister in both appeals.

My watch was taken, so it is unusual to be guessing the time from the light through the glazed obscure windows and prison routine.

An improved estimate of my state of mind, which was good from the outset, meant I received a small electric kettle and a TV. I watched very little as my case still predominated.

From the first day I was allowed to keep my breviary and a pair of prison rosary beads was placed in my room, after my own beads were confiscated like most of my possessions.

Was introduced to the small grotty exercise yard. A major disappointment, approximately fifteen metres by ten metres with high walls and half the area exposed to the sky through overhead bars. It was no botanical garden.

Kartya was pleased, she explained when she and Paul called, with an article in *The Age* by a regular police columnist, John Sylvester,[17] who asked how an uncorroborated accusation accompanied by twenty contrary prosecution witnesses could even come to trial.

Paul shared my approval of Frank Brennan's *Australian* article[18] and was also disappointed with his *7.30 Report*[19] appearance. Others were more favourable, recognizing he was placing severe doubt on the conviction. Two such were Cait Tobin[20] and Greg Smith.[21]

The food is too plentiful, large volume with at least three veggies of different colours. Met the prison governor. A large man, impressive and straightforward. He explained that my safety was paramount, and Sr Mary O'Shannassy, the chaplain, explained that during his two-year term he had worked to make the institution more courteous.

The bed and toilet seat were very low, and no chair was provided in my cell. This was making the tendons on my left leg (especially) sore, so I asked for a higher chair. The governor explained that he did not want to be accused of giving me a more comfy chair, and I replied that it was only a higher one! Three plastic chairs were

[17] "Beyond Reasonable Doubt: Was Pell Convicted without Fear and Favour?", *Age*, 27 February 2019.

[18] "Father Frank Brennan on Cardinal George Pell Guilty Verdict: 'I Still Hope for Truth, Justice'", *Australian*, 28 February 2019.

[19] "Father Frank Brennan on the Conviction of George Pell", *7.30 Report*, Australian Broadcasting Corporation, 26 February 2019.

[20] Cait Tobin is a friend of Cardinal Pell's.

[21] The Hon Greg Smith is senior counsel and former attorney general for the State of New South Wales.

superimposed on one another, which was sufficient, and a raised toilet seat arrived also.

Sr Mary O'Shannassy, a Good Samaritan Sister, is a sister of Monica Mackie, a school principal I worked with in the Ballarat Diocese, and Jake O'Shannassy, who was ahead of me at St Patrick's [College], Ballarat, and a good footballer, perhaps centre halfback.

She remembered me celebrating the last Christmas Day Mass at Pentridge jail before it closed in 1996 and that I was late leaving because I was playing pool with the younger inmates. I told her how they couldn't believe I was so hopeless at the game.

God our Father, help all my loved ones to cope and find some peace during this time of my troubles. I thank you that my faith remains firm and that I have a good measure of peace; probably one tangible fruit of the torrents of prayers offered up for me.

Friday, 1 March 2019

My purchases came back from the canteen, but the cheap watches they sell were out of stock. I can check the TV for the time, but I still miss a watch.

Quieter today with fewer interviews as the daily routine commences. I was woken by the guards at the cell door at 6:30 am, as I slept well. A long window of bars and opaque glass or plastic, about eight feet by two, is next to the bed. No blinds or curtains, of course, so it is possible to follow the progress of night and day.

My clothes arrived, many of them useless for any jail purpose, as well as three books and a couple of *Spectators*. I returned my Jerusalem Bible, as Sr Mary had already provided a copy. I thought I was allowed six books and six magazines and hoped to receive Peter Brown's *Through the Eye of the Needle*, on money and the ancient Church, in lieu of the Bible. I was able to obtain a *Herald Sun* through the canteen and saw Richter was obliged to apologise for his reference to "[plain] vanilla sex", which I had not noticed.[22] Most of the

---

[22] "Pell's Lawyer Makes Apology", *The Herald Sun*, 1 March 2019. Richter used this phrase in court during the plea hearing on 27 February in arguing "that the offending was at the lower end of the scale for sex abuse cases".

letters to the editor queried or opposed the jury's verdict, and Paul and Kartya, who came together, remarked that there had been no similar debate on the legitimacy of a verdict in Australia since the Lindy Chamberlain case.[23]

Strange not celebrating Mass each day, although I have no pressure of other duties to distract me from my daily prayers. A Muslim must be imprisoned nearby, as I can hear him praying in the evening. Apparently some of the other prisoners in the protection units are coming off ice [crystal methamphetamine]. Certainly some have psychiatric problems.

Exercised a couple of times for a half hour in the heat of the afternoon, for the second one in a new exercise pen or space, a bit cleaner and brighter than the first one. After twenty-five minutes of walking with my stick, forward, backward, sideward, I am happy to take a rest.

During the second exercise period, the energetic head of Segs,[24] who had brought me here in handcuffs, came to explain that his section would search my cell each month and that he would be taking me to the sentencing. Pointing to the slight bruises on my left wrist, I asked if the handcuffs would be larger next time. Certainly, he replied, but the handcuffs would be attached to a belt and the van would be different! All this because I am in some special category. A correct man, but not brimming with sympathy.

Writing this in the evening, as I propose to do regularly. Starting to develop a routine, beginning with the Prayer of the Church,

---

[23] In 1982 Lindy Chamberlain was convicted of murdering her infant daughter Azaria on a family camping trip at Uluru in the Northern Territory in 1980. Her husband, Michael, was convicted of being an accessory to the murder. Azaria's body was never found. The case was attended by extraordinary levels of controversy and media attention, arising from the Chamberlains' claim that Azaria had been taken from their tent by a dingo [Australian wild dog]. Despite the evidence supporting this claim, the Chamberlains became the object of considerable public hostility, fuelled by, among other factors, public suspicion of their Seventh Day Adventist faith and their alleged lack of emotion in public appearances. Their appeal to the High Court of Australia in 1984, on the grounds that the jury's verdicts were unsafe and unreasonable in light of the evidence presented against them, was dismissed. In 1986 a further item of clothing Azaria was wearing at the time of her disappearance was discovered at Uluru. This new evidence led to a judicial inquiry, which resulted in the exoneration of Chamberlains and the quashing of their convictions in 1988.

[24] Segs refers to the prison's "segregation units", where twenty-three hours out of every twenty-four are spent in solitary confinement. These units are designated for especially dangerous prisoners or those at risk of harm from themselves or other prisoners.

followed by a meditation later in the morning. Moving through the Epistle to the Hebrews, a favourite of mine. Utterly Christocentric as Paul (or his follower or imitator) shows Christ embodies the promise of the Jewish scriptures.

My three plastic chairs have been replaced by a splendid higher health chair, as the hospital had recommended to me in the past.

Some confusion over visiting times. Not Saturday and Sunday, as on the lists, but Monday and Thursday. I have a slot on Monday 4 March at 1:00 pm for three people. Not sure David can make it.

It has been interesting to have a number of people, from Ruth to prison staff, explaining to me that my faith would be a great help at this time. My first instinct was to respond tartly that I knew this already, but the comments were kindly meant and interesting, even a little poignant, coming from people without faith. They are true.

God our Father, I pray for those caught up in the bushfires in Gippsland; and for all those jailed in this prison, some of them desperately unhappy, some without faith and hope. I pray, too, for all the prison staff, that the courtesy and decency shown to me may be the norm and that they will refuse to sink toward the violence, anger, and hatred of the worst of the prisoners.

Saturday, 2 March 2019

The first reading in the breviary today (week seven) is from the Book of Ecclesiastes; sophisticated, pessimistic, and the most pagan of the Old Testament books. "Light is sweet; at the sight of the sun the eyes are glad" (Eccles 11:7). Neither in my cell nor in the corridors is there clear glass in the assessment prison. Iron lacework separates my double-glazed cell window, and even the upper half is somewhat opaque. I miss the sun, and the cityscape and the countryside, having only a square of sky, seen through bars, in the exercise yard. This morning the sun came into one corner briefly before I finished my half-hour exercise.

For many years I looked down my nose at the cosmology of the creation account in Genesis, where light and darkness are created long before the sun. Probably, however, this was a put-down for those who claimed the sun was a god, or even the supreme god. I can imagine ancient searchers for meaning or truth groping in this direction of deifying the sun.

Prison is a place of punishment, despite being run by decent people. Requests are always responded to tardily, confusions abound. A couple of days' delay is customary, and the spartan conditions in the cell and the impeding of the light are part of the pattern. While every silver lining has a cloud, the opposite is true, so that while no windows can be opened, we do have air conditioning. The only jail in Victoria to have it.

Tried to phone my brother three or four times, and on each call it sounded as though his phone were switched off. Eventually I asked them to check if the correct number was programmed into the list. One digit was missing, and the sympathetic boss promised to get it corrected; but nothing happened today.

Kartya called, and we finalised an initial list of visitors, which can be varied once visits are made. Charlie Portelli[25] has been furious and upset by a false claim in some local newspaper of collusion between him and me. He had the report pulled down. However, I asked Kartya to pass on to him Francis of Assisi's message of *"pace e bene"* [peace and goodness], explaining a bit of background. Kartya herself thought it beautiful.

Sr Mary brought me Communion, and we went through a small service together with Sunday's readings. I miss saying Mass and was grateful for the Communion. Am always uneasy when we start to chat immediately after Communion. On visitation, people presumed it. Probably I should suggest a couple of minutes' pause before the chat. The chaplains do a fine job, and Sr Mary says their work is appreciated by the prisoners, 35 percent of whom, she claims, still say they are Catholic.

The two leaders of the Segs squad, which will accompany me on any visit outside the prison, explained my status and their role. Use of handcuffs seems to be mandatory. I explained, and they agreed, that I was unlikely and unable to run away and am no threat to anyone. It is all done to protect me.

---

[25] Msgr Charles Portelli, parish priest (pastor) of Keilor Downs, Archdiocese of Melbourne, formerly master of ceremonies to Archbishop Pell.

Watched Winx[26] win her thirty-first consecutive race, her twenty-third in Group One—a world record.

God our Father, help me to yearn for you, just as I yearn for the light and sight of the sun. Help all of us, teachers in the Church, to show this light to the many who are unconcerned by their blindness and sometimes unaware of it.

---

[26] Australian thoroughbred racehorse. The race referred to was the Chipping Norton Stakes, run at Randwick Racecourse Sydney on 2 March 2019. Winx recorded thirty-three consecutive wins, twenty-five of them Group One races, before being retired in April 2019.

WEEK 2

Ash Wednesday in Solitary

3 March–9 March 2019

Sunday, 3 March 2019

This is the first Sunday for many decades, apart from illness, that I have not attended or celebrated Sunday Mass—probably for more than seventy years. I wasn't even able to receive Communion.

The first reading in the breviary today has Job's troubles just beginning. It all lies ahead for him. [Robert] Richter, who is not a theist but Jewish, mentioned him to me a couple of times as a model. I replied that I took some consolation from Job, because his good fortune was restored in this life, unlike the good Lord's, and I still believe that the only just verdict for the judges is to quash the convictions.

Paul [Galbally] and Kartya [Gracer] called this afternoon to say that Paul will be discussing the way forward with [Bret] Walker on the utility of lodging an application for bail with the Court of Appeal. A bail grant is very rare, but they might bring the case forward. As Richter told Judge Kidd when I was sent down, "You have just removed the bail of an innocent man."

Paul and Kartya told me of Paul Kelly's first-rate article in *The Australian*,[1] the best of all, according to Paul; and Tess [Livingstone] sent me a copy of her Thursday on-line article[2] (which had the highest number of hits for two days) and her Saturday article.[3] Paul

---

[1] "Pell's Conviction and Fall from High Public Esteem Is a Question of Judgment", 2 March 2019.

[2] "George Pell: This Saga Has a Long Way to Go Yet", also published in the print edition of the *Australian*, 1 March 2019.

[3] " 'Faith, Innocence' Sustain Stoic Leader in Darkest Hour", *Australian*, 2 March 2019.

is pleased there is so much debate, equalled only by the Chamberlain case,[4] and he feels sympathy is moving in my direction, especially among the lawyers.

He doesn't want me to respond to the Friday letter of James Gargasoulas. When I explained that I felt a bit guilty as a priest in not giving him any sort of reply, he suggested I write to him when I am free. "Galbally is worth his money", I told Kartya. Two more of these mad (literally) messages arrived today. Gargasoulas is the man who murdered six people in Bourke Street with his car rampage.[5]

All is set for David, Judy, and Sarah [Pell][6] to visit at 1:00 pm tomorrow, and I have completed the list of the ten people I can phone. The friendly guard, Polish B, took my laundry and put it through the wash. He and E, the boss, are regularly helpful.

A very hot day 40°C [104°F], with bad fires around Bunyip and Nar Nar Goon [in Gippsland, Victoria]. Many houses gone.

Muslim chants floating into my cell. I wonder who he is, perhaps not Gargasoulas. I am not sure what religion he follows as he claims to be god or a messiah. A bit noisier tonight with at least one fellow shouting out in distress.

Still following through with Hebrews, a great piece, which develops Paul's central task of explaining Jesus' role in Old Testament or Jewish categories; that he completes the work and message of the first Covenant. Fidelity to Christ and his teaching remains indispensable for any fruitful Catholicism, any religious revival. This is why the "approved" Argentinian and Maltese interpretations of *Amoris Laetitia*[7] are so dangerous. They go against the teaching of the Lord

---

[4] As noted in Week 1, n. 23, Lindy Chamberlain had been convicted in 1982 of murdering her infant daughter on a family camping trip. Her appeal to the High Court was dismissed. But new evidence found in 1986 resulted in her exoneration in 1988.

[5] James Gargasoulas was convicted in 2018 of murdering six people and injuring twenty-seven others when he drove a car through the Bourke Street pedestrian mall in central Melbourne in January 2017.

[6] David, Judy, and Sarah Pell are the brother, sister-in-law, and niece of Cardinal Pell.

[7] Apostolic exhortation published by Pope Francis in 2016, following the Synods on the Family convoked in 2014 and 2015. The document caused controversy among Catholics, especially for its treatment of the traditional teaching that Catholics who are divorced and remarried without annulment of their previous marriage cannot be admitted to Holy Communion. Pastoral guidelines for applying the approach to this matter set out in *Amoris Laetitia* were issued by the Catholic bishops of the Buenos Aires region in Argentina in September 2016, and by the bishops of Malta in January 2017. Both sets of guidelines permitted divorced

on adultery and the teachings of St Paul on the necessary dispositions to receive Holy Communion properly.

Called unexpectedly for a medical check this morning. All was well, although my blood pressure (standing 120/80) was low, as I suspected, because I was feeling a little lethargic.

God our Father, I pray for all my fellow prisoners, especially those who have written to me. Help them all to see their true selves; indeed, help me, too, to do this better myself. Bring all of them some peace of mind, especially those who most certainly do not possess it.

Monday, 4 March 2019

In the breviary, Job's problems continued and worsened, as Satan was allowed to infect him with malignant ulcers. Job didn't condemn God, although his embittered wife urged him to "curse God and die." Job uttered no sinful word. "If we take happiness from God's hand, must we not take sorrow too?" (Job 2:9–10).

On many occasions, when I was asked about undeserved suffering, I used to reply that "God's Son, Jesus, didn't get a very good run." For Christians, this always causes them to pause and consider, and I sometimes asked them also to recall their blessings.

I learnt this in my first Easter as a priest in 1967 in the village of Notaresco in the Abruzzi mountains, Italy, when most of the men of the town lived and worked in Switzerland or Germany, sending home the money for the family and coming home for annual holidays. As a new, totally inexperienced priest, I wasn't sure how to console these wives and mothers. Several lines did not help, but when I said simply that Jesus suffered, too, they took consolation from this. God's Son suffered as they were suffering.

I didn't like writers, even great Christian writers such as St John of the Cross, who emphasised the essential and necessary role of

---

and remarried Catholics to receive Communion under certain circumstances. Pope Francis endorsed the Buenos Aires guidelines in a letter to the bishops of the region in September 2016; and the publication of the Maltese guidelines in *L'Osservatore Romano*, the newspaper of the Holy See, in January 2017 was seen by some as an official endorsement of these guidelines as well.

suffering if we want to come closer to God. I never read much of his work, finding it a bit frightening, while I did manage to finish *The Interior Castle* [1588] by St Teresa of Avila, who followed a similar robust Spanish theology.

My approach was more like Jude Chen's grandfather, a friend of Sun Yat-sen,[8] according to Jude. His grandfather prayed to God for small troubles, because without them he would become proud, and through them he wanted to avoid big trouble. The Chens were faithful members of the underground Church in Communist China. All lost everything, suffered greatly, and some received long jail terms until there was a measure of liberation in the late eighties and nineties, when Jude escaped to Australia. We became good friends, and the family helped him, until he migrated to Canada because we could not promise him permanent residence here. We have kept in contact, and I know how upset he and his wife, Monica, would be with my predicament.

David, Judy, and Sarah made their first visit, and it went well (obviously) with a good deal of laughter. I was strip-searched beforehand. We met in a larger room, with clear windows and children's images in bright colours on the wall. I managed to fit into the required overall, but put it on back to front with the zip at the front!

David didn't think there was any chance the Court of Appeal would give me bail, and so it proved, when Paul, Kartya, and Ruth [Shann] came down later to explain that nothing would be gained by an appeal soon after sentencing, when the prosecution would not have tendered their reply and the court might have been irritated by a premature approach. Ruth explained that she could find no precedent of bail being given because of the strength of the appeal. I had decided that if this advice were to be given, I would follow Ruth, provided she was giving her own views and not those of her senior. She replied that she was a bit of a rebel and always gave her own views.

Was disturbed that Nick [Pell][9] was off work and upset and suggested that Charlie [Portelli] be asked to contact him. Paul said he

---

[8] Sun Yat-sen (1866–1925), a Chinese physician and politician, received a Western education and was baptised in Hong Kong in 1884. He became the first president of the Republic of China in 1912 after the fall of the Qing dynasty.

[9] Nick Pell, nephew of Cardinal Pell.

would phone Nick to try to help. David reported that Marg[10] was forgetful, but otherwise not too bad. Paul spoke with her and felt she was lucid and coping.

God our Father, give peace and calm, especially to the close members of my family, who are deeply distressed. Help Nick to cope and be open to help. And I thank you, good God, for the public debate that is emerging over the verdict. May this struggle in the strangest of ways strengthen the resolve of the faithful Catholics to stick with Jesus so we all recognize that he is our only salvation.

Tuesday, 5 March 2019

In the breviary reading today, Job has snapped, "spat the dummy", in the older Australian vernacular. He didn't attack God, but laments his own birth: "May the day perish when I was born, and the night that told of a boy conceived. May that day be darkness." Later on in chapter 3, he regrets that he did not die as a newborn: "Whatever I fear comes true, whatever I dread befalls me" (Job 3:3–5, 25).

His situation was extreme; family killed, property destroyed, a disgusting disease, expelled to the ashpit, lost in silence. It is not surprising that he complains.

Obviously, Job did not know Christ, while his concept of the afterlife did not seem to discriminate between good and bad, the fortunate and unfortunate. Certainly for him in the shadows, "bad men bustle no more, there the weary rest", "high and low all are one" (Job 3:17, 19); but the one true God is not seen as the ultimate and only Judge, who will not only reward the good, but bless with, and in, eternal life those who have suffered, those who are poor and unfortunate. Job's afterlife, to the extent he acknowledges it, is an escape for all with no clear concept of a separation between the sheep and the goats, of redress for those who have suffered.

Kiko Arguello[11] says that one major doctrine separates Christians and secularists, and that is the different attitudes to suffering. Secularists

---

[10] Margaret Pell, sister of Cardinal Pell.
[11] Kiko Arguello (b. 1939) is the Spanish cofounder of the Neocatechumenal Way.

want to hide suffering or put an end to it. Hence the enthusiasm for abortion and euthanasia. We Christians believe suffering in faith can be redemptive, that salvation was gained for us by Christ's suffering and death, and that the worst can be redeemed. Equally, no group works harder than the Christians to alleviate pain. The Jews were not expecting a Messiah who would suffer and be beaten, and Job did not have Christ as his model in his suffering.

Neither did he have the concept of heaven or hell, reward or punishment, where those who have suffered more than their share in this life will find the scales of justice and mercy are weighted in their favour.

Heaven means the worst human disaster is not the last word, and I think that one of our good God's main tasks in the next life will be to take special care of the billions of *anawim*.[12]

Tragedy possesses another brutal and final dimension when God does not control life after death, is not just, and does not reward and punish. I knew the ancient Greeks did not believe in our heaven, but only years afterward did I realise that when I studied Sophocles (sixty years ago!) I read him through Catholic glasses, subconsciously mitigating the finality of death and destruction and shame for Sophocles and his audiences.

Today was a quieter day, the first of many, with only a visit from Kartya. We discussed the possible length of my sentence (five to seven years?), recognizing that [Chief Judge] Kidd has a reputation for stiff penalties. The appeal date is likely to be June 5.

Hearing the sentence will be unpleasant, and I elected to stand, although the judge offered me the possibility of sitting. What should I be doing then? My thought is to pray for the judge, while saying to myself as I look at him that he too knows the sentence is unjust. He is caught in a bind, the procedures have to be followed, but I hope he answers his conscience and does what he can toward the appeal, not doing a Pontius Pilate.

I felt greater resentment during the trial toward the prosecutor, who obfuscated and confused, blurring and sometimes contradicting

---

[12] Hebrew for "the humble", and in particular those who have been humbled or bowed down by oppression. In both the Hebrew scriptures and in the New Testament, *anawim* also carries the sense of God's promise to raise up the humble, precisely because of their lowly and oppressed condition.

the facts to enable the jury to make their bizarre decision. Ruth nailed Gibson[13] repeatedly in our appeal, but surprised me by suggesting he probably did not believe the jury would accept such a melange. She thinks his unexpected concessions in court for the pleas indicate his unease.

Obtained a broom and swept my small cell. The paint is still chipped on the floor, there is no curtain, and the open toilet is a bit more than a metre from me as I write, but this is home for the moment.

God our Loving Father, help me to keep hatred out of my heart. Not only should I speak the truth in love, but I should think the truth in love.

Ash Wednesday, 6 March 2019

Never realised this until Sr Mary gave me the readings of today a couple of days ago. She gave me the ashes and brought Communion. Earlier I had been visited by Father Philip Gill, Anglican prison chaplain from St Peter's, Eastern Hill, who offered me the ashes. I consented, saying I had no problem with Anglican ashes, to which he countered that his were Catholic in origin because they became from Sr Mary. I asked him to telephone her because I did not want to start a turf war. I explained I had been to St Peter's many times, had donated a kneeler for the Knights of St Lazarus Chapel (which seems to have disappeared), and I could not think of my friend [John] Hazelwood's name (Anglican Bishop of Ballarat, whose funeral in St Patrick's Cathedral in Ballarat I attended). Nor could I remember then Graham Walden's name, later Bishop of The Murray, with whom I co-chaired the Anglican-Catholic dialogue group in the Ballarat diocese. Good and happy times.

Job (chapter 7) has well and truly hit his stride as he lists his woes, months of delusion, nights of grief, vermin, scabs, and pus all over him. He is no understated Stoic, but an eloquent Jew, vehement and explicit.

He expects little after death. "As a cloud dissolves and is gone, so he who goes down to Sheol never ascends again." He scolds God,

---

[13] Mark Gibson, prosecutor in the commital and trials.

whom he accuses morning after morning of testing him, at every instant, in fact.

It is not as though he is asking a God who is good and kind what he is up to. It is as though he is rebuking a difficult and interfering God. "Why do you choose me as your target?"

We are some distance here from the famous passage in St Augustine's *Confessions* on the good God. "Late have I loved you", Augustine wrote, "O Beauty so ancient and so new", who had chased away his blindness, so that Augustine now "burned for (God's) peace". This is the breviary's second reading of the day.

Neither is Augustine any Stoic, but when he will be united with the Lord, "there shall be no more grief and toil, and my life will be alive, filled wholly with You." That was not Augustine's situation as he wrote, as he goes on and on listing his woes and calling on God's mercy.

One thought in particular is encouraging. "Who would choose trouble and difficulty? You (God) command us to endure them, not to love them." Christ at Gethsemane in the garden was an example of this, sweating blood in his anguish. I find this easier to understand than St Paul rejoicing in his weakness, so the power of God would be manifest in him (2 Cor 12:7–10), although personal weakness is different from external misfortune.

As I don't have my next volume of the breviary for Lent, I am more than pleased to stay with Job as he struggles on.

Ruth called for a chat and noted that the front page of *The Age* was highlighting Walker replacing Richter for the appeal. When asked, Richter rose magnificently to the occasion, proclaiming that he was too emotionally involved in the case. The verdict was perverse, he insisted, and an innocent man is in jail. All on the front page of *The Age*.[14]

---

[14] "Robert Richter No Longer Part of George Pell's Legal Team for Appeal", *Age*, 5 March 2019:

> Leading criminal barrister Robert Richter will not be in George Pell's legal team for the appeal against the Cardinal's conviction for child sex offences, partly because he was too emotionally involved in the case and angry at the guilty verdict.
>
> Mr Richter QC told *The Age* and *The Sydney Morning Herald* that he felt he did not have "sufficient objectivity at this stage" to participate in the challenge set to be heard in Victoria's Court of Appeal.

E's replacement, a tall man, is less sympathetic, and my Polish friend is away. Shaving should be done in the morning, he replied, when I asked for my shaving kit in the afternoon. He would make an exception this once. He didn't, and the kit didn't arrive. A couple of assistants go out of their way to be helpful and chatty, and the others are cordial. Nothing serious at all.

Spoke to Marg and David by phone. She was pretty good and asking when she could visit.

Have been on "retreat" this week, reciting the daily breviary three times and meditating thrice to replace the daily Eucharist and the customary lectures. I was overdue for a retreat.

[Cardinal] Parolin sent a message via the nuncio and Sr Mary expressing his support. I was touched and pleased. The copy of the appeal [submissions] must have been useful here.

Some rain in the last twenty-four hours and snow on the Alps. A day or so ago it was 40°C [104°F]. My watch arrived, and I managed to set the time correctly, and the TV wouldn't work.

God our Father, I pray once again for my family and friends, that they will not be too wounded or disturbed. May my predicament help to strengthen their faith and goodness, especially Sarah and Nick, Bec and Georgie, so they can pass on the faith to young Sonny.

Thursday, 7 March 2019

A quiet day. Tim and Anne [McFarlane] came in this morning for a pleasant hour on the other side of the glass.[15] Not an enormous amount of news. Apparently Geoff Horgan QC [Queen's Counsel],

---

"I am very angry about the verdict," he said, "because it was perverse".

However, he has denied that he "quit" the legal team, and said if need be, he was available to be consulted.

Mr Richter said Cardinal Pell, who has been convicted of five counts of sexually assaulting two choir boys in St Patrick's Cathedral in 1996 and 1997, would be "better served by someone more detached".

"I think the man is an innocent man and he's been convicted. It's not a common experience."

[15] That is, a noncontact visit in a booth separated by glass.

former prosecutor and painter of the two cathedral icons,[16] had a strong supportive letter published,[17] and I learned that the [character] references had been published in many papers. [Bill] Shorten objected for some reason, but was rebuked publicly by his shadow attorney general, Mark Dreyfus [QC].[18] [George] Weigel has penned a couple of strong pieces, comparing my case with the nineteenth-century Dreyfus case in France,[19] and [Fr] Raymond de Souza has vigorously joined the fray.[20]

Dave Bell, Ruth's husband, suggested that as Richmond has dropped me as vice patron, I might switch to Melbourne![21] Happily, Matilda[22] returned from the sleep hospital a reformed sleeper. A successful outcome.

Resettlement lady called and asked the routine questions. Was I intellectually retarded? she enquired. She commented that I was laughing, not at her, but at the question. "I don't think so", I replied.

Had a good chat with Charlie, the Salvation Army chaplain, whom I couldn't remember meeting. We hadn't, explained Charlie, despite Sr Mary's claim. An ex-Anglican, he went to the Anglican Eucharist because he missed it. A strong disciple of the Lord.

Received about fifteen to twenty beautiful letters, some of them from fellow prisoners. I will reply to most of the prisoners.

---

[16] The icons *Christ* and *Our Lady with the Christ Child* are on either side of the Great West Door inside St Patrick's Cathedral in Melbourne.

[17] "Not Up to Pell to Prove Innocence", Letters to the Editor, *Australian*, 1 March 2019.

[18] On 29 February, the then–Labor Opposition Leader Bill Shorten criticised former Prime Minister John Howard for "an error of judgement" in providing Cardinal Pell with a character reference prior to his sentencing. Mr Dreyfus defended Mr Howard's right to do so as an important part of the normal process in sentencing convicted persons.

[19] "The Pell Affair: Australia Is Now on Trial", *First Things*, 27 February 2019; "Our Dreyfus Case", *First Things*, 6 March 2019. Alfred Dreyfus, a French Jewish artillery officer, was wrongly convicted of treason twice, in 1894 and 1899, based on false evidence. He was finally exonerated in 1906, pardoned, and released from prison.

[20] "Calling Cardinal Pell's Prosecution What It Is: Religious Persecution", *National Catholic Register*, 1 March 2019.

[21] Cardinal Pell has been a lifelong supporter of the Richmond Australian Rules football club. He signed to train for the professional men's team at the end of high school in 1959, before deciding to enter the seminary the following year. In 1997 he was made a vice patron of the Richmond team, which revoked the honorary title on 26 February, the day the suppression order on his conviction was lifted.

[22] Matilda, granddaughter of Tim and Anne McFarlane, who is the daughter of Dave and Ruth Bell.

Today Job stands rebuked by his friend Zophar the Naamathite, not a sympathetic character. He objects to Job's babbling and wordiness, and more specifically to Job's claim to be faultless and free from blame. Not so, explains our corrector. "It is for sin that he (God) calls you to account." He praises the ungraspable mystery of God and urges Job to "renounce the iniquity that stains your hands". Then good times will come, and Job will live "unwavering and free from fear" (Job 11:11–15).

The Book of Job was written to grapple with the problem of the suffering of the innocent, while Zophar denies the question and links Job's woes to the sins he has not acknowledged.

The wages of some sins are real and obvious; for example, from drugs or alcohol or lies, etc. But many evil people lead charmed lives, even if it is with deadened sensibilities rather than peace of mind; and many, too many, suffer through no moral fault of their own.

Jesus' teaching represents an enormous advance. Those killed by the collapse of the tower of Siloam (Lk 13:4), he explained, did not die because of their own sins or those of their ancestors.

Gregory the Great's commentary on Job for the day explains that the law means charity and cites Paul's long list of duties that follow from the law of love. It is a beautiful piece of theology, a comprehensive moral program, but when it is all spelt out so consecutively, I tend to feel a bit deflated and imperfect. Which is probably what is intended. We have to lift our game. Certainly it is difficult to see the direct connection with Zophar's sermon.

On my return from my visit, I expressed my disappointment to the commandant that I did not receive my shaving gear before my visit, as I had asked for it yesterday in the afternoon and asked a couple of times this morning. But not when I was receiving my breakfast, both guards quickly volunteered in response to his question. "Well," I said to one of them, "if I didn't ask you I didn't ask you!" I will take closer note next time. No permanent harm seems to have been done.

Saw the nurse this morning and talked this afternoon by video with Dr McIsaacs from St Vincent's about my heart. Pressure was 120 over 80, and I explained that I sometimes feel a bit off and lightheaded when my pressure is in 120 range. It has been in the 140s for decades, on good days! Jail life is very quiet.

Did quite a bit of work for my China review of Overholt's book.[23] Guard got my TV to work again.

God our Father, help me to offer up the quiet and the tedium for the good of the Church and for your work in the world. Continue to give me strength and peace of mind and help my fellow prisoners, especially those who are bad or disturbed or desperately unhappy.

Friday, 8 March 2019

Received a letter from the Supreme Court stating that my appeal would be heard in the Green Room on the 5–6 June. Ruth will have to delay her holiday, and Tony[24] has consented.

Likely to be transferred after sentencing on next Wednesday. Said I would prefer a more congenial exercise area, a later lockdown, and a bit of company. My safety is their main concern—and mine.

With the doctor this morning, and I wasn't surprised that my blood pressure was 106(?) over 62 or 63. It was no wonder that I felt seedy—not dizzy; perhaps my balance was a bit worse than usual. In the evening, they took me off the Prazosin. Let's see how we are tomorrow morning, although I gather the tablets are slow moving.

One or two of the lads noisy and distressed—especially around lunchtime. Might be Gargasoulas. A lot of suffering in this place.

Drug people came and gave me the regular briefing offered to all. Very cordial, and I said I didn't have any questions.

Sr Mary brought me Communion, and we went through the Sunday readings, which she left with me. She carried [Br] Mark O'Connor's[25] greetings and said Barney Zwartz had a hostile article in *The Age*, quoting Helen Last.[26] Told her of how I planned to approach Kidd during sentencing (in charity), and she emphatically

---

[23] William H. Overholt, *China's Crisis of Success* (Cambridge: Cambridge University Press, 2018). The review, "China: What Next?", was published pseudonymously in the final number of *Annals: Journal of Catholic Culture* (130:9–10), November-December 2019.

[24] Tony, partner of Ruth Shann.

[25] Br Mark O'Connor is a Marist Brother who has been active for decades in social justice area.

[26] "Church Knew Pell Was at Centre of Decades-Old Lurid Sex Claims", *Age*, 7 March 2019.

agreed.[27] She was impressed when I told her Walker thought it the strongest appeal he has seen. She brought Pope Francis' Lenten message and *Melbourne Catholic* on women and faith. I will read them both.

Sung Muslim prayers have just started to float into my cell. Was able to obtain fish for main (3:30 pm!) meal and avoided the meat in the luncheon salad.

Poked around with my China review and put down some random notes on my time at St Patrick's, perhaps for a series "Different Worlds".

Someone once said to me that every priest has three or four or five or six decent sermons in him, but after that, one has to work harder and be more careful to avoid repetition. That seems to be the situation with keeping a jail diary and particularly with the theological reflections.

Job's speech in reply [to Zophar; see Job 12:3–4] is not particularly congenial as he tells his interlocutor that "I can reflect as deeply as ever you can, I am in no way inferior to you." I have no reason to doubt his claim, but it seems to me that he weakens his position by making it. My reaction might be a bit old-fashioned Anglo.

Job resents being a laughingstock, mocked yet blameless (chapter 12). Those who challenge God make a god of their two fists. But "this state of things is all of God's own making." God is blamed for the droughts and havoc, for turning judges into fools and untying the belt of kings. God raises some up; then strikes them down and destroys.

With no scales of justice in Sheol, an interventionist and punitive God, and no concept of redemptive suffering or of a God who permits evils and suffering for a long-term purpose (rather than causing it), Job is in trouble. But he never doubts that God is in charge.

I think it was Father Michael Hollings, the Catholic chaplain during my time at Oxford, whom I first heard explaining that God writes straight in crooked lines. I always believed in Christian providence, but when I saw how Tolkien brought all the characters and the narrative together at the conclusion of *The Lord of the Rings*, I thought of how much better our infinite loving God is able to adapt his purposes

---

[27] See entry for 5 March above.

as a consequence of our choices, good or sinful. Job never doubted God was in command, but he attributed the woes directly to God.

Receiving Pope Francis' Lenten message reminded me to pray for him and the universal Church. I am not sure I am missing the regular updates from Rome. However, I did see on SBS[28] that Cardinal [Philippe] Barbarin [archbishop of Lyon] received a suspended six-month sentence and offered his resignation.[29] He is travelling to Rome in the near future. Apparently he did not act quickly enough to report a paedophile priest. If he goes, it will be a loss as he is regularly on the side of the angels.

So, Lord Jesus, in these tempests around the world, help the Church leadership to be wise and courageous, to identify the main challenges and battles, and rally the faithful to remain loyal and active.

Saturday, 9 March 2019

I have received one hundred letters since I arrived here at Melbourne Assessment Prison (MAP), most of them in the last three days. About a dozen of them are from fellow prisoners. I sent off a couple of replies to two prisoners, one of whom addressed me in Latin.

Many of them attached poems and prayers, often beautiful in every sense and nearly always expressing the sender's deep faith and understanding of Jesus' suffering and death.

Naturally I feel uneasy and embarrassed being compared to the Lord; or even to Thomas More or John the Baptist (the alternative choices of one husband and wife couple who wrote to me). I can't remember anyone mentioning John Fisher,[30] who has been swamped by More in the popularity stakes after Robert Bolt's *A Man for All Seasons*, and now in the notoriety stakes after Hilary Mantel's two

---

[28] Special Broadcasting Service (SBS), largely funded by the Australian government, airs free radio and television programs.

[29] Philippe Cardinal Barbarin's conviction for not acting quickly enough to report a paedophile priest was overturned by an appeal court on 30 January 2020.

[30] St John Fisher (1469–1535) was an English Catholic bishop, cardinal, and theologian, who was executed by Henry VIII for refusing to recognize him as supreme head of the Church in England.

novels.[31] Will she ever finish the third volume where her "hero" Thomas Cromwell comes to grief? And I think one could almost say, receives his just desserts from that moral monster Henry VIII. So many deaths, especially of those close to him.

My fate has serious repercussions for the Church, especially in Australia, but more widely because of my advocacy of "crucifixion Christianity". There seems little doubt that my social conservatism and advocacy of the Judaeo-Christian ethic have sharpened popular hostility, especially among the militant secularists.

I believe in God's providence; I never chose this situation and worked hard to avoid it; but here I am, and I must strive to do God's will.

Cardinal Sin from Manila, who was a formidable churchman, opponent of Marcos, and a great showman ("welcome to the house of Sin"), used to say that he was like the donkey Jesus rode into Jerusalem, on what we used to remember as Palm Sunday. I am happy with a similar comparison for my mediocre self; faithful in my prayers and duties, once hardworking, but spiritually ordinary. God sometimes chooses strangely.

I am caught in a struggle between good and the spirit of evil. I have felt this more strongly of late. A friend of mine, a senior woman professional and academic, was in the court when the jury gave their guilty decision (the worst moment of her life, she claimed). She is a genuine believer, Catholic, but most un-mystical, and she claimed she sensed the presence of evil in the jury and the courtroom. I didn't, as I was so stunned. Everyone, and all the pundits, had told me I could not be convicted on the evidence. Even the magistrate said this, among other things.

One of the Dominican nuns from Ganmain sent me a handwritten copy of James McAuley's beautiful poem "In a Late Hour", written I think for Bob Santamaria.[32] I know it well.

McAuley professes his loyalty to the Lord, his simple thankfulness. I am not sure that the "Antirealm" has conquered, but it "is here", to use

---

[31] *Wolf Hall* (Picador, 2010) and *Bring up the Bodies* (Picador, 2013). The third volume in the series, *The Mirror and the Light*, was published by Henry Holt in 2020.

[32] B. A. (Bob) Santamaria (1915–1998) was an Australian Roman Catholic, a writer, and a political leader. He was an important figure in Australia for sixty years.

his phrase. Even more than in his time, for many today "the sense of nature (is) gone." Today "from wounds deep rancours flow", and I join my prayer to his: "While the mystery is enacted I will not let you go."

McAuley is my favourite Australian poet, and the best (with apologies to Les Murray).

A Thurgoona woman sent me a copy of Ecclesiasticus 2:1–11 recommended by Bishop Columba Macbeth-Green. I did not remember the passage about the chosen being tested by fire and in the furnace of humiliation. My situation exactly.

Job continues apace in the breviary reading (as my Lent and Easter volume has not yet arrived): "Let him (God) kill me if he will; I have no other hope than to justify my conduct in his eyes" (Job 13:15). He blames God for pursuing him, "measuring my footprints, while my life is crumbling like rotten wood" (Job 14:27–28). He acknowledges God's supremacy and asks to be left alone.

A quiet day, the quietest, no outing after lunch of any sort. Cleaned the cell with broom, disinfectant, and cloths and watched the horse racing from Flemington and Randwick. In the evening, turned to SBS for a show on Morocco and the renovation of Big Ben. Said the Office of the Dead for the repose of soul of Mike Willesee.

My Lord Jesus, I pray that I may do as I should as we move through this mess, so that your will and the Father's will not be damaged by my weakness or perversity or lack of wisdom.

I pray, too, in a special way for all those praying for me, many or all of whom have their crosses, large or small.

WEEK 3

Sentencing

10 March–16 March 2019

Sunday, 10 March 2019

Another Sunday without the Eucharist. I pray my other prayers with some extra zeal to mark the Lord's day. The food is a bit better for Sunday, with the main meal about 11:30 am and a nice salad with a jam roll, a Swiss roll, as we called it in my childhood, for the 3:30 pm meal. Not too bad, either. I suspect I am putting on a bit of weight, despite leaving a lot of the calorie-heavy food uneaten.

A surprise visit to the doctor this morning to check my blood pressure, which was 145 over 80 something. I was still ever so slightly off the pace, but better than yesterday.

As my feet come near to the end of the bed that abuts onto a stone wall, they were cold. I had some trouble getting to sleep. I put on socks and took off my jail top, which was too heavy under a couple of blankets. Woke up around 2:00 am, but resorted to saying the rosary, which did the trick as it usually does for me, and I went to sleep.

I used to tell the teenagers and young adults that if they did not pray when they were in trouble, then their faith was weak indeed. It follows from this that I should not feel guilty or rather uneasy here in jail when I pray because I feel needy. I find I can turn to God to pray in the empty times, when I have no work or distraction, and I thank God for this small progress.

Even when I am a bit uneasy and I start to pray, I do not always ask for anything, although I often ask for peace and strength and pray for all those whom I have omitted to pray for when I should have.

I always offer part of my daily breviary prayer for the Church victims of paedophilia in Australia, not only for my accuser in these trials, as has been reported. To require accusers to prove their case is not to be antivictim, but to establish that they are victims. Many have been falsely accused, including myself many times, and we do not have justice unless justice is given to all parties.

Courage was often lacking in those who should have tackled this abuse early on, and courage can be lacking when the pendulum changes direction and swings to excess.

The Truth, Justice and Healing Council bore the brunt of work for five years for the Church in the Royal Commission,[1] but they should have reserved their right to cross-examine complainants, even if they had done so rarely. This would have encouraged sobriety.

They also failed to acknowledge properly the success, partial and flawed as it was, of *Towards Healing* and the Melbourne Response.[2] Even Gail Furness, counsel assisting [Justice Peter] McClellan, conceded that the rate of offences fell substantially from the early 1990s. In terms of slowing or stopping the offending, we had broken the back of the problem from at least 1996–1997. It is not accurate or truthful to suggest the Church officials did nothing before the Truth, Justice and Healing Council was set up. Nor is it accurate to suggest the Church had no "good" bishops before some unspecified date, that they were all "company men" who placed the Church before the victims. This is unfair and grandstanding, playing to a hostile crowd.

The paedophilia crisis remains the greatest blow the Church has suffered in Australia. So many terrible crimes, and so many among them horrendous. If anyone in the mid-nineties knew the extent of the problem, they did not say so publicly, or to me privately. We thought the Melbourne Response would finish its work in a few years.

---

[1] The Royal Commission into Institutional Responses to Child Sexual Abuse (2013–2017) was established by the Australian government to examine complaints of abuse in educational, religious, youth, sporting, and state institutions.

The Truth, Justice, and Healing Council (2013–2018) was formed by the Australian Catholic Bishops' Conference and Catholic Religious Australia to oversee the Church's engagement with the Royal Commission.

[2] *Towards Healing* was the official response in March 1997 of the Australian Catholic Bishops' Conference to the problem of sexual abuse. The Melbourne Response was the policy the Archdiocese of Melbourne adopted at a public forum in October 1996 in response to the problem of sexual abuse.

In the breviary, Job is battling on eloquently making two points, i.e., blaming God for his troubles and insisting that God has the power to do something about it. He is in charge. Man can achieve very, very little. God's verdict is that wisdom "is the fear of the Lord" and understanding is "avoidance of evil" (Job 28:20–28).

It was a relief to move on to the responsory from 1 Corinthians (2:6–8); God's secret wisdom for us is Christ.

The second reading is another beautiful and famous passage from Augustine's *Confessions*. To praise God is our joy, "For you have made us for yourself, and our hearts are restless till they rest in you."

How does the soul first move toward God? Must we know God before we can implore him? Augustine is a superb psychologist, able to write about himself with eloquence and insight. But he is even better when he talks about our God of love. "Surely not to love you is already a great woe."

Let these words of Augustine be my prayer tonight:

[O Lord, my God,] say unto my soul, you are my salvation. Let me come in haste to lay hold upon you. Hide not your face from me. Let me see your face even if I die, lest I die with longing to see it.

Monday, 11 March 2019

The event of the day was of course the visit of Chris Meney, although close behind, made possible only by the visit, was the fact that we could meet in the garden. The non-arrival of Nick and Rebecca[3] was a disappointment. Heaven only knows what might have stopped them as Nick spoke by phone to Chris this morning saying his appointment was at 12:30 pm. I had never mentioned such a time and thought all three were coming for the hour.

The authorities have worked to make the outside visiting area attractive—nicely paved, with round tables surrounded by fixed metal benches, a covered area of ferns in the centre with a pagoda-type top, and an aboriginal garden in the corner. A memorial to our fallen soldiers, a plaque telling us the area was opened by Pauline

---

[3] Nick and Rebecca Pell, nephew and niece of Cardinal Pell.

Toner,[4] and above the entrance a Venetian scene with something like the Bridge of Sighs over the canal. In a corner, almost hidden away, were some decent roses, in bloom with red and white flowers (I think). We sat for half the time and also walked around in the almost balmy weather of this Labor Day holiday. A lovely day. Watched the Moomba parade[5] for ten to fifteen minutes on TV this morning and found it pretty ordinary, although the kids marching were pleased, and so were the youngsters who, allegedly, designed the floats.

As always, strip-searched and locked into an overall before the visit, which I put on correctly this time, not back to front. I had a 3XL, but needed the biggest size, probably 5XL.

Chris seemed a little hesitant, perhaps worried by my possible response, to claim that my problems and jailing were part of God's providence, although he did not know clearly what was afoot and what might be good consequences. He was probably reassured when I enthusiastically concurred that God, the Spirit, is always at work. Chris thought it might tell the faithful that the general situation is unlikely to get easier, although I hope that not too many too soon will have to repeat my experience.

Chris has been a great friend and invaluable support. Mary Clare and Jess[6] are in Medjugorje, praying for me I hope, among their other intentions.

As well as my garden exercise, I also had two half-hour walking sessions in our grotty exercise pen. A radical contrast, but the small area of sky that was visible contained the sun this morning.

Chris brought the next volume of the breviary, so it will be interesting to see when it arrives to me. The guards said it will come up automatically, and I will not need to sign out anything.

Job is in much better form, deeply eloquent today, but still following his hard line in blaming God. He recalls the good times when God's lamp shone over his head (Job 29:3). Once treated with respect by the young and the rulers, now he is a laughing stock. Terrors turn

---

[4] Pauline Toner (1935–1989) was elected to the Victorian Parliament in 1977 and served as minister for Community Welfare Services in the Cain Labor government, 1982–1985, in which capacity she was responsible for prisons (among other areas).

[5] Annual festival in Melbourne, held on the Labor Day weekend in the second week of March.

[6] Mary Clare and Jess Meney, wife and daughter of Chris Meney.

to meet him, and he is gnawed by wounds that never sleep. God is severely reprimanded: "You take no notice. You have grown cruel in your dealing with me" (Job 30:20–21).

Job was so underequipped to deal with his appalling situation, with his fierce indignation and plain speaking. I remember Cardinal Lustiger[7] from Paris, a convert from Judaism, whose people came from the same village in Poland as Jim Spiegelman's[8] family, fiercely wondering why God allowed four or five bishops from France to die young, as he had picked them out as likely archbishops. Lustiger confronted modernity as it should be met, with the full Christian call to faith and repentance. At one stage, he had more young priests and seminarians than the rest of France combined. I followed something of Lustiger's model when I reformed the Melbourne seminary. Jewish traditions of being outspoken are long-lived.

We know that God is never cruel to us, no matter what is allowed to happen. God is not like a superior who abandons us or refuses to continue supporting our best efforts, who turns against us. God is always with us, turning our suffering to good, uniting it with Jesus' suffering and death. God is always listening, especially when he is silent. Our sufferings have a purpose. Job did not know of a suffering Messiah.

God our Father, I join my small suffering with that of your Son, Jesus, so that it may be used as you will, when you will, for the spread of the Kingdom, especially in Australia.

Tuesday, 12 March 2019

Today I sent a carefully worded letter to James Gargasoulas, the Bourke Street murderer, in response to his many letters and card. He is either mad or competent in appearing to be mad. Yesterday I received a card from Sophie O (unknown to me—the writing on the

---

[7] Jean-Marie Cardinal Lustiger was born into a Polish Jewish family in 1926. He converted to Catholicism in 1940. He was bishop of Orléans from 1979 to 1981 and archbishop of Paris from 1983 until his retirement in 2005. He died in 2007.

[8] Jim Spiegelman was the chief justice of the Supreme Court of New South Wales from 1998 to 2011 and the chairman of the Australian Broadcasting Corporation from 2012 to 2017.

envelope was obscure) urging me to ask James to pray for forgiveness. Despite my lawyer's advice, I felt it the better thing to do as a priest. Told him plainly I did not think he was the Messiah and gently urged him, like us all, to seek enlightenment and repent.

Finished my retreat on last Friday—a five-day program from the preceding Monday. It was more haphazard than my retreats normally, but it was something. Did not find it difficult to pray.

Lent in jail looks after most of the penance dimension, leaves time for prayer, while the alms giving is out—unless I use Michael Casey[9] as my attorney. Felt a bit down this afternoon and earlier this evening at the prospect of tomorrow's humiliation of the sentencing. For some reason, I feel a bit better now. God will provide, and it will be the last public hurdle before the appeal.

Saw the doctor this morning, who found my blood pressure was up. I explained I was a bit tense about the sentencing, and we decided she would review the situation in a couple of days.

Sr Mary called to give me Communion in the afternoon. For one reason or another, she was knocked back three or four times this morning, refused access. One or two of the guards were a bit uncooperative. My breviary has not arrived, and neither did my laundry. Strangely, one of the two guards came and gave me an extra plastic bottle of milk, which I happily accepted.

Today is the final reading from Job in this volume of the breviary. I will have to backtrack with my prayers if volume 2 for Lent doesn't arrive tomorrow.

Job is again eloquently sticking to his guns proclaiming his basic goodness: "If he (God) weighs me on honest scales, being God, he cannot fail to see my innocence" (Job 31:6), which is exactly my prayer in this bizarre cathedral case. Not one of the twenty witnesses supported the complainant's claims, and I had four people who provided alibis; the master of ceremonies, the sacristan, and two altar servers. God's will be done; his permissive will.

Job lists his good deeds as well as his avoiding evil. Then he concludes, "I have had my say, from A to Z, now let the Lord answer me."

At least at this juncture the breviary does not quote the final chapter 42, where God rebuked Job's three adversaries, Eliphaz, Bildad,

---

[9] Michael Casey, former secretary to Cardinal Pell, 1997–2014.

and Zophar, then restored Job's "fortunes and gave him twice as much as he had before" (Job 42:10). He then lived to see his descendants to the fourth generation.

This is a good Old Testament, this-world ending, and please God my appeal will also succeed.

I had expected Paul Galbally to call this afternoon; to no avail. I was hoping to receive news of the missing nephew and niece.

Just interrupted over the intercom to be told I will be woken at 5:00 am.

Dear Lord Jesus, give me the strength to retain my composure tomorrow, to carry myself with Christian dignity and not give into anger at the injustice of it all. May Mary, your mother, our mother, and therefore my mother, be with me so I offer up a valid offering for the good of the Church. I feel that St Mary of the Cross MacKillop[10] understands my situation; as would John Fisher and Cardinal Thuan,[11] whom I knew and admired.

Wednesday, 13 March 2019

Well I managed to get through the sentencing, which the judge organized to be live-streamed. It was harrowing, but I coped by looking straight at the judge all the time, while I was sitting, or standing for the recitation of the penalties. Ruth also said she, too, looked straight at [Judge] Kidd all the time. I kept repeating in my mind, "False. Unjust." Occasionally I agreed with his reasoning on my moral leadership and responsibility with the choir. Then I repeated, "The premises are wrong."

---

[10] St Mary of the Cross MacKillop (1842–1909) and the religious order she founded, the Sisters of St Joseph of the Sacred Heart, were important in expanding education in Australia. She was the first Australian to be canonized and is the patron saint of the country.

[11] Francis-Xavier Cardinal Nguyen Van Thuan (1928–2002) was bishop of Nha Trang in South Vietnam (1967–1975), and was appointed co-adjutor archbishop of Saigon in 1975. He was jailed by the Communist government of Vietnam in 1975, spending nine years in solitary confinement before his release in 1988. He was allowed to leave Vietnam for Rome in 1991 and was appointed president of the Pontifical Council for Justice and Peace in 1998.

As mentioned, the previous hearing had an Alice-in-Wonderland dimension, as my team, who believed in my innocence, had to make, or at least respond to, hypotheses of why I acted as alleged. The situation and circumstances around the allegations argue for implausibility, not for the (stupid) arrogance the judge alleged.

I finished up with a non-parole sentence [period] of three years eight months, which was better than my erroneous calculations while in the court of four years six months.

Robert [Richter] had estimated a little less, and Ruth something more. It is important to win the appeal.

Robert asked whether I was inclined to ask for a reduction of sentence during my appeal. I replied that my first instinct was to say no, as I did not want to offer the judges any wriggle room to weasel out with a "compromise". Richter said he was not surprised at my response and heartily agreed. Ruth concurred, saying the only possibility in any case was for a few months off.

The courtroom was packed, and possibly another room was available for the overflow. I recognized few people, only Mary Helen Woods,[12] Peter Westmore,[13] and Anne Lastman.[14] I did not see Patrick Meney.[15] Phoned David [Pell] afterward, and he said the media were saturated with the news. Phoned Margaret three times, but the phone was only receiving messages. Apparently Joseph and Susan Santamaria were with her.

Ruth pointed out that the judge dissociated himself quietly by his remarks from the jury decision. Such was not his business, but theirs. The appellate judges would note this, she said.

Ruth also explained how difficult his position was in sentencing me as he accepted I was innocent. What of the prosecutor, who only turned around once, and furtively, to glance at me during the proceedings?

Apparently my categorisation as a reviled prisoner liable to prisoner violence places me in the same category as a terrorist. Handcuffs were fitted to my wrists for all travel, but when I arrived in handcuffs for

---

[12] Mary Helen Woods, friend of Cardinal Pell.
[13] Peter Westmore, president of the National Civic Council from 1998 to 2018.
[14] Anne Lastman, advocate for victims and friend of Cardinal Pell.
[15] Patrick Meney, son of Chris Meney.

the interview with the lawyers beforehand, Richter intervened and claimed he had never spoken before court with a handcuffed client. After some consultation, they were removed for my chat with them, and I intervened to tell the team that the guard affixing the cuffs, imposing the humiliations, was OK. In fact, he was cordial and genuinely helpful, unlike his Central European colleague and assistant who brought me from the County Court to MAP [Melbourne Assessment Prison] a fortnight ago.

Every stage of the progress to the court was accompanied by delays—an hour or so at one stage on my return. Probably this is primarily part of the ritual humiliation, but it might give people time to settle down.

My blood pressure was up when tested before leaving: 158 over 100. The nurse asked me innocently if this was OK! Tonight I am back on the Prazosin. I also had a second Lasix (furosemide) tablet today because of my swollen legs, but I did not take them until I returned from court.

Here in prison, you are often told that "it will occur" and it doesn't. At 9:00 pm on Tuesday night, I was told I would be wakened at 5:00 am. The call came at 5:45 am, which was no problem, and I was given twenty-five to thirty minutes to be ready in my civilian clothes. We headed off about 7:30 am. I did not have a belt (which was retrieved from my locker as we set off), which meant my trousers fell down a couple of times. I attached the trousers to my shirt using a button, and this, with the belt, avoided any public embarrassment.

I was told we would be returning immediately after the hearing. I explained that I expected to speak with my legal team afterward, which did happen and very usefully, and we finished coming back to the prison, coming "home", in the early afternoon. The court session began at 10:00 am.

A couple of guards asked about my appeal, and I told them my case was very strong. One replied that he had already heard this.

I had to sign the Register of Sex Offenders in the court, but so far the DNA swab has not yet taken place. I have no objection to this.

I was relieved after the hearing, pleased to be through the experience and coping with the sentence, given the strength of my appeal. I did remember to bow to the judge as I left the court.

Ruth and Robert agree that the foundation of the appeal is the fact that I only celebrated Mass in 1996 at the cathedral on 15 and 22 of December. A second offence a month later is not possible in 1996, and on three occasions J[16] insisted the offences were in the 1996 choral year.

I also explained vehemently that I had alibis from four witnesses, none of them accused of lying. "How many alibis are needed?" I insisted, while Paul Galbally smiled quietly in agreement. He will also speak with Adrian Barrett[17] as a few more choir boys have phoned offering help.

I prayed most of the way to the court in the special silver van, which I had to enter backwards to fit in the narrow space for the bench; also while I was waiting beforehand and then a couple of rosaries of thanks afterward while waiting to return.

Jail means plenty of penance for me this Lent, which will balance out a little the absence of stiff penances over many years. I do not deeply regret this, although more should have been done, because I was always busy. It is a consolation that you can offer up your humiliation, suffering, and inconveniences with the Lord's for the good of the Church.

My Lenten breviary still has not arrived, being with the lawyers, who thought the book fragile and liable to be knocked about further by the jail processes. And here I was blaming the jail for the delay!

Lord Jesus, thank you for getting me through this day. May the damage done to the Church by the news of these jail terms be balanced out at my appeal, and may faithful Catholics be strengthened to battle harder for Christ, his Catholic Church, and the wider Christian cause.

Thursday, 14 March 2019

A word or two about my lodgings in cell 11, unit 8 of the Melbourne Assessment Prison, where I am locked up with a Muslim terrorist (I think he is the one singing his prayers now this evening, but my

---

[16] J the complainant.
[17] Adrian Barrett, former cathedral choir member and friend of Cardinal Pell.

identification could be wrong) and Gargasoulas, the Bourke Street murderer. Basically, I do not know who they are. At least a couple of the prisoners in the dozen or so cells often shout out desperately at night, but not for long generally. It is interesting how you become used to this noise, and it becomes part of the background. I am in solitary confinement, allowed out for exercise for up to one hour and for visits from lawyers, officials, friends, the doctor, etc. The guards vary in their level of sympathy, but all are correct, most are cordial, and a few are friendly and helpful. I can receive mail and phone out when on exercise.

My cell is about 7 or 8 metres long, more than 2 metres wide under the opaque window where the bed is; a good bed with a firm base, a not too thick mattress, sheets, etc., and two blankets. As we have no windows to be opened, we have air-conditioning, which was useful in the heat of a week or so ago.

As you enter, there are shelves on the left wall with a bench for my kettle and television and an eating space. Across the narrow aisle on the right as you enter, we have a basin with hot and cold water, an open toilet with a high seat and arms (given my knees), and a very strong shower recess with good hot water. Unlike many posh hotels, a good reading lamp is in the wall above the bed. It is very cosy, with all essential services to hand like a Chinese apartment of some underground Church members in Shanghai that I visited. There they had a stove, toilet, and basin together at the end of the small apartment. Everything seems to be low in the jail, so my higher hospital chair is a blessing together with the rubber neck brace I brought with me. Not much space for clothes, although we have to wear the green prison uniform of tracksuit pants and top. The paint has peeled in many places from the yellow concrete floor. No carpet.

This morning a visit from a couple of women from the placing service (which is not its correct name), including Vicky the boss wearing a cross. I requested a bit more space to walk and a more congenial space (than the yard I currently use), a later lockdown, and a bit of company. Given my status, the last two requests are not possible, and a cell with its own small exercise area, always accessible, would seem to be the only option. Whatever happens with that, Vicky suggested I was likely to be around Melbourne when I leave here.

My blood pressure was not too bad when I visited the doctor, but I think the automatic monitor needs recalibrating. The readings were too high.

Had a lovely hour with Tim O'Leary[18] and Bernadette Tobin.[19] Quite a deal of news about the fierce divisions in society on my situation.

The most consoling piece of news was from Tim's parish, where Fr Kevin [McGovern] preached well on my predicament and the Mass numbers seemed to be up! Shane Healy, the Melbourne Arch-diocese press man, said he had heard similar news.

A couple of reports were disturbing, although neither is likely to come into effect. Frank Brennan, SJ, was to receive an honorary doctorate from the Melbourne College of Divinity; or, more cor-rectly, its university status successor. He was informed it was not going ahead because of his support for me. Apparently now the news is the award will be conferred at a later time.[20]

Greg Craven, Australian Catholic University vice-chancellor, has also been strongly attacked for his support, with the head of the ACU branch of the academic union saying he should be sanctioned and writing to that effect to the ACU chancellor.[21] Naturally, Greg also has support, but the storm was or is considerable.

Tim also wrote to the principal of St Patrick's, Ballarat, [John Crowley] objecting to the removal of my name from a wing of buildings, who phoned him to say he has received a lot of criti-cism from the Old Boys, but support from the parents of the year sevens. "Yes," said Tim, "because they don't know George Pell." Tim had heard from all the members of his crew, Bruce Ryan, Rick Murphy, and Peter Leonard, who in his small piece for [the school's magazine] *The Shamrock* (I think) listed me as an important influence in his life. Please God my predicament will provoke some strengthening among those who have drifted a bit, as well as among the strong Catholics.

---

[18] Tim O'Leary is the senior executive of the Archdiocese of Melbourne and a friend of Cardinal Pell.

[19] Bernadette Tobin is the director of the Plunkett Centre for Ethics; her husband, Terry, is a Queen's Counsel.

[20] Fr Frank Brennan, SJ, is a Jesuit priest, author, and lawyer, as well as rector of Newman Col-lege, University of Melbourne. The postponement of the award was subsequently made public.

[21] "Australian Catholic University Staff Want Greg Craven Disciplined over Pell Support", *The Guardian*, 5 March 2019.

Tim reported a good article in *Quadrant*,[22] [George] Weigel in *First Things*,[23] and good stuff from Raymond de Souza.[24]

As my breviary still has not arrived, I returned to week one, and the second reading today was from Athanasius on God, the all-holy Father of Christ, who is the Supreme Steersman, who guides and orders the universe for our salvation through the work of our Lord and Saviour, the good Word, the sole Word of the good God, living and active. Athanasius anticipates the response to the deist notion of God as a clockmaker, who winds up the universe and then leaves it entirely to its own devices, by explaining that God's continuing care is needed to prevent creation from returning to nothing.

Probably the universe is a bit more messy and wasteful than Athanasius envisaged, and certainly the universe is larger than he ever dreamed.

I do not know why God created such an immense universe, any more than I know why he created dinosaurs. What is interesting is the uniqueness of human life, and probably intelligent life, on this tiny planet in a remote corner of the universe, created 14.3 billion years ago. Similar to the coming of the Redeemer, God's Son, Jesus, born a poor child in a backward and troublesome province of the mighty Roman Empire. What is the providential purpose of all this? Part of the answer must be that God acts like the gentle breeze of Elijah; or the dew descending, mentioned in the second Eucharistic Prayer. God plays a long game, and for most of the time he goes very quietly; but not always, as with John the Baptist and his successors. On many occasions, we do not know what God is doing.

Lord Jesus, help me settle in here for the next few months and use my time productively to pray, read, and write. I pray for all my friends, all those who are defending me, that you will keep them from harm.

Friday, 15 March 2019

Eighty letters arrived today, and it took me a couple of hours to read them. Very moving. During the whole of my priestly life, except

---

[22] Keith Windschuttle, "George Pell and the Jury", *Quadrant*, 12 March 2019.

[23] George Weigel, "The Holy See and Cardinal Pell", *First Things*, 13 March 2019.

[24] "Cardinal Pell to Be Sentenced: A Case of Justice or Corruption?", *National Catholic Register*, 12 March 2019.

perhaps for the last four-year spell in Rome, I was always strength-ened and inspired by the quality of the faith of the people I served. So many good people, generally going quietly about their lives.

In the *Herald Sun* today, a short article appeared reporting that the number of calls to helplines had increased during the publicity around my jailing and sentencing.[25] This would follow the normal pattern.

I was worried by the number of those who might leave the Church or stop practising because they judged me guilty. I do not have evi-dence on this.

What did come as a surprise was Tim O'Leary yesterday claiming the Mass numbers were up in his Melbourne parish. Three Sydney letters today followed a similar line.

Jim and Genevieve McCaughan[26] wrote: "Ash Wednesday saw a veritable multitude attending Mass—far, far more than in previous years." Like a big number of others, they claimed, "We are pawns in a raging cosmic battle."

Drs Cathy and Richard Lennon[27] sent a card with a dozen photos, most from my life as a bishop, writing: "Already we have heard of people returning to the practice of the faith because of your coura-geous witness."

Mary Clare Meney, just before leaving for Medjugorje, wrote a bit more expansively:

> You may be surprised to hear this but your situation has changed the Catholic landscape within Australia and I feel much good is going to come from it. I see already some very positive things happening. I have heard of a number of lapsed Catholics suddenly return to Mass; and the "shock waves" have caused many practising Catholics to "step up" in their spiritual life. This is a "wake-up" call for all of us—and I believe it is all in the plan of Divine Providence.

I had remarked jokingly to one or two close friends that I could not detect any improvement in myself despite the deluge of prayers and penance over the last few years from around Australia, the UK, US, and Ireland particularly and more widely. All the leadership of

[25] "Helpline Calls Rise", *The Herald Sun*, 15 March 2019.
[26] Jim and Genevieve McCaughan, friends of Cardinal Pell.
[27] Drs Cathy and Richard Lennon, friends of Cardinal Pell.

the Neocatechumenal Way[28] from around the world are interceding. Now we see God's providence at work in a way I never anticipated.

Whatever the extent of this development and whatever the time it continues, it is a mighty reason to thank God and recommit myself to using my jail time well in a religious sense. And I must take care that false words or false steps of mine do not damage the spiritual ecology. *Deo gratias.*

Also received a beautiful letter from Fr Francis Denton, Fr Anthony's younger brother, and a copy of a splendid sermon on me and the general situation. A young priest with brains, insight, and intestinal fortitude (and a fine painter). He added: "One has the strange sense that events are coming to a head, and the entire Church finds herself on the threshold of her final purification. Whatever the case, God in his providence will order all things to the good of those who trust in him." In different ways, usually less elegantly and less extremely, many of the letter writers are aware of a bitter showdown between good and evil, faith and hostility, relativism and the Judaeo-Christian tradition. Let us see.

An anonymous Russian-Australian named George sent me a text on the saintly life from St Anthony the Great, the early hermit or monk from Egypt, included in the *Philokalia.*[29] I had not read it previously. Good and profound with a deal of common sense. The virtuous life "is not attainable for everyone in equal measure". Spiritual people should not talk too much, which is probably correct, but his views on material reality went too far for me: "What is alien to man is everything created. So, disdain all things." We can be led astray by God's creation, but it is regularly beautiful and good.

Lord Jesus Christ, help me not to give in to exasperation, anger, despondency during the months ahead. Bless all those who are praying for the Church and for myself, and strengthen all those who have been moved by the Spirit to come closer to yourself and the Church. May the tares not choke them.

---

[28] Catholic international lay movement founded in Spain in 1964, which draws inspiration for its forms of prayer and worship from the early centuries of the Church, and is centred on missionary work especially among marginalised people.

[29] A collection of Greek texts about Christian monastic and ascetical life, first published in 1793. It gathered the unpublished writings of the major hermits of Eastern Christianity up to the fourteenth century. *Philokalia* means "love of the good and beautiful".

Saturday, 16 March 2019

A quiet day today with a new commandant in the unit, blond, silent, somewhat disapproving. I had asked in the morning for a broom to sweep my room and to have my laundry done. Neither eventuated.

Saw the Muslim doctor this morning. My blood pressure was 140 over 80, which suits me perfectly. As I have developed over the past couple of days a heavy cold or the flu, I mentioned this also to Dr Muhammad, and he placed a swab up my nose to identity what was ailing me. If it is influenza, I would be the first in the prison! The medicine he prescribed would arrive tonight (it did not) or tomorrow. On my return, I managed to obtain some salt so that I could inhale warm salty water as the Indian peasants do and as recommended to me by Dr Trachtenberg (to relieve nasal congestion).

My Lenten breviary still has not arrived, although Kartya is promising action, so I went back to the first week of Ordinary Time for the readings. I have had my fill of the Wisdom literature, of Ecclesiasticus, for the moment, and I could not find too much inspiration in the worthy letter ascribed to Clement of Rome.[30] Apparently it was considered for inclusion in the New Testament canon, but I am not surprised it did not make the list. Much less strange than the Apocalypse, but a bit ordinary.

I also struggled to complete my twenty pages of St Anthony the Great. We have to curb "the body as an enemy and adversary of the soul",[31] which is certainly true but not the whole story. We are entitled to be comfortable for some of the time.

Naturally, as Anthony is one of the founders of the monastic movement, if not the founder, in the East and an expert in the interior life, my hesitations or dissent touch only on some particular points.

He gives us plenty of reason to ponder as he writes, "When a man is not good, it means he does not know God. The only means to know God is goodness."[32]

This obviously reflects the psalmist explaining that only the man with clean hands and pure heart will climb the mountain of the

---

[30] First Letter of Clement, ca. AD 96.

[31] *Philokalia*, St Anthony the Great, "On the Character of Men and on the Virtuous Life", no. 117

[32] Ibid., no. 29.

Lord.[33] But is there anything else to be said? One of the mysteries of our age is the rise of unbelief, sometimes in men and women whose moral lives are or seem to be blameless. Augustine claimed that our hearts are restless unless they rest in God,[34] but so many lapsed Catholics seem to have no angst on the issue at all, as though they have happily become tone deaf. I am reluctant to conclude that all those who do not believe are not good. I think of my father, who was a good man while religiously tone deaf, although he became more sympathetic to the Church as time passed. And I think of one first cousin, the kindest of men who cared for a difficult mother in her last years and his wife of a happy marriage when she fell ill. To my surprise he had a completely non-religious funeral.

On a broader level, I feel that the love of prosperity, sometimes a genuine materialism, and the sexual revolution have dimmed the capacity to see God. And many people are uneasy and restless, as we see through marriage breakdowns, alcohol, drugs, addiction to pornography.

The teachers in our schools are now in the front line trying to help and heal the children suffering from the mistakes, the defeats of their parents or stepparents or "uncles". I remember the piece of Brazilian graffiti: Divorce contracts are written in the tears of their children.

Whatever these mighty sociological tides might be, part of the Church's problem is self-inflicted. If Christ is the Son of God, his teaching has a unique authority, and his teaching when lived brings human flourishing. Despite G. K. Chesterton's pessimism, many good people over the centuries have tried and succeeded in living the Christian life. When we believe we can improve on Jesus by eliminating the hard teachings or downplaying prayer, faith, the cross, etc., then we should not be surprised that people leave or do not join. A religion that is too easy is a false religion.

What do some of the reform forces in the Church want to change? They never put all their cards on the table. It was a moment of awakening for me when I claimed to a high European prelate that the first criterion for a good bishop is that he would witness to the Catholic and apostolic faith. My interlocutor frothed with indignation and disapproval.

---

[33] Psalm 23.
[34] Augustine of Hippo, *Confessions* (ca. 400), book 1.

God our Father, keep us always faithful to your Son, our Redeemer, and help Church leaders see that the only Catholic unity is around the apostolic tradition.

The alternative is certain decline.

WEEK 4

Sublime Company

17 March–23 March 2019

Sunday, 17 March 2019

St Patrick's Day and probably for the first time in seventy years I did not mark the feast in any special way, except for a few extra prayers for Ireland. The television is full of the appalling massacre in the mosque in Christchurch, perpetrated by an Australian fanatic addicted to gaming. However, I did not come across anything on Ireland on SBS, which is probably more left of centre politically and socially even than the ABC.[1]

The Church is declining in Ireland, which still has too many priests and almost no seminarians, although Mass-going nationally is supposed to be above 30 percent. A strong core remains faithful, attending pilgrim centres such as Knock and Croagh Patrick in good numbers. Certainly at Knock a few years ago they had many confessions.

I worked hard with Pope Benedict to obtain stronger bishops in Ireland. He was sympathetic, but not good at translating his wishes into action. When [Archbishop] Charlie Brown was appointed nuncio [to Ireland 2012–2017], I had hoped for an improvement. Certainly there do not seem to have been any "bad" appointments, but all the newcomers, like their older confreres, so far are captive to the bishops' conference. With strong leadership, a repeat of the Holland and Quebec collapse should be avoided. A bishop needs to raise the flag to announce that he is reforming the religious education

---

[1] The Australian Broadcasting Company (ABC) is a national, government-funded television and radio network.

curriculum and setting up a new seminary. If Ireland has any life left, a good number should rally.

I am surprised by the passivity of the Irish Catholics, very different from their cousins in Australia until fifty years ago. As I asked rhetorically at Cork in an after-dinner speech in 2011, "Has all the good Irish blood gone overseas?" No lack of fight in that room, however. As one good lady commented, "Oh my God, I was ready to march."

I am sympathetic to Kathy Sinnott's Newman College project, a Catholic liberal arts college like Campion here in Australia. It is struggling (if it still exists). To have any chance, such a project needs a strong academic leader (which they have in Nicholas Healy, who was at Ave Maria University in Florida and previously in Michigan), a suitable building, and money. Another necessity, of course, is a decent number of students, which seem to be in short supply, and at least some wealthy donors. Not sure how many of these are about in Ireland, either.

Paul and Kartya called, informing me that the Appeal Court overturned the conviction of a Christian brother accused of paedophilia crimes in the 1960s, which is good news.[2]

Still waiting for my breviary, but Kartya assures me it has arrived at the prison. I await new magazines and some books, also.

Another twenty-four letters were delivered today, which is very encouraging. *Deo gratias*.

After finishing my meditations on the Epistle to the Hebrews, I decided to move through the Book of Revelation.

When I was Archbishop of Melbourne, a classmate, Fr John Williams, came to tell me he was dying. A dedicated and faithful priest, and an alcoholic with a dry sense of humour, he smiled and said he was not sure he would have stopped drinking if he had realised he was to die so young! He added that so far he had not thought much about life after death, but was commencing meditation on

---

[2] "Freedom for Frail Cleric after Appeal Court Dumps Child Sex Conviction", *Age*, 15 March 2019. Br John Francis Tyrrell was convicted on the evidence of his accuser alone, despite manifold problems with his evidence. The conviction was overturned by a unanimous decision of three judges of the Victoria Court of Appeal. One of these judges was Justice Mark Weinberg, whose dissent from the Court of Appeal's decision on 21 August 2019 to dismiss Cardinal Pell's appeal attracted considerable notice.

Revelation. This still seems to me a good idea and one reason for my choice. I have no premonition of death at all, but at my age it will not hurt to start to prepare, even as I hope it is a remote preparation!

St John the Apostle is hard on most of the seven churches he is addressing. I would be pleased to be like the church in Philadelphia, who have kept the Lord's command to endure patiently, and I am not "dead" like the church in Sardis (Rev 3:1, 10). Perhaps I fit in Smyrna: "I tell you, the devil will put some of you in prison to test you, and you will suffer persecution for ten days. Be faithful" (Rev 2:10).

God our Father, I thank you for all those who worked heroically if imperfectly to plant the faith in Australia. Bless and reward all the sons and daughters of St Patrick who built the church in Victoria, and raise up leaders in Ireland for a fightback, to stop the rot and at least steady the situation. Lord Jesus, give them good seminarians and priests and religious, and raise up more Catholic lay leaders like David Quinn.[3]

Monday, 18 March 2019

I might be losing a bit of spiritual momentum as I slip into a daily routine. Sr Mary did not call once again. I should ask to see her. I would like to get a missal especially for Holy Week. No problem with the daily round of prayer, although as I am not waking during the night (generally), that means one less rosary! Strangely, I do not particularly enjoy my exercise sessions, but I am aware I need the exercise and the rosary is a congenial and valuable help while I walk, just as it was on the exercise bike in Sydney.

Woken every morning around 6:00 am to receive my medicine (the poor man up the corridor who had been shouting madly has just stopped). As the bed is low and the concrete floor slippery, I place my right foot into my prison gym shoe to give me enough traction to rise. I now go back to bed until 7:15 am, when the siren sounds (the Muslim prayer singing has just started). Not at all sure where Islam fits

[3] David Quinn is the director of the Iona Institute, Ireland.

into salvation history as there are so many good Muslims. The worst of them are in another category, as Aquinas believed.[4]

Breakfast comes around 8:00 am, after I have made my bed. It is important to ask for my razor and mirror at this time. Today I also repeated my request for a broom, was promised the same, which did not arrive. Am enquiring about another prison uniform dull green tracksuit top, as this one I am wearing, despite my cleaning, is beginning to look like a dinner jacket. Some stains are intractable.

We have roll calls twice a day, when we have to place our hand on the small trap, which they open in the cell door. The main meal is around 11:00 am and the final meal at 3:30 pm, which I postpone if the food is cold. Bananas, apples, oranges available.

Have developed a better system with my leftover food, paper plates, plastic cutlery, etc., which I wrap in newspaper and store in the large brown paper bags that are available, before consigning to rubbish in evening.

Watch Channel 7 *Sunrise* for breakfast, perhaps at the late morning lunch, and then SBS 6:30 pm international news, followed often by an ABC or SBS program. Saw another episode on the Kennedys tonight covering the Cuban Missile Crisis. I had not known, or perhaps not remembered, that the US had pulled its missiles out of Turkey as a *quid pro quo*, although I had some vague recollection of a deal. I wonder if this Turkey deal is mentioned in my Sorensen and Schlesinger biographies of JFK.[5]

Bobbie was my favourite Kennedy, whom I met on Capitol Hill when I was serving at the new Cathedral of Mary Our Queen, Baltimore, in 1967. Johnnie Weigel[6] was with me. Kennedy was full of Irish American charm and respectful toward a young Aussie priest. When he was shot, I said then my love affair with America was over. It returned, but changed.

---

[4] Muhammad "can also be figured for the dragon in the same Apocalypse which says that the dragon swept up a third of the stars and hurled down a third to earth. Although this line is more appropriately understood concerning the Antichrist, Mohammed was his precursor—the prophet of Satan, father of the sons of haughtiness." From Thomas Aquinas, *On Reasons for Our Faith against the Muslims, Greeks and Armenians* (New Bedford, Mass.: Academy of the Immaculate Publishing, 2002).

[5] Theodore C. Sorensen, *Kennedy* (New York: Harper & Row, 1965) and Arthur M. Schelsinger Jr, *A Thousand Days: John F. Kennedy in the White House* (New York: Time, Inc., 1965).

[6] Dr John Weigel, brother of George Weigel.

Usually take my shower late in the afternoon and write this diary just before bed.

David called, and we had a good hour together. I told him I had no intention at this stage of ever moving to Bendigo, and we agreed to return to the question of Margaret's will after the appeal is heard.

The Court of Appeal judgement on Tyrrell exonerating him arrived from Paul this morning. I galloped through it and was very heartened by the systematic forensic examination of all the pieces of evidence.

My Lenten breviary arrived today, with cover intact; fragile to some extent after more than forty-five years' use.

I continued with the meditation on the Book of Revelation, where the Lamb opened the seven seals (chaps. 5–9). Frightening stuff, although even today in Syria, for example, we see wars and suffering on a diabolical scale. Life is inescapably a mighty struggle between good and ill, although in Australia, a peaceful English-speaking democracy, this is played out more staidly, often under the surface, than in places like South America, Africa, and China. Christchurch is a terrible exception.

In Australia, as the secular minority has increased to become the second largest "religious" group after the Catholics, the struggle to rid the law of Judaeo-Christian influence means the disputes are more open and bitter, and this in turn means anti-Catholicism. Tony Abbott[7] suffered from it. I feel deeply that there is more than a whiff of the spirit of evil at work in my legal struggle, also.

Lord Jesus, raise up leaders here in Australia who will continue the public struggle for love, righteousness, and the natural order. Give them wisdom, discernment, and especially courage, which is often in short supply.

Tuesday, 19 March 2019

Today was an unusual day in my quiet prison life as I never stepped outside my cell. Someone had mentioned that I would visit the doctor today, but nothing happened during the morning. When lunch

---

[7] Anthony John Abbott (b. 1957), prime minister of Australia 2013–2015.

was served about 11:00 am, I mentioned that I was happy to get my half hour of exercise, whenever it was convenient. The guard replied that because I had influenza I would not be allowed out. I complained about the injustice of this, and he said the boss of section 8 would speak to me.

(Our mad friend is shouting again.)

I felt a bit disconcerted, more powerless than ever, and even wondered whether I had stood on someone's toes.

After lunch, I wrote a note asking to see the doctor and the boss to discover why I could not take exercise alone, despite my influenza. (You slip your note under the door into the corridor.) Eventually the boss arrived wearing a surgical mask and standing back a metre from the door. He had the decency to laugh with me at the spectacle. I suggested they ring a bell as I approached the exercise pen so the guards could keep their distance. He was apologetic, amiable, and said he would speak with his superiors, but had to follow the regulations.

I started Tolstoy's *War and Peace*, which Rebecca had brought at my request. I remembered visiting his lovely old house in Moscow with Kris Sadowski,[8] or did he simply organize the trip? No, I think he was there.

Then the older Anglo doctor, whom I had seen yesterday, called to talk about my blood count, which was above 3, a bit high, and said I should take Warfarin in the evening, not the morning. He spoke about my cough and explained I did not have influenza. On hearing this, I appealed to the local boss, who was listening, pointing out that, as I did not have influenza, I should be able to exercise. Then he explained the whole prison was quarantined, presumably against the flu. This was probably true as we had no afternoon count.

The doctor was clear that no exercise was not his recommendation, but he would not make his views known as he only worked at the prison a couple days a week.

Sr Mary had called and could not be admitted, although the boss said that the three of us together would set times for a couple of visits each week for the future. A good solution. Nothing heard from

---

[8] Kris Sadowski, leader of the Polish Catholic community in Melbourne and friend of Cardinal Pell.

my lawyers, who I presume would have been barred, also. I am still coughing up a lot of rubbish, but my cold is a bit better. The quarantine should be lifted tomorrow.

Used my Lenten breviary for the first full day. Exodus is the first reading and already "on the fifteenth day of the second month", the Jewish people are blaming Moses and Aaron for leading them into the wilderness to die from hunger and lamenting the lost flesh pots of Egypt (Ex 16:1–3). God came under attack also and, hearing their cries, sent the quails and the manna (Ex 16:11–15). Plain speaking was the tradition; Job was not an innovator in his outspokenness.

To my delight, a couple of *Spectators* arrived, which contained high quality and sympathetic articles on my case. Charles Moore had a useful paragraph, also.[9] I had previously donated my earlier *Spectators* and other magazines to the prison library, so that I could receive new magazines—up to six.

Michael Davis of the *Catholic Herald* writing in the *Spectator* was critical of Robert Richter for not allowing me to take the stand.[10] This is misstated, as I made the decision.

Until halfway through the first trial, I had presumed I would be in the box, but Robert explained that he never allowed this, and only one client had gone against his advice. I was relieved and never gave it too much thought.

Frank Brennan was always keen for me to be in the box, especially after the hung jury decision. Eventually I decided I should give evidence, despite the entire legal team and my own advisers being opposed. Terry Tobin[11] came around to my point of view.

I only decided not to take the stand after the prosecutor had dealt with Charlie Portelli and especially Max Potter.[12] I was so cross with the treatment they both received, I was frightened that my hostility might turn a majority for acquittal into a split decision. The basis of my reasoning was quite wrong.

---

[9] Melanie McDonagh, "Why I Find the George Pell Verdict Hard to Believe", *Spectator*, 27 February 2019; Charles Moore, "A Re-run Trial in Australia Has Convicted Cardinal George Pell of Child Sexual Abuse", *Spectator*, 2 March 2019.

[10] Michael Davis, "My Personal Thoughts on George Pell's Conviction", *Spectator*, 9 March 2019.

[11] Terry Tobin, a friend and Queen's Counsel.

[12] Maxwell Potter, former sacristan at St Patrick's Cathedral, Melbourne.

I have no complaint with Richter's work. Forensically, we clearly won the trial, and I thought he demonstrated this more effectively in the second trial than the first. Robert is a friend whom I admire, an outstanding QC who is very upset by the "perverse verdict", his phrase, and professed his belief in my innocence on the front page of *The Age*.[13] It is impossible, for me and all the legal team, to conjecture the forensic path, the logic the jury used to come to a unanimous verdict of guilty. Philip Breene's article in the 9 March *Spectator* on Joh Bjelke-Petersen probably explains what happened in my case.[14] Public opinion was too deeply hostile to me.

God our Father, I do not know how many people over the centuries and around the world have been condemned unjustly like your Son. Take care of these victims. I pray for our justice system here in Australia, that all practitioners will be scrupulous in their work for justice, and I pray especially for all my fellow Australians who have been wrongly convicted.

Wednesday, 20 March 2019

An unusual day, although ultimately closer to the normal pattern. At breakfast, the guard informed me, as I heard him explain to my unknown neighbour (I have not seen another prisoner in this section of twelve), that the whole jail would be closed down and in quarantine today. I thanked him for letting me know and thought this would not go down well with the great majority of prisoners, if they have to stay in their cells again all day.

Unexpectedly, at 11:30 am, I was asked if I wanted a walk, because they had lifted the ban in our section, where no one had influenza. My coughing was decreasing and drying up. Naturally I was pleased to get outside for thirty-five minutes, although the phones were inactive. I had marched on the spot yesterday every hour or two for one hundred steps, which is not the same as moving, even if the space is

---

[13] See "Church Knew Pell Was at Centre of Decades-Old Lurid Sex Claims", *Age*, 7 March 2019.

[14] Philip Breene, "Prosecuting Pell", *Spectator*, 9 March 2019.

confined and grubby. It was warm, so I took my cardigan off, but overcast, although still nice to be outside. My prison top needs a wash (I have been promised laundry tomorrow), so I wore my long-sleeved blue and white shirt under the old dark blue cardigan. I must say I felt a bit better for the change.

About a week ago, one of the Ganmain Dominican Sisters, who had been a physiotherapist, told me not to forget my upper body fitness. I had done nothing, but then commenced a simple routine.

Another twenty-five to thirty letters, including beautifully long letters from Rebecca and Georgie and an unexpected couple of pages from Margaret. Georgie had multiple suggestions and a quiz, so I will have to do my homework before I meet with her on Monday.

Obviously, the letters are encouraging, and many give evidence of the deepest faith. A real tonic. Some thank me for the measures I took to try to strengthen the faith in the community, and I am grateful this is acknowledged and the particular initiatives are identified. God gives the increase, but the moves were well intentioned and, I deeply believe, coherent and consistent with the only strategies that might produce growth. We have been in the lean years, and prayer, orthodoxy, and loyalty cannot guarantee genuine growth. However, we have to be united to the vine, and we will certainly not nourish genuine vitality without faith, prayer, and sacrifice.

Too many, even some bishops, are too reconciled to decline, and some do not even know where the battlefield is. Some of the functionaries for the coming Australian Catholic Plenary Council 2020 are in this category. If things go wrong, the council could finish up restarting the slide toward a rout, like the collapse suffered in Quebec, Holland, Belgium. But the young priests, the young women religious (to the extent we have them) are faithful, prayerful, and know where the main game is to be played. Overwhelmingly, also, the smaller number of regularly worshipping young adults are faithful and prayerful.

The situation now is almost the opposite of that after the Second Vatican Council, where all of us young priests and religious were "progressive", committed to the conciliar reforms, as the differences slowly emerged between those committed to following the text of the council documents and those who saw the texts as mere compromises to be used as springboards for other and "better" options.

Thirty thousand men left the priesthood, and even more religious departed. Ratzinger, de Lubac, Daniélou, von Balthasar[15] clarified the options between continuity or rupture.

One correspondent wrote that the measures I introduced saved her life. *Deo gratias*. Jim Wallace[16] also wrote and was not flattering about our judicial system.

My meditation this morning was a bit of a disaster as I dozed for two-thirds of the allotted time and twenty minutes beyond it. My recollection is hazy, but I think the Little Flower, St Thérèse of Lisieux, said that sleep remains "valid" prayer, as the intention is good even if the flesh is weak.[17]

One lady suggested that the Lord is getting me to do reparation for McCarrick, whom I had met many times.[18] I would be happy to play a small part in this, as he has done much damage, which was then deepened by the cover-up and his revival when Benedict was gone. She also hoped I was not being treated as badly as St John of the Cross was when his religious brothers imprisoned him. I am not being treated badly.

This reminds me of a conversation I had with Fr Kolvenbach, the superior general of the Jesuits, after I had clashed on television with the Australian Jesuit provincial [Fr William Uren] about St John Paul's magnificent encyclical on morality *Veritatis Splendor* in 1993 or 1994. At least, I claimed to Kolvenbach, I am not like St Charles Borromeo, the sixteenth-century reformer and archbishop of Milan, who was the victim of an assassination attempt by some of the religious in his archdiocese. "Not yet", he responded. A magnificent

---

[15] Joseph Cardinal Ratzinger, Henri Cardinal de Lubac, Jean Daniélou, and Hans Urs von Balthasar.

[16] Jim Wallace, national director of the Australian Christian Lobby, 2000–2013.

[17] *The Story of a Soul: The Autobiography of St Therese of Lisieux* (1898), chap. 8: "I should be distressed that I drop off to sleep during my prayers and during my thanksgiving after Holy Communion. But I don't feel at all distressed. I know that children are just as dear to their parents whether they are asleep or awake and I know that doctors put their patients to sleep before they operate. So I just think that God 'knows our frame; He remembers that we are dust'."

[18] Theodore McCarrick, Archbishop of Washington, 2001–2006, was suspended from priestly ministry in June 2018 after a Church investigation upheld allegations of sexual abuse made against him. He resigned from the College of Cardinals in July 2018 as a result of further allegations of abuse committed against children and adult seminarians, and was laicised by Pope Francis in February 2019.

linguist, Kolvenbach was an intellectual, moral, and I think spiritual heavyweight, worthy of leading the Jesuits, even if I wondered about one or two of his utterances. What is absolutely certain is that in Rome generally, not universally, we no longer have this intellectual sophistication.

I saw on SBS television that the Holy Father has not accepted Cardinal Barbarin's resignation, because Barbarin is appealing.

Dear Lord Jesus, help me to be charitable in my judgements, honest and accurate; but charitable. Bless those who are working effectively for gospel renewal and give the gift of discernment to those good people who mean well but don't see clearly. "Set pools of (prayerful) silence in this thirsty land." [19]

Thursday, 21 March 2019

The biggest development in my quiet prison life was the first AFL[20] games of the season at the Melbourne Cricket Ground [MCG] before 84,000 people between traditional rivals Carlton and Richmond. Richmond finished up with a solid win of thirty points after a blitzkrieg of a first quarter, where we scored five or six goals holding the Blues to one point, their lowest first quarter score ever against Richmond. [Alex] Rance, the champion Richmond backman, an All-Australian for five years,[21] badly injured his knee, which will be an enormous loss if he cannot return for the finals.

---

[19] When he was archbishop of Melbourne, Cardinal Pell had these words from James McAuley's poem "A Letter to John Dryden" (1954) engraved on a fountain at St Patrick's Cathedral:

> Incarnate Word, in whom all nature lives,
> Cast flame upon the earth: raise up contemplatives
> Among us, men who walk within the fire
> Of ceaseless prayer, impetuous desire.
> Set pools of silence in this thirsty land.

[20] The Australian Football League (AFL) organizes competitions for professional men's Australian Rules football, which is a game more like rugby than American football.

[21] That is, selected for the (nonplaying) All-Australian team, comprising the best players from all teams each year.

My routine was destroyed, as this is being written next morning rather than between 9:00 and 11:00 pm. It will be interesting to see whether I finish up watching more football than at any time of my life, or whether it will become too much. We shall see.

It is sometimes said that I chose to study for the priesthood rather than play VFL (as it then was called—the Victorian Football League). The bigger choice for me was between going to university and a professional career, on the one hand, or priesthood. I went to the seminary feeling I needed to do so to follow God's will, so I was much less joyous and generous than many of my peers.

A number of VFL clubs were asking me to sign in 1959, my last year at St Patrick's, Ballarat, although I had by then almost reluctantly decided to go to the seminary. I never even managed to train with Richmond, although I did sign with them, and they promised me a place on the training list and the payment of my university fees. Another problem was that Newman College at Melbourne University did not allow students to play league football then, and I was keen to go there. Richmond was not the powerhouse it now is or became in the late sixties and seventies, nor was the preparation in any way as rigorous and professional as today.

I do not regret becoming a priest, although my life has been turbulent, as I do believe I did God's will, however imperfectly. I gave my life to a cause of ultimate significance—and a priestly way of life with many human consolations.

At the Royal Commission [into Institutional Responses to Child Sexual Abuse], some lamented the excessive reverence and deference given to the clergy by many Catholics. Without doubt, a minority of clergy abused this outrageously, but the respect, often love, shown to priests was not the result of some Church decree. It had been earned by generations of hard priestly work and prayer. Moreover, the people's devotion and loyalty were not indiscriminate; they were tolerant, but individuals and families made their judgements and choices.

An unexpected visit from a gentlemanly Indian-Australian physiotherapist, who worked on my left arm and shoulder, as my knees seemed to be progressing, although still swollen in an ungainly fashion.

A pleasant visit from Tim and Anne McFarlane, who told me that public opinion in the legal fraternity was strongly in my favour, even among those who disagreed with my views.

The second reading in the breviary was an excerpt from St Hilary of Poitiers on "Blessed is everyone who fears the Lord."

Fear of the Lord is not approved of by the progressive wing, because God is so loving, understanding, and all-forgiving. They do not always join these sentiments with the obvious premise that one needs to repent before God can forgive. I remember a vehement condemnation of "fear of the Lord" by a senior bishop, and indeed a majority of bishops voted to remove "the fear of God", or "of the Lord", from the liturgical translations at one of the Australian bishops' meetings.

Hilary explained that fear of the Lord had to be learned, through prayer and the search for wisdom and understanding, unlike our natural fear of being hurt through sickness, threats, or natural disasters.

I am in favour of fear of the Lord, properly defined, and not because I believe God is cruel or unpredictable or hostile. In many discussions over the decades, I usually began with the Scripture teaching that only "perfect love casts out fear" (1 Jn 4:18), and none of us can claim to love perfectly.

God is often reduced to being like a benevolent great uncle or grandfather, off the pace, kind, non-demanding, and ineffectual. It is extraordinary over the years how little time in our religious education programs was given to boosting and explaining God's profile. In my dialogue sessions with school students before their confirmation when I was an auxiliary bishop, we regularly struggled to obtain answers on what was meant when the Church teaches God as "Spirit".

I welcomed the new Mass translation of "with your spirit" for "*et cum Spiritu tuo*", as it brought the concept into regular prayer and, therefore, notice. It was harder to ignore.

God is the Spirit of love, who created the universe through his Son and will forgive every crime when there is genuine repentance. Even Stalin, Hitler, Pol Pot, and Mao would be eligible. This is extraordinary.

If Christianity continues to decline, society will be less forgiving. Constantine was the first Christian Roman emperor, whom I much admire, because he created sociological currents that carried people toward God and goodness. Peter Brown, the best living historian of early Christianity, said many were lapsing into Catholicism. For some unknown reason, Constantine had his son Crispus killed, and his pagan opponents claimed he became Christian, where his sin could be forgiven, as paganism did not forgive the killing of adult children. Abortion, of course, was rife.

Lord Jesus, raise up among us new Elijahs, men and women, to keep the flame of Christian monotheism burning, especially in Australia. We do not want our country to become a dry, weary wasteland, where there is little yearning for the Transcendent, while being mightily superstitious.

Friday, 22 March 2019

A second day that was different, not because of the second AFL match between Collingwood and Geelong, but because H, the sympathetic boss, a big plainspoken man, gave me three outings in the pen. The first was in the cool of the morning around nine, the second about 11:00 am, and the last about 4:00 pm, as the sun was thinking of setting. It was a beautiful afternoon with the sun reflected on the neighbouring skyscraper—and I could hear some birds singing and chirping. I have always loved the singing of birds, although singing is not quite the word for many Australian birds such as the kookaburra. Generally, we take the blessings of birdsong for granted. Unit 8, where I reside, is on the fifth floor, so the birds are some climbers.

Was also called twice to the medical centre to give blood as the first sample was insufficient. The Indian nurse taking the blood is not experienced in this procedure, does not hide it, and was teased a bit as a result. A more senior Irish nurse was able to advise. The test was simply to confirm whether my blood was thin enough to help avoid a stroke. No health problems, although my cold continues, despite some newspaper reports that I am in hospital. I am not sure who or what is behind such rumours.

A small senior delegation interviewed me to see how I was coping. I said I was going OK, no complaints and too much food. The drug and alcohol man asked if I had anything to say, and I replied that in my present position I had access to neither. The boss of the group, Miss Kendall, wished me well in my appeal.

The day was also unusual because I did not have time for all my daily routine!

At H's suggestion, I changed my sheets and blankets to help rid myself of my cold. In place of two old thin blankets, I received another of the same ilk and one heavy new dark blanket, which made a difference. I thank God for the kindness of the suggestion and am grateful for another small mercy.

Life is pretty basic at the moment, with the occasional small nuisances, such as a short-handled toothbrush, which bends during use, and weak plastic knives that cut inefficiently. Both of these are designed to prevent them being used as weapons.

My rubbish disposal technique is improving as I try to obtain a large brown paper bag, wrap my rubbish in newspaper, and dump it in the bag for the daily collection just before lockdown around 4:00 pm. The shower water is hot, like it was at St Patrick's, Ballarat, for the boarders in the late forties and fifties. The prison food is better and more plentiful than St Pat's food was then.

Newspaper reports have me in solitary confinement for twenty-three hours a day. Life is not like a silent retreat, as I have a television, some contacts with the guards, who are not hostile, visits (for example) to the doctor, conversations with the lawyers, and twice a week outside visitors on Monday and Thursday. My hour of exercise, generally in two half hours, is also in isolation.

Unfortunately, Rance's ACL[22] is completely ruptured, so he is out for twelve months; but, more happily, Geelong beat Collingwood in a great game. Collingwood wasted many opportunities, especially in the second quarter, and all six newcomers for Geelong played well.

Some of my closest friends and my closest cousins support the Pies.[23] On my confirmation dialogue rounds between 1987 and 1996 as an auxiliary bishop, someone would always ask what team I supported. I would ask for silence, which arrived invariably, and explained that I barracked for two teams: Richmond and any team playing Collingwood. Different levels of pandemonium ensued. Actually, I have a hidden soft spot for Collingwood since they organized collections among themselves to help us [Richmond] remain in Melbourne, decades ago, when "they" wanted to exile us to Queensland.

---

[22] Anterior cruciate ligament.
[23] The Collingwood AFL club, known as the Magpies.

The letters of support continue to arrive, some of them beautifully written and deeply spiritual, when not theological. One New South Wales correspondent, among quite a few others, compared my situation to that of Lindy Chamberlain, whose baby was taken by a dingo [Australian wild dog]. She, too, was roundly condemned by public opinion.

The correspondent reminded me that God's holy warrior angels surround me and that I am protected by the helmet of salvation, the shield of faith, and the sword of the Spirit. She urged me to forgive, bless, and pray for my accusers; which I do, and without enormous difficulty.

She pointed out that St Paul, the Pilgrim of *Pilgrim's Progress*, and Lindy Chamberlain all wrote about their jail experiences, and she urged me to do the same to affirm God's goodness and so "give hope to many others, who are going through trials of their own, to stand strong in their belief of God's saving power, love, and faithfulness to his Word."

I know all the prayers for me will not be wasted in God's plan, and this diary might be part of such a plan.

A beautiful letter arrived from the four remaining members of the John Paul II Institute for Marriage and the Family, which I helped start in 2001 and has now been closed because of financial pressures in the Melbourne Archdiocese, which recently spent tens of millions on a new office block. One of the worst decisions in the history of the archdiocese. A fine letter of thanks to me also from Owen Vyner, originally from West Australia, a graduate of JPII and now lecturing in Christendom College, Front Royal, Virginia, in the US.

Anna Silvas, a prominent theologian from Armidale in New South Wales, also put pen to paper. She was too generous to me, because God sometimes has to use defective instruments, but she spells out a "sublime" context of faith.

This day I have been very conscious of Cardinal Pell in prison and indeed in solitary confinement. Our Lord loves him too well to spare him this. Why, so holy a man as John the Baptist was not spared imprisonment in Herod's dungeons, and while there, he suffered, in my estimation, something of a very purifying Dark Night that tested the inmost cords of his heart. Our Lord's last word to John while he was alive is shattering: "Blessed is the man who is not scandalized in me." Hence I believe John was Our Lord's forerunner even in the Passion. Our Lord endured abandonment—John of the Cross calls it annihilation, with reference to the Latin text of Psalm 72—in all the psychic Reality of his human nature. This is the sublime company Cardinal Pell now has the privilege of keeping.

God our Father, we join our trials and tribulations to the redemptive sufferings of your Son. May something, many good things, come out of this mess, so that the Kingdom is spread and more believe God is good for them (and us).

Saturday, 23 March 2019

Big storms last night in Melbourne, especially in the eastern suburbs with some flooding. I was completely unaware of any rain, with my double-glazed opaque and barred window. The one consequence for me was that it was still raining this morning when I was asked to exercise, so I chose to take the time in the afternoon, as the youngish friendly Indian female guard was frightened I might slip. Today is the second day when I am going solo without my walking stick, as I no longer feel a bit wobbly every now and again.

No visit from either Sr Mary or the legal team, but both are likely to come tomorrow for Sunday. David told me on the phone that Kartya would definitely be here.

Margaret had a fall at St John's Hospital in Bendigo and remains there with a urinary tract infection. When they have space, she will go into rehabilitation for a fortnight. No bones broken, thank God.

The letters continue to arrive, and I opened about twenty today. Only a few are "strange", theologically or psychologically, or both. Most are beautiful and manifest a deep faith. H the supervisor said that when he arrived at the jail at 6:00 am yesterday, a couple of women were already outside praying. Plenty of support and plenty, plenty of hostility—but not in jail in unit 8, at least among the guards.

A letter from Greg Craven explained that Frank Brennan's honorary doctorate from the University of Divinity was delayed to avoid upsetting victims' feelings.[24] The protest against Greg at his staff meeting amounted to a quarter of the staff wearing stickers, no disruption, and a couple of hostile questions. His meeting with the academic staff at Aquinas campus, Ballarat, was completely harmonious. It is a sad reflection of the division and bitterness, and an expression of identity politics, that a call for justice for me is seen as antivictim. I repeat that we have no justice unless there is justice for all. When I win my appeal, and even if I do not, I will not be antivictim; but it is imperative that it be proved legally that complainants have been wronged.

The first breviary reading is again from Exodus and relates the promulgation by God of what we have tidied up into the Ten Commandments (Exodus, chap. 20). As an adult, and even as a child, I always regarded them as essential. Fifty years ago, I remember reading that Bertrand Russell, a famous atheist philosopher, claimed the Ten Commandments were like a final exam of ten questions, where only six needed to be attempted. Clever, but too convenient.

On another occasion, when I was explaining to a psychologist that the commandments were like a railway track or a highway to travel along powered by love, she responded that the countryside is more interesting off the highway. You can see a lot from a train without getting caught in the desert!

At the two Synods on the Family,[25] some voices loudly proclaimed that the Church was a hospital or a port of refuge. This is only one image of the Church and far from the most useful or important, because the Church has to show how not to become sick, how to avoid shipwrecks, and here the commandments are essential. Jesus himself taught, "If you keep my commandments you will remain in my love" (Jn 15:10).

Jim Wallace, a good friend and former director of the Australian Christian Lobby, which works to preserve Judaeo-Christian values in society, wrote me a strong letter of support, lamenting the weakness of the Australian legal system and nominating the four Scripture texts he had been using as he prayed for me and in his morning study.

---

[24] "Pell Support Puts Award on Hold for Frank Brennan", *Australian*, 16 March 2019. Greg Craven was the vice chancellor of the Australian Catholic University from 2008 to 2020.

[25] Convoked in 2014 and 2015. See Week 2, n. 7.

To my surprise, all were from the Old Testament, and it occurred to me that I had never meditated regularly on any Old Testament text, except perhaps Ezekiel. I continued my study of the Old Testament over the years (I think of Leon Kass' wonderful book on Genesis), learned to love the prophets and the psalms, and became a devotee of Elijah, because I believed he saved monotheism under Ahab and Jezebel. The parallel with today is obvious. I am not a Marcionite, as I believe God speaks through the Old Testament.

All four of Jim's references suited my situation, especially perhaps Samuel 17:47, where David is addressing the Philistines: "For the battle is the Lord's and he will give all of you into our hands."

Let me make my prayer today that of the soon-to-be canonized John Henry Newman:

Make us trust in thee, O Jesus ... Make us sure, O Lord, that the greater is our distress, the nearer we are to thee.

WEEK 5

Spiritual Mediocrity

24 March—30 March 2019

Sunday, 24 March 2019

Finished the day watching a TV show on Princess Diana[1] telling her side of her tragic story. How the establishment reckoned that a twenty-year-old, with not even university experience, from a broken family and after an unhappy childhood could cope with becoming Princess of Wales is still a mystery, although I haven't seen it much discussed.

No doubt there is another side to the story, but Charles' continuing relationship with Camilla[2] from the time of the marriage was intolerable for a young, inexperienced bride. Neither is it compatible with Christian teaching. A battle-hardened thirty-year-old cynic might have recognized a marriage of convenience and managed to survive, but Diana was already ill with the strain from her changed circumstances at the time of the ceremony.

She obviously did not want to bring down the House of Windsor, because of William, but she broke ranks and told her story to the public, caused the monarchy to wobble (much helped by John Major),[3] and took her revenge on Charles.

She was stunningly beautiful, and I still marvel at the depth and extent of the love and devotion for her. The public forgave her faults and recognized a victim.

---

[1] Diana, Princess of Wales, a member of the British royal family, married to Prince Charles and mother of William and Harry. She died in an automobile accident in 1997.

[2] Camilla Parker Bowles was romantically involved with Prince Charles prior to and during their first marriages. She later became the second wife of Prince Charles and uses the title Duchess of Cornwall.

[3] John Major served as prime minister of the United Kingdom from 1990 to 1997.

Soon after her death in 1997, Cardinal [Jozef] Tomko, prefect of the Vatican Congregation for the Evangelization of Peoples appointed me as apostolic visitor to the seminaries for the preparation of priests in Irian Jaya and Sulawesi in Indonesia. In northern Sulawesi, the first-year seminarians were segregated from the main seminary in Manado, about twenty kilometres [12.5 miles] along the coast. The seminarians, and they were many, lived in groups of six or ten in separate houses around a compound. Most houses had conventional Catholic names, but one was dedicated to Princess Diana. With a little affected severity, I asked how on earth this could have happened. The head of first-year formation rose to the challenge, claiming it was named after the princess to remind the students of how possible it is to go the wrong way! I did not recommend any name change and found the incident touching, although remarkable. Communications have brought strangers on two sides of the world together, captivated by the mystique of tradition, beauty, Diana's genuine and regular humanitarianism, and the tragedy of her life and death.

Diana was buried with a pair of rosary beads in her coffin, placed there by her butler, and she had met Mother Teresa, but Nigel Boonham, the sculptor, who had her sit for him as he prepared her statute, was clear that she had little religious sensibility.

A beautiful day, clear, and the sun was visible through the open top of the pen during both my exercise sessions. When the sun is out, it is a help, as overcast days can dampen the spirit. I still remember my first three weeks at Oxford University in 1967, where I spent nearly four happy years, when the sun never broke through the damp clouds once. By 1971, I think I could then have lived in England (if my family had been there). Growing up in the forties and fifties in Ballarat, I coped with Oxford winters, but I missed the Australian summers. During my first summer in England, I didn't go for a swim on a good warm day, saying to myself that I would wait for it to get a bit hotter. A big mistake as that day was the high point of the summer.

Until today I still hadn't managed to obtain a broom, but Sr Mary explained that you normally asked to clean your room when given time for exercise. This had never been explained to me, so at exercise time I raised the issue and finished up with a vacuum cleaner, a blue and white swipe, and a eucalyptus spray disinfectant. A little less dust might help my cold disappear.

Switched off a couple of Aussie Rules [football] matches, as either too one-sided or a bit lacklustre. Despite the quietness of prison life, I must confess I am still something of a sport snob.

The readings today were not the richest, not the most helpful for meditation. Augustine dealt well with the Samaritan woman and her continuing spiritual incomprehension, and the seven angels in Revelation brought to a conclusion their grim work. The puzzle is not merely the extent of the destruction, as millennia of history furnish similar terrible incidents, but the angels are doing, in apocalyptic language, God's work.

God our Father, help us to love your creation and be grateful for its beauty and goodness, which outweigh all the evil and suffering, even in this life. While I don't believe we are in the best of all possible worlds, neither do I have a black-armband view of salvation history. Help us believe in the strength of your love.

P.S. Both Kartya [Gracer] and Paul [Galbally] in the morning and Sr Mary in the afternoon visited. Mary said it was two weeks ago that she was last able to come, and we agreed she would come at 1:00 pm on Tuesdays.

Monday, 25 March 2019

I have never seen any other prisoners, and there are twelve of us in Unit 8. All are in solitary confinement. I don't know who the others are, although Gargasoulas is probably one and perhaps a Muslim terrorist. At least a couple are mentally disturbed.

This morning in my exercise half hour, the pen next door was occupied by a highly agitated prisoner, shouting profanities, as he spoke with a friend or adviser, perhaps lawyer, whose voice I could not understand or hear clearly.

Later when I returned from my visit with Georgie, my niece, a squad of guards was in the common area putting on white uniforms and accompanied by an Alsatian dog. I presumed it was for some practice routine. As I entered my cell, I asked what was happening and was told I would find out.

Later it emerged that one prisoner was refusing to leave his cell, so the squad was called to gas him out. At one stage, the dog was whining in a strange way, voices were raised, and some confusion ensued. The boss H came to the small window on my door and asked was I all right. Not knowing what was going on, my response was that of course I was all right.

By coincidence, I tried to pass a note under my door into the corridor and found the opening was blocked, obviously against the gas, as I now realise. And that was that. The prisoner was removed, I was told. No loud shouting. No profanities.

Nearly every night, two of the prisoners, one of them near to me, used to shout out to each other in rich Aussie accents, but occasionally in a foreign language.

So far tonight, we have heard no such dialogue and no Muslim prayers. Perhaps the forcibly departed guest was the Muslim terrorist.

Spent a pleasant hour with Georgie, who came down from Bendigo. Margaret seemed to be holding her own in the hospital in Bendigo, and Georgie was keen for me to keep a journal or diary as a way of coping, of dealing with my feelings. I was able to explain that this was already underway. She was interested to hear of my daily routine.

Must confess a small lapse. Every contact visit is preceded by a strip search, an undignified procedure. A new guard, whom I had not met, was very directive, telling me, among other things, to take my socks off. He then told me to stop taking off my socks. Exasperated, I interjected that it was only one minute earlier that he had told me to take the bloody things off.

No more was said. He was younger, officious, perhaps a bit hostile, but not malevolent, I think, and I thanked him as I left. Not even a storm in a teacup, but . . .

A batch of letters arrived from Galbally's office, all of them encouraging, and many of them homing in on the Easter theme of Jesus' redemptive suffering.

Others range more widely. One prisoner has written a couple of long, sophisticated messages, full of support, useful advice, and interesting odds and ends. After explaining that he did not participate in a conversation with some fellow prisoners on my situation, he quoted this Chinese proverb. "Don't try to teach a pig to sing. It wastes your time and annoys the pig." Paul Galbally, like me, was delighted, saying he would add it to his repertoire.

Sr Mary gave me a copy of an excellent sermon by Mary M. McGlone, a Sister of St Joseph from the US.[4] Moses was her subject, and she rejected the magnificent muscled persona, with the tablets in his hand, of Michelangelo's statue in Rome. Rather "he was a runaway criminal who relied on his father-in-law for a job." True, but a lot more was to follow.

McGlone's main theme was that "Jesus' Father has a habit of choosing to work through the most inauspicious people and circumstances." God lacks highly qualified agents, she claimed. I found all this comforting and encouraging.

I am not pretending that I don't have some worldly capacity and have not achieved this and that, whatever of my failures and omissions; but I do not feel spiritually adequate to the drama that is being played out around me. My adventures and how they conclude are important for the Church in Australia, and I am consoled to hear of God using spiritually mediocre people.

Lord Jesus, help us all to follow in your footsteps, to concentrate on the essentials of faith, hope, and love.

Also, let me once again make my own another passage from John Henry Newman, taken from one of my favourite poems:

> *Lead, Kindly Light, amid the encircling gloom,*
> *Lead thou me on!*
> *The night is dark, and I am far from home,*
> *Lead thou me on!*
> *Keep thou my feet; I do not ask to see*
> *The distant scene; one step enough for me.*[5]

Tuesday, 26 March 2019

Most of my theorizing on the gassed prisoner is awry. This morning I could hear some Muslim prayer chants, but they were muffled, from

---

[4] Mary M. McGlone, "Third Sunday of Lent: Catching Fire", *National Catholic Reporter*, 23 March 2019.

[5] John Henry Newman, "The Pillar of the Cloud" (1833).

farther away. Then early tonight, not long after lockdown, some shouted dialogue did take place, briefly and perhaps with a different and third voice. Later in the evening I could hear a distant Muslim prayer chant.

All in all, I am none the wiser. It is possible that the prisoner was returned to his cell after being gassed out. I will try to find out that much tomorrow, if I can.

Apparently, I was on the front page of the *Herald Sun* today, with headlines about Pell, Hell, and my cell, claiming my cell is next to Gargasoulas'.[6] From comments made today by the guards, it seems this could be true. They told me TV crews were at the entrance as they arrived as well as a group praying for me. Sr Mary thought the article might win me a bit more sympathy.

My concerns were somewhat different. This morning, two members of the Sentence Management Unit called to talk about my future lodgings. The boss still thought I would be moving either to the Remand Centre or some other centre not far from Melbourne. I would not be going to Port Phillip, which has been privatised and is not favoured by the prisoners—or the guards here.

The major, indeed only, significant issue is my personal safety from prisoner violence. This publicity might make it more difficult to maintain this in a new location. H feels that I am likely to remain here until my appeal. While this would not be a catastrophe, I would prefer more freedom to be outside, less confinement, and perhaps easier and more frequent visiting hours. We shall see.

Sr Mary called to give me Holy Communion, and she remained for a good chat, asking one of the female guards to move away from the bookshelf behind us, as we were entitled to speak together privately. The guard took two books and left us. Mary is feisty and formidable, and I can see how she has all the auxiliary bishops celebrating Mass in the jails and a Mass every week in each jail.

Managed two exercise sessions outside on a nice, partly overcast day. Phoned Margaret, who has returned to Mirridong, bruised after her fall, but in good form and perfectly coherent. I thanked her for her letter, asked about the crosswords, which she was still doing, and said we both need to keep exercising.

---

[6] Aneeka Simonis and Mark Buttler, "Pell Cell Hell", *Herald Sun*, 26 March 2019.

The first reading in the breviary recounts Moses' delayed return from Mount Sinai to find that the people and Aaron had concluded that he was not coming back and had fashioned a molten calf, to which they brought burnt and peace offerings before sitting down to eat and drink, then rising up to play.

God was furious, but Moses placated him and then went down to deal with his unruly followers, smashing their idols, grinding them to powder, which he scattered upon the waters and made the people drink.

The issue is so shameful that we must have a core of historical truth behind the story. What is most remarkable is Aaron's treachery. Despite that, the Levites rallied to Moses, slaughtering three thousand opponents. Obviously, high office is no guarantee of probity, and Aaron is an early example of weak leadership.

The second reading is from St Peter Chrysologus,[7] who also has a beautiful sermon on Christmas in the breviary. After jail, I should get myself organised to read more of him.

His message is that prayer, fasting, and mercy constitute the essential activities for Lent, reinforcing one another. They are inseparable, so that "if a man has only one of them, he has nothing."

In Australia, Lent is known as a time for extra prayer. Project Compassion for aid and development overseas has continued to grow, but fasting is not conspicuous.

Each year in Sydney, to break the fast of Ramadan, I had an interfaith dinner to which all the religious leaders came at Cathedral House. I remember one evening sitting with the Sunni Mufti on my left, the Shiite leader on my right, Jews, Buddhists, Hindus, etc., Protestants, and bishops from the Eastern Churches. In the early years at least official Anglican representatives did not attend.

Usually we had a guest speaker, but one year she did not attend as she was transplanting a heart, rather than talking of the operation. As the only alternative available we had to talk to one another, and on our table the topic became the practices for fasting in the different faiths and Christian traditions.

Obviously, the most spectacular practice and probably the toughest fast was the Muslim abstinence from food and drink from dawn to

---

[7] St Peter Chrysologus (406–450), a brilliant homilist, was the bishop of Ravenna.

dusk, even more particularly in hot countries with long days. Every faith tradition fasted, and all the Eastern Christian Churches had strict fasting programs. Only the liberal Protestants fasted less than the Roman Catholics.

One of my great grandmothers, Irish Catholic, used to fast on black tea and bread and dripping on the Fridays of Lent. I realised our loss, my fault, too late, but I did in recent years support the practice of abstinence from meat on every Friday, as the English Catholic bishops have recommended for all English Catholics. It is a practical penance and a useful sociological marker. We need to define our identity in many ways.

This year my Lent in jail will compensate for the too easy penances of many years.

God our Father, help us to prepare well for the feast of Easter, when the suffering, death, and then the glorious Resurrection of your Son are celebrated. Help us do this through prayer, works of mercy, and fasting.

Wednesday, 27 March 2019

Four weeks since I entered jail. Something of a milestone, but also a reminder that a couple of months remain. Much better to take the situation day by day, like Alcoholics Anonymous, and work toward high points, especially Holy Week and Easter.

The prisoner who was gassed out of his cell was transferred to another jail. The shouted dialogue was loud and clear tonight, perhaps with a third voice. Muslim prayer chants could be heard this morning still muffled, but so far tonight I have heard nothing. I wonder whether he prays quietly on those occasions or has a rest from prayer.

Michael, Ruth, and Rachel Casey[8] sent me three small beautiful cards of a da Vinci Madonna and Child, Holbein's portrait of Thomas More, and a fifteenth-century Paradise Garden. They are on the shelf behind me as I write.

---

[8] Michael Casey is the former secretary to Cardinal Pell, 1997–2014. Ruth and Rachel are his wife and daughter.

On *Sunrise* this morning, the news captions on the bottom of the screen told the world that a big number (in fact, thirty-three) of editors, reporters, newsreaders have been charged with contempt of court for breaching the suppression orders on my case. I am not sure whether this will help in the court of divided public opinion, but it is certainly not to my disadvantage.

I must say I am pleased, because my reputation was destroyed among many people by their activities. Nor do I think my approval is unchristian, although a beautiful letter of Sr Mary Therese, founder of the Immaculata Sisters and now in Tasmania, quoted Luke 6:27–36 and reminded me of Jesus' teaching to "love our enemies, do good to those who hate you, bless those who curse you, pray for those who abuse you".

As a matter of fact, I have felt more exasperated by one or two of the opposition lawyers and some journalists than with my accusers. Instincts are at one level, but need to be purified and sometimes redirected.

Like a number of insightful and devout Catholics, Sr Therese feels that many graces are coming to the Church in this time of suffering. But her final sentence is blunt. "I will be praying hard for you to forgive those who have sinned against you, so that you may show the world what Jesus looks like." She is right, and I do forgive.

During my visits as bishop and archbishop to preconfirmation groups, I soon adopted Dame Edna Everage's[9] technique of asking questions and relying on the answers to progress the dialogue. In grades five and six, students will respond to questions, as they often will in the first two years of senior school. I always asked questions for forty to fifty minutes and allowed the students to ask me anything for ten to fifteen minutes.

I received questions from grade sixers suitable for a postgraduate theology seminar and others that might have come from someone in grade two or three. Occasionally parents made suggestions to their children.

On one occasion, a young boy asked the meaning of the passage in today's breviary from Exodus. What did God mean when he

---

[9] Dame Edna Everage is a popular comic character who has appeared widely on stage and television, created and performed by Australian comedian Barry Humphries.

told Moses, "You shall see my back; but my face shall not be seen" (Ex 33:23)?

It is a commonplace that no one has seen God; Jesus and Our Lady and many saints have been seen in many apparitions, but not the Transcendent Trinity.

By a happy coincidence, I had been reading one of the Greek Fathers, the ancient theological teachers, not of the Roman tradition, but of those we now know as the Orthodox. In those days, Greeks and Latins were still united in one Church, but with different liturgies, pieties, and theological styles and interests.

I think the author I was reading was the fourth-century St Gregory of Nyssa, and his explanation was that we can only see God through the beauties of nature, which reflect God's goodness, greatness, and intelligence. The young lad was quite satisfied.

Lord Jesus, always help us to see the unseen Father, the Transcendent Light, through the wonders you, as Word, created. Let us not be distracted, much less submerged, by the evil and ugliness. Lord, I confess that I have been irritated by unctuous professions of forgiveness from some churchmen. It seemed too easy, even glib. This might have been my fault, cynical, the stirrings of a black Irish heart. But I pray that all of us, especially myself, strive to forgive as you did on Calvary, to practise what we preach in this ultimate test.

Thursday, 28 March 2019

I awoke this morning with a spring in my step (so to speak), because my nephew Nicholas was visiting and because of the big clash tonight between the ancient rivals Richmond and Collingwood. Many Irish-Australian Catholics had lived in those two Melbourne suburbs until the Second World War, so there was great rivalry in my mother's tribe between the two teams, in which I still join happily.

It was a busy day, by my prison standards, as I had a visit to the physiotherapist for my shoulder, which was helped by last week's session, and then a visit to the medical centre to give blood to check the viscosity. As usual, a couple of attempts were necessary to obtain the volume for a successful sample. I bit my tongue and battled not to show what I thought of the level of efficiency. But there is no shortage of adequate medical care, at least in my case here in jail.

Then a pleasant three-quarters of an hour with my nephew Nick, who looked well and spoke energetically. He has to be careful to avoid influenza and pneumonia. Still receiving quotes for the construction of his new house, which he estimates will take seven months to build.

My case has brought pressure on him at work, hence a couple of days off. The hatred of Catholics is intense. He has always had the faith, although once in a while it was submerged, but my problems and the hostility to Catholicism have turned him into an eloquent defender of Holy Mother Church, leaving medals at different places on his work site! In defending me, he categorized me as a John Paul the Great man (his phrase) and compared the implausible accusations at the cathedral to accusations in the dressing rooms at the MCG[10] after a big match. He rightly observed that the dressing rooms, like the cathedral sacristy, were busy places at that time. Unfortunately, he explained, many of his Maltese Catholic workmates, initially at least, were caught up by the avalanche of hostility in the media. When I pointed out that I did not receive one hostile comment moving around Sydney during the last eighteen months and many expressions of goodwill, he was surprised. On this issue, Victoria is a different country. He also shared my dismay at the rapid disavowal by my old school St Patrick's Ballarat. Not even a murmur about innocent until proven guilty, about the importance of due process, or, more recently, about the necessity of seeing what the appeal judges decide.

The letters continue to arrive; yesterday H explained there were "eighty-eight" letters for me then in the office, but, as they had to be read by the guards, I would only receive them at the weekend. In fact, about fifteen arrived today, including a note of encouragement from Archbishop Barry Hickey, emeritus of Perth, giving me two good quotes from 2 Corinthians and Ephesians. "Finally, be strong in the Lord and in his mighty power" (Eph 6:10). A beautiful letter from Kingaroy, Queensland, spoke of silence: "The silence at dawn, before the trooper's bugle, a bird's first call maybe". She concluded, "Make silence your friend and you shall win through."

---

[10] The Melbourne Cricket Ground, the largest sports stadium in the Southern Hemisphere.

Collingwood thrashed Richmond, which was outthought and outcoached. Grundy dominated in the ruck. Dusty Martin is still a good player but only a shadow of the magician of two years ago. In fact, Richmond was beaten nearly everywhere, with an extraordinary difference in the statistics. No Tiger premiership this year. And Jack Riewoldt was injured—as a bonus. De Goey was magnificent for the Pies with five goals, while Lynch (Tiger) is on the improve with three goals once again.

The Brexit fiasco drags on in Britain, probably toward a no-deal exit. No one could say the negotiations were successful, but since many Remainers refused to accept the decision and opinion was so divided in the House of Commons, to escape the present mess would have required more strength, wisdom, and luck than May[11] possessed.

The intransigence of the European leadership is a long-term guarantee for disaster, and their fears for the future of the Union fuel their obduracy. No group of governors can run an empire while prescribing the shape of bananas and the composition of meat pies and preventing family members in Ireland from preparing their relatives' graves, because this is a task for gravediggers.

My daily life in my cell is far removed from these important and unimportant issues. Football is a pleasant recreation, but nothing more.

Lord Jesus, help me use the abundance of silence to come closer to you and so contribute to healing the division in our society and the wounds of the victims.

Friday, 29 March 2019

My technique for survival and coping has changed and improved since my arrival. My return to bed to doze or sleep from 6:00 am, when I receive my medicine, until the siren sounds at 7:15 am is now an important part of the daily ritual. I am told an Opus Dei penance is to spring from bed as soon as you awake, but I always liked five minutes more after the alarm.

[11] Theresa May served as prime minister of the United Kingdom from 2016 to 2019.

My Sudoku book has 250 puzzles, and I try to complete two each day, one from about one-third of the way through, which seems to reflect the grade of difficulty. I didn't want to complete all the easy ones and then be doomed to perpetual frustration in my last weeks before the appeal from being unable to solve anything. I have improved, am solving them both most days. Sometimes I alternate by tackling the "very easy" Sudoku from the Monday, Wednesday, Friday *Herald Sun*, the only newspaper allowed. To my embarrassment, I originally had some difficulty with this "very easy" category.

I nearly always exercise twice a day for half an hour in one of the grotty pens. Today I asked the guard if he would give me a broom to clean up the small yard, and he consented. I had been thinking about it for a while but wondered whether such a request would rock the boat. At any rate, the job is now done, not so much as an act of altruism, but self-help, as grot is a bit depressing. I shall try to clean up the second one tomorrow, or as soon as permitted.

The birds were singing nearby at about 3:45 pm when I was outside, only the second time I have heard them, while the squawking of the gulls could also be heard. You can use the phone in the exercise pen; in fact, I tried to contact Archbishop Fisher[12] today, but could hear the office receptionist at the Polding Centre[13] conclude the call. I have never been eloquent on a phone and did not use a mobile until I returned home a couple of years ago. All calls are monitored, of course.

We can order odds and ends three times a week from the canteen, so I have my Lipton and camomile tea bags, two blocks of Cadbury's milk chocolate (only four small pieces a day), toothpaste, hair shampoo, and even Vaseline skin lotion. It is not luxurious, but these are small blessings. I am quite "attached" to my kettle and television set.

In the Werribee seminary, where I began preparing for the priesthood fifty-nine years ago, we were urged not to become too dependent, "too attached" to created things. Obviously, I could live in jail without a kettle or TV, but I hope this won't be necessary. Often life provides strange and welcome consolations.

[12] Anthony Fisher, OP, is the successor of Cardinal Pell as the archbishop of Sydney.
[13] Polding Centre is the administrative office of the Sydney Archdiocese.

One verse from Psalm 68 in today's breviary easily became my own.

> Let those who hope in you not be put to shame
> through me, Lord of hosts;
> let not those who seek you be dismayed
> through me, God of Israel.

"Amen" to all that.

My daily meditation on the Book of Revelation has continued, a disconcerting tale of woe punctuated by beautiful mystical moments such as the great multitude that no one could count, from every nation, tribe, people, and language, worshipping and praising God before the throne of the Lamb; the 144,000 virgins on Mt Zion; and the pregnant woman "clothed with the sun, with the moon under her feet and a crown of twelve stars on her head" (Rev 12:1).

But underlying these moments of triumph was the execution of divine justice, as the Lamb opened the seven seals before "ten thousand times ten thousand angels" and the seven angels with the seven bowls went spreading God's wrath on the earth, sparing the white-robed martyrs "made white in the blood of the Lamb" (Rev 7:14).

What might we make of all this? This book is part of the revealed word of God, so it cannot be set aside, easily dismissed, as we are obliged to wrestle with the text and understand what we can.

Two preliminary points can be made. The supernatural is an essential part of the Christian message, and when Catholicism is reduced to an agnostic service organization, the tradition is betrayed, converts disappear, and the exodus quickens. "When the Son of man returns, will he find faith on earth?" (Lk 18:8) are the most sobering lines in the New Testament.

Christ spoke of a rich life after death, beautiful or terrible, quite beyond our limited intellectual horizons, and the Book of Revelation starts us on this imaginative journey. Heaven will be different from a well-earned holiday over the Christmas break or even a special long trip to strange parts as we commence our retirement.

Jesus spoke many times of heaven and hell, and on the Last Day God will not be inclusive, [but] separating the sheep from the goats.

A second point from the Apocalypse is that life is a struggle between good and evil that no one can avoid. Great Babylon falls, a dwelling for demons and a haunt for every unclean spirit; war broke out in heaven as "Michael and his angels fought against the dragon", and we have this same red dragon with "seven heads and ten horns" trying in vain to destroy the child of the woman crowned with the sun who "will rule all the nations with an iron sceptre" (Rev 12).

A pre-Vatican II atheist is alleged to have explained that the only Christian dogma he accepted was the teaching on original sin, that each human heart as well as the structures of society are flawed, tempted to evil as we aspire to the good and beautiful.

The "culture wars" of the English-speaking peoples, which we are losing, are not a recent invention. The Apocalypse was written nearly 1,900 years before the invention of the contraceptive pill. Most of us want a quiet life, some of us don't manage to achieve it, but everyone has to choose one side, not the other. Struggle is necessary.

Lord Jesus, help us all to choose your Father, by following you and your teachings in your community as we opt for truth, goodness, and beauty.

Saturday, 30 March 2019

The packet of "eighty-eight" letters arrived as had been promised. I didn't count them, remembering the trouble King David had from God when he organized a census for his kingdom. I am not sure exactly what the problem was, although it must have been connected to David's excessive pride, his assertion of self-sufficiency rather than relying on God's providence. Neither have I looked up the commentaries for a more learned explanation.

All the letters are beautiful, a strong and welcome consolation. Many take up the Lenten and Easter themes and apply them to my situation. A few have quoted Cardinal Francis George, the late and great archbishop of Chicago, who predicted three generations of worsening trouble for bishops before a restoration. In defending his dire predictions to me, he noted that most commentators ignored his fourth-stage rebound, the return to better times aided by Christian teaching.

Unfortunately, President Trump is a bit of a barbarian, but in some important ways he is "our" (Christian) barbarian. His two appointments already to the US Supreme Court will slow down the secularist advance, because the court there has immense power to shape society, much more than the Australian High Court possesses. To my mind, the Australian system, where Parliament makes more of the decisions, is better. It was to protect this local balance that I opposed an Australian Bill of Rights, where the courts would decide more through their interpretations. Parliamentarians can be removed by the voters, unlike judges.

Not one of the letter writers has expressed hostility to the victims of the paedophilia crisis, and this is exactly as it should be. Quite a number acknowledge the terrible damage done to victims and the standing of the Church.

One senior retired politician explained to me that the Royal Commission [into Institutional Responses to Child Sexual Abuse] demonstrated that the problem was not unique to Catholics, as she had long thought. Public opinion, however, cannot grapple with the sad reality that 95 percent plus of the sexual abuse of minors occurs outside institutions.

One writer wrote a page or more on the evil of an accused person claiming falsely to be innocent of the listed crimes and so eliciting popular support. He knew I was not guilty of this, he added. I agree with him completely that such a deception would be almost worse than the original crime.

Managed to take both my exercise sessions and to phone Margaret and Chris Meney. In the evening, not only was a bird or two singing, but one small bird was within the barriers above the pen. Two systems of bars at right angles to one another cover the open space, and between them is a pattern of interesting metal strips, a mesh with rectangular spaces. I am not sure a small bird could enter, but this one, about the size of a sparrow with brown to light orange plumage, was poking around. I frightened it off, telling it that if it entered, we might never be able to return it to freedom.

The mother of a good young priest wrote me a beautiful letter quoting G. K. Chesterton, the English Catholic writer, brilliant, quirky, and provocative, whom I have quoted a number of times over the years: "We who drink the blood of God go gaily in the dark." I am not completely in the dark, and I am not sure how many do manage to go gaily in such a situation. But the phrase certainly made me stop and ponder.

G. K. Chesterton's reputation has survived better than that of his Catholic contemporary Hilaire Belloc,[14] not least because of his Fr Brown detective stories. By a strange coincidence, Elizabeth Anscombe, one of the greatest philosophers of the twentieth century, who was lecturing at Oxford when I was a student there, became a Catholic after reading the Fr Brown stories. She was probably the most formidable intellect I have ever encountered, and we Christian youngsters at Oxford, interested in the world of ideas, walked taller and stronger as a result of her courage and brilliance. She objected to President Truman receiving an honorary doctorate at Oxford, because of the atomic bombing of Japan, and knelt publicly outside the Sheldonian Theatre saying the rosary during the ceremony.

God our Father, grant all our public leaders and especially to the Holy Father, the cardinals, and the bishops the gifts of wisdom, prudence, and perseverance, but especially give them courage, which is regularly in short supply. May Jesus himself be our model.

---

[14] Hilaire Belloc (1870–1953) was a French-British author, historian, and poet, as well as one of the most prolific and versatile writers of the early twentieth century.

WEEK 6

Eroding Social Capital

31 March—6 April 2019

Sunday, 31 March 2019

This morning for the first time in prison I watched the Archdiocese of Melbourne's *Mass for You at Home* celebrated at 6:00 am on Channel 10. It isn't even listed in the *Herald Sun* TV guide, hidden under the generic title "Morning Programs". Sr Mary mentioned it was on as I wasn't sure it had survived. When seminary rector around 1985–1986, I celebrated for them on a few occasions, and while we did not have a prime-time slot, I don't believe we were reduced to a 6:00 am appearance.

The Mass was celebrated beautifully, with faith and a scrupulous regard for the rubrics, and I did not recognize the celebrant. To my surprise, it was Mgr Tony Ireland, who had been assistant with me at [St Patrick's Catholic Church] in Mentone. I had not seen him for twenty-five years, and he was now a little plumper with a toothbrush moustache. On Monday, I received a supportive letter from him.

Because of time constraints, the sermon on the Prodigal Son was short and concentrated on the older brother, conjecturing whether he eventually went to the welcome home party.

Nearly fifty years ago when I was part-time chaplain at Eton, going down on Saturday night for a couple of classes and Mass on Sunday morning, I remember giving a lecture on the Prodigal Son, when the entire group noisily shouted out their support for the older brother. Overwhelmingly, they were good young men, some very innocent, but I thought at least a few of them would have been better advised to support the younger brother.

Lord Caccia, the provost, blackballed me from conducting the Eton Remembrance Day Service, but I believe I was one of the first, if not the first, Catholic priests since the Reformation to conduct a prayer service for the entire school. The Anglican chaplains arranged this as a consolation prize.

My memories are happy. One student told a master he thought I would do well in the colonies, and another lad explained to me that the problem with the new headmaster (Chenevix-Trench) was that he did not realise he was no longer at a minor public school. One night after supper, a housemaster lamented that he was not sure now what he was preparing the boys for, as the British Empire had ended. In fact, Etonians like David Cameron[1] became busy running Britain.

Three little anecdotes, tall tales perhaps but true, should not give the wrong impression, as the college was a healthy community, privileged and traditional, but serious academically and basically happy. The Catholic students then numbered about sixty or seventy.

But to return to the Mass. An Alma Mercy nun from the US (a reformed Mercy Order of highly qualified women, devoted mainly to education and medicine, and thriving) wrote that "being deprived of (celebrating) the Eucharist must be the most difficult part" of my being in prison. Sr Mary, the chaplain, brings me Communion twice a week, and this is a blessing. At times I have felt deeply the inability to celebrate, but for most of the time I realise it is not permitted or possible and get on with my daily program of prayers. I believe that one of the keys to surviving in prison, and especially in a solitary regime, is to concentrate on doing what one can rather than lamenting what one cannot do.

Spent some hours opening and reading the latest batches of letters. As always, they provided plenty of food for reflection. For the third time, a letter included a message about me from Our Lady to Irish visionary Christina Gallagher (or so it claimed), where Our Lady pronounced that "the reason the power of darkness overshadowed him (me) with false accusations" was the work I had been doing to correct financial wrongdoing and sexual misbehaviour in the Vatican.

---

[1] David Cameron served as prime minister of the United Kingdom from 2010 to 2016. His successor Boris Johnson also studied at Eton.

All the major agents for financial reform at the Vatican were attacked, especially in the press, and a number of these senior figures in Rome feel my Australian problems are connected there. We have no proof of such a connection, although I don't discount the possibility, but Our Lady must know more than I do if the locution is genuine.

A bishop should be respectful of such locutions and apparitions, but deeply sceptical, because one of the bishop's special roles is to test the charisms, being slow to give the seal of approval.

Let me make my own a prayer of St Thomas More, sent me by a young Melbourne priest.

O holy Blessed Saviour, Jesus Christ, who willingly didst determine to die for man's sake, mollify mine hard heart and supple it so by grace, that through tender compassion of thy bitter Passion, I may be partner of thine holy redemption.

Monday, 1 April 2019

Last night as I was watching the third TV show in a series on building the new three-billion-pound sewer system in London, a huge engineering feat. Canon Alexander Sherbrooke, parish priest of St Patrick's Church in Soho, appeared on the screen to bless the workers and the machines. As usual, he was not overdressed in his black shirt and plastic collar and a jumper. A small stole completed the uniform for the blessing with holy water and prayers.

Alexander is a true and loyal friend of many years with a vibrant parish in Soho, an area not renowned for religious devotion. He restored the church beautifully, and I was pleased to launch his campaign for funds. The hungry are fed regularly by parish volunteers, and the parish has a group each night praying before the Blessed Sacrament, and anyone is able to phone in and ask for a prayer. No counselling is given. Alexander has been an invaluable support for me in my troubles, organizing prayer vigils and fasting. As a seminarian, he was a "convert" of Mother Teresa of Calcutta.

My day was quiet and uneventful except for a very pleasant visit from my sister-in-law, Judy. David was caught up on business. The weather was overcast, but not cold, when I went out in the afternoon for my only exercise session.

The food continues to be plentiful, too plentiful, but the main meal, which we can choose from four alternatives, is never hot and often unappetising. Sometimes I have to force myself to eat, for health reasons, as we had to do during my years as a seminarian in Rome at Propaganda Fide College (1963–1967). We had students from sixty-three nations, and the diet was not Italian, but hybrid international, not suited to Aussies. We had no fruit and no cereals, to mention a couple of problems, and the wine was the worst I ever drank in Italy. I maintained my health by continuing to eat, but some of the Australians were diagnosed with malnutrition when they returned to Australia. I learnt my lesson to keep eating even when the food doesn't appeal.

Another fifty or sixty letters arrived today, and the senior officer suggested I consign the three hundred or so which had already arrived to my lawyer, Kartya Gracer. With some misgiving, I included the first pad of written diary entries with the idea that Margaret O'Reilly, my part-time secretary in Sydney, might begin typing them. I hope they arrive safely, or more accurately, that Kartya can pick them up from the property office without any problems.

Often the letters make me stop and think. One woman thought that "the beginning of our Catholic persecution" was when I refused Communion to those wearing rainbow sashes in St Patrick's Cathedral, Melbourne. This was about the time of the visit of John Cardinal O'Connor of New York for the centenary of the cathedral celebrations (1997). She might well be right. With the referendum deciding in favour of homosexual marriage, we can expect to see further pressure to limit our religious freedom to give Christian teaching on family, marriage, and sexuality in our schools and churches and parishes.

One of my major concerns is the long-term consequences of my problems for the Church in Australia. The short-term damage is beyond dispute, but the benefits or blessings in the short- and especially the long-term are more difficult to discern.

A Sydney lawyer was encouraging, repeating the claims made by others that Lent has seen an increase in daily Mass-goers in parishes and at Polding Centre. She added, "But believe me there is something already stirring in the hearts of so many that will in time bear great fruit. Your time and suffering in jail could well be for many an aid to their own salvation." Whatever of this, the prayers of so many thousands of people for me will not be wasted and will benefit the Kingdom of the Lord in some way.

Once again, I have a writer citing yet another James McAuley poem for my consolation. This is one aspect of his contribution that I had not appreciated. His poem, which has been turned into a hymn, is addressed to Our Lady, Help of Christians, and is especially apt for us in Australia today.

> *Help of Christians, guard this land*
> *From assault or inward stain;*
> *Let it be what Christ has planned,*
> *A new Eden where you reign....*
>
> *Take from us the coward heart,*
> *Fleeting will, divided mind,*
> *Give us sight to play our part,*
> *Though the world around is blind.*[2]

Tuesday, 2 April 2019

Am writing this in the evening, following my usual routine, after watching the conclusion of Treasurer Frydenberg's budget speech and the ABC panel discussion. At the moment, I don't find much difference between the party programs, as most of the conservative Liberals have been sidelined.

We have reason to be grateful to our politicians because of the level of prosperity and peace we Australians enjoy. After returning from Italy to drive around suburban Sydney, I was in a world different from suburban Rome. We ride on the back of our mines, but our leaders have avoided recession for twenty-eight years, and this was not inevitable. Very few Australian politicians become rich from their time in Parliament, and they don't fully deserve their low ranking with the public.

Our main challenges are elsewhere, connected with the decline of Christian influence. Paul Kelly from *The Australian*[3] has written well

---

[2] James McAuley with Richard Connolly, "Help of Christians, Guard This Land".

[3] Paul Kelly is the editor-at-large of *The Australian*. He was previously the newspaper's editor-in-chief. He writes on Australian and international politics and is the author of several books.

about the consequences of this for Australian society generally, rather than focussing on the damage to the Church communities themselves. In our discussion of this over a meal in Rome, we agreed that while older people are inclined to be pessimistic, it is a fact that social capital is eroding. This can be quantified. Schoolteachers with some decades of experience testify to this. We share this decline with much of the Western world, but that is no consolation.

Many of my correspondents are sensitive to this, perhaps hypersensitive. One lady wrote, "These are dark times for our world, and everywhere the glue of trust and grasp of Truth is being melted away and the fabric of society is un-ravelling and many souls are frightened." The challenge is to work together cooperatively to show that this level of pessimism is not warranted. It will be no easy job to slow down the rot and impossible to stop it in the short term.

Major changes in social values often have unforeseen consequences. Democracies need an accepted core of common assumptions or traditions, because the principle of diversity is insufficient by itself and needs to be buttressed by a commitment to civil discourse, human rights, and freedom of speech. Some, but too many, are prepared to close down discussion, deny freedom of speech, because particular ideas are offensive to them. If this were an option for Catholics, public debate would be curtailed radically.

While I was not surprised that many disagreed with my supporters as they made claims about the perverse jury verdict and the pollution of public opinion, I was surprised that at least a couple of these supporters had to defend themselves against attempted "punishments".

Meanwhile, back at the ranch, Sr Mary brought Communion and stayed for a chat, telling me of the long-term prisoner who lamented never seeing the stars for years and of another who was overjoyed when he was transferred to another prison to see grass and be able to walk on it and touch it.

The day was clear, with a few clouds. Autumn is the best time of the year in Melbourne.

I was also chosen at random for a drug test, which is preceded by a strip search. When the brief procedure was concluded, I said to the amiable warder, "That was easy enough." He said, "Apart from the humiliation", and I replied that here you get used to that.

Spent some hour or so reading the remaining twenty letters from the last batch, some of them from the US as well as New Zealand, Ireland, and England.

An unexpected boost came from an anonymous "brother in arms" from Spain, written in simple, imperfect English and containing the original Spanish of a short mystical poem that explained it was not heaven or hell that was the motivation to be good, but Christ's suffering and death on the Cross. He provided an English translation, which he correctly said needed improvement, inviting me to do the job. Unit 8 at the Melbourne Assessment Prison does not have a Spanish dictionary!

He also included an article from the Spanish newspaper *El Mundo*, by Felipe Fernández-Armesto,[4] "a friend of you". I had met Felipe, now a professor at Notre Dame University in the US, here in Melbourne and in Boston at Professor Claudio Veliz's Conversazione series. An accomplished author and historian, he is perfectly bilingual in Spanish and English, as exotic a personality as his name suggests, and a public defender of Catholicism. He spoke of a persecution of the Church and vigorously defended me personally and because of the evidence presented in the case. For him, the Church contains saints and demons, but it does not follow from this that there are more sinners in the clergy than among the people generally.

God our Father, help us to be grateful for the many blessings we enjoy in Australia, to realise the extent of these good things as we also dedicate ourselves to remedying society's wounds. Help us to avoid cynicism, pessimism, and the paralysis that follows from them. Inspire many young Christians to commit themselves to these public struggles.

Wednesday, 3 April 2019

Few distractions today as we had no visits to doctors, nurses, or physios, and no outside visitors, as Kartya was unable to come. Exercised a couple of times with the weather clearer in the morning.

Domestically, I asked permission to sweep my small cell, and they provided me with a mop and bucket as well as a broom and dustpan.

[4] Felipe Fernández-Armesto, "Persecución a la Iglesia católica", *El Mundo*, 7 March 2019.

As usual, nothing explained to you about these procedures, and you have to rely on your common sense or friendly advice as to when and how. We don't do our laundry, which is handed over to the guards. Lint is the danger. Everything is pretty rough and ready, and no ironing of course. I wash my own socks in the shower, which helps preserve them a little better.

Another ten or so letters arrived today, and I moved through them before the 11:00 am lunch. Yesterday, a letter from solicitor Peter Breen told of his client's success at the High Court in her case for malicious prosecution with $4.2 million damages.

In the afternoon, a writ arrived from one of my accusers against the State of Victoria, a religious order of Sisters, Child and Family Services, and myself for a wide variety of alleged offences.

His accusations against me had been withdrawn by the prosecutor before going to the Supreme Court. The accuser was a drug user with a criminal record. The accusations alleged inappropriate behaviour at an institution I visited only a couple of times in eleven years, in a swimming pool I never frequented and never knew existed. He "recognized" me from television after claiming to have seen me once in the pool forty years earlier. A nolle prosequi (which I obtained) is equivalent to a not guilty verdict, so the claim is probably of nuisance value.

Have moved through and completed my meditations on the Book of Revelation, and think I would change the advice I have given previously to those thinking about life after death to meditate their way through the book. Now my advice would be to concentrate on the last four chapters and read the earlier sections quickly.

In 2012, I visited Mary's house, revealed in a vision in the nineteenth century, outside Ephesus, not far from the cave where John is supposed to have written his bizarre Apocalypse. The cave was big enough, complete with a niche in the wall John is supposed to have used as a pillow, overlooking a beautiful valley. The shrine's message was quite clear that it was the same John who authored the Fourth Gospel. An exotic setting for the origin of a remarkable piece of religious writing, which was received into the canon of Scripture, or list of "revealed" books, only with great difficulty and after much discussion.

Mary's house had a long queue of pilgrims, apart from ourselves, waiting to enter and pray in devotion to Our Lady, the Mother of

Jesus Our Lord. Most of them were Muslims, who regularly frequent Christian Marian shrines in many countries.

A Polish priest who had worked in Australia was in charge of this sanctuary, and he asked me if he could speak to my fellow pilgrims, who were Catholic schoolteachers. I wasn't sure what he would say, but I was happy to agree.

His message was simple. He grew up in Poland, where nearly everyone is Catholic, and he now works in Turkey, once Christian, now Islamic Turkey, with a tiny minority of harassed Christians. Your task, he said to the teachers, is to see that a similar fate does not befall the Church in Australia.

It is the beautiful vision in the last chapter of Revelation of "the river of the water of life, as clear as crystal, flowing from the throne of God and of the Lamb" that inspires the Pilgrim Way, with its long fountain of running water, in front of the south transept of St Patrick's Cathedral, Melbourne. The Lamb is enshrined at the source of the fountain, surrounded by the Revelation quotation. The trees now overshadow the walkway with a half-dozen other small fountains, each accompanied by a biblical quotation on water. Down below, the water runs over a plaque with a superb prayer from James McAuley.

> *Incarnate Word, in whom all nature lives,*
> *Cast flame upon the earth: raise up contemplatives*
> *Among us, men who walk within the fire*
> *Of ceaseless prayer, impetuous desire.*
> *Set pools of silence in this thirsty land.*[5]

Thursday, 4 April 2019

A very busy day by prison standards, as the physiotherapist arrived as I was finishing my cup of tea about 8:30 am to work on my left arm and shoulder, which he is improving.

Not long after, Kartya arrived, and I was interested to see whether she had received the letters and diary. She enquired after being with me, and nothing had come to "property" as yet. The Breen letter and

[5] James McAuley, "A Letter to John Dryden" (1954).

the writ were also still en-route. My morning half hour of exercise followed; then I telephoned Margaret, who was pleased because the heart specialist gave her an "all clear" and does not want to see her for fifteen months.

Toto and Rita Piccolo came for a visit through the glass at 1:00 pm. They are the founders of the Neocatechumenal Way in Australia, coming as a family in mission with almost nothing about forty years ago. Now seventy-five communities exist across Australia with two seminaries, one in Perth and one I invited to Sydney, which has already produced about ten priests. I believe the finger of God is on them, as they, like Opus Dei, are able to hand on the faith to their young ones as well as provoking many conversions.

Their community way of life is demanding, although they are now part of the landscape and provoke much less hostility from other Catholics, especially in Sydney. I remember a senior Sydney priest, friendly, not hostile, who advised me soon after I came north that in Sydney neither Opus Dei nor the Neocatechumenal Way was regarded favourably. "Then these are two things that need to change", I replied. Both here and around Australia and in many parts of the world, thousands of "Neo-Cats", a name many of them don't like, are praying for me.

Kiko [Arguello], the cofounder, and Fr Mario[6] sent their regards from Rome, and Toto asked if I had any message for them. I urged them to continue the prayers and informed them I was well enough and that, in God's providence, friends were reporting movements of grace, even conversions here and there. God is always at work in some way.

I then had a strange brief interview over the phone with a female member of the Placement Assessment Unit, who asked two questions of me. This was organized by a quiet, courteous man, who remained with me after calling up my questioner. "Did I know the choir boys who had been molested in the cathedral?" I replied that I could not see the point of the question as I was completely innocent of these charges. In fact, I did not know either boy or their families then or subsequently, as had been made clear in court. "Did I intend to lodge an appeal?", I was then asked, as they had no record of this. This was surprising as the appeal was lodged before my sentencing,

[6] Fr Mario Pezzi, presbyter of the international leadership team.

and I already have the date for the appeal hearing on June 5-6. That brought the phone call to a courteous conclusion. "Life is sometimes strange", I commented to my young companion as we left.

Naturally my breviary readings have continued each day with Moses and his querulous followers almost in Canaan. Their spies had returned with grapes, pomegranates, and figs to announce that the land was flowing with milk and honey, with large fortified cities. Unfortunately, however, the spies also pointed out that the inhabitants were huge and strong, so that they felt like grasshoppers. Another big problem to be followed by renewed lamentations and complaints. There is a lot to be said for reticence.

As I am still locked up in Egypt, Moses' long, hazardous journey across the deserts did not speak to my situation like Job's story, but it is a perfect preparation for Easter.

Another forty-five letters arrived today, which I read gratefully. A day or so earlier, I had received a letter from Fr Matthew Baldwin, a Melbourne priest doing doctorate studies in Rome. One of the consolations today in our local turbulence is that so many of the young priests are spiritually solid and theologically orthodox, unlike us after the council in the sixties and seventies, when we were often confused and unnerved with the whiff of revolution in the air. Matthew, a good friend, wrote that it was as if he were writing to Thomas More or John Fisher, "yet your incarceration seems so much more inglorious in the eyes of the world." This is true. He concluded by quoting Christ's words to St Peter: "When you were young" you "walked where you liked", "but when you grow old" ... "someone else will put a belt on you and take you where you'd rather not go" (Jn 21:18). Also true.

God our Father, I ask the mother of your Son, Mary the Theotokos, the God-bearer to keep her mantle over our young priests so they remain men of prayer, regularly serve their people, and lead with wisdom and perseverance.

Friday, 5 April 2019

After I had received my tablets at about 6:00 am and gone back to bed, I was awoken again at 6:45 am by a loud mechanical drill working on the other side of my cell wall, or so it seemed. I don't know what it was about or even whether they were working in a cell, but it was a strange time to start. I could hear a prisoner banging on his cell wall in protest.

After more than five weeks in my cell 11, I noticed that an earlier inhabitant had scratched "home" into the white paint that framed my barred and opaque cell window. I wondered if it was "Wiggy", who had scratched his name into the glass wall of the shower, where the water continued hot, who wrote the word and whether he was bitter. I suspect not, as this is my home for the moment, and it is not a terrible place.

Kartya arrived unexpectedly to pick up the two legal documents, which were delivered while she was still with me, and she gave me the good news that she had collected the first bag of letters and the diary with them. She was surprised by my unusual telephone call.

Letters continued to arrive, and one of the guards almost apologised for the delay in delivery, explaining that the jail had only one censor, and my hundreds of letters were jamming the system.

However, the big news of the day came with the arrival of a six-person senior committee, who looked after placements. I explained once again that I was going well enough and that nothing would be gained for anyone if I fell in a heap.

The whole meeting was cordial and courteous, and the upshot was that I probably will be moved to Unit 10, where I will be able to interact with other prisoners. The move would not take place immediately, as I will go to the gymnasium with some of them to see how the interactions develop. When asked my reaction to this proposal, I acknowledged that their first concern was my physical safety and that, provided I was not hit on the head with a brick or involved in countless altercations, I would be happy to "give it a go". The committee knew nothing of yesterday's phone call, and the director commented that the incident was unusual and that they would make enquiries to see that I had not been deceived in some way. We shall see whether a change is as good as a holiday or, if not quite that, at least an improvement.

One week after cleaning the first exercise pen, I obtained a broom and pan and swept out the nearest exercise space next to the warden's office. It is an improvement, even though the space was not as dirty as the second pen.

A couple of letters in particular caused me once again to pause and consider. One woman wrote on Jesus' command to Peter to forgive seventy-seven times, quoting *Lent with Mother Teresa,* by Heidi Hess Saxton (a book I did not know). "Seventy-seven times forgiveness acknowledges that I do not see the whole story, that God does not love me more than he loves those with whom I am in conflict. It is absolute surrender and love, an extravagant kind of grace, and undeserved forgiveness that holds out a hand that may be refused."

This came as a shock. I accept the obligation to forgive my enemies and pray for them, but I choked on the idea that God loved one or two people, e.g., prominent personal opponents and enemies of Christianity, as much as he loved me. But, of course, that is true, and such a claim says nothing about their or my responses to God's love. None of my accusers fall into this special category because I find it easier to see and understand that they are deeply wounded.

Another writer wrote profoundly about the spiritual crisis in the West. For him "the United States is the (last) best hope for mankind. . . . If US exceptionalism fails, then the West, as we have known it, falls; individual freedom balanced by limited constitutional government will enter a long Dark Age for many decades, perhaps for generations."

While there are "green shoots" of hope, though none of them are in Australia, and there is no successor to B. A. Santamaria, he praises in particular the agnostic Jordan Peterson,[7] who found "the Logos was buried in the heart of the Christian West", as perhaps a new Boethius, certainly surpassing "the sad and limited Marcus Aurelius". I agree with this last thought as I was severely unimpressed by the emperor's *Meditations.*

He also mentioned an online petition, which they hope to present to the Legislative Assembly in Victoria, requesting permission for me to celebrate Mass privately while I am in jail. This would be beautiful and is deeply appreciated, but I hold out no hope it will be successful.

God our Father, I ask you to send your Spirit to our leaders, civic and religious, so that they will understand we are in a period of profound

---

[7] Jordan Peterson (b. 1962) is a Canadian clinical psychologist and professor of psychology at the University of Toronto as well as a popular author and public speaker.

change, which will accelerate with automation, where ideas remain of
basic and primary importance as we shape our responses in faith, hope,
and love.

Saturday, 6 April 2019

Last night I watched a two-hour show on SBS television on Winston Churchill, covering the four days before the victorious landings
in Normandy in the Second World War, on June 6, 1944, D-day.
Winston came through as an old man under enormous pressure and
drinking too much (nothing surprising in this after four years of
world war), who was terrified that too many troops had been committed to this venture, that it would be a failure, too many deaths,
like the Gallipoli landings in World War I, for which he was blamed,
or that the troops would be pinned down interminably as they had
been thirty years earlier on the Western Front. I remember reading
that even Bismarck acknowledged that he had to deal with God over
the young men who died in war under his command. Churchill was
always a depressive, with his "black dog".

And he has always been one of my heroes since I read and then
heard his wartime speeches. I was captured and captivated by his
language, by the perils of Britain's situation, and by his defiance and
leadership, which so disconcerted in those early days many of his
Conservative party colleagues. I now know much more of Churchill
and of his dark side, of how he was wrong on many issues, but he
recognized Hitler for what he was, and, without him, Britain would
have capitulated. He is still a hero for me, and he himself lamented
his lack of faith.

I took two recordings with me to Rome in 1963; his wartime
speeches and Joan Sutherland singing in *Lucia di Lammermoor*.

Have also just finished reading the biography of the Vietnamese
cardinal Francis Van Thuan, whom I was privileged to know and
regarded as a friend.

The cardinal belonged to a distinguished Vietnamese family,
strongly patriotic, who had served in leadership positions for three
generations, despite their Catholicism, in a Buddhist country. The
Catholics in Vietnam are still not free and have a history of 244
years of intermittent persecution that produced 150,000 martyrs and

occasionally some vigorous self-defence. In 1885, at An Ninh, the site of Thuan's minor seminary, seven seminarians commanded one thousand Christian volunteers organized in seven companies, who successfully defended the site against a Can Vuong militia,[8] who had burnt the two nearby churches to the ground. Each year this victory was commemorated in the seminary.

Thuan's uncle was Ngo Dinh Diem, prime minister of Vietnam under Emperor Bao Dai in 1954 and then first president of Vietnam during the war with the Communist north. Always vulnerable because of his minority Catholicism, Diem was brought down by Buddhist opposition, inflamed by the mistakes of his sister-in-law, Madame Nhu, and by the Western press backed by the US government, who had concluded a regime change was necessary. Diem was overthrown by a military coup and executed by a bullet in the head on November 2, 1963. I remember how upset we were that this began under President Kennedy's leadership and tried to console ourselves by believing the US would never have consented to his execution.

When the US was defeated in Vietnam in 1975, Thuan was appointed coadjutor archbishop of Saigon with the right of succession. Soon afterward, he was arrested by the Communists and eventually spent thirteen years in prison with two spells of solitary confinement. Later Thuan told me that one of his major achievements was to avoid going mad, especially in the first period, when the cell was damp, had no windows, one electric light, which either was turned off for hours or days, or left on; and not even the guards spoke a word. His only human contact was with his interrogators, and he sometimes lay on the floor to try to obtain fresh air from the opening under the door.

One of the many good things my Ballarat bishop, Ronald Mulkearns, did was to encourage schoolchildren to write to the archbishop, and eventually he was freed in 1988.

Before he was made president of the Vatican Council for Justice and Peace [CJP], the archbishop was living in Rome in the via Sachetti and receiving no financial help from the Vatican. Bob Santamaria urged me to try to remedy this during one of my regular

---

[8] Can Vuong (Loyalty to the King) was a Vietnamese insurgency against the French colonial rule of Vietnam. Its militias murdered about 40,000 Vietnamese Christians for being alleged allies of the French.

Roman visits, and I spoke to the Australian cardinal [Edward] Cassidy then working there. I don't know when support commenced, but he was appointed first as secretary for the CJP and then as president. Pope John Paul II was a strong supporter, but many in Rome were unaware of his moral and spiritual eminence. I was irritated by the apartment allotted to him in Trastevere, which was noisy, but I knew the cardinal did not care at all.

He produced a string of beautiful books, sourced mainly from his time in prison, many of them on the theme of hope. He shared his experiences. He was fond of these lines from the French poet Charles Péguy:

> For faith only sees what is, and Hope sees what will be.
> Charity only loves what is, and Hope loves what will be.[9]

God our Father, help us always to be people of Christian hope even when, humanly speaking, the situation seems hopeless. May we always believe in the Resurrection as well as the crucifixion and be sustained by the promise of eternal life with you, your Son, and the life-giving Spirit.

---

[9] Charles Péguy, *Le Porche du mystère de la deuxième vertu* (1911).

WEEK 7

Perfection through Suffering

7 April—13 April 2019

Sunday, 7 April 2019

The day began with a small fiasco. I wanted to watch *Mass for You at Home* at 6:00 am on Channel 10, relying on the medicine delivery around that time to wake me. Contrary to my usual schedule, I had woken around 4:00 am, drifted back to sleep, and then awoke at 7:15 am, more than an hour after the start of Mass (or so I thought). When the tablets finally arrived, I asked the guard why he was late, and he merely laughed and said, "You had an hour's extra sleep." I [had] briefly wondered whether Summer Time[1] was finishing but concluded foolishly that I would have seen something on television. Only later did the penny drop. As I had just received a copy of *St Pauls Holy Week Missal* from Sr Mary on Saturday, I read through the Mass text as a compensation. I hope to do this now every day.

Paul Galbally and Kartya Gracer arrived in the early afternoon after an unusually tasty roast chicken, which was still warm, with peas, potatoes, and pumpkin. Paul outlined the extent of the substantial costs that remained to be paid and the suggestions of Danny Casey[2] on how to meet them. I said I would take the question on notice and speak to Danny and Michael Casey this afternoon, but I would try to have it all concluded during the week. After the phone calls, I

---

[1] Summer Time is a name used for Daylight Saving Time in Australia. When it ends, the clocks go back one hour.

[2] Danny Casey, close friend of the cardinal, former business manager for the Catholic Archdiocese of Sydney, and former director for the Secretariat of the Economy.

endorsed the proposed course of action. An expensive business, but I am well served.

Managed to obtain a broom and mop, so my cell is now as clean as I can manage. As the exercise pen had a whiff of urine about it, I mentioned this to the senior guard, who promptly said he would throw a bucket of hot soapy water down the drain. I suspect we have a newcomer to the unit as someone was working out next door energetically and noisily; the first time I had heard this. One of the guards claimed that I shuffled around the small space, but I do this for the whole half hour with a variety of unoriginal routines. When I first attempted my version of the slow march with my walking stick, I still had some balance problems, but these are now gone. Regularly exercising with my arms also, and the left arm is improving.

Holy Week is fast approaching, and we switched today in the breviary to the Epistle to the Hebrews and a commentary from Athanasius, which I used as well as moving through Mark's Gospel, which I had chosen for meditation after the Book of Revelation.

I love all the Gospels, but Mark is number four on my list. Originally Matthew was my first preference, but he has been replaced by Luke and then John, which is a rich source for meditation, but often more difficult as the basis of a sermon. I did not set out to do so, but I have published less about Mark than any of the other Gospels.

Meditating on Mark will give me an opportunity to reassess my attitudes toward him. Thank God I am not finding it too difficult to pray at the moment; I am not afflicted with that spiritual dryness which has often been my lot. My present method of meditating is pretty basic, nothing too sophisticated, simply a very slow Lectio Divina (i.e., a slow meditative reading of the Scripture text). I have supported the introduction of the Fr John Main[3] type of meditating, so ably spread by Fr Lawrence Freeman, OSB,[4] into our Catholic primary schools in Sydney, and it works well for the children with a teacher who understands it and is also ready to practise it with them.

[3] Fr John Main, OSB (1926–1982), was a British Benedictine monk who taught the use of a prayer phrase or mantra for meditation.

[4] Fr Lawrence Freeman, OSB (b. 1951), is a British priest and Benedictine monk who established the first Christian Meditation Centre in London, a part of the World Community of Christian Meditation.

This approach advocates the repetition of a single phrase, e.g., "Jesus, Son of the Living God, have mercy on us", and I meditate like this during nearly every meditation for some periods.

But when I am under pressure or preoccupied, I need some more structure, because I am so readily distracted. The Jesuits ran my first seminary at Werribee, and I can see the advantages of the structure that St Ignatius recommended: the choice of a Gospel passage, the composition of the place, his three points.

Young people are often open to meditation today, precisely because their lives are so noisy and often frantic. No previous generation has been able to distract themselves continually as this generation can. It is unhealthy and not conducive to spiritual equilibrium. Most of our new seminarians find it difficult to put aside their mobile phones on entering the seminary. Look at teenagers walking along the street with their heads buried in their phones.

It is a blessing for the Church and psychologically healthy that young adults often love the silence, the call to mysticism, to prayer before the Blessed Sacrament. I never expected this, because after the Second Vatican Council, among the enlightened class (where I felt myself to belong), the celebration of Benediction and adoration were regarded as totally out of order, medieval relics that had been rejected. None of us then would have thought it remotely possible that we would have a Synod of Bishops on the Eucharist in Rome in 2005 that would conclude with the Holy Father, bishops, and all other participants celebrating Benediction and praying in silent adoration.

God our Father, at the moment I am blessed with many hours of silence each day. Help me to use this well to move forward toward you, to pray for the Church, for the large number of people who have asked me to pray for them, and for my successful appeal.

Monday, 8 April 2019

I'll begin with the least important activity in my prison routine: my daily attempt to complete two Sudoku puzzles. Pride comes before a fall. After a sluggish start, I was solving most of them, but for the last six puzzles I have been unsuccessful. I feel a bit like an Australian

Test[5] batsman of old, perhaps one of the Chappells,[6] who was enjoying a terrible run of failures, but explained that he was still batting well, presumably in the nets. With a bit more care, I should improve and stop this losing streak.

Enjoyed a couple of exercise sessions as usual, where I have increased slightly my work rate with more exercise and a number of circuits on the trot, rather than just walking. I haven't exercised for one hour a day every day since I was at secondary school, and even then I probably had a day or two off each week.

Chris Meney and his wife, Mary Clare, came at 9:00 am this morning. They were down from Sydney for birthday celebrations and to see Melbourne play. The Aussie Rules team suffered a third inglorious loss. Unfortunately, Chris did not bring me the recent copies of *The Spectator*, but he insisted they were arriving by mail.

We discussed briefly the consequences of my jailing for the Church, and Chris felt it could be good especially for the young clergy to help them sort their priorities and alert them to the possibility that rough times lie ahead of them. He is probably correct on both counts.

Mary Clare is an energetic Catholic activist, involved in many different apostolates. In her [circles], she felt new life was stirring. She knew of the Irish visionary Christina Gallagher, noting that she had gained the disapproval of her bishop and was a bit into doom and gloom. Chris also informed me that Fr Joe Hamilton's[7] brother had died in Ireland somewhat unexpectedly some weeks ago, and I offered up my daily prayers for the repose of his soul.

In my breviary, I have a commemorative card for Bob Santamaria with a [James] McAuley poem, "Retreat", on the back of it. I hope the final verse fits my situation.

> Nor is failure our disgrace:
> By ways we cannot know
> He keeps the merit in his hand,
> Behold the kingdom grow!

---

[5] Test is a form of the sport of cricket noted for the long duration of its matches (five days).

[6] Greg and Ian Chappell were notable Australian cricketers.

[7] Fr Joe Hamilton is a Sydney priest and friend of the cardinal who is working on a PhD at Oxford University.

I haven't received any new letters either yesterday or today, but the last bundle contained the usual number of helps and pearls. One US writer from an Ordinariate[8] parish wrote: "A kind word warms for three winters." So be it.

A South Australian woman gave good practical advice. "I pray that you can forgive and that the meekness of Jesus possesses your soul. I suffer from anger problems, and I really don't want you to suffer in this way because it is very painful and a trap."

She also told me of her eleven-year-old daughter, who "drew a picture of you in Heaven with Mary's hand on your shoulder while you received a trophy from Jesus with the words, 'Well done, good and faithful servant'." That would be nice.

On a different tack, a good friend of mine, Fr Luke Joseph, who had been a seminarian when I was rector of Corpus Christi College and with whom I had enjoyed many a shouting match over the decades, mentioned the woes Cardinal George predicted for his successors, with the hope that these "not be completely fulfilled in your person". One could even claim that by the cardinal's prediction, I am ahead of schedule!

Mark's Gospel recounts Jesus' parable about the Kingdom of God, which is like the seed scattered by the sower on the ground to become grain. "Night and day, whether he sleeps or gets up, the seed sprouts and grows, though he does not know how" (4:27).

God our Father, I pray that we may believe that your Spirit is always at work, in every desert and in every disaster. Help us to be grateful for our friends and their kindness and to preserve our sense of humour, which is an antidote to self-centredness. May we priests always remember that we are here to serve.

Tuesday, 9 April 2019

The jail was locked down for a good part of the day, although I managed to get my exercise session in the morning. It was beautiful, crisp

[8] The Ordinariate of the Chair of Saint Peter is the equivalent of a diocese for people from Anglican or Episcopalian churches in the US and Canada who wish to become Catholic. It was created by the Vatican in 2012.

Autumn weather around 15°C–20°C [59°F–68°F] and good to be outside. The phones were temporarily disconnected.

I didn't know what prompted the lockdown, but it meant that when Sr Mary visited, we couldn't sit at the table in the central area as we usually do but were forced to dialogue through the small trap of the prison door. In this section, this is her usual practice.

We went through our prayer service, and I received Communion. She did not have much news, but was busy organizing all the prayer services in the Victorian jails for Holy Week. She will return on next Tuesday for an early Palm Sunday celebration. I am using her Holy Week missal to read through the Mass every morning.

Ruth Shann, the junior barrister, who is working with Bret Walker for the appeal, called unexpectedly, although I was aware that she was coming at some stage to talk of the approach Walker was taking. He did not change anything in the appeal document, but he is organizing the material to meet the norms the High Court follows. Naturally, he is not emotionally involved in the case as we are, and Ruth found it reassuring that he, too, thought the evidence extraordinarily weak. Apparently, Walker has an Anglican background (perhaps his father was a priest or minister) and knows about vestments and sacristies.

The judges do not have to consider what line of reasoning the jury might have taken, not least because the jury does not give any reason for their decision, but simply consider the evidence on its merits. It will be interesting to see what line of reasoning the prosecution uses when they present their written case some time next week. Ruth commented that the prosecutor in his final address ignored the testimony of Jeff Connor[9] that he and his fellow servers were in and out of the sacristy at the time of the alleged attack. She regards him as our best witness and Geoffrey Cox's[10] evidence as also being extremely valuable. My ranking puts Charlie Portelli at the top of the list; he is an honest man who provides a complete alibi. Ruth repeated her claim that the prosecution did not expect the jury to accept their line of reasoning and were also surprised by the verdict.

She said that Robert Richter was still upset, but a successful appeal would be reassuring as his confidence in the law has been shaken somewhat.

---

[9] Jeffrey Connor was an altar server at St Patrick's Cathedral, Melbourne.
[10] Geoffrey Cox, former deputy music director, St Patrick's Cathedral, Melbourne.

As Holy Week comes near, the breviary links together the prayers and readings, using the Epistle to the Hebrews with a commentary today from the fifth-century pope St Leo the Great, who played a pivotal role in the Council of Chalcedon, which defined the two natures, divine and human, in the one person Jesus Christ.

Leo is not as prolific or imaginative in his writings as St Augustine, nor as elegant in his prose and reasoning as our own Pope Benedict, but he is a formidable homilist and theologian. "For your (Christ's) cross is the source of all blessings, the cause of all graces. Through it those who believe receive strength from weakness, glory from shame, life from death ... for you are the true Lamb of God who takes away the sins of the world."

A Sydney woman who was disturbed by my plight gained great comfort by singing to herself the ancient Latin Benediction hymns "Tantum Ergo" and "O Salutaris Hostia". I understand this; they are classics, and they still resonate in the most unexpected places. Years ago, I attended the beautiful open-air consecration Eucharist for Chris Saunders, the new bishop of Broome. The ceremony was preceded by an aboriginal smoking ceremony, reverent and appropriate.

Afterward I was talking with a local when an older indigenous lady joined us. She agreed it was a beautiful Mass and liked the smoking ceremony. But she said, "You can't beat those old Latin hymns" and tottered off into the dark singing the "Tantum Ergo".

I should mention that Ruth went to the women who were outside the jail praying and holding a placard stating that it is wrong to imprison an innocent person and spoke with them. She was impressed, as someone is there every day to pray and witness.

On a less exalted note, we have a noisy newcomer to our twelve-cell unit. He often has a shouted conversation in the late afternoon or early evening after the 4:00 pm curfew with those closer to him at the other end of the corridor. Tonight, he gave me a few honourable mentions, and, while I heard the word "cardinals", I could not make out what he was saying, although it didn't sound completely hostile.

More importantly, I managed to solve one of the Sudoku puzzles, an easier one, although even here I fear they are becoming more difficult as I progress farther into the text.

God our Father, help us to deepen our faith in Jesus your Son, our brother, who is both God and man. So much depends on this. We are consoled that Jesus as a man suffered like us and grateful that his Divinity meant that we are redeemed, our sins forgiven when we repent, so that an eternity of happiness is open to us. Lord, we believe; strengthen our little faith.

Wednesday, 10 April 2019

No lockdown in the jail today, and the phones were functioning during both my exercise sessions. I tried twice to call my sister, Margaret, in Bendigo but was unsuccessful. The weather was a little colder and overcast, but it was still pleasant to be outside. I look forward not only to the exercise, which is not particularly enjoyable given the confined and grotty space, but to the fresh air, to being outside, to being able to see the sky and clouds and sometimes even the sun. These opportunities, a good hot shower, my television and kettle, and the cordiality of the guards help make life a bit better than bearable.

Yesterday I forgot to order my *Herald Sun* for today, which has the week's TV guide, but the boss of the unit bent the rules to order one. I appreciated it. Incidentally, I am moving more with the times because I frequently eat my meal on the customary narrow shelf watching the television. Teachers have told me that in many, perhaps most, areas, too many families eat their evening meal around the television set. I have even heard of a young fellow from a more conventional Catholic family who asked his mother, as a birthday present, to be able to eat his meal while watching television!

Philip Gibbs, the Anglican chaplain, called, and we had to chat through the trap of the prison door. I suggested he enquire whether we could talk at the table in the common area, but he was told the space was occupied. Somehow, we came to discuss the Rev Johnson,[11] the Anglican clergyman with the First Fleet. Philip had read his letters with their harrowing tales of his difficulties. For years, the colony of New South Wales had no church building, a fact that scandalised the

[11] Richard Johnson (1756–1827) was the first Christian cleric in Australia.

Spanish sailors who came across the Pacific from Lima, Peru, around 1794. One of their aims was to estimate the military strength of the settlement, because they were seriously considering trying to take over the colony. Napoleon's invasion of Spain put an end to all that. When the church was built, it was burnt down by persons unknown, not by the Irish Catholics, I hope, who were forced to attend the Anglican services.

Still no new letters, so I enquired of the boss, who said the censor was probably dealing with the other 240 prisoners' mail. Another guard said that the number of my letters was unprecedented for them.

Fr Martin Maunsell, a Sydney priest who was always friendly, loyal, and supportive, sent me a copy of his statement to his parish, explaining that "the crucified, risen Jesus Christ", not myself or any Church leader, defines the Church. He also mentioned my appeal, to be heard by three judges, so that my "case is still in the process of taking place". His letter explained that I had "overwhelming support" among his parishioners and that "support for you is actually growing." Ruth, too, said she was not surprised by this, given the support our team is receiving in the legal profession.

The breviary is now using the Epistle to the Hebrews, written by Paul or some anonymous author from Paul's followers, who reassured his people that God would not be so "unjust as to forget all you have done, the love that you have for his name, or the services you have done or are still doing" (6:10). Hebrews is not claiming that good works entitle us to heaven, but this is closer to James' "faith without works is dead" (2:26) and to Jesus judging on the Last Day in Matthew, chapter 25.

God our Father, help us not become complacent, too pleased, when we are thanked or praised, so that we forget the other side of the picture, our sins, failures, and weakness. May we also remember that we are saved only through the suffering, death, and Resurrection of your Son, Jesus Christ.

Thursday, 11 April 2019

Thursday is the busiest day of the week now that the physiotherapist is coming on that day when I regularly have visitors. Paul Galbally also called, which reminds me that I should suggest they come on some other day when I have no diversions except my exercise sessions. I had recently noticed that in the second pen some prisoner had twice scratched "beer" (apparently quite important to him) into the paint work, which is less picturesque than one or two other pieces of graffiti. To my surprise, I haven't heard any curses or blasphemy, although I don't know whether this is unusual or typical. Our noisy friend was shouting and swearing in his cell for many hours during the day. One small miracle was that his voice never gave out. He is much disturbed and unhappy. Sad. I have no idea what his crime was.

The physiotherapy is helping my left arm a lot, and I commended that previous physio to his replacement, who, it turned out, is his boss. Naturally he was pleased with my commendation.

The McFarlanes came at 11:00 am and were waiting in a cubicle different from where I was sent. This was quickly remedied. They were to come at 9:00 am, because they were leaving tonight for San Francisco to stay with their son, young Tim and his family, who is working there. At about 8:00 am, I was asked if I could contact them to come later as the guards had a union meeting. I think the McFarlanes were pleased with the later time. Their grandson Edward is now walking, and young Matilda is apparently as beautiful as ever, sleeping well after her training and sitting up by herself.

One sad piece of news was that a close friend of theirs had gone bankrupt, lost his business and house, and there were financial irregularities to boot. I, too, knew him quite well, so the news was a blow as well as a surprise.

The most important information Paul Galbally brought was that the Court of Appeal had decided to live stream the appeal and make a visit to the cathedral. Apparently, both decisions are unusual, and the first might be unprecedented. They also want to view the evidence giving of Portelli, Potter, Finnigan,[12] and Mallinson[13] (perhaps). Paul explained that we had no objection to this, but he also suggested they watch the films of Connor, the adult altar server and diarist, and Cox, the assistant choir master, giving evidence. I approved of all these developments.

[12] Br Peter Finnigan was the choir marshal at St Patrick's Cathedral, Melbourne.
[13] John Mallinson was the music director at St Patrick's Cathedral, Melbourne.

We then discussed a couple of other cases in which I was involved, including one where it was alleged that I had some responsibility for a Christian Brother offender, whom they mistakenly identified as a priest. Paul was pleased we had arranged payment of the fees.

The most erudite of my prisoner correspondents sent a typed four-page letter with a good deal of sound advice and interesting observations. He kindly mentioned that he, some chaplains, and his small circle of Christian and Muslim friends believed in my innocence, insisted that as I was "doing the porridge", i.e., serving the sentence, I was required to go with my gut feelings, as they "bring a clear guidance from our Heavenly Father", and "must keep a strong hand on the reins". God certainly does not speak through all my gut feelings.

By an interesting coincidence, on the day I received his letter, in which he was correctly warning that "we live in the 'Me Too' era where there is now a reversed onus placed on citizens" so that all sorts of allegations can be made, sometimes unsupported by any evidence, that are published and damage the accused, Geoffrey Rush, the Shakespearean actor, won his case for defamation against the Sydney *Daily Telegraph*. I welcome the decision, as due process is always required if we are to maintain the presumption of innocence as the basis of Australian criminal proceedings.

He again praised Sr Mary the chaplain very highly, explaining that the prisoners, because of her more than twenty-five years of service in the prisons, refer to her as a "boob head", that is, a lifer.

Before I left Sydney, one of our young priests who had called to see me regularly, asked whether I was following any saint or school of theology to help me through my travails. I almost felt uneasy (a passing feeling that I rejected on reflection) as I replied that I was relying on the elementary New Testament narrative about Jesus' redemptive suffering.

God our Father, help us to understand this always and more deeply, so that we can make our own the conviction mentioned in the Hebrews reading of today's morning prayer. "It was appropriate that God, for whom everything exists, and through whom everything exists, should make perfect through suffering, the leader (Christ) who would take them to their salvation" (2:10).

Friday, 12 April 2019

As anticipated, today was quieter than yesterday, with my daily routine undisturbed except for a visit by Kartya. Took my customary two exercise sessions; the air was crisp in the morning, the sky clear, and the sun appeared in the bottom left-hand corner of the large skylight. The weather was overcast this afternoon, but not cold and no rain. One of the guards said it was very fresh for him coming to work.

Kartya informed me that it had been announced that Archbishop Wilson, emeritus of Adelaide, was suffering from bowel cancer. Although he was cleared on appeal, it is difficult to think he would have been charged with not reporting a sexual abuse offence if he had not been archbishop of Adelaide and chairman of the Australian Catholic Bishops' Conference. At every significant juncture in my adventures of the past few years, he has written a supportive letter. I am grateful for this.

Kartya clarified those whom the judges wanted to watch. Naturally J the complainant topped the list, with Portelli and Potter, as I thought, and McGlone.[14] Our requests are that they should add Jeff Connor, Finnigan, and Cox. Kartya enquired, and it was confirmed that the cathedral visit and the viewing by the judges are most unusual. She felt it destroyed any claim that I was being treated just like anyone else, but I repeated my support for the measures, believing that whatever might help the judges to obtain an accurate understanding was to be welcomed.

I was also more enthusiastic about the live streaming of the appeal to balance up the fact that only the judge's sentencing, and nothing of the two trials, was put to air, which meant I was horribly disadvantaged. She had been enormously impressed by her first meeting with Bret Walker, QC, for the appeal, when he discussed (with the other team members) the case and its precedents for four hours without any notes or material. She had also discovered that he is selective in the briefs he accepts for the Courts of Appeal, generally opting to battle against injustice.

We both agreed that it was encouraging to realise that the judges had already started work. I must clarify what will happen at the

[14] Daniel McGlone, a lawyer, was an altar server at St Patrick's Cathedral, Melbourne.

appeal, if anything, beyond the interventions of the prosecution and the defence and their being questioned by the judges.

As you become older, it is important to utilise the thoughts that come to mind, because they can disappear quickly. Yesterday when I was waiting in a room, which used to be a library, for about twenty minutes for the physiotherapist to arrive with his bench, I used the time to take some exercise, as the room was larger than the exercise pen. To my delight, I noticed that at each end of one of the large windows, the glass was not too opaque, while not being perfectly clear, and I could distinguish cars going up and down some street, perhaps Spencer Street. It was a pleasant bonus.

Have received quite a few letters from friends who are numeraries of Opus Dei, which is composed mainly of lay members but led by priests and a prelate. It was founded in Spain in 1928 by Fr Josemaría Escrivá. Its members have strengthened Church life wherever they have gone and have been great supports to me, not least when I was working in Rome. I attended their monthly recollections there at the Church of San Eugenio, and they have provided me with a confessor each month for quite a few years.

I invited them to come and work in Melbourne when I was archbishop, explaining I would not do so if the Senate of Priests was against the move. I explained that no one would be obliged to join them or work with them, and the senate voted to support the invitation by a small margin.

One of my correspondents was an early recruit to Opus Dei who has remained as a layman or numerary. He was educated by the Jesuits at Riverview in Sydney, and the mythology is that late in the evening at a Riverview old boys' reunion, when most there were quite relaxed, they decided to get together a party of warriors to rescue him and release him from the sectarians who had captured him. He survived and is still working effectively and happily.

God our Father, help us to remember that your Spirit is still with the Church, so that just as the Benedictines in the sixth century, the Dominicans and Franciscans in the thirteenth century, and the Jesuits in the sixteenth century rose up to meet the challenges of the times, so too today groups like Opus Dei and the Neocatechumenal Way will help us hand on the faith.

Saturday, 13 April 2019

I woke up at a quarter to five, about an hour earlier than usual, to the low sound of Islamic chanting and loud banging from our noisy friend at the other end of the corridor. He was to be in good voice during the day.

A pleasant surprise came with my 6:00 am medicine delivery. A woman whom I did not recognize bent her head down to the door trap and asked how I was. When I replied that I was OK, she said sympathetically that my situation must be very difficult. She told me there was no need to get out of bed as she could place the tablets on the shelf herself.

As the bed is very low and the painted concrete floor is slippery, I need to put on my prison gym shoes to gain the traction necessary to rise. It requires a small effort, so I was pleased to be able to avoid this rigmarole. I was touched by the nurse's kindness. A kind word warms for (three) winters.

The letters are once again arriving to my cell, dozens of them on most days. When I received a large envelope from a legal firm, I was mildly apprehensive, but on opening I found only a beautiful printed card with my coat of arms in colour on the front cover and a large spiritual bouquet, listing the many Masses, prayers, and penances a group of people had performed for me.

A mysterious photocopy of a letter from the Vatican also arrived with no signature visible. It was very encouraging, explaining that "through all the weeks, with my prayer and my sympathy, I remained with you on this difficult way." The author was saddened by my sentences and then went on, to my surprise, to write, "You have helped the Catholic Church in Australia, with success, to come out of a destructive liberalism, guiding her again to the wideness and beauty of the Catholic faith.... I am afraid that now you have to pay also for your unshaken Catholicity, but thus you are very close to the Lord." He concluded by promising me "my constant closeness to you in prayer".

Many people write asking me to pray for them, some of them claiming my prayers are strong at the moment because of my situation. Previously, I would usually celebrate Mass in response to special requests, but as this is not an option now, I immediately say after receiving such a request the Memorare, a medieval prayer to Our

Lady composed by St Bernard of Clairvaux in the twelfth century,[15] and then commend the matter to God, who already knows what is in our hearts. I feel my poor inadequate prayers are stretched beyond their capacity, but God will provide if he chooses.

Have been moving in fits and starts through Mark's Gospel alternately with the breviary prayers and readings for fodder for my meditations. Providentially I have arrived at chapters 9 and 10, not long before the Passion narrative commences.

For many years I have been intrigued and puzzled by Our Lord's claim that, if we wish to enter heaven, we must become like little children. I vividly remember the mother of a young family coming to me after I had preached on this theme to state emphatically that if heaven was to be full of little children, she did not want to go there. Jesus is not making exactly this point here in Mark's Gospel, explaining that those who welcome a child in his name welcome him and then going on to proclaim the terrible indictment of those who corrupt children and do not repent.

Children who are loved are not only simple but loving, hopeful, open to the truth, trusting, and regularly looking forward to the future. Obviously, Our Lord is commending all this to us as adults. But children are also innately selfish, egotists, whose lives revolve around themselves. Jordan Peterson claims the crucial breakthrough occurs between the second and fourth birthday, but it is the work of a lifetime to become unfailingly altruistic. I am sure Jesus is not recommending childish weaknesses to us.

One of the guards said that our noisy neighbour has never grown up. He banged loudly from his cell off and on during the day and, in the early evening, had a ferocious and obscene argument with a neighbour for about an hour. It was sad and distressing.

Watched the football last night and tonight. None of the teams will be premiers, but in both games the pace and standard picked up in the second half. The football has made jail life easier for me.

However, the day belonged to Winx, the champion racehorse, who scored her thirty-third consecutive win, a world record, so garnering twenty-six million dollars in prize money. Just as no other country has

---

[15] Bernard of Clairvaux (1090–1153) was a Cistercian monk and theologian, Doctor of the Church, and founder and abbot of the monastery of Clairvaux.

a horse race that "stops the nation" like the Melbourne Cup, so no other country would give such publicity and adulation to a racehorse. It might not be ideal, but many alternatives would be worse.

Let me conclude with a blessing sent to me from a family in Sligo, Ireland.

May you always sleep well in the darkness,
and may the gentle Mother of God
watch over you in all your waking hours.

WEEK 8

Holy Week

14 April—20 April 2019

Palm Sunday, 14 April 2019

I managed to celebrate Palm Sunday with appropriate solemnity given the limitations of my situation. My prison watch enables you to set the alarm, and I followed the instructions to rise at 5:58 am. The alarm didn't go off, but I woke just before 6:00 am and was able to join *Mass for You at Home* on Channel 10 very soon after six. Fr Fabian Smith, Indian born and a seminarian when I was archbishop here, celebrated correctly and with reverence. He had changed since I last saw him more than fifteen years ago, but I recognized him, especially through his voice. Given the reading of the Passion, which also was abbreviated, there was no sermon because of the customary time constraints. I noticed that Geoff Hobbs, who was a seminarian when I was Corpus Christi College rector from 1985 to 1987, is still the producer after twenty or thirty years.

Jesus is not remembered for this small triumph, the enthusiastic welcome into the sacred city of Jerusalem, before it was captured by the Romans in A.D. 70–71, the Jewish priesthood and Temple destroyed, and the animal sacrifices terminated. The practice of Judaism was quite changed by these events, and one rough and inexact comparison would be Catholicism without a priesthood or Eucharist and without a St Peter's in Rome. I had good relations with Rabbi John Levi in Melbourne and Rabbi Jeremy Lawrence and Alan Crown[1] in Sydney. Jewish-Catholic friendships after nearly two

---

[1] Alan Crown (1932–2010) was a professor of Semitic studies at the University of Sydney.

millennia of often bitter hostility must reflect God's will as well as being a significant human advance. I believe Australia regularly has more news of Israel and things Jewish in its media than many European countries, reflecting less anti-Semitism here.

But to return to Palm Sunday. For many years, I exaggerated in my own mind the likely size of the welcoming crowd, thinking of something like an AFL finals crowd at the Melbourne Cricket Ground. It was a crude and elementary mistake because the numbers probably were not greater than a few hundred, with many women and Northerners from Galilee. I don't believe that most, if any, of these would have later joined the crowd shouting for Jesus' death and the freeing of Barabbas.

The second reading in the breviary is taken from the eighth-century writer St Andrew of Crete. "Since we have clothed ourselves with God's grace," he wrote, so we must spread ourselves under Christ's feet, "not (coats) or lifeless branches or shoots of trees, matter which wastes away and delights the eye only for a few hours".

The spiritual power that Jesus generated came, not from his local successes or from the love and loyalty of his disciples, but from his suffering and death. This was the means and path to his Resurrection and our salvation, and it was this that St Peter found so hard to accept. He loved the Lord and, like us, did not want a loved one to suffer. I have a great deal of sympathy for him in his humane worldliness. I, too, would have been insisting to Jesus that we should work to avoid the worst, that the worst is not inevitable, etc., although I am not sure I would have rebuked Jesus as Peter did.

Jesus' response to Peter is equally interesting, because Jesus did not say that he realised Peter loved him and wanted what was best for him. He didn't treat Peter gently at all. "Get behind me, Satan! You do not have in mind the concerns of God, but merely a human concern" (Mk 8:31–33). *Sic ad nos*. This is something for us to ponder, also.

But God enabled Peter to do great things as the "rock man" of the Church. God's power is real and available to us. This is as remarkable as the way Jesus made this available through his suffering and death.

An unknown supporter from France recommended to me some verses of Psalm 86. I make them my own.

Hear me Lord, and answer me
for I am poor and needy. . . .
Save me, because I serve you
just as my mother did.
Give me a sign of your goodness,
that my enemies may see it and be put to shame,
for you, Lord, have helped me and comforted me.

Monday of Holy Week, 15 April 2019

As the Epistle to the Hebrews continues to explain Jesus' life in traditional Jewish categories, the author has Jesus, the Supreme High Priest, entering the sanctuary. "So as we go in" with him, he writes, "let us be sincere in heart and filled with the faith, our minds sprinkled and free from any trace of bad conscience and our bodies washed with pure water" (10:22). He urges his listeners not to stay away from the meetings of the community, an exhortation I will not be able to follow here in prison. But I will be present in spirit.

In the breviary's second reading, the incomparable St Augustine explains the basic lesson of Holy Week by stating that when St Paul boasted about Jesus, he did not boast of the Lord's miracles or that he was Creator, much less ruler, of the world. He gloried only "in the cross of our Lord Jesus Christ".

Paul was unable to found a Christian community in Athens, and so we have no letter to the Athenians. A commentator claims that one reason for this failure was that St Paul in his speech in the agora in Athens did not mention the crucifixion, the mystery of the Cross. This is true. Whether or not there was any relationship of cause and effect between these two facts, St Paul never made the same mistake when he founded the lively community in Corinth.

David visited today with Sarah and Rebecca, and we met for an hour separated by glass. Others had beaten us to the time slot in the personal contact program. Rebecca, a senior teacher, has settled into the high school for year twelve in Bendigo, and no one has harassed her over my situation. Sarah has just returned from Nepal, where there was some sort of analogue replication of living on the moon, which did not go well, and a meeting in Paris for those involved in some way in the space travel programs. A happy relaxed time. David informed me that Fr Robert McCulloch, the Australian Columban priest who is his order's procurator in Rome, and a close friend, hopes to visit me on 22 May. I subsequently discovered this is not a Thursday or Monday visitor's day.

Also had a brief surprise visit in my cell from the boss of the jail, a man much taller than I. I repeated my usual and true line that I had no complaints. He asked whether there was any news of my shifting, and when I explained a decision would be taken early next month, he insisted that a change would be an improvement. I wrote a few notes of Easter greetings to three of the prisoners who had written to me, including my neighbour Gargasoulas. In response to his question, I repeated that I did not think much of his logic!

Yesterday, when I was in the small exercise pen saying the rosary as I completed the first part of my routine, the prisoner in the next pen broke into an Islamic prayer chant. I believe he is guilty of planning a terrorist attack; while we are both serious believers in the one true God, we are worlds apart in our thinking.

Some Catholics have argued with me that Christians and Muslims do not pray to the same God. However, there exists only one God, described in quite different ways in these two monotheistic traditions.

The situation was ironic and prompted a couple of basic thoughts. All the great religions are not the same, but radically different. Secondly, these religions are lions not lambs, for good generally, but sometimes for ill, a point made famously by G. K. Chesterton.[2]

Islam not only has different roles for women and the family from Christianity, the Quran and the New Testament have different teachings on love and violence, while Islam does not believe in a Trinitarian God or the Incarnation.

The Buddha did not speak of God, and Christians do not believe in reincarnation.

Hinduism is a blanket term coined by the British in India for a census to cover the multiplicity of local religions and philosophies, often sophisticated and sometimes beautiful, that are not Christian, Muslim, or Buddhist.

[2] G. K. Chesterton, "The Paradoxes of Christianity", chapter 6 in *Orthodoxy* (1908).

Christians built a civilization, Christendom, which shaped Europe and her colonies for more than fifteen hundred years, and Christian institutions, such as schools, parishes, hospitals, retirement homes, and welfare agencies, play an increasing role in Australian life.

However, Islamic terrorism has fuelled the secularist accusation that religion is the cause of war, all wars. If all religions are thrown into the same category, the accusation gains strength.

I remember being invited out for Sunday lunch at Manly in Sydney soon after September 11, and no sooner had I sat down at the table than the religion and war connection was alleged against me. I replied that I didn't think the greatest war criminals of the twentieth century were Christians, citing Stalin, Mao, Hitler, and Pol Pot, to start the list. I believe there can be a just war. I am not a pacifist, but while Christians must plead guilty to wars of aggression, they are not guilty on all counts. In fact, I suspect the vast majority of aggressors are not Christians, but this is a question of fact to be decided from history.

The thirty-six editors, writers, and announcers accused of breaching the suppression orders on my situation appeared in court today, and their case was held over until June.

An unknown friend from the US (I think) sent me this beautiful prayer to Our Lady.

Mary, Mother of the Church and mother of the hermitage, pray that we will be instruments of the Spirit. Pray that we will know when to act and when to wait, when to speak and when to be silent. Teach us how to listen and to know the voice of God in our hearts.

Tuesday of Holy Week, 16 April 2019

The big news of the morning when I switched on the television was the destruction by fire of Notre Dame Cathedral in Paris, which dates back to 1163. More than a national mausoleum like Westminster Abbey (a church I love, nevertheless), Notre Dame was a strong centre of daily worship and prayer. It was heartening to see the crowds outside the ruins, some kneeling in prayer.

Although the kings of France were not crowned there, the cathedral was the best-known symbol of Christian France, more than seven hundred years older than the Eiffel Tower. It was there that the goddess of reason was enthroned in the 1790s after the French Revolution, displacing Christ. Napoleon crowned himself there in the presence of Pope Pius VII, who was invited to do the job, and, much more importantly, the solemn Te Deum was sung there to celebrate victory over the Nazis after World War II.

France has been divided religiously since at least the 1789 Revolution, and contemporary paganism has devastated many areas. But, just as France produced a dramatic flowering of new religious orders in the nineteenth century after the destruction of the Napoleonic wars, so today orthodox Catholicism in France is a vigorous minority. A lot of this is due to Cardinal Lustiger, the late archbishop of Paris, who showed how the Church can contribute and survive in a heavily secularised society. The present archbishop of Paris, Michel Aupetit, who was a medical doctor, is in the same tradition, and I hope he will soon be a cardinal. With a few more years of experience and effective leadership, he should be eminently "papabile", a worthy possibility to be the next pope.

The weather was beautiful this morning as I took my exercise around 9:00 am. I saw a Qantas plane pass overhead, and a small bird came by. I tried to telephone Danny Casey to request him to contact Jean-Baptiste de Franssu[3] to tell him I was thinking of him and thank him, Hélène, and all the family who had written to me.

Sr Mary called to give me Communion, but our time was cut short by the arrival of an Alsatian dog and squad. I don't know what was going on, although there was no noise or fuss, except a few yelps from the dog.

She returned unexpectedly two and half hours later to give me the blessed palm that she had forgotten and tell me my Latin-speaking correspondent was pleased to receive my note with its Latin sentence! He is in another unit in this prison.

It was not possible for me to take my afternoon exercise. When I enquired, they replied that it had been a busy day. Kartya's recently purchased clerical collar (to replace the one that mysteriously disappeared)

[3] Jean-Baptiste and Hélène de Franssu. Jean-Baptiste, a close friend of the cardinal, is the president of the board of supervisors of the Institute for the Works of Religion, also known as the Vatican Bank.

arrived in the usual brown paper bag but is not long enough to do up around my neck.

Spent some time reading Kai-Fu Lee's *A.I. Superpower*, which I have nearly finished, and each evening in bed I read a section of Tolstoy's *War and Peace*. After three hundred pages, I am not long past Napoleon's victory over the Russians and Austrians at Auster- litz. A vast sprawling masterpiece about aristocrats and eccentrics, arranged marriages and emptiness, bravery and cowardice, imperial romanticism and folly. In short—about war and peace.

John's Gospel from today's Mass recounts Judas' betrayal and Our Lord's prediction of Peter's triple denial before the cock crows. Judas and Peter represent two different types of betrayal by friends.

At this stage, Peter was impulsive, given to bluster, and afraid of embarrassment or perhaps some type of punishment, or at least exclu- sion from the group. His weakness was not premeditated, and he quickly wept and repented. He was then one of the apostles St John Fisher mentioned in his 1508 sermon who were still "but soft and yielding clay", not yet "baked hard by the fire of the Holy Ghost".

Judas is another story, his motivations a mystery. John tells us he was in charge of the money and a thief, but this itself does not suffice to explain his treachery in betraying Jesus. Perhaps he thought he should be with the special trio, Peter, James, and John. Perhaps he had high political hopes for Our Lord and became bitterly disappointed when he recognized Jesus was not interested in political success. Neither is greed alone a sufficient cause, because he could have simply robbed the common purse and departed. What bitterness drove him to betrayal by a kiss? And then his despair and suicide?

God our Father, the stories of Peter and Judas are a warning to us all, particularly to those of us who are priests and even more so to us bish- ops, successors of the apostles. May we always be aware of our hidden weaknesses and pray that when we are standing firm, we might be wary lest we fall.

Wednesday of Holy Week, 17 April 2019

Last night I watched a BBC program on the last week of Jesus' life, narrated by Hugh Bonneville, who plays the lord of *Downtown*

Abbey. He spoke with a wide variety of scholars, one of whom, the Israeli writer Amos Oz, went to bat for Judas, claiming he wanted to avoid violence and disturbance by working with the authorities. Many of the speakers assumed, without any argumentation, that differences in the Gospel narratives were devised for political or theological purposes and that truth was a secondary concern. At the conclusion, I think the narrator was himself moved by the story and surprised at himself.

Unseasonably warm, around 30°C [86°F], so that I had to take off my cardigan for both exercise sessions. Unfortunately, I was required to take another drug test, the second in a week or so, complete with a strip search in my cell. The guard administering the random procedure was very reasonable and agreed with me, as did the Unit 8 commander, that such a repetition was intrusive and ridiculous. I wrote a letter of protest, saying that the selection procedure needed to be improved so that low- or no-risk prisoners who passed the test should be exempt for some months at least from another test.

Kartya called and gave me a copy of our reply to the judges on the live streaming of the appeal and their request to watch Portelli, Potter, and McGlone give evidence. Our request that the unchallenged evidence giving of Connor, Finnigan, Cox, Mallinson, Rodney and David Dearing,[4] and two other choristers should also be viewed (with my interviews) was a masterly, systematic demonstration of the impossibility of the accusations. Very heartening. On this second set of evidence alone, no jury would or should convict.

A couple of members of the placement team called for their weekly visit, confirmed that a decision would be made on my situation early next month, with a week where I went to the gymnasium with Unit 10, a second week spending from 10:00 am to 4:00 pm with them, while still sleeping in Unit 8, and then moving there if things went well. I asked about the differences in daily routines from Unit 8.

A couple of thoughts before Holy Thursday tomorrow. Today's breviary reading from Hebrews, chapter 12, has one of my favourite scriptural passages, where the author described meeting with the transcendent God. "What you have come to is nothing known to the senses: not a blazing fire, or a gloom turning to total darkness,

---

[4]Jeffrey Connor, Peter Finnigan, Geoffrey Cox, John Mallinson, Rodney Dearing, and David Dearing were witnesses in Cardinal Pell's trial.

or a storm; or trumpeting thunder or the great voice speaking which made everyone that heard it beg that no more should be said to them" (v. 18). No, what they have come to now is Mt Zion and the city of the living God, the heavenly Jerusalem, to God himself, the supreme Judge, and to Jesus, the mediator who brings a new covenant.

It is a wonderful passage to be read aloud to a congregation, provided it is read well, because it evokes the Transcendent, brings our minds and imagination to begin thinking of being in God's presence. So many of us are tone deaf to the Supernatural, not tuned into any godly wavelength.

My second thought is from Mark's Gospel, chapter 11, which I am following, and occurs after Jesus' entry into Jerusalem, when he drove out the money changers and dove sellers from the Temple, denouncing them for turning a house of prayer into a den of robbers. If the good Lord was to return to earth again for a similar purpose, I would be able to suggest a couple of places where he might start.

I had been a priest for some decades before I read somewhere that Jesus condemned the love of riches more than he condemned hypocrisy. I never made an exact count. But I continue to believe the claim is correct. I was shocked, although I was quite clear already that one could not love and serve both God and money and that it was more difficult for a rich man to enter the Kingdom of heaven than for a camel to pass through the eye of a needle. But surely a love of money, within limits, was not worse than hypocrisy?

It was while I was working with money during my years in Rome that I was told of Mother Teresa of Calcutta's claim that priests are often faced with two major challenges: sex and money, and that money is the greater danger. I am not prepared to dispute that proposition.

I do not want to make a mountain out of a mole hill, and there is not a mountain of financial corruption around the world in the Church, much less in Australia. But the love of money can be corrosive without any descent into illegality.

God our Father, help us to understand and accept your Son's teaching on riches, about the dangers of greed and materialism to our faith and moral well-being, so that we always opt for God and not for mammon, whether we are rich or poor or, as 80 percent of Australians claim to be, middle class.

Holy Thursday, 18 April 2019

Prison is certainly not the best place to celebrate the Easter feast. Being unable to attend the Holy Thursday Mass of the Oils with the priests is hard, just as it is hard to miss the evening Mass of the Lord's Supper. While the ceremonies in Sydney are always celebrated with dignity and genuine reverence in that splendid neo-Gothic sandstone cathedral, and the music led by what is now the best choir in Australia, it is not this splendour's absence that I lament most of all. It is the inability to celebrate these central mysteries in my community according to the ancient prescribed rites of the Catholic Church. These sacramental celebrations in any setting, provided they are reverent, set out the events commemorated and draw us into their mystery.

Sr Mary came especially for Holy Thursday Communion service at 1:00 pm, but we were interrupted at our table in the common area three times. Twice I had to return to my cell while other prisoners were moved (we never see one another), and then a message arrived to say that a television link meeting with the St Vincent's Hospital heart specialist had been arranged (unknown to myself) at 2:00 pm, when I was to meet with John Clifton from Ballarat. Which of the two was to go ahead? I quickly replied that the meeting with my visitor had priority and the doctor could be seen later, on some other day. The guard volunteered that as John was already down below, I could see him immediately and then go to the medical centre for the doctor. I had received Communion, so we hurriedly concluded our prayers, and I went below.

John Clifton had been a good Aussie Rules footballer whom I had coached at Villa Maria school in the 70s. Coming from a large Catholic family with a strongly Catholic mother and a non-Catholic father, very supportive, he had been a pilot in Britain in the Second World War and was, with the family, a Footscray supporter, now the Bulldogs.

I had not met John for about thirty-five years, but I remembered him because of his family and the fact I had played him at centre-half forward, normally where I played my best player. He emerged in Ballarat as my strongest public defender, speaking on radio, in the press, and on television.

Apparently, the local ABC reporter in Ballarat could find no one prepared to support me publicly, when John knocked on his door to volunteer. Naturally, I thanked him for speaking up, for "sticking out his neck for me", and he replied that just as I had "stuck out my neck" for good causes, he wanted to do the same. He is a man of strong Catholic faith, as well as being a man of courage.

I caught up on his personal story, on some of his siblings (I had blessed the marriage of his older sister), and some of his school friends. It was a great visit.

Took my two usual exercise sessions. During one of these, the principal shouter and banger from the other end of the unit was on the phone, shouting as usual, in the exercise pen next to mine. It was impossible not to hear him as he protested his love, threatened to bash someone, made arrangements to spend some money—all in colourful language at the top of his voice. The saddest moment was when he informed his friend that he had already soiled himself a half a dozen times, from stress and anxiety, as he rightly explained. I prayed for him as it is hard to see the situation improving. He is again shouting and banging in his cell as I write this.

The daily Eucharist has been at the heart of my priestly life, just as the Mass is constitutive of each Catholic community. That is why there are no priestless parishes, even when the priest is not resident or visits only rarely.

We consume the consecrated bread and wine, fruit of the earth and work of human hands, according to the adapted Passover ritual that Jesus instituted. Unthinkingly, I had long thought of the Lord as serene and majestic as he is depicted in Da Vinci's *Last Supper* in Milan. But Jesus was under enormous pressure, knowing what was likely, and grieved by the betrayal of one of his chosen Twelve, as he instituted the Eucharist.

En route to the Cologne Youth Day with the Sydney pilgrims in 2005, I had an unfortunate experience with the church at Gethsemane. Each day in Jerusalem, I went out with a different pilgrim group, and on this occasion, I was with the secondary students, who went up and down every hill in Jerusalem at the gallop.

We prayed together a Holy Hour in the evening in the church next to the garden at Gethsemane where Jesus prayed, and when the light dimmed, I soon fell into a doze, not once but twice, as I was truly exhausted. On two occasions, scripturally literate university types tapped me on the shoulder to ask: "Can you not watch one hour with me?"

Holy Thursday is also the feast of the ministerial priesthood, and once again St Peter Chrysologus provides beautiful material on the wider but basic notion of Christian priesthood. "How unique is the duty of Christian priesthood! For there a man is himself sacrifice as well as priest; there a man does not look for something outside himself to offer to God; there a man brings with himself and in himself and for himself a sacrifice to God; there the victim is not consumed and the priest never completes his task; there the victim is slain but lives." Let me conclude with St Peter's exhortation.

Do not throw away the privilege granted to you by divine authority. Put on the vestment of holiness; buckle on the belt of chastity. Let Christ be the veil for your head; let his cross always be on your forehead to protect it. Place on your breast the sacrament of divine knowledge. Keep ever burning the sweet-smelling incense of prayer. Take in your hand the sword of the Spirit. Set up the altar of your heart. And so without fear bring your body to God as his victim. Amen.

Good Friday, 19 April 2019

I started this sacred day by praying the Stations of the Cross in the traditional style of St Alphonsus Liguori, founder of the Redemptorists. I didn't sing the "Stabat Mater", but warmed as always to the short introductory prayers, the priest's meditation on each station followed by the congregation's response and prayers.

I have always attended the Good Friday stations, generally in the morning. In Ballarat, we walked as an ecumenical group from most Christian churches, starting from the summit of Black Hill and descending to finish at St Columba's Church, Ballarat North. The movement is good for everyone, especially the children, and it is an easy form of prayer. In Melbourne when I was archbishop, we started an ecumenical Way of the Cross following a set of stations built into different buildings in the central business district.

Naturally I had no visitors today and did not have my morning exercise session, discovering there had been a prison shutdown due to a disturbance in another unit. By a coincidence, the shouter put on one of his loudest and longest shouting and banging performances. I discovered he has not been in jail previously and claims he will be released in May. One possibility is that he is partially deranged by ice.

Managed to speak with my sister on the phone after four earlier attempts. Didn't turn on the television, except for the evening news, not watching the televised AFL game, a development I regret. There was a strong push when I was Melbourne archbishop for a game on Good Friday, which I publicly opposed with the support of the Richmond Football Club president Leon Daphne, who said he would not be opposing his archbishop on the issue. Most of the players then had no enthusiasm for another playing day.

While the Good Friday Appeal for the children's hospital continues strongly, the television stations were almost completely silent on this religious feast. For too many, I suspect, the day remains a holiday for reasons similar to the survival of the Queen's Birthday holiday. Neither Italy nor the US stops work for the day. The biggest religious news of the week by far was the fire in Notre Dame Cathedral, Paris. It seems as though President Macron, like Julius Caesar, has declared himself great high priest as he announces what will be done with the building in the reconstruction.

One message of this feast is that the Son of God suffered like us, and indeed much more than nearly anyone else. He is our brother in pain as well as our Saviour, and people understand this and are consoled.

I remember a Muslim taxi driver telling me he could not follow such a weak God who allowed his Son to suffer and die like this. A similar point was made on television by Richard Dawkins,[5] and he was very pleased with himself for it. "Who could follow a God who would do this to his Son?" he asked. But there are many brave and good parents who are proud of their sons for making the supreme sacrifice in a great cause.

Understanding what we are celebrating on Good Friday, and why, is easier for Christians than outsiders. In merely human terms, it remains strange. Cardinal Van Thuan, the white martyr from Vietnam, summed up our claims nicely. Jesus' "arms and legs nailed to the Cross,

---

[5] Richard Dawkins (b. 1941) is an English evolutionary biologist, ethologist, and author of The God Delusion. He debated Cardinal Pell during a live televised Q&A about God and religion on 9 April 2012. The ABC program was watched by a million viewers.

and life draining out of his body, it was then he accomplished the most for humanity. At his weakest moment, Jesus redeemed the world." One of my many correspondents, an older lady from Singapore, sent me this quotation for my consolation.

The foundations of our understanding come from the chapters on the suffering servant in the Old Testament prophet Isaiah. The suffering servant is without beauty and majesty. "He was despised and rejected of men, a man of sorrows and acquainted with grief", the lines immortalised in the music of J. S. Bach's *St Matthew Passion*.[6]

Yet ours were the sufferings he bore; he was pierced through for our fault. God himself says, "By his sufferings shall my servant justify many, taking their fault on himself" (Is 53:11).

Isaiah clearly knew about redemptive suffering. What was new was that the suffering servant was to be the Messiah, not a powerful religious and political leader, a national liberator like David or Solomon. And the suffering servant is the Son of God. The salvation of the world truly hung on the wood of the Cross.

God our Father, we pray that through the death of your Son and in the hope of the resurrection pardon may come, comfort be given, holy faith increase, and everlasting redemption be made secure.

Holy Saturday, 20 April 2019

The first verse of the breviary prayers explains today's significance.

> His cross stands empty in a world grown silent
> Through hours of anguish and of dread;
> In stillness, earth awaits the resurrection,
> While Christ goes down to wake the dead.

From an earthly point of view, this day is an interlude now that the hard work of redemption has been done and the unexpected comeback, the Lord's Resurrection from the dead, occurs tomorrow. In earlier days, the penances and fasting used to finish at midday

---

[6] This line from Isaiah 53:3 is in George Frideric Handel's *Messiah*.

on Saturday, and I remember as a child sitting poised and ready with my box of chocolates for midday to strike. Incidentally, we did not have a Project Compassion collection in Lent before the Second Vatican Council to help focus our self-denial into service for others. This collection continues strongly, doing as much good spiritually for the donor as it does for the recipients, the overseas partners of Caritas Australia.

I spent much of the day reading dozens of letters. One jail official claimed I was receiving a hundred a day, which only come to me slowly and irregularly. Most pleasing of all was a warm and theologically well-constructed letter signed by each seminarian at Good Shepherd Seminary, Homebush, where I had been living. They asked me to "offer some part of your suffering for us, seminarians in formation, here in Homebush and further abroad", and then went on: "We know that your trials and sufferings, your white martyrdom, will be a source of great fruit for the Church in Australia, and the Church at large." I pray that this will be so, not least to counteract the damage, confusion, and disillusion provoked by the conviction.

Another note from Cardinal Tim Dolan of New York, a regular supporter, and a beautiful couple of pages from Cardinal Roger Mahony, the emeritus archbishop of Los Angeles. "So many of your brother cardinals are totally supportive for you, and this bond remains deep and solid", he wrote. He recalled we had been together on the Vatican's fifteen-member Council of Cardinals for the Study of Organizational and Economic Problems of the Holy See in Pope Benedict's time, "when so many of our questions were never answered satisfactorily and where our recommendations were never taken seriously".

In those days, we council members did not know what we did not know, but we did know that we were not in charge. The situation is now improved, but not sufficiently, as the Secretariate for the Economy's efforts at financial reform were thwarted and inconclusive.[7]

[7] In 1981 Pope John Paul II established the Council of Cardinals for the Study of Organizational and Economic Problems of the Holy See. Amid rising concerns about corruption and mismanagement in the Vatican, in 2013 Pope Francis formed an international panel of cardinals, which included Cardinal Pell, to advise him on reforms of the Roman Curia. The following year the pope created the Secretariate for the Economy and named Cardinal Pell its prefect. In June 2017 the cardinal took a leave of absence from this office to stand trial in Australia.

One woman correspondent said she became a Catholic after I visited her Uniting Church community (I am not sure I was the catalyst for many other adult conversions), and one ex-seminarian who had lapsed from regular worship, but not from belief in God, explained that he had returned to Sunday Mass because of my trouble, but he was not sure this practice would last!

Fr Eric, the rector of Redemptoris Mater Seminary in Sydney, wrote on behalf of staff and students to wish me a good Easter. They, too, are rock solid in their loyalty and prayer for me.

The ancient homily on the Lord's descent to hell, which is today's second reading in the breviary, is another of my favourites. I liked to read it publicly during the Tenebrae service, something I achieved regularly in Melbourne but managed only once (I think) in Sydney. "Today there is a great silence over the earth, a great silence, and stillness, a great stillness because the King sleeps. The earth was in terror and was still, because God slept in the flesh and raised up those who were sleeping from the ages. God has died in the flesh, and the underworld has trembled."

At one of the discussion days I chaired for new bishops in Rome, one US bishop claimed that our entire pastoral approach is conditioned by how many people we believe will be saved in heaven. He was correct. If everyone goes to heaven, whatever they have written by their lives in the Book of Life, a dimension of urgency has gone (to say the least).

For decades I preached my hope that few would finish up in hell, although I always emphasised the need for repentance and the need for an efficient purgatory. Everyone can be saved if he repents, but a repentant Stalin or Hitler would need a lot of dry cleaning (penance in purgatory).

God loves each of us, and Jesus promised heaven that very day to the good thief dying on the cross next to him. I still believe that those in hell decide to go there and turn their backs against the light, but I probably did not pay sufficient attention to Our Lord's warnings. Jesus said, "Enter through the narrow-gate. For wide is the gate and broad is the road that leads to destruction, and many enter through it. But small is the gate and narrow the road that leads to life, and only a few find it" (Mt 7:13–14).

For those like myself who have lived sheltered lives, never being caught up in wars or terrorist attacks, etc., we can be inclined to

underestimate the evil in societies and the damage done to many
people, victims. Evil people exist, and evil too is a mystery.

The final judgement is not our decision. Each of us should pray for
mercy for himself and be content with the judgement of the Lord,
who sees into the recesses of the heart and mind. God understands
us better than we understand ourselves, and I still hope against hope
that many, many will be saved, that the risen Lord was fully occupied
during his time in Hades reinstating multitude upon multitude on the
thrones of heaven.

*God our Father, help us to believe that you are a God of infinite love
and mercy, who is also the just Judge who will separate the sheep from
the goats on the Last Day.*

WEEK 9

Easter Week

21 April–27 April 2019

Easter Sunday, 21 April 2019

Liturgically, the Easter Vigil is part of the Easter Sunday celebrations, just as a Saturday evening Mass fulfils our Sunday obligations.

The Easter Vigil concluding with the first Easter Sunday Mass is the centrepiece and highpoint of the Church year. Larger congregations probably come to Mass at Christmas, because less faith is required to celebrate a birth, even the birth of the Son of God, than is needed to celebrate the redemptive death of a good young man, especially if that man also has a divine nature. In Australia, we even have more performances of Handel's *Messiah* at Christmas than we do around Easter. Christmas is an easier feast for the less interested and those of weaker faith and can be celebrated by those with no faith. A new baby, a good marriage, a supportive wider family are generally appreciated even by those who do not enjoy them. Faith is needed for an Easter celebration.

The Easter bunny is a small, sad creation, and in Sydney I strongly supported the Polish Michaelite Fathers in the production and distribution of their chocolate Paschal lambs. Long-settled customs are hard to change, but if Coca Cola could create Father Christmas in the 1920s, it is worth persevering with the chocolate Paschal lambs.

The Resurrection is the culmination of the ultimate struggle between good and evil, between the Light and the powers of darkness. Paul himself said that if Christ is not risen, then "our preaching is useless and so is your faith" (1 Cor 15:14). So the Resurrection does not mean that Jesus' soul goes marching on or that his memory

143

remains as a powerful influence. No, the Christian claim is that Jesus rose body and soul from the dead. The tomb was empty, and the tomb is empty.

It is because Jesus is truly risen that

> The sanctifying power of this night
> dispels wickedness, washes faults away,
> restores innocence to the fallen, and joy to mourners,
> drives out hatred, fosters concord, and brings down the
>   mighty

in the words of the Exultet.[1]

I cannot remember the last time I did not celebrate Easter with a community or in a church. This has probably been my invariable practice since before I reached the age of reason. I have celebrated the Easter ceremonies as a priest for nearly fifty-three years. But not this year.

When phoning friends and family during my exercise spells outside (the only permitted time to phone), I was asked a number of times whether I was able to attend Mass, receive Communion during the Triduum, or even participate in an ecumenical service. My answer was no.

I was not able to prepare the Easter candle outside the cathedral affirming that all time, all ages, all glory and power belong to the (risen) Christ.

I was not able to turn in the sanctuary to face the congregation and see the light from the newly lit candles spread slowly but surely in fits and starts through the dark vault of the cathedral.

I read each of the beautiful readings of the escape from Egypt, of the terrible story of Abraham and his willingness to sacrifice Isaac, but I did not hear them proclaimed.

I was not able to bless the baptismal waters, a magnificent prayer.

I renewed my baptismal promises quietly to myself, not with the newly baptised and the cathedral congregation. And, of course, I could not consecrate the bread and the wine or receive Communion.

---

[1] A proclamation sung during the Easter Vigil in the Roman Rite of the Mass.

But I knew that everywhere around Melbourne, throughout Australia, and indeed through every country in the world, Christians were gathering to offer sacrifice to the Paschal Victim, life's own Champion, who had been slain, but now once again lives to reign.

> *Christus vincit.*
> *Christus regnat.*
> *Christus imperat.*
>
> *Christ conquers.*
> *Christ reigns.*
> *Christ rules.*

Easter Monday, 22 April 2019

This evening, I just watched the third and last instalment on SBS television of Queen Victoria and her nine children. I was surprised to discover she was so unpleasant to her children and immensely self-centred. I suppose that it would be hard work to be otherwise, if you were Queen of England. Strangely, it is Sydney, not the state of Victoria, which has two large statues of this woman, one in George Street outside the Queen Victoria Building and the other at the Hyde Park end of Macquarie Street, where the Queen stands outside St James' Church, allegedly with one eye on her beloved husband, Prince Albert, whose statue is across the road, and the other eye on what was the Mint,[2] down the street a little.

While I could find very little religious television on Good Friday, this was not the situation on Easter Sunday, and I watched every program as a religious substitute for the real thing. At 6:00 am, I began with the Easter *Mass for You at Home*, once again celebrated by Msgr Ireland[3] (who had sent a second encouraging letter) and

---

[2] The oldest public building in Sydney's central business district, the Mint was originally part of a hospital, then became a mint with a coining factory nearby. It is now the head office of the Historic Houses Trust of New South Wales. Some of its offices are open to the public, and it houses a well-known restaurant.

[3] Msgr Anthony Ireland, a former rector of Corpus Christi seminary in Melbourne, was a seminarian when Cardinal Pell was the rector.

celebrated well. Hillsong[4] followed, where Senior Pastor Houston[5] orated effectively for thirty minutes, twenty minutes of which were before an inert congregation (not completely inert, but nothing like a charismatic gathering) of 1,500 to 2,000 people. The backdrop contained no religious symbolism. A cross was nowhere to be seen. I had expected no readings from the Scriptures, but thought there would be an Easter theme. Christ was hardly mentioned, Easter not at all, as the theme was wisdom, largely referenced from the Old Testament. This wisdom required common sense and hard work which would bring success in your marriage (it would last) and success at work, which usually meant promotion. The weekly ABC *Compass* program also had no Easter theme, but told us of Catholic life in Bishop Columba Macbeth-Green's vast Diocese of Wilcannia-Forbes in western New South Wales. The countryside is now ravaged by one of the worst droughts.

The English program *Songs of Praise* was a beautiful Easter service celebrated in St Mary's [Anglican] Church Portsmouth, UK, many hymns, with a couple from Handel, including "My Redeemer Liveth". In the evening, the ABC showed a documentary on the restoration of the Edicule, the marble shrine around the place of Jesus' burial in the ancient Basilica of the Holy Sepulchre in Jerusalem, which houses the site both of the crucifixion and burial and of the Resurrection. The news clip of the Holy Father's Easter Sunday Mass in St Peter's Square showed an immense congregation filling even the Via della Conciliazione. It is strange that Christian programs at Easter don't address the central message.

I have spent a good part of the last three days opening letters of support and Easter greetings. They nearly always promise prayers, which is consoling, and often contain good advice, prayers, poems, or holy cards.

I found today something of an anticlimax after yesterday's feast, so when one message urged me to remember that each day passed meant that one less remained, I was heartened. The thought is almost banal, but it cheered me. Yet another copy of Cardinal Newman's

---

[4] Hillsong is a charismatic Pentecostal church based in Australia with some 150,000 members in twenty-three countries.

[5] Brian Houston (b. 1954) is an Australian pastor and evangelist, senior pastor at Hillsong Church, and from 1997 to 2009 was national president of the Australian Christian Churches, the Australian branch of the Assemblies of God.

prayer "The Mission of My Life" arrived (five in all from different people), where the central thought is that God has committed to each of us some work which he has "not committed to another". The soon-to-be-canonised cardinal concludes, God "may make me feel desolate, make my spirits sink, hide my future from me. Still, he knows what he is about."[6]

I had a grateful letter from Sr Theoktisti in an Orthodox monastery in Anatoli, Agia, Greece, whom I knew as Nicky and helped when she was at Notre Dame High School in Oxford after the death of her mother. Another told me George Yeo, a good friend on the Vatican Finance Council and a former foreign minister in Singapore, had gone on social media to affirm that I should not have been convicted.

A woman from Altona North[7] sent me a copy of Rudyard Kipling's poem "If", which is not religious, but contains wise and worldly advice to his son on how to become a man:

> If you can wait and not be tired by waiting,
> Or being lied about, don't deal in lies,
> Or being hated, don't give way to hating,
> And yet don't look too good, nor talk too wise.

Good Anglo common sense, like the teachings of Confucius and the Greco-Roman Stoics, all constitute a decent stepping-off point for developing the Christian virtues.

Letters from close friends are special. Those from Bernadette, recounting a small legal triumph in court of her husband, Terry, in the "layering" defamation case, from Caterina Pagani,[8] telling me the children are praying for me daily (and that they have bought a big dog), and from Gabriele Turchi[9] with his family news, provide a human and a spiritual boost.

God our Father, I thank you for so many good friends; keep them in your care, reward them for their kindness, do not allow them to be put to the test too often, and keep their children faithful, good, and happy.

---

[6] St John Henry Newman (1801–1890), who was first an Anglican priest and then, after his conversion, a Catholic priest and cardinal, was canonised on 13 October 2019.

[7] A suburb of Melbourne.

[8] Caterina Pagani, friend from the Neocatechumenal Way.

[9] Gabriele Turchi, friend from the Neocatechumenal Way.

Easter Tuesday, 23 April 2019

The siren to wake us went off fifteen minutes late this morning, giving time for extra rest until 7:30 am. This diary, too, is still behind in recounting each day's events.

The breviary is using the First Epistle of Peter for the Scripture readings, when the material is expressed concisely and systematically. Peter is talking of Christ "the living stone, rejected by men, but chosen by God", who is a fundamental cause of division between the good and the evil. He, Christ, "proved to be the keystone, a stone to stumble over, a rock to bring men down. They stumble over it because they do not believe in the word" (1 Pet 2:4–8).

Accusations of one kind or another have been circulating about me for nearly three years, and slowly, indeed, reluctantly, I began to believe there was more than a whiff of evil and, in fact, the presence of the Evil One in the accusations against me. They were so many and, with the exception of the cathedral charges (which I thought would be the easiest to disprove because of the availability of witnesses and the bizarre nature of the claims), all have fallen by the wayside. I don't know how many were fantasy, how much was fiction.

On Holy Saturday, I received from Tim O'Leary photocopies of four articles from the magazine *Quadrant* online, dating from early April. For present purposes, the most important was Keith Windschuttle's "The Borrowed Testimony That Convicted George Pell", recounting the details of a sex abuse case, in Philadelphia in 1998, of a priest abusing an altar server in a church sacristy. The accusations in the US were made by "Billy Doe", a drug dealer and petty thief, whose evidence was inconsistent and who, Catholic lawyers claimed, had been given "red carpet treatment" by the district attorney, who was himself later sentenced to jail on unrelated bribery charges. The original convictions were overturned and reversed.

The *Rolling Stone*, a US magazine circulated also in Australia, wrote up the Philadelphia case in September 2011. But in 2016, Ralph Cipriano in *Newsweek* exposed another hoax story *Rolling Stone* ran on an alleged gang rape by seven men at a college party and revealed a good deal of the local politics involved in the three-year legal struggle over the Church accusations in Philadelphia.

Windschuttle lists seven similarities between the Philadelphia and Melbourne accusations, with significant differences on a second "incident", which is found in both stories. According to Windschuttle, "There are far too many similarities in the stories for them to be explained by coincidence. The conclusion is unavoidable."

It will be fascinating to discover where all this leads, and Windschuttle concludes his article with the hope that there will emerge one investigative journalist "somewhere, willing to follow these leads into the bowels of the Victorian police operations". Tim O'Leary, in speaking to me by phone today, informed me that Chris S. Friel from the UK[10] has already published interesting further information, which I have not seen.

I do not know what legal weight judges might give to the information we have already, but it would have been of interest to a jury.

Naturally what lay behind J's grotesque allegations was a long-term point of enquiry and interest to me and my legal team. I always claimed they were the invention or fantasy of a person who had never seen a busy cathedral sacristy after a pontifical Sunday Mass. Had something similar happened in his parish? Or elsewhere?

I suspect the information will prove to be important, because I do not believe J has either the intellect or the imagination to construct by himself such a story, despite the flaws and impossibilities in his account. He changed his story twenty-four times during the trial.

God works in strange ways, because it is only weeks since I was grumbling (but not too badly) and asking the Holy Spirit to put on his skates! The enormous volume of prayer is being answered.

Naturally, I mentioned all this to Ruth and Paul from the legal team when they visited on Easter Sunday. Neither had read the article, although Paul was aware of it and will speak to Windschuttle by phone. My brother David, Rebecca, and Georgie were also very interested when I informed them on Easter Monday.

The routine of prison life continues. On most days, I manage two periods of exercise, when I walk for twenty minutes and now rest for ten. Yesterday, I swept the cell and changed my bed sheets and

---

[10] Chris S. Friel is a theologian and philosopher located in Wales, UK, who wrote a series of more than 130 analytical papers on the Pell case, which he made available online at Academia, https://independent.academia.edu/ChrisFriel.

towels. Today, Sr Mary brought me Communion, looking fresher than she was last time, but limping more noticeably. The guards are now cordial and generally friendly, so I sometimes am given extra biscuits or a half litre of milk. One letter writer suggested my life resembled that of a seminarian or a Trappist monk. There is a bit of truth in each suggestion, although I am not praying as much as a monk, while sharing the Trappist quiet. I don't know if the monks are allowed their own kettle, but they certainly wouldn't each have a television set. I would meet the daily prayer requirements for a semi-narian, but not share the community interaction, which is essential to their formation. Nonetheless, an old-style pre-Vatican II seminary is not a bad preparation for prison life.

I will conclude by returning to Cardinal Newman's prayer, with adaptations.

God our Father, I will always trust you. Whatever, wherever I am, I know I can never be thrown away. Whether I am sick or perplexed or in sorrow, I may still serve you, and these difficulties may be necessary causes to some great end, which is quite beyond me.

You do nothing in vain, and you know what you are about. Amen.

Easter Wednesday, 24 April 2019

I awoke early this morning and heard the trucks emptying the rub-bish bins five stories below as well as the hum of Islamic prayer chant. A near neighbour banged loudly in his cell three or four times—then quiet again. Our shouter and banger was silent yesterday, so I don't know whether he is still with us.

Christine from the volunteer observers at the prison called for a pleasant chat. I had no complaints and told her I was doing as well as might be expected.

When I mentioned the five hundred or so letters I have read already, she commented that they must bring me consolation. They do so very much, and they present such a wide offering of advice, anecdotes, expressions of gratitude, comments on the case and on society generally, etc.

One lady claimed that "Our Lord wasn't being kind when he called us sheep—he was being brutally accurate." But he still loves us.

Another Catholic schoolteacher and principal told an amusing story, which I had not heard, about taking her preparatory grade to a St. Patrick's Day Mass which I celebrated. A poster of St Patrick was on the lectern, and when I entered with mitre and crozier, the preppies stood, hugged one another, and clapped. "It's St Patrick—he came to our church", they gasped.

The comment of a four- or five-year-old boy standing with his father at the entrance of an overcrowded Brighton church when I came to confer confirmation was less spiritual. "Dad, Dad," he said, "it's the King." "No, son," I replied as I swept past, "it's only the archbishop." Those were the days. Vanity of vanities.

Thank God for our schools, whatever their imperfections. Many times, today, the youngsters who come to us early have little or no religious formation. I heard of two preppies chatting in the church before their first school Mass. "What do you think is going to happen?" asked one, to which his friend replied, "I think it might have something to do with a wedding." Then came the last word, "Don't be silly, you don't go to church for a wedding."

A former US prosecutor told me he was invoking the aid of the Little Flower, St Thérèse of Lisieux, for me. My case recalled for him the Castro show trials conducted from a sports stadium in Havana, which prompted his mother to immigrate to the United States.

A doctor from Königsdorf in Germany pointed out: "It appears that Cardinal George's prediction became true rather earlier in Australia."[11]

Paula [Shah] from the office at St Mary's Cathedral in Sydney, a good friend, urged me to keep going by quoting St Thomas More's statement to his daughter, "God gave us a brain, intellect, and does not expect me to go as a lamb to the slaughter."

A fellow prisoner insisted that I must not yield an inch to fear. He claimed Julius Caesar was terrified by thunder (something I feel is

[11] Francis Cardinal George, archbishop of Chicago, had predicted, "I expect to die in bed, my successor will die in prison and his successor will die a martyr in the public square. His successor will pick up the shards of a ruined society and slowly help rebuild civilization, as the church has done so often in human history." Quoted by Tim Drake in "Cardinal George: The Myth and Reality of 'I'll Die in My Bed' ", *National Catholic Register*, April 16, 2015, https://www.ncregister.com/blog/cardinal-george-the-myth-and-reality-of-ill-die-in-my-bed.

unlikely) and that Dr Johnson would not enter a room left foot first. If he did, he re-entered with his right. I wonder if this is the origin of the saying that we should put our best foot forward.

Fr Frank Brennan, SJ, in his Easter greeting, exemplified Paula's approach. "I continue to insist with people that there is a need to distinguish honesty and reliability. There is also a need to distinguish evidence of a complainant from suggestions put by the prosecutor." Amen to all that.

Dr Gerald Fogarty told me of the impressive work of Opus Dei at Warrane College, University of New South Wales, and Fr Danny Meagher, rector of Good Shepherd Seminary, kept me up to date with developments there. The seminary continues to go well.

And finally, I should mention the letters promising prayers from the director and students, mainly priests, of the Program of Church Management at Santa Croce University in Rome. They were most supportive.

During my financial work in the Vatican, I became aware of the challenges there and elsewhere and the occasional mishaps which have occurred on every continent. Personal honesty and goodwill are no excuse for incompetence, which makes corruption so much easier.

I felt the need for a course in management and finances in Rome for priests, religious, and laity, which could be followed in a variety of ways, e.g., part- or full-time. One did not need to be Einstein to recognize the need, but the Santa Croce authorities took up the idea expertly and quickly. Their enterprise and efficiency are not universal in Rome, and in February this year (2019), the first cohort finished their course.

As other avenues of attack become exhausted, our enemies will be keen to exploit any weaknesses in the Catholic world of finance.

Kartya and Ruth from the legal team came with the prosecution response to our appeal, basically leaving unchanged their trial approach, which often obscured or ignored the truth. To my disappointment, which I expressed, Ruth had not read Windschuttle's article, much less those of Friel. The prosecution is between a rock and a hard place, which might explain the presence of Mark Gibson, QC, the prosecutor in the trials, as the second QC in the prosecution team. Apparently two QCs together are unusual in appeals.

Kartya also told me that my cousin Bob Burke's wife, Yvonne, is dying with leukemia. He requested prayers, and of course I will pray, but, unfortunately, I cannot offer Mass for her.

Anzac Day, Thursday of Easter Week, 25 April 2019

Since I was at school, I have always tried to celebrate Anzac Day,[12] whenever it was possible, no matter the country I was in; just as I always visited Australian war graves whenever I happened to be nearby. I regularly offered Anzac Mass for the deceased Australian soldiers and admired their courage.

Few countries have a National War Memorial museum like we have in Canberra. Is this evidence that we are warmongers? I don't think so. That is not the national sentiment. We are not a people who support their country right or wrong. A priest friend from Canada, Fr Raymond de Souza, who is an excellent writer and defender of my cause, when he visited Canberra with me remarked that Canada had no equivalent centre. I also realised how unusual and British our tradition is when I arranged for the Neocatechumenal seminarians, largely from South America, Italy, and Spain, to visit our Canberra landmarks.

The Commonwealth War Cemetery in Rome near the Aurelian Wall is unusually beautiful as well as being typically well maintained. All the graves, no matter what the rank of the deceased, are the same except for the different religious symbols. There is an annual Anzac service in the cemetery and at Domus Australia, Rome.

I had hoped to watch the French and Turkish Anzac ceremonies, but exercise sessions, which are not scheduled predictably, and my visitors prevented this. The twenty-minute ceremony at the MCG [Melbourne Cricket Ground] last night, Anzac Eve, with tens of thousands of lighted candles, was impressive and appreciated by the seventy-thousand-plus Aussie Rules football crowd. Richmond had a good win.

---

[12] Anzac Day commemorates all of the Australians and New Zealanders who served and died in all wars, conflicts, and peacekeeping operations. Originally the national holiday honoured only the members of the Australian and New Zealand Army Corps (ANZAC) who served in the Gallipoli Campaign in World War I.

Anzac Day is celebrated as strongly as it ever was and also among the young. It has resisted the Marxist-style iconoclasm and hostility to tradition which have engulfed whole sections of society and infected Christian churchgoers, too, when it hasn't enticed them to lapse out of practice and, indeed, membership.

Patriotism, love of country, and a willingness to serve and make sacrifices are not the refuges of scoundrels. That is a nasty nationalism, often used by unscrupulous leaders to distract from internal political or economic problems. This will be a particular temptation in China, with all its wealth, as it faces up over the coming decades to demographic decline, the imbalance of the sexes from the now abandoned one-child policy, huge debt, little or no pensions, and the necessity of continual expansion of the economy to incorporate the 300–400 million Chinese subsistence farmers still outside the market. China is a world leader with the US in artificial intelligence, robots, automation, but the challenges there will be acute, as they will be everywhere.

A final word about the Anzac tradition which commemorates a defeat. The British do not issue medals for defeats. The recently federated Australia (1901) was still an adolescent in 1915, and the sixty thousand war deaths brought Irish Catholics and Anglo Protestants closer together. The Catholic military chaplains were often the first priests non-Catholic soldiers had met, and their contribution across the board was crucial to this improvement. Our military chaplains are still well respected, and I strongly supported their recruitment, recognizing the need for chaplains with our forces, especially when they are in action. Anzac Day pays tribute to redemptive sacrifice, one fruit of our Christian tradition.

Deacon Ronnie Maree and Roberto Keryakos, a senior seminarian, came down from Sydney especially to see me. I asked them to pass on my thanks for the wonderful letter from the Good Shepherd seminarians. They said congregations were up in the parishes, larger this year than last year, for the Easter ceremonies. In Ronnie's parish of Bankstown, the congregation for the long Saturday night vigil was as large as on Good Friday afternoon. Our future priests will be outnumbered, but in Sydney, at least, they are well prepared, and they will serve well. We need more, but, thank God, we don't have a seminarian drought as bad as Ireland's. The evidence demonstrates clearly that orthodox bishops, teachers of the Catholic tradition, who have a good seminary will attract priestly vocations. When the bland are leading the bland, we produce a contraceptive Catholicism, which looks healthy on the surface but cannot produce new life.

God our Father, on this Anzac Day, we pray for continued peace and for the repose of all those who have died in war.

Strengthen our priests, give us more seminarians, more religious, and more lay leaders.

Friday of Easter Week, 26 April 2019

I am receiving quite a few letters from Queensland, indeed, from nearly all parts of Australia, except perhaps the West. I opened about a hundred today, regularly being encouraged, sometimes surprised and enlightened.

One lady from Kingaroy in Queensland began, after proclaiming that Christ is risen, in this way: "Grandma told us that the sun dances on Easter Sunday. You may not be able to see the sun, but I tell you it shines on you and dances with the shadows."

And so, she concluded her letter, "The birds are calling to each other outside. A light breeze moves the sunlit leaves. A plane growls overhead, and the grass far below is still happening. Remember three things because they are still happening. Remember God's beauty and whispering gentle ways. Yes, the sun dances on Easter morn." I don't think you could find a better Easter greeting than this for someone in solitary confinement in a prison.

In a more conventional way, a professor of English from University of Dallas, Texas, was equally encouraging: "I am praying that the truth of your innocence will become known, for your relief, for the joy of the Christian people, and for the glory of God. I pray that God sustain you and provide the consolation of faith."

In the evening, SBS television had a two-hour film[13] on a remarkable Indian mathematician Ramanujan, who began life as a poorly paid accounts clerk in Madras, where for a long time he couldn't find

---

[13] *The Man Who Knew Infinity*, a 2015 British film starring Dev Patel as Ramanujan and Jeremy Irons as Hardy.

anyone competent enough to evaluate his mathematical writings. With the help of a more senior accountant, he received confirmation of the quality of his theorising, which he had never doubted. At the beginning of the twentieth century, we were in a different world, where the British were still ruling India and racial prejudices were often explicit. Despite all this, he wrote to a senior mathematician, G.H. Hardy, at Trinity College, Cambridge University, claiming that one of his theorems was incorrect. Hardy recognized his genius and brought him to Cambridge, working with him so that he could prove the truth of his claims in a way which would be academically acceptable. Ramanujan's work was published and his genius recognized while he was still young, so that he was elected a Fellow of the Royal Society and a Fellow of Trinity. During the First World War, when Trinity was used as a military hospital, Ramanujan contracted tuberculosis, returned to India, and was dead within a year.

Unlike his mentor, he was a deeply religious Hindu, who believed his goddess sent to him his mathematical theories as truths. The film has G.H. Hardy, an atheist, also acknowledging that mathematicians do not create their theorems but discover them as they exist and function in the physical world.

God is a fantastic mathematician, many, or at least some, of whose higher mathematical workings are still beyond our comprehension. For me, the beauty and simplicity of the mathematical principles which rule the universe are evidence of a Supreme Intelligence, and I believe that human geniuses somehow draw down from that sublime intellectual Mystery, whether they are scientists or mathematicians, musicians like Mozart or J. S. Bach, artists like Michelangelo, or writers like our Shakespeare.

It is a further step in faith to accept that the Supreme Intelligence is benign and interested in us like a good father, but the Creator cannot be less than what "he" creates, so cannot be less than personal. In that sense, recognizing a "personal" God is more accessible to reason, less a matter of faith, than acknowledging that God is good.

Every human is a great mystery, in the image of God, and Christ proposed the child as a model for those who wish to enter his Kingdom. Great saints like Mother Teresa of Calcutta rank with, and indeed above, geniuses in other fields. None of this can be denied by a Christian, but great intellects, too, can point us to God.

The universe is either the product of chance or the work of a transcendent Creator, outside and beyond space and time. Whether we are at the macro or micro level, talking of DNA or the theory of the Big Bang, first devised by a priest, Fr Georges Lemaître, the odds against the random development of these functioning complexities are impossible. Scientists and mathematicians are our allies in defence of the notion of objective truth; not my truth or your truth, but truth that tells us accurately of reality.

Knowledge is one essential part of wisdom, just as truth is; and in God's creation, we can find patterns and signs of his existence, an existence which is not a matter of opinion. It is a matter of fact, true or false, to be accepted freely or denied. Because I believe there is a man in the moon does not change the moon one iota. Truth matters, and the truth of God's existence matters.

Ramanujan's nationality reminds me of a piece of folklore from forty or fifty years ago. It was claimed then that Indians are the most religious people in the world and the Swedes the most irreligious.

In those days, Peter Berger, the renowned sociologist from New York, was arguing cogently against inevitable secularisation in modern societies, and I think he was the one who claimed that the US was a society of Indians ruled by Swedes. Since then, the "Swedes" in the US have made spectacular gains, but the United States remains much more religious than Western Europe and more religious than Australia even today.

God our Father, help us to remember that ideas are important and that we come to recognize and discuss your creation only through words and spoken ideas.

Make us more than practical, common-sense individuals, but seekers for truth, lovers of wisdom, and servants who strive to live their lives in faith, hope, and love.

Saturday of Easter Week, 27 April 2019

Yesterday and today the breviary readings from the Apocalypse shift from John's messages to the individual church communities to the post-Resurrection world in heaven. Yesterday, we had the vision of the throne, occupied by Someone whose face gleamed like precious stones and who put out flashes of lightning, sounds, and peals of thunder. The elders were worshipping the Lord God almighty, who lives forever and is worthy of receiving glory, honour, and power.

Today we hear of the Lion of Judah, who alone was able to open the seven seals on the scroll held by God almighty.

He is also the Lamb who has been killed and by whose death men of every tribe, language, nation, and race have been bought by God. Thousands and millions of angels were praising God and the Lamb, singing with the whole of creation.

Over the years, I have experienced some difficulty with the series of Gospel readings from John between Easter and Pentecost, trying to avoid repeating what was said in the previous sermon and what I had said in previous years. I struggled to make them interesting. But a series of sermons on the Apocalypse might be too interesting, too confronting.

If I put a lot of work into a sermon to good effect, I did not hesitate to use it with a different congregation, always making some additions or changes. I have filed away nearly every Sunday sermon since ordination, noting time and place.

During my time as archbishop in Melbourne and Sydney, I only once repeated an earlier Sunday sermon. I was short of time and justified the repetition which was delivered in Sydney, because the original was in Melbourne. To my surprise and dismay, I received an email from a good friend, a former choirboy from Melbourne, rebuking me for my sin of repetition. In my later years in Sydney, I put my sermons on the diocesan website, where friends and foes took the regular offerings, and I ran head to head to top the list of hits with those who were searching for Mass times.

It is not difficult to preach about the Lord, because he was the greatest of teachers and had such an interesting and tumultuous public life for three years. However, I believe it is particularly difficult to portray Jesus in films, although I admired Mel Gibson's *The Passion of the Christ*. I would not have followed some of the Christ figures in other films across the road, let alone given up my life for them.

The Christ figure on a crucifix should depict suffering, so as a consequence of this, I changed the crucifix in the Good Shepherd Seminary Chapel because Jesus looked too comfortable. Louis Laumen's bronze replacement crucifix meets every criterion of faith and art, so that the seminarians are now praying before Isaiah's suffering servant, the Son of God in distress. A lot of good prayer takes place there regularly.

Paintings of Jesus also present a challenge. I am not surprised that those painting icons in the Eastern tradition are required to fast and pray while they are working. Some paintings of Christ, not too many, are faithless. The best of the contemporary images of Christ have been painted by Kiko Arguello, cofounder of the Neocatechumenal Way. Christ appears as a Jew and as a man whom I would be prepared to follow.

As I write this, opposite me at the head of my prison bed is a large card, sent to me by my dear friend Gabriele Turchi, with Kiko's latest face of Christ. It seems to me to be different from his earlier versions, with large kind eyes, but an aura of majesty and, indeed, challenge, which is somewhat confronting. We find no hint of a slight sneer or the curl of his lip which can be found in some Greek and Russian icons. Jesus is majestic, the Redeemer, merciful, and a reluctant judge.

My day was quiet, with no visitors and no televised important horse races. Yesterday, the lawyers were in for a couple of pieces of business. The day itself was cool and cloudy while I took my two exercise sessions.

God our Father, I pray that my family, friends, and supporters will experience the peace of Easter, growth in faith, and eventually eternal life with you, your Son, and the Spirit.

WEEK 10

Divine Mercy

28 April–4 May 2019

Divine Mercy Sunday, Second Sunday of Easter, 28 April 2019

Today is Divine Mercy Sunday, the Second Sunday of Easter, and my sister's birthday. She is seventy-five today and unfortunately is in St John of God's Hospital in Bendigo with a stomach infection. As always for her birthday, I managed to send her a dozen long-stemmed red (I hope) roses. She has been a wonderful support and friend to me over the decades, my constant companion on holidays at Torquay for thirty years and at Manly for more than ten years. She is now in a retirement home in Bendigo, where my brother, David, lives, who is very good to her. Her health has deteriorated.

I regret not being able to offer Mass for her on this day, just as I am sad that I cannot offer Mass for any other purposes, such as the approaching wedding of Daniel Hill and Leah. The Hills are strong and prayerful supporters. By offering Mass, I felt I could do something worthwhile to answer requests and help those suffering. A Mass is so much better than my poor personal prayers. Quite a number of those writing to promise me prayers and offer support ask for prayers for their intentions. I try on every occasion to recite a Memorare to Our Lady immediately when I receive each request.

A goodly number of those who write are devotees of the Divine Mercy, promulgated by St Faustina. Our world senses that we need mercy, more than we merit.

The day passed quietly, with no visitors, as Paul Galbally did not arrive, as I thought he might. When I exercise, I sit down in the open for ten minutes each session to enjoy the fresh air and look at the sky; not as good as looking north up the coast at Manly, but still pleasant.

A half a dozen small birds were hopping around the roof of the next-door pen, but none seemed to want to enter, and then suddenly they were gone, flying off very quickly.

The morning started poorly as I forgot to try to set the alarm on my watch and missed the 6:00 am *Mass for You at Home*. I read through the Mass text instead. *Songs of Praise* came from the Methodist Central Hall in Westminster, a splendid building next to the House of Parliament. While I didn't particularly like the hymns, which I didn't know, I have a great admiration for John Wesley, a small man, the eighteenth-century founder of Methodism. A Catholic St Vincent de Paul group works from the hall with the battlers, the deprived. Once near Soho in a Methodist church, I came across a pulpit Wesley had used for preaching. I placed my hand on it and prayed that some of his evangelical zeal would pass to me.

Only half a dozen letters were passed on to me yesterday, but about thirty arrived today. Over the past few days, I had put together three written pages on the prosecution response to our appeal. I read it to Paul Galbally, who basically agreed and assured me I had not made any legal mistake! I was cross with the way the prosecutor dealt with Max Potter, eighty years of age, and Fr Charles Portelli and for the obfuscation and confusion his suggestions must have produced in the jury in the last trial. A prosecution has to prove the case beyond reasonable doubt, and that is not achieved by putting out suggestions and possibilities unsupported by evidence. This general approach has continued in the appeal response.

While I watched much of Carlton's brave but unsuccessful battle to defeat Hawthorn in the AFL, most of the day was spent reading the seven dense, information-packed articles Chris Friel from Wales had posted on my case and my general role in the Australian paedophile crisis. Once again Tim O'Leary had sent them on to me.

I don't know Friel and had never heard of him previously. It is fascinating to conjecture how and why he became interested from distant Wales. Terry Tobin commented simply, "He is a Catholic." I suspect Friel's work will continue, but he has already unearthed a mine of information, organized so that it is comprehensible and brilliantly analysed.

He doesn't share Keith Windschuttle's conjecture that the Billy Doe hoax in Philadelphia is the trope or the model of the accusations against me. He might be a bit too cautious. While there are certainly at least a couple of differences between the two accounts and one additional similarity beyond the seven Windschuttle listed, it would be too obvious to have everything in parallel.

Whatever of that, Friel has worked to try to produce a timeline for the construction of the allegations. The story evolved. Originally, we find no reference to the incident being after a Mass in Advent or to a sacristy. He effectively exposes the muddle which Louise Milligan's[1] *Cardinal* presents, and he discovers that [Vivian] Waller, J's solicitor, knew of the 2011 *Rolling Stone* article which recounted Billy Doe's story and that the tweeter Lyndsay Farlow is an anonymous proxy for Waller. Something of the ambiguity and inefficiency of the police work, especially in the initial investigations, is exposed, and he has begun to explore the wider police involvement and their interactions with lawyers, activists, and complainants.

His verdict on Milligan's 2017 version is illuminating. The "overly suspicious", he wrote, will "find in Milligan a mind on the move", where "the shifts in the narrative are not governed by a gradual appreciation of what really happened." Rather, we have "a picture created by a deranged imagination ... forced to accommodate itself to the rigors of cross examination".

Over the years I used to ask those plagued by serious religious doubt to pray each day this simple prayer: "Dear God of love, if you exist, bring me to the truth."

God our Father, I know that you exist and that you are love itself. In this wretched case, guide us to discover the truth.

Monday, 29 April 2019

Today was an eventful day, but not too much, in my quiet prison life. It began well with the gent who brings my tablets at about 6:00 am, once again simply leaving them on the bench through the trap door rather than requiring me to put on my shoes so that I can rise

---

[1] Louise Milligan is an investigative reporter for ABC TV and the author of *Cardinal: The Rise and Fall of George Pell*, which was published in 2017 and fostered a negative view of Cardinal Pell before his trial.

from the low bed to go to the door, give my number, and collect the medicine. This meant I could continue to rest and doze in bed until 7:15 am. Small mercies are appreciated.

I swept my cell, changed the sheets and towels, had my laundry done and returned before lunch. The guard explained that usually prisoners should change sheets and towels on each Sunday. I explained that I had never been told of any such procedure but would be happy to cooperate from next Sunday.

Unexpectedly during the morning, I had a visit from the big man whom I know as the boss of this prison, whose name (I discovered) is Sidinsky, the deputy commissioner of operations for Corrections Victoria [Nick Selisky, general manager of the Victoria Department of Justice and Regulation]. His message was courteous and simple: Tess Livingstone's phone number had been removed from my list, and she could not visit, because she was a writer at *The Australian* and this fact had not been reported to them. I was unaware of this requirement, which Sidinsky acknowledged, and he explained that I was in no trouble. He mentioned the bad luck, which meant I had two drug tests in ten or so days. It was the luck of the draw, he explained. I replied that my suspicion was that the draw was not random. He mentioned again the possibility of a change in my living arrangements, the difficulty of being in solitary for a long period, and explained that I could request a computer. We both agreed that we would reconsider this after the appeal and hoped it would not be necessary.

The Tobins were due to arrive at midday for an hour-long contact visit, an improvement on a half hour through the glass, which had been thought necessary because of overcrowding. At 12:10 pm, I knocked on the cell door to explain that I was expecting visitors at midday. "The visitors were late arriving" was the excuse. Terry and Bernadette had arrived well before the due time, and I am not sure what occasioned the confusion.

I asked Terry to inform Tess of the unfortunate developments, swapped news, told them prison life wasn't too bad, and was reassured to learn they thought I looked well and had perhaps lost some weight. I must try to check this during my next visit to the medical centre.

They had watched the football at home with Peter O'Callaghan, the founding independent commissioner of the Melbourne Response to the paedophile crisis. Terry remarked, quite rightly, that Peter is a wonderful man. "How did you choose him?" I replied that he had been recommended by my brains trust, but the last word came from my friend Bob Santamaria's enthusiastic endorsement of the recommendation.

We spent a good deal of time discussing Friel's contribution, which Terry also described as remarkable. He, too, was more inclined to agree with Friel than with Windschuttle on the role of the Billy Doe story. I repeated my claim that J had to have been given the story from somewhere, because he lacked the capacity to develop it from nothing. There was no chance meeting, nothing to build on.

A week or so ago, I received a letter from a fellow septuagenarian from Box Hill North, which concluded, "Each man brings his stone, however humble, and thus plays his part in building the City of God."

God our Father, help us to build stone upon stone in this case so that we arrive at the truth, for the good of all involved, everyone, and for the good of the Church.

Tuesday, 30 April 2019

The day started with a small regression because the 6:00 am medicine bringer, presumably a different person from yesterday, required me to rise from my lowly couch to collect the tablets at the door. It was hardly a major regression.

However, the pendulum swung back in the afternoon, which was beautiful autumn weather, cool with clear skies, when I was allowed to stay outside for nearly an hour. Thoroughly enjoyable. It couldn't be said that I am a stargazer, because they are all lost in the sun's superior light in the day, but I did spend a good deal of the time looking heavenward (if that is not too anthropomorphic a way of speaking).

Last night I watched the first TV debate, televised in West Australia, between Prime Minister Morrison and Bill Shorten, the ALP [Australian Labor Party] leader. Neither man is a Howard or a Hawke,[2]

---

[2] John Howard was the prime minister of Australia from 1996 to 2007. He was a member of the Liberal Party. Bob Hawke, a member of the Labor Party, was prime minister from 1983 to 1991.

but both compare well with Jeremy Corbyn, Labour leader in the UK, and Trump in the US. Many Aussies are too hard on their politicians, and we are inclined to take our prosperity for granted. Wages, however, could do with a boost, and the number of casual workers should be diminished through more permanent contracts. I still believe the climate change debate proceeds on the wrong premises, i.e., that increases of carbon dioxide certainly raise the temperature and that we have the human capacity to modify climate (weather over a thirty-year period). We should remember King Canute, who realised he couldn't stop the incoming tide. The climate change movement is now a world-wide financial colossus, ruthless and intolerant, colossally expensive, a useful substitute for religion for too many.

Unfortunately, many in the Vatican have jumped onto the climate change bandwagon, despite the encyclical *Laudato si'* twice acknowledging that the Church should leave science to the scientists. It could be a mistake like the one the papacy made with Galileo.

Kartya called to clarify where we are with prospective visitors and to ensure all will be well for the video link-up at 2:00 pm tomorrow with Bret Walker, our new chief barrister.

Sr Mary came for our weekly Communion service and a chat, bringing me another Sr Mary McGlone Sunday sermon, which was typically excellent. Her principal theme on chapter 20 of John was about peace and the forgiveness which generates peace. She claimed that, with the Spirit, "the disciples were commissioned to make forgiveness of sin the purpose of their lives." When commenting on Thomas' demand that he see and touch Jesus, she wrote, "No physical expression proves love. At best, the physical is a sign of what exists on a much deeper level."[3]

A week or so ago, Bernadette Tobin sent me a copy of her husband Terry's article on the Notre Dame disaster, pointing out, from the evidence of family friends, that the cathedral was a living centre of community worship.[4] He lamented that the three-hour BBC commentary on the disaster was almost completely a religion-free zone and quoted the comments of the editor-at-large of the *Wall Street*

---

[3] Mary McGlone, "Sunday of Divine Mercy: Are You Convinced?", *National Catholic Reporter*, 27 April 2019.

[4] Terence Tobin, "The Pompiers and the Cross", *Catholic Weekly*, 26 April 2019.

Journal: "The spectacle of the second most famous Church in Christendom consumed by fire in this, the holiest of weeks for Christians, was for many as good a symbol of the collapse of a historic culture before the advancing flames of atheistic, multicultural relativism as any terrorist attack or act of malicious desecration." The editor went on somewhat bitterly about the ambition to rebuild the cathedral: "It's not a church that these leaders want to build but a museum. How fitting. For the political and cultural establishment, that is where religion, the faith that built this great cathedral, belongs."[5] France is much farther down this track than Australian society, but the cultural establishment here who share their goals, especially in Victoria, are picking up their pace.

From an entirely different starting point, another letter and enclosed article also moved in Tobin's direction. A retired High Court judge sent me a 1997 book review she had written about repressed memory, usually of childhood sexual abuse, and the ritual witch-hunt; of how "conscious hunches and resentment can be crystallised by protracted therapeutic suggestion."[6]

The book examined twenty Australian prosecutions based on recovered memory where the therapists never questioned the truth or accuracy of the memories. The intellectual roots of this "formidable socio-political movement" are Freud, feminism, and Foucault or, more broadly, deconstructionist theory. For Foucault, the concept of the individual is a fiction, a creation of bourgeois ideology, and so "there are no facts, only interpretations." Some therapists encouraged women to invent new stories to empower themselves.

Freud follows a somewhat different line, because for him repression meant suppressing knowledge, which always existed and could always be invoked. Moreover, feelings of dread or gladness could be the residue not only of real life, but of fantasies, wishes, and images of absurdity. The motto of his famous book *The Interpretation of Dreams* comes from the Latin poet Virgil: "If I cannot bend the higher powers, I will move the infernal regions."

[5] Gerard Baker, "The Crisis of Values in the Flames of Notre Dame", *Wall Street Journal*, 19 April 2019.
[6] Susan Crennan, review of *Talk of the Devil: Repressed Memory and the Ritual Abuse Witch-Hunt*, by Richard Guilliatt, *Australian Law Journal* 71 (1997): 1001–1004.

The review concludes that "some modern epistemologies seriously challenge the rule of law insofar as they strive to make the inquiry into truth meaningless."

More than twenty years later, the former judge wrote recently, "Somehow I think the 'moving of the infernal regions' to which Virgil referred has occurred collectively in our society and cultures. It is not easy to predict a return to equanimity and received notions of justice."

The elite are often wrong, as many are or were Marxist; or like watermelons, red inside and green outside. Before the Second World War, many in Europe were Fascist or Nazi, as democracy was "old-fashioned". And the Church has seen worse times. But we are in a period of radical social change.

One surprise is that only two people have sent me the Serenity Prayer, once given to all members of Alcoholics Anonymous. I thought it was ascribed (wrongly) to St Francis of Assisi, but one writer insists it came from the North American Protestant theologian Dr Reinhold Niebuhr.

> *God, grant me the serenity*
> *To accept the things I cannot change,*
> *Courage to change the things I can,*
> *And wisdom to know the difference.*

Wednesday, 1 May 2019

Today is the feast of St Joseph the Worker, a response to the Communists' May Day celebrated today, introduced by Pope Pius XI. A good idea.

It is time to mop up with some information on ongoing activities. First of all, a confession. The breviary readings I discussed on 27 April are incorrect, as I was a week ahead of myself. I dropped my breviary while I was meditating (dozing again), and I misplaced the ribbons which had fallen out of place. Paul's Epistle to the Romans has replaced the Gospel of Mark for most meditations.

About ten days ago, I finished Kai-Fu Lee's book *AI Superpowers*, and I will put together a few thoughts soon. Have just completed the first two volumes of *War and Peace* and look forward to reading a section each night before I sleep. A good measure of how much I am enjoying a book is how far I continue reading into my normal sleep period; *War and Peace* passes that test with flying colours. Natasha's disastrous plan to elope has just been scotched.

The shouter has been quiet for some days, so I asked whether he was still with us. The answers were enigmatic, although one warder mentioned medicine to quieten him down. Apparently we are not to be told anything of the other prisoners in this section for solitary confinement. By a strange coincidence, while I was eating breakfast an hour ago, there was a prolonged period of banging and anguished shouting. However, the voice sounded different, somewhat lighter, from that of the earlier outbursts. I still haven't read Pope Benedict's article on the paedophilia crisis.

The major and welcome change from what I anticipated is the huge number of letters. Sidinsky [Selisky] said I was receiving sixty to seventy a day, although they only come to us in fits and starts, e.g., the letters from Jackie Toakley and her children (she is Michael Casey's sister), which she sent before Easter, have not yet arrived. These letters take a good deal of time to read on most days and provide regular food for reflection and meditation as well as encouragement. They also explain why my reading program is behind schedule.

My regular practice of doing two Sudoku puzzles a day continues, and I am improving. Apart from an occasional glitch, I am now able to solve all the easy puzzles. Even more satisfying is the fact that I have solved the last two of the more difficult section, which is unprecedented for me. As I don't do much with numbers, this activity is undertaken to help keep me on my intellectual toes and slow the inevitable decline which comes with age! The major literary disappointment is that my copies of *The Spectator*, apart from a couple early in my jail career, have not arrived. I miss them, the daily *Australian*, and the weekend *Financial Times* from London (and the *Annals* of course).

If I were unfortunate enough to fail in my appeal, I suspect a significant long-term loss would come from the prison food. It is ample, too much so, nourishing, if heavy with calories, but it is never served hot. Small light plastic cutlery is (not) ideal. All in all, I am not at Alfredo's, my favourite Sydney restaurant.

There is every opportunity to pray and no sufficient excuse for not doing so. While it is unpleasant not to celebrate or attend Mass for a few months, it would be an awful cross to be prevented from celebrating for years.

I finished the evening last night watching an excellent film on General [John] Monash, Australia's greatest soldier. A Renaissance man with three degrees, but primarily an engineer, he was only a part-time soldier originally. The Australian victory at Hamel, France, meticulously planned for a coordinated air, artillery, and infantry assault, became a model for further battles and was an important breakthrough in the stalemated First World War, while the Australian capture of Mont St Quentin was equally a remarkable feat of arms.

The film did not romanticise war, showing the ferocity of the battle-hardened Australian troops, whom the Germans feared as killing machines, the destruction of life, the terrible wounds of many who survived, the results of gas attacks. And the miserable aftermath for many of them when they returned home to Australia, suffering often from neuroses that were little understood then, from unemployment and niggardly pensions. There were many ex-soldier suicides.

Sixty thousand Australian soldiers died from a population of almost five million. The two countries farthest away from the European battlefields had the highest pro-rata death rates. Only New Zealand's was higher than Australia's.

Monash was knighted on the field of battle by King George V, a rare distinction, and lionised after the war in London, becoming something of a friend to the King. They could converse together in German.

The Australian prime minister, Billy Hughes, who was also in Europe then, often had to play second fiddle to Monash, which he strongly resented. He became a foe, and our greatest soldier suffered as a result. He was never made a field marshal, something my good friend Tim Fischer, former deputy prime minister and Australian ambassador to the Vatican for the start of my time there, tried to remedy by having him so promoted nearly one hundred years after the end of the Great War. Tim is a character, who is at present badly ill, but always a loyal friend. Despite his sickness, he visited me on numerous occasions during my recent trials.

They shall grow not old, as we that are left grow old;
Age shall not weary them, nor the years condemn.
At the going down of the sun and in the morning
We will remember them.
[Lest we forget.][7]

God, all merciful Father, grant eternal peace and light to all those, civilians and soldiers, who died in war.

Thursday, 2 May 2019

Word has come in that my cousin Bob Burke's wife, Yvonne, has passed away. She was a good person and a devoted mother. A sister of Carmen Callil, the writer and feminist who has lived in London for decades, Yvonne was a regularly worshipping Catholic. May she rest in peace.

Les Murray, our most renowned Australian poet today, has also died. A convert to Catholicism, he made no secret of his theism and robust Catholicism, the antitype of political correctness. Unfortunately, I never met him, but I admired his work a lot. A few years ago, he sent me a copy of his collected poems with a kind inscription. Recently *Quadrant* magazine, where he had been poetry editor and done a huge amount to encourage poets and young writers, invited other Australians from the world of literature to explain his contribution and express their gratitude. It was a blessing that he was alive and able to accept this acknowledgement of his contribution. May he, too, rest in peace.

Yesterday I met with my legal team once again and with Bret Walker, SC, for the first time. After a few minutes, they were unable to hear me speaking, although we could see one another. The warder supervising me was as useful technologically as I am, so he contacted the communications office at the jail, and we continued our half hour by audio contact only. Walker explained that he would begin

---

[7] The "Ode of Remembrance", the fourth stanza of the poem "For the Fallen", by Laurence Binyon.

his case by outlining the importance of examining the evidence, before presenting the evidence, to obviate any claim that examining the evidence is the role of the jury. I asked one or two questions and concluded by stressing the importance of reading Windschuttle and Friel as important background to understanding what happened before the charges were laid, even if this cannot be used in the appeal.

Today Katrina Lee, who had been in charge of archdiocesan communications when I was in Sydney and is still looking after me for this case, came to see me, as did Tim O'Leary. To my profound embarrassment, he was not on my list, through my mistake, and he had to go back to work. I phoned him this afternoon to apologise personally, and he informed me he had been in contact with Friel, passed on my points, and that Friel was now somewhat more sympathetic to Windschuttle's claims.

Katrina brought me up to date with Sydney archdiocesan news and with her continuing contacts. She has ordered another book from the US which tells of paedophilia cases there, with references to "the kid", which might contain further similarities to the accusations against me. The investigative work is continuing on a number of fronts.

I also had my weekly treatment from the visiting physiotherapist, who was accompanied by a warder supervisor from the medical centre. He identified the Holbein portrait of Thomas More on the card from the Caseys, which is on my shelf, so we had quite a chat about Henry VIII, More, Anne Boleyn, and Hilary Mantel's historical novel *Wolf Hall* on the infamous Thomas Cromwell.

It rained lightly for most of my morning exercise session, but the weather was fine and cloudy in the afternoon. Phoned my sister without success.

Read a chapter of Cardinal Van Thuan's booklet *Five Loaves and Two Fish*, a meditation on the Eucharist, which had been sent to me and slipped past the censors as my books are limited officially to six. I will read a chapter a day.

Not praying as easily as during my first weeks in jail; perhaps I have too many distractions on the evening television, or, more likely, I am slipping back into more usual patterns. Naturally I continued all my prayer routine; it is simply that it is more difficult. I switched my meditation method to the style recommended by Fr Laurence

Freeman, the mantra-type repetition of a prayer such as "Lord Jesus, Son of the living God, have mercy on us." This helped. I don't try to meditate by emptying my head so the good God can enter, as he is crowded out by distractions.

Today is the feast of Athanasius (d. 373), archbishop of Alexandria, by then heavily Catholic, and a tough, controversial bishop, champion of the divinity of Christ in the Arian crisis. Arius, a priest of Alexandria, denied the divinity of Christ and was condemned by the assembled bishops at the Council of Nicaea in 325. One or two of the emperors after Constantine were Arian or semi-Arian, so Athanasius was exiled three or five times. In an excess of enthusiasm, Bob Santamaria claimed that Archbishop Mannix[8] was the greatest bishop since Athanasius. Mannix remains one of my heroes, but Bob's claim was a bit over the top.

On many occasions I have explained that so much depends on Jesus having both a divine and human nature in the one person. If Jesus is divine, then his death and Resurrection can be seen properly as transforming the brute matter of evil and suffering into all-powerful, transforming, and healing spiritual energy.

All human suffering is transformed if it can be associated for some good human purpose with Jesus' redemptive activity. Naturally I am offering my difficulties for a successful appeal, for the Church, for all victims, but also for a good friend, that her cancer may continue in remission, and for a young couple, that they may be able to have their own children. The prospect of a reward of heavenly happiness brings another beautiful dimension to the stoic and dignified endurance of human misfortune.

If Jesus is divine, his teaching has a unique authority; it brings the "Maker's instruction" so that it cannot be rejected, cannot be radically corrected or improved, something we are able to do even with theological classics such as Athanasius' *On the Incarnation*.

Let us pray with St Augustine.

---

[8] Archbishop Daniel Mannix (1864–1963), an Irish priest who became archbishop of Melbourne in 1917, was controversial both for demanding state aid for the education of Roman Catholics and for his opposition to drafting soldiers for World War I and to Communism. He was a promoter of Catholic Action and was responsible for establishing 181 schools and 108 parishes.

May the Lord Jesus give [us] a heart to love him, a will to choose him, a reason that may always adhere to him. And may the God of love and mercy love [us] eternally. Amen.

Friday, 3 May 2019

Only one surprise punctuated a typical prison day. In the afternoon, I was told a legal visitor had arrived. Presuming it was one of my lawyers, I received permission to take down my legal notes. To my surprise, I was directed to the large contact meeting room, where a policeman served me with a subpoena requiring my presence on 12 August in court for a hearing in a dispute about the wills of Bishop O'Collins and Bishop Mulkearns.[9] As I know nothing about either will, I shall not be able to contribute much.

I then went to speak to my lawyer Kartya Gracer, who had arrived by chance at the same time, had heard police were speaking to me, and demanded to be present. It was a pleasant anticlimax for her when she heard the nature of the discussion, and I was able to pass her the documents.

She was well pleased with the team meeting with Walker, as I was, and I told her I had one point to pass on. One starting point is to state that the jury found J a convincing witness. My view is that the more likely starting point was that the jury felt I was reprehensible, deserving of punishment on issues outside the trial, where something "must have happened". To put it in other terms, which I did not use with Kartya, I was a victim of identity politics, as white, male, in a powerful position, who belonged to a church whose members had committed vile acts and whose leaders were believed to have conducted a cover-up until very recently (despite the twenty years of good work and the dramatic improvement in offence statistics since the mid-nineties, at least). The judge's warnings against scapegoating were overridden by years of hostile publicity. This demonstration of the difficulty, even impossibility, of my receiving a fair trial by jury in

---

[9]James O'Collins (1892–1983), bishop of Ballarat (1941–1971), and Ronald Austin Mulkearns (1930–2016), who succeeded him as bishop (1971–1997), were both accused of covering up child sexual abuse.

Victoria might be of interest to a judge who required more than an examination of the evidence.

Had a couple of pleasant exercise sessions, with some extra time sitting in the fresh air. Not raining. One of the warders has started the process to enrol his son at St Pat's, Ballarat.[10] I commended him for this and endorsed St Pat's as a good school. Once upon a time, I could have provided a family reference, but I fear it would not be helpful at this time. He explained that he wanted his son exposed to Christian values and could not afford to send him to [Ballarat] Grammar.[11]

Spent most of the day reading and sorting the letters which have arrived. As always, they are a regular source of enlightenment and instruction, beyond their function as a morale booster. An Opus Dei numerary wrote that she was visiting a South American woman jailed here for drug trafficking, who has no visitors. That would be terrible. Almost certainly she would also be isolated by her limited English. It is one thing to read a language, another thing to be able to conduct a basic conversation, and quite different again to be able to converse in a sophisticated way expressing accurately what you want to say. I remember studying German in Germany, separated by language deficiencies from the friendly people who surrounded me. And there is the much sadder situation of migrant grandparents unable to converse with their Aussie grandchildren.

God works in strange ways, because if I had not been in jail, I would not have received this huge number of letters, where quite a few express their gratitude for my work.

When you publish something you have written, you can never know where it might finally arrive. One woman from Texas said that in the "glorious time" after she became a Catholic twenty-five years ago, I was "one of the first Catholic authors she read", which helped her to come "into the heart of the Church and prevented me getting stalled at the periphery". Another woman from Bermagui in NSW [New South Wales], who had taught at Kilbreda College in Mentone, thanked me for my Legatus summit lecture, delivered

---

[10] St Patrick's College is a Catholic secondary school for boys founded by the Christian Brothers in Ballarat, Victoria, in 1893 and attended by Cardinal Pell.

[11] In Australia, a grammar school is a private, often high-cost secondary school.

in Naples, Florida, in 2006 on "Islam and Western Democracies". She wrote, "You spoke when everyone else was silent, Truth."

Clare McCullough wrote from London to encourage me and told me of her own legal troubles, seeking my prayers for her cause. She is among those appealing against Buffer Zones outside abortion centres, and they have suffered "many lies and accusations". Their appeal will be heard on 16 July. May their work for life be blessed.

An [Anglican] Ordinariate nun from Torquay in England sent me this prayer from Isaac of Stella written around 1169.

May the Son of God who is already formed in you grow in you so that for you he will become immeasurable and that in you he will become laughter, exultation, the fullness of joy, which no one will take from you.

Saturday, 4 May 2019

The big news of the day is the arrival of the 16 March number of *The Spectator*. Although I received a couple of copies early on, it has needed nearly two months of requests, badgering, and encouragement to achieve today's result. The last page includes an excellent and accurate column by David Flint,[12] pointing out the impossibility of my acting as accused.

Fr Paul Stenhouse[13] recently wrote informing me of the death of another *Spectator* stalwart, Peter Coleman, who was writing well almost until the end. A distinguished Christian man in every sense, he often spoke sympathetically to Fr Paul about my situation. May he rest in peace as he deserves.

The unit has changed. No longer do I hear Islamic prayer chants; shouted conversations in the evening seem to be a thing of the past, although Gargasoulas is probably still next door. His writings are a jumble, to put it politely, but he is not without insight. He sent me a two-page article from a magazine on an older Melbourne priest

---

[12] David Flint (b. 1938) is an Australian legal academic who writes and lectures in both Australia and the US.

[13] Fr Paul Stenhouse, MSC (1935–2019), was a distinguished scholar and writer. From 1964 to 2019, he edited *Annals*, the longest-surviving Catholic journal in Australia.

(which I read with interest), then writing in his letter, "Fr X is your adversary." He is right.

My early morning routine has stabilised for the better, as those delivering my tablets soon after 6:00 am now leave them on the inside shelf near the cell door, as I requested. This means I don't have to scramble out of my low bed.

The small Scripture reading for morning prayer, which I have read hundreds of times over the years, struck me today as useful and important. It is from Paul's Letter to the Romans. Incidentally, I am not finding Romans to be rich soil for meditation. Paul is brimful of ideas, deeply intellectual, and I find it, often, a bit much for quiet meditation. But these four lines are different. Linking in, only indirectly, with one of the letters I received.

He wrote, "None of us lives for himself only, none of us dies for himself only; if we live it is for the Lord we live, and if we die it is for the Lord we die. Whether we live or die, then, we belong to the Lord" (Rom 14:7–9).

One of the women who wrote to me explained that she had plenty of problems herself, but when she was tempted to fret too much over this and feel sorry for herself, she remembered that so many others are in worse situations. That is exactly my situation, as the guards are courteous, regularly say thank you, and not just to myself, the food is sufficient and nutritious, the water in the shower is hot (very important), and the toilet works. My books are limited to six, which is more than sufficient for any one time, and no one disturbs my reading, writing, or praying. It is so much more comfortable than the prison conditions of my Catholic prison heroes Fisher, More, Kolbe, Van Thuan,[14] etc., and, please God, it will be briefer. It is also a religious opportunity for me to join myself to Christ and lay a few stones to strengthen God's Kingdom by not giving in to ill humour and recrimination.

Many letters remind me and encourage me to do my duty, to do the right thing with as much joy as I can muster.

One young priest, now up in country New South Wales, has been very sick for years, in regular pain, and in and out of hospital for the

---

[14]John Fisher (1469–1535), Thomas More (1478–1535), and Maximilian Kolbe (1894–1941) were all imprisoned and martyred for their faith. Francis-Xavier Van Thuan was imprisoned for the faith but died in exile.

past couple of years. He is offering all his sufferings, his cross, for my intentions.

Another writer from Toowoomba, who has given up reading fiction until I am exonerated, told me of a friend who caught the flu and prayed, "Dear Lord, I offer up all my sufferings for Cardinal Pell." She then deteriorated, caught pneumonia, cracked her ribs through coughing, and had to suffer a colonoscopy to examine whether she had an internal rupture. Her prayer changed, "Dear Lord I am so glad to suffer for him, but ... tell a few more people to pray."

She need not have worried about any shortage of people praying. On nearly every day, a small group is outside the jail praying publicly. "They are not a nuisance, not doing any harm", one warder told me.

The Missionaries of Charity from Wagga sent me this prayer of Mother, now Saint, Teresa of Calcutta.

Remember that the passion of Christ ends always in the joy of the Resurrection of Christ, so when you feel in your own heart the suffering of Christ, remember the Resurrection has to come.

The joy of Easter has to dawn. Never let anything so fill you with sorrow as to make you forget the joy of Christ Risen.

WEEK 11

Hostile Operations

5 May–11 May 2019

Third Sunday of Easter, 5 May 2019

A variety of people bring the morning tablets to my trap door soon after 6:00 am. Today, it was the tall, fair woman who had spoken kindly to me on earlier occasions. She was surprised to find me up already. "I am watching *Mass for You at Home*", I explained. "OK," she said, "it's as though you are on retreat. I hope you enjoy it." I had to remind her before she moved on that I wasn't quite enjoying it.

The celebrant was Bishop Terry Curtin, auxiliary bishop in Melbourne, who preached a truly excellent sermon in the brief time allotted on Jesus' question to Peter: "Do you love me?" This is an almost childlike question, which we would rarely ask, he explained. Why didn't Jesus put it differently, for example: Will you be loyal in the future?

Decades ago, I was with a Neocatechumenal pilgrimage group by the Sea of Galilee, where Jesus cooked fish (no potatoes then) and asked the question. They re-enacted the scene with anyone who wished to answer. I participated as a respondent and found it deeply moving.

With every successive group of pilgrims I brought there, we also re-enacted the scene, with a non-authority person asking the question for anyone who volunteered to answer. "I am Jesus. Do you love me?" As far as I could see, every young pilgrim participated. A beautiful tradition which I hope continues and spreads.

The second reading in the breviary today is from the second-century St Justin Martyr. He is known as the first "apologist", not someone who apologises, but one who strives to explain to outsiders what Christians do and believe. As the secularist acid damages individuals and families more severely, an increasing number will be looking for a way out, for help and answers, and there will be increasing opportunities for new "apologists".

The passage deals with a central problem in the pastoral life of the Church: Who should receive Communion? I am not talking about the small number of divorced and remarried without an annulment who wish to receive Communion, but about Christmas, Easter, weddings, funerals, and school Masses when nearly everyone receives. Justin's teaching remains in force today and follows St Paul. Only those "who believe", those who are baptised—"washed in the bath which confers forgiveness of sins and rebirth"—and those "who live according to Christ's commands" (regular worship and a lifestyle congruent with Church teaching or a recent genuine confession) should receive Communion. The others, if they wish to approach the priest or minister of Communion, should ask for a blessing.

It will be very difficult pastorally to reform the "open house" inclusive approach, because many regard the reception of Communion as being like accepting a biscuit and a cup of tea. And any restriction by the bishops will be seen, at least initially, by many as the Church announcing she will not offer a cuppa to whole groups of persons.

Justin is also explicit about the Real Presence: "Food which nourishes our flesh and blood by assimilation, is the flesh and blood of this Jesus who became flesh." I fear that many going to Communion would not see the Host as the Body of Christ, but as a somewhat sacred biscuit. In an age of religious indifference and ignorance, the indiscriminate reception of Holy Communion is against the tradition and bad for the spiritual health of the Church. I have written many times that sinners in the Church are also an ancient tradition, but the call to repentance is not optional, and following Christ is not value-free. Reverence has to be taught and encouraged, especially in Australia, and when we encounter the Holy of Holies, the Mystery of Mysteries, through the reception of the Lord's Body, this should be a moment filled with awe.

Every type of Catholic should realise there is an exclusion zone around the Eucharist, where adults without faith and without basic good practice should not enter. Years ago, a prominent criminal who was in jail was known to be Catholic. "Does he come to the jail Masses?" the chaplain was asked. "Yes" was the reply. "Does he receive Communion?" The chaplain explained, "No, he doesn't because he has faith."

A Polish-Australian warder brought me a pile of letters. "George," he said, "you receive as many letters each day as I have received in a lifetime." The letters are a great help. One in particular touched me, from a woman I can't remember whom I met in 1996. "You were a great help to me then", she wrote, as she was suffering from a phobia which crippled her psychologically. She finished the letter with the words: "You were the helping hand I desperately needed. You in fact saved my life." *Deo gratias.*

God our Father, we pray that more people may come to know and love your Son, our Brother and Lord. Purify our Eucharistic faith and practice to give us the perseverance and insight to live our daily lives as your Son has taught us to do.

Monday, 6 May 2019

This morning the podiatrist arrived unannounced and dealt with my feet, scraping away a troublesome corn, cutting my toenails, and treating what had become an ingrown toenail. Life moves slowly and often unpredictably in jail, because about ten days ago I asked for a pair of scissors to do an inexpert job myself and enquired whether help from a podiatrist was possible. I hadn't really expected it would be.

Solitary confinement places a person at a disadvantage in knowing what is going on elsewhere outside our section, but I have been surprised at the basic decency of the interactions. One warder explained that they treat prisoners the way prisoners treat them; but it is better than that, because some inmates of Unit 8 are damaged and unreasonable, and they are treated well enough. I am sure there were no podiatrists in the Gulag! Once or twice I have heard large groups of prisoners laughing outside on exercise. Nonetheless, this is not the Hilton. All are in their cells from around 4:00 pm, and small humiliations are built into prison life.

Had a contact visit, face-to-face, with my brother, David, and his daughter Sarah, which went happily. Margaret might be improving in the Base Hospital in Bendigo (not St John of God's), and everyone otherwise is well. Sarah had attended Yvonne Burke's[1] funeral at Nazareth House, where the Mass was celebrated with dignity and music from her children and grandchildren. Four out of Bob and Yvonne's five children are professional musicians, lecturers, and teachers. Bob gave an eloquent eulogy, according to Sarah, sometimes going beyond his printed text!

David van Gend is not a Catholic, "only halfway across the Tiber", to quote his own words, but is certainly a formidable cultural warrior. He sent me a copy of his article, scheduled for publication in *The Spectator*, which begins with these lines: "Is it too much to hope that in our multicultural society there might still be found space for the culture that gave us Notre Dame, Bach, free speech, and Izzy Folau?"[2]

Before explaining the presence of Israel Folau in such distinguished company, I must mention J. S. Bach's tribute to Notre Dame,[3] which dates from the twelfth century. "Our debt to you remains eternal", he said, not least because it was the Notre Dame School, late in that same century, that invented polyphony and harmonisation, which made possible the glories of Western music.

Now back to Izzy. Folau is a brilliant rugby union player, originally from Tonga and a devout man of simple Christian faith, an old-type Protestant, who has no time for the Catholic feasts of Christmas and Easter, much less for devotion to Our Lady.

He paraphrased and changed St Paul's list of those who will not "inherit the Kingdom of God", posting his warning on Instagram: "Drunks, homosexuals, adulterers, liars, fornicators, thieves, atheists, idolaters. Hell awaits you. Repent."

Rugby union officials sacked him for hate speech, and initial negotiations began on Saturday and could continue indefinitely through the courts, even for years.

---

[1] Yvonne was the wife of Cardinal Pell's cousin Bob Burke.

[2] David van Gend, "Our Lady of Paris and Our Man Folau", *Spectator* (Australia), 27 April 2019.

[3] J. S. Bach, *Köthener Trauermusik* BWV244a.

Big issues are at stake, and starting the Christian defence of freedom of speech and freedom of religion with Folau is not ideal. God condemns an unknown number to hell, a condemnation which is beyond our human competence and knowledge. But can a Christian follow St Paul and teach publicly that those practising certain activities will not inherit the Kingdom of God (1 Cor 6:9–11)? Will Catholic schools which receive government funding continue to be able to teach all Catholic teachings?

Religious freedom was never and never should be unlimited, but neither should it be limited except to avoid a greater evil. Nor should religious freedom survive only through legal exemptions.

The destruction of Notre Dame has sparked some beautiful writing. Van Gend wrote that we watched Notre Dame burn "with the sense of being aliens in a now hostile culture". Henry Ergas in *The Australian* set out the framework for the discussion. "It is hard not to see in that tragedy both the greatness of the civilization we inherited and the scale of the perils it now faces."[4]

The cathedral builders in the thirteenth century were confident of the marriage of faith and reason, of the rational structure of God's creation. The rediscovery of Aristotle in the West around this time, when a Spanish bishop commissioned a Latin translation of the Greek originals, produced a confident Scholasticism, which laid the foundation for the spectacular scientific advances in the Western world and Western predominance.

Ergas believes that for many today, past and present have drifted apart, that an awareness of historical continuity has been swamped. Coming closer to home, to Folau as precursor, for Ergas, "reason uncoupled from faith has too often degenerated from believing nothing into believing anything, morphing into a vicious intolerance of those for whom religion continues to matter." There we have it.

Ergas is pessimistic, believing that an "all consuming present" has swamped the biblical commandment to remember, to "remember the days of old, consider the years of ages past" (Deut 32:7), to remember the exodus from Egypt.

He concedes that Anzac Day is a counterexample, but so is the whole of Catholic life; priests, pope, bishops, the New Testament,

---

[4] Henry Ergas, "Much to Learn from the Stones of Notre Dame", *Australian*, 25 April 2019.

baptism, Eucharist, the sacraments were all born in the age of the apostles. Eighty percent of the prayers in the Roman Missal are one thousand years old.

Faithful, knowledgeable Christians will have an important cultural role in the dark ages which are threatening, if we remain steadfast and loyal to the good God, to the Lord, and to the tradition.

The symbolism of the destruction of part of Notre Dame will be decided by the next generations of Catholics, either as a call to arms, like a beacon in a time of war and trouble, or as a prototype of uncontested collapse, the heart destroyed, some remnants of the structure surviving.

God our Father, your Son commanded us to celebrate the Eucharist in his memory, to celebrate his death until he comes again. May we always remember that he visited us and saved us. May we always remember with gratitude the good things we have received from our parents, family, parishes, schools, and from all the Australians who built the nation to which we belong.

Tuesday, 7 May 2019

Have not long returned from my morning half hour outside in the pen. The weather was fresh and clear, delightful, with no clouds above the skylight. While resting on the metal bench, I noticed that a new storey is being added to the nearby building, perhaps at the ninth or tenth level.

We have a new shouter, more pathetic and less coherent than his predecessor, whose protests and profanities were confident, clear, and direct. A neighbouring prisoner got fed up with our newcomer's "carry on" and started to mock him loudly, so that at the moment we have silence.

A couple of guards came in to check the smoke alarm high up in the wall near the entrance to the shower. His lighted smoking taper took a deal of time to provoke any reaction, but they left without comment.

Swapped out a couple of books on Sunday so that I now have the poems and plays of T. S. Eliot, donated by Shane Kevin Gleeson with "Mitleid" [sympathy], and Brant Pitre's book *Jesus and the Jewish Roots of Mary* (2018), donated by the Abraham family, which Scott Hahn[5] described as "the best biblical study of Mary I have ever read". High praise, indeed. I am reading twenty pages a day.

In the breviary today, the Lamb has broken the seventh seal, the trumpets are blowing, and the destruction continues. St Augustine's message is more helpful, as he discusses the Christian obligation to sing to the Lord a new song. "So the new man will sing a new song and belong to the new testament."

Augustine has remarkable insight and eloquence with a distinctive style of thought, often contrapuntal, which is not difficult to recognize. "Everybody loves; the question is, what does he love? Consequently, we are not told not to love, but to choose what to love." He explains in sermon 34 the reason why we love God is because "he first loved us."

Sr Mary called to give me Holy Communion, informing me that Fr Pat Moroney, OMI, once an outstanding principal at Mazenod College here in Melbourne, had celebrated a prison Mass for her and was excellent with the men. I wasn't surprised. She also brought the sad news that Fr John Pierce, the Passionist who had been parish priest at Marrickville during my time in Sydney, had died suddenly yesterday as he was boarding a small plane in New Zealand. May he rest in peace. God knows best, but he was too young to go.

I mentioned to Sr Mary the numerary who was visiting a jailed drug runner from South America, who had no one to visit her. She mentioned there were many foreign "mules", drug runners, in our jails, quite a few from Vietnam and Mexico, who had no one to help them. She added that too many other prisoners shared this isolation.

This morning on the news it was announced that the Duchess of Sussex, Prince Harry's wife,[6] had given birth to a son. Harry did well at the announcement, happy and informed. He has inherited some of his mother's winning ways.

I am watching more television now than at any other time in my life and am amazed at the amount of time the commercial stations

---

[5] Scott Hahn (b. 1957) is an American Catholic theologian and apologist.

[6] Prince Harry (b. 1984) is the younger son of Charles, Prince of Wales, and the late Diana, Princess of Wales, of the British royal family, and is married to Meghan, Duchess of Sussex.

give to the royals and the number of excellent BBC programs on SBS. The results of the Premier League soccer in England are also relayed every morning.

When I studied in England, I watched the soccer on television twice a week, thoroughly enjoying it as a Manchester United fan. I continued to watch it for a while when I returned but lapsed as I had no one to talk with about it. Australian soccer then as now fails completely to capture my interest.

In some ways, Australia and Britain are closer than ever through modern travel and communications, although we are long past the days when my passport as I sailed to study in Rome in 1963 was marked "British passport, Australian citizen". London remains a great international city and one of Australia's larger cities because 300,000 Aussies, not counting tourists, live and work there. Before the great financial crash in 2007–2008, the number was higher.

If the Labor Party wins the election, the republican debate[7] will probably be rerun, and with no more success than last time. John Fahey, the former premier of NSW [New South Wales] and federal minister, has written me a long letter of support. We had worked together on the pro-republic side at the Constitutional Convention in 1998,[8] and he informed me, "I have only recently let my Republic Movement lapse, informing the movement I will re-join when the president is not an atheist as Peter FitzSimons is." It is hard to think of any other appointment or activity which would do more to push Christians into the royalist camp than having FitzSimons heading the republican organization. It indicates that they regard the religious voters as a lost cause or of no political significance, or both.

In my view, the maintenance of the Westminster system is paramount in the discussion. I am more hostile than ever to the idea of a directly elected president (which was my earlier position) after the election of Trump and the comedian president in Ukraine.

[7] Since the nineteenth century, there has been a movement in Australia to change its system of government from a constitutional parliamentary monarchy to a republic, which would remove the power of the monarch of Australia, who is currently Elizabeth II. The Australian Labor Party made republicanism its official policy in 1991.

[8] The 1998 Australian Constitutional Convention was called by Prime Minister John Howard, a member of the Liberal Party, to discuss whether Australia should become a republic, with the head of state appointed by Parliament. A referendum to implement the model was rejected by the Australian electorate in 1999.

Australia has always had a powerful big brother, first Britain, and now the United States. We need to stand on our own two feet, but we need allies and need to remember we are a Western culture, a Western nation on the distant rim of Asia.

After such an Irish stew of thoughts, religious, biographical, and cultural, we should conclude with some lines from Psalm 67 in today's Office of Readings.

> *May the Lord be blessed day after day.*
> *He bears our burdens, God our Saviour.*
> *This God of ours is a God who saves.*
> *The Lord our God holds the keys of death.*
> *And God will smite the head of his foes,*
> *the crown of those who persist with their sins.*

Wednesday, 8 May 2019

A busy morning—so to speak. First of all, the call came to go to the medical centre for a couple of reasons. The dressing on my left big toe, formerly ingrown, needed to be changed, and I had asked to see a doctor because of a red spot on the inside of my left shin, which I had only noticed a couple of days ago. The doctor came and said it did not look cancerous, which was my only concern, and the nurse changed the bandages on my toe.

En route I met briefly with the management team in the common area. My projected transfer to Unit 10 seems to be inching ahead but has yet to be signed off by the director of prison services. A couple of prisoners have to be transferred out of Unit 10, so the initial mixing might begin in a couple of weeks. An update was promised for next week.

While I was having my morning exercise session, the Anglican chaplain, Philip Gibbs, called, and we chatted together in the pen on one end of the metal bench. Someone a bit earlier had split milk over the other end, which the officer in charge said he would fix up when I mentioned it. I had offered to do it. This was the area I swept a few days ago. It wasn't too bad but collects dirt more quickly than the first, or closer, exercise area. Philip mentioned that the Lambeth Conference[9] was on later this year, and I replied that the Church in Australia had a council next year, which I hoped would not do too much damage.[10] Fifty percent of prisoners say they have no religion, according to him.

I received only a few letters yesterday and about twenty or so today.

Am fresher today as I slept better and somewhat longer. I must try to go to bed earlier, although I often write in the evening, and try not to read *War and Peace* for too long once I go to bed. I am more than halfway through the masterpiece; Napoleon and his troops have progressed deep into Russia, Rostov has been decorated for the brave cavalry charge he initiated, even though, unknown to the authorities, he refrained from killing the French officer with the dimple, and Natasha is back to health after her disastrous attempt to elope.

It was overcast for my second exercise period with a large puddle of rain on one side of the pen, which meant I walked diagonally rather than around the small area. Again, I received an extra fifteen minutes outside, which I appreciated.

The Dominican Sisters at Ganmain are among my strongest advocates and supporters, and one of them, who claims to be the most outspoken, wrote of the opportunities for new contacts and influence which follow from my predicament. While her examples were not all accurate, she is right about the blessings brought by the letters.

Another Dominican Sister from Berala recounted how my close friend Fr Peter Joseph, parish priest of Flemington, warned his flock on Good Friday about the local council parking rangers, who were "like Judas seeking to profit from the Lord's Passion".

News itemising a huge spiritual bouquet from Toronto, Canada, arrived. A young Dominican priest wrote about coming to the jail and praying the rosary for me. He has a group studying C.S. Lewis' *The Great Divorce* on the virtue of hope, which distinguishes sharply between fame on earth and fame in heaven. He enquired whether I

[9] The Lambeth Conference is an assembly of Anglican bishops from throughout the world. It is convened by the archbishop of Canterbury every 10 years to discuss current issues. The first conference took place in 1867.

[10] In October 2020 the Catholic Church in Australia was to hold its initial assembly as part of its first Plenary Council since Vatican II. Due to the COVID-19 pandemic, Assembly 1 was postponed until October 2021 and Assembly 2 was rescheduled for July 2022.

was "conscious of an extra burst of consolation" while he prayed the rosary for me, but I am afraid I wasn't. Perhaps too much a man of the age and spiritually insensitive.

A convert wrote to thank me for my weekly articles in Sydney's *Sunday Telegraph*, which ran for thirteen years and "played an important role in helping me to understand and appreciate the Catholic viewpoint, which in turn helped lead me into the Church".

A good friend of mine, a parish priest in a small country parish, exemplary in faith and prayer (not all of my friends are obviously in that category), wrote, "St John Paul II, as I recall, spoke of people's hunger for God. It's something I rarely, if ever, see." When I reply to him, and soon, I will tell him something of the hundreds of letters (one thousand?) which I have received already.

Another friend, Ireland's loss and Australia's gain, Fr Brendan Purcell,[11] told of his valiant defence of my innocence, on the day of my sentencing, on the Joe Duffy radio show in Ireland, which has the largest listenership in the country, and of being roundly abused for his pains. Counselled against mentioning my name in his cathedral parish sermons, he preached on Cardinal Newman and Cardinal Mindszenty,[12] adding, "I think everyone knew I was referring to you."

The letters are valuable, not because they please me, but as expressions of faith and explicit commitment. Hostile pressure can bring the best of the Church to the fore.

Let me conclude today in faith and confidence with these lines from Psalm 88 in today's Prayer of the Church.

> *Love and truth walk in your presence. . . .*
> *Happy the people who acclaim such a king,*
> *who walk, O Lord, in the light of your face.*

---

[11] Fr Brendan Purcell, who previously taught philosophy at University College Dublin, is now assistant priest at St Mary's Cathedral, Sydney.

[12] Jószef Mindszenty (1892–1975), was cardinal archbishop of Esztergom and leader of the Catholic Church in Hungary from 2 October 1945 to 18 December 1973. During World War II he was imprisoned by Hungarian Nazis, and after the war he was arrested and tortured by the new Communist rulers. After eight years in prison, the Hungarian government released him during the 1956 uprising, and he lived the rest of his life in exile, first in the United States and then in Austria.

Thursday, 9 May 2019

Another busy day, judged by the standards of prison, with a couple of pleasant distractions beyond my two exercise times. Heavy rain was threatened, but it was clear for both my outings. The physiotherapist came and worked effectively on my left arm, shoulder, and neck, saying he would return in a fortnight. He is a Hindu from Delhi, married to a Sikh, one child, who was educated at a Catholic secondary school in Delhi. He follows the school motto: "Do unto others as you would have them do to you." We discussed the various religions' sacred books, and he described the three "gods" of his tradition and of the search for Karma. The nurse replaced both bandages on my left foot and covered the spot on my shin in case I knocked it.

The highlight of the day was the visit of Archbishop Anthony Fisher, my successor in Sydney. He looked well and happy, and I congratulated him on his splendid Easter sermons, saying how delighted I was to hear that the apostles were not aristocrats, but Hillary Clinton's deplorables, and to hear him quoting Churchill, telling the House of Commons, when their backs were absolutely to the wall in the early stages of the struggle against Hitler, when they were alone except for the Dominions like Australia, that he had "nothing to offer but blood, toil, tears, and sweat". Despite that, he went on to ask: "What is our aim? I can answer in one word: Victory. Victory at all costs. Victory in spite of all terror. Victory, however long and hard the road may be."

As a teenager, I thrilled to these words. I am certainly a greater devotee of Churchill than the archbishop, but I never invoked Churchill explicitly in the cause of Christ and the Church.

The Catholic Church in Australia is not on its knees as Britain was at that time, but we are under great pressure, which is one reason why I need to win my appeal. And we do have our appeasers, groups and commentators who believe the only way forward is to jettison our old-fashioned ideas on marriage, family, sexuality, and life issues in the light of superior modern knowledge. This is capitulation and is not an option no matter how small our numbers might become. And recent history has shown in Holland, Belgium, Quebec, and other places that selling out to the world, downplaying the transcendent, denying hell, and falling silent on heaven empties the churches in a couple of generations, faster than any alternative. It is a great consolation that Archbishop Fisher knows where the battles are and will certainly lead in the right direction.

I have appealed at different times to a couple of incidents in British history to illustrate the religious points I wanted to make. In 1995 when I was pointed apostolic visitor to the seminaries of Papua New Guinea and Solomon Islands, I visited the seminary at Mt Hagen in the Highlands led by a redoubtable Dutch rector; the accommodation was spick and span, and the gardens magnificent. The student body was uneasy, not one hundred miles from a strike or rebellion which had occurred a couple of years previously. At morning Mass, I explained briefly the story of the Battle of Trafalgar and how Nelson had sent a message to the fleet that "England expects every man to do his duty."

Even at the time, I wondered what on earth they might make of it, but they all knew of tribal warfare which still occurred. On a plain outside Mt Hagen, many of the Christians gathered around a large cross on each Holy Thursday to renounce tribal warfare or to do penance for a skirmish.

On more than one occasion, I told the story to gatherings of Catholic university students of General Montgomery, who had just been appointed to the command of the Allied troops pushed eastward across North Africa by the Germans under Rommel. When he arrived at headquarters near Alexandria, Montgomery found them drawing up plans once again to withdraw south to the source of the Nile. He called all the staff together, publicly burnt the plans, and said: "Here we will stand and here we will fight—when we are prepared." On these occasions, the youth leaders knew what I was saying, even if some were unable or unwilling to follow.

The archbishop reassured me that the Australian Catholic Bishops' Conference, which he was attending here in Melbourne, was not doing any damage and that things were moving in the right direction. He also said all the bishops were supportive of me. Let us turn again to Psalm 88 from yesterday's Office:

> *Yours is a mighty arm, O Lord;*
> *your hand is strong, your right hand ready.*
> *Justice and right are the pillars of your throne....*
> *For you, O Lord, are the glory of their strength;*
> *by your favour it is that our might is exalted.*

Friday, 10 May 2019

This morning the siren to tell us to get up sounded at 7:30 am, or twenty-two minutes late. This meant some extra time to sleep or doze. I had been awake since my tablets were delivered around 6:00 am. Once again, I had read later than I intended, but the new Russian commander in chief, the old gouty, overweight Kutuzov, had just been appointed, and I wanted to see what he was up to. Tolstoy's hostility to the theory that great men decide the outcome of events, which he thinks depends more on coincidence and its ebb and flow, is difficult to reconcile with the history of Napoleon, but it is more compatible with the Russian response, if Tolstoy is in any substantial way accurate in his description of the remarkable incompetence and divided command of the Russian army (up to Kutuzov's appointment).

Apparently, it rained heavily in Melbourne overnight, 25–40 millimetres [1–1.5 inches] in different suburbs, and heavy snow was falling in the Victorian Alps, a month before the opening of the skiing season. Ballarat had even heavier rain.

The two exercise pens used to be one, so that only the far pen has a drain outlet. The puddle therefore was larger and deeper than I had seen it in the first area. When it rains heavily, only about one-third of the exercise area is under cover. While outside, I phoned the lawyers to express the hope that they would be coming today as I had not seen them since last Friday.

Not surprisingly, Kartya and Ruth Shann the barrister arrived in the afternoon. Kartya explained she had been busy preparing folders for the judges, where our evidence and the evidence of the prosecution on the many and various points are placed side by side. We have informed the prosecution that we are doing this and asked their agreement to our presenting it early to the judges. It would be interesting and indicative if they did not agree to this, because I believe that the prosecution cases to the jury in the second trial (at least) worked effectively to obfuscate and confuse the jury. They didn't want it to be clear, e.g., when and why Potter waited five to six minutes before he opened the sacristy, and they tried to swamp Portelli's evidence in possibilities, which he explicitly limited or excluded.

The prosecution is still objecting to the online streaming of the appeal proceedings, but the court has affirmed that this is going ahead, and we announced that we now support this, rather than not opposing. I feel that the more information available, the better for a proper understanding of the fiasco and for my long-term reputation.

It seems likely that Justice [Peter] Kidd from the trial will file a "Judge's Report" to the hearing, something which is no longer done regularly. As informed opinion holds that he did not agree with the jury verdict, which he studiously avoided endorsing in the sentencing, we don't anticipate the report will be unfavourable. Ruth is not sure what the judge is likely to say.

She is very impressed with Walker, who now is also convinced of the deep failure of the law in my situation and therefore emotionally committed to the cause.

I went through a dozen or so points I had prepared on Ruth's comments on the prosecution response, and I asked her and Bret to consider running in some form [Peter] Horgan's (the Queen's Counsel and former senior prosecutor) point about the impossibility of my receiving a fair trial by jury in Victoria. Ruth outlined one major difficulty with this, i.e., that we had not run this line at the trials (Ruth explained she had underestimated the hostility toward me, and I added that this existed also among Catholics), and there was another secondary consequence. It is in my long-term interests for the impossibility of the accusations to be established from the evidence, rather than having the case settled on a "technicality".

The Appeal Court has also called for the evidence from the committal hearing, where the magistrate did not halt the case going forward but did maintain in her ruling that if the evidence of Portelli and Potter is accepted, "no jury could convict." This can only be good news, like the judges' consenting to view all the evidence we requested.

God our Father, the healing of hearts and minds can only be achieved by arriving at the truth. May the appeal bring us to the truth.

Saturday, 11 May 2019

Life returned to normal this morning as the siren sounded at 7:17 am, which is as close as we ever get to precision here in the jail. Delay is built into the system as a reminder to us, as prisoners, of our status. Once you accept this basic premise, life is simple and the warders are not unpleasant. One of the various nurses who distribute the warfarin each evening has been difficult on occasion, inventing this or that requirement, but I have resisted this successfully so far.

While the day was overcast, the rain has stopped, and I was able to take both my exercise sessions. Three of my phone calls missed their targets; one out and two not answering. The warder who brought me back to my cell reminded me that tomorrow is an important day, Mother's Day, so I wished his wife a good day.

I spent this morning reading the five online articles Tim O'Leary had sent me by post: one from Keith Windschuttle and four from my unanticipated Welsh ally Chris S. Friel, philosopher and theologian, a formidable and intellectually ferocious bloodhound.

Windschuttle wrote of the intersection of the law, politics, and the need to mould public opinion through social media and traditional media.[13] He outlined seven consecutive stages in the "Get Pell" operation (a term created by Robert Richter, QC), when Operation Tethering was set up by the police at least twelve months before they had an accusation against me.

He referred to Paul Kelly's claim (from *The Australian*) November 2012 that the royal commission on paedophilia was a perfect fit for Julia Gillard's[14] political strategy, "the combination of a moral crusade, a cast of victims and coming systemic dismantling of the Catholic Church".

I was well aware from the beginning of the commission's capacity to foment anti-Catholicism, much of which was deserved, but not all of it. And the commission[15] demonstrated beyond contradiction that the Catholic cab was not the only one on the rank. Rather than such a grand strategy of dismantling, I had surmised the commission was an attempt to wedge the then opposition leader, Tony Abbott,[16] with a royal commission into Catholic institutions only, which it would have been difficult for him to resist. I had been on the record as not

[13] Keith Windschuttle, "The Course and Consequences of Operation Get Pell", *Quadrant*, 6 May 2019.

[14] Julia Gillard (b. 1961) was the prime minister of Australia and leader of the Labor Party from 2010 to 2013.

[15] The Royal Commission into Institutional Responses to Child Sexual Abuse was established by Prime Minister Gillard in 2012.

[16] Anthony John Abbott (b. 1957), a member of the Liberal Party, was leader of the opposition from 2009 to 2013 and prime minister from 2013 to 2015.

opposing a commission into all institutions and conveyed this view to the cabinet.

Although the then premier in New South Wales Barry O'Farrell conceded to me later that it had been a mistake to confine his New South Wales enquiry to Catholic institutions, the enquiry itself was much more evenhanded under Crown Prosecutor Margaret Cuneen, SC, who condemned Bishop Leo Clarke's conduct[17] as inexcusable, but who also found that the inveterate foe of Catholics, detective Peter Fox, had made many exaggerated claims and that by 2010 he had lost his objectivity and become a zealot.

I believed neither then nor now that there was any chance of the Church being dismantled, least of all by the characters Windschuttle lists, but the Church is wounded, and they have caused more damage than they probably anticipated.

Windschuttle concludes by pointing out that if the foundational principle is jettisoned—that a person is innocent until proven guilty beyond reasonable doubt—and if my appeal is unsuccessful, mine will not be a "one off misadventure. In the current climate of sexual politics, it is bound to be a model for the persecution of many others."

Chris Friel's papers have a focus different from Windschuttle's (to some extent) and give evidence again of immense labours, of an outstanding capacity to organise and analyse vast amounts of material to make them comprehensible, with the insight and intuition of a top barrister.

He follows the evidence to outline the relationships between the complainant J, his lawyer, Dr Vivian Waller, the police, especially Doug Smith, former head of Operation Sano on historic sex crimes, Louise Milligan, journalist and author, Dr Bernard Barrett from Broken Rites, an organization which supports complainants, and the mysterious tweeter Lyndsay Farlow. Is she a proxy for Waller, a team, linked to Broken Rites, or?

On 25 May 2015, Farlow tweeted about the Billy Doe incident in Philadelphia, which has eight points of similarity with the accusations

---

[17] Bishop Leo Clarke (1923–2006) was accused of covering up child sexual abuse by two of his priests while he was responsible for the Diocese of Maitland-Newcastle in New South Wales.

against me, and, on 18 June 2015, J lays his complaint with the police. Is the Billy Doe story an example to Australia of what priests get up to in sacristies and/or the model which shapes and develops J's accusations? The witch-hunt and smear campaign against me were already well under way by June 2015. Friel opines that this evidence, and much else which he outlines, merits further scrutiny.

I am surprised by Friel's revelations, because I never anticipated so much could or would be discovered and because of the extent, persistence, and complexity of the operations hostile to the Church and myself. I suspect it is a surprise to my lawyers, also.

Once again I remember St Ignatius of Loyola's advice that we should act as though everything depends on us and pray as though everything depends on God. I accept this and believe in self-help under God, because God has no hands but ours. But it is not difficult to become absorbed in the activity and let the prayer slip.

We should balance this advice with the prayer of another great Spanish saint and reformer whom we revere as Teresa of Ávila.

> *May nothing disturb you, nothing frighten you.*
> *All things pass, God does not change;*
> *Patience can cope with anything.*
> *One who has God lacks nothing.*
> > *God alone is enough.*
> > *Solo Dios basta.*

WEEK 12

Questions without Answers

12 May–18 May 2019

Mother's Day, Second Sunday of Easter, 12 May 2019

Our new shouter breaks out regularly, occasionally incoherent with rage. As I am writing this on Sunday evening, an animated dialogue, on the top note, is being conducted at the other end of the unit. We quieter types are placed together about twenty metres from them. I can't make out what the argument is about, although others are also shouting for quiet. As the walls are very thick, they need to shout, so their voices collapse after some time—usually. The main protagonist is mentally disturbed, according to one of the warders; I don't know whether this has been caused by ice, but it is all something of a contrast to the SBS feature on Kensington Palace I was watching.

The AFL football season has made a welcome difference to my weekly program as I regularly watch the three free-to-air televised games, provided they are either close or classy.

The day has passed quietly, overcast during my two exercise sessions, but with no rain. Unfortunately, I missed the 6:00 am *Mass for You at Home*, as I have not mastered how to set the alarm on my watch. I followed the instructions without success. I was awake at 5:15 am, but then dozed off. *Songs of Praise* was excellent as usual; genuine worship, usually a short story about some good work and melodious traditional hymns, from a (High Anglican) church in Bristol with statues of Our Lady, to tie in with Mother's Day. I managed to cover all bases with telephone calls yesterday or today for this secular feast, which is a good thing.

Unexpectedly I have become an SBS fan of Michael Portillo's TV series *Railway Journeys* in the UK and now in North America, and I have also been through Ukraine and am travelling on the Silk Road from China in the footsteps of Marco Polo with other guides. Tonight, we arrived at Baku on the west coast of the Caspian Sea.

The daily breviary readings vary, of course, and some of them are not suitable for my mood or situation as food for thought and meditation. I had already moved through the Book of Revelation soon after incarceration, and the avenging angels are a bit grim for Easter celebration. The Book of Job was excellent as I settled into prison life, and the Holy Week readings were beautiful. I enjoyed meditating on Mark's Gospel, left Paul's Epistle to the Romans to one side after a week or so, and am now using Cardinal Thuan's *Five Loaves and Two Fish* on the theme of the Eucharist. For some reason, my meditation is not proceeding as happily or easily as in the first six weeks, as I am more regularly distracted or dozy.

Silence has returned to the unit after a fifteen-minute fireworks display.

Today I was helped a lot by the breviary's homily 14 of St Gregory the Great, an outstanding pope, who sent St Augustine [of Canterbury] and his Benedictine missionaries to England in 596. The Roman emperor had shifted to Constantinople in the time of Constantine, a providential development which gave greater freedom to the popes in Rome, both religiously and politically, as the pope and bishops in Italy came to provide more and more of the social cohesion damaged by regular invasions.

Gregory apparently was often sick but proved to be both a fine administrator and a brilliant writer and psychologist. His classic work *Moralia* on the many different psychological types among people and clergy was required reading for bishops in many countries for hundreds of years.

Today, he is writing on the Good Shepherd, who knows his sheep. I once had a close friend, a university professor, who objected to the sheep analogy for the laity as sheep are necessarily silent, regularly fleeced, and often led to the slaughter! Every analogy limps in some way.

Gregory speaks directly of the sheep who will come to the pastures of eternal happiness if their love is expressed in action through obeying the Ten Commandments. He is even more explicit about the shepherd: "The love which leads me to die for my sheep shows how much I love the Father."

Both priests and people, shepherd and sheep, are to follow the same instructions. "No misfortune should distract us from this happiness and deep joy; for if anyone is anxious to reach a destination, the roughness of the road will not make him change his mind." Neither should we be misled by the charms of prosperity, "for only a foolish traveller, when he sees pleasant fields on his way, forgets to go on toward his destination".

Another great writer of the nineteenth century, English cardinal John Henry Newman, prayed along parallel lines.

> *Lead, Kindly Light, amid the encircling gloom,*
>   *Lead thou me on!*
> *The night is dark, and I am far from home,*
>   *Lead thou me on!*
> *Keep thou my feet; I do not ask to see*
> *The distant scene; one step enough for me.*

Monday, 13 May 2019

When I entered the exercise area this morning, the shouter was next door, noisily asking if there was anyone in my pen. I didn't reply, which is my general practice. Moreover, I didn't know whether he would conclude who I was (my speech patterns are different from most or all of the others) and whether this would make him even more angry. The shouting continued, punctuated by five or six ferocious bangs on the metal partition between us. The warders came in swearing furiously. The warder in charge then opened my door and asked whether I was all right. I responded in the affirmative, and he explained to me that jail can be like this!

Just after midday, this same warder called at my cell to enquire whether I knew Fr Portelli, who is known to his father. My reply was that Charlie was one of my closest friends, a "great bloke", and an important witness in my trial. By coincidence, the recent Andrew Bolt article on the alleged tapping of Charlie's phone was on the bed beside me, and I mentioned it.[1] The lawyers were disturbed that

[1] Andrew Bolt, "What Bugged a Priest about His Private Call to Pell", *Herald Sun*, 21 April 2019.

Charlie had gone public. Whatever of that, and a successful outcome to the appeal is the overriding priority, I completely endorse his claim that the prosecutor was trying to bamboozle him and Potter, each of whom provides an alibi for me.

On last Friday, Pope Francis issued a new set of Church procedures, whereby paedophilia allegations have to be reported to a church superior, and protocols were announced to deal with allegations against cardinals, bishops, and religious superiors. Reactions were mixed, but all this must be a step in the right direction as awareness of the problem varies among nations, and national patterns of offending are likely to differ substantially. The Holy Father's directions come from his meetings earlier this year in Rome with all the bishop presidents of national bishops' conferences.

On 10 April, the pope emeritus Benedict XVI published an eleven-page reflection on the sex-abuse crisis, since he had been in positions of authority at the public outbreak of the crisis and now wished to contribute toward a new beginning for the Church.[2]

Despite his eighty-nine years of age, the document is typical of Benedict at his best, expressing elegantly and cogently his views on three topics. He begins by examining the world between 1960 and 1980 from a German perspective. These were the years of the sexual revolution, after the invention of the contraceptive pill, and he spells out the consequences of this revolution on priests and the formation of priests. The last one-third of the document answers Lenin's famous question: What is to be done?

I was initially somewhat surprised that Benedict began by writing of the Creator God of love who communicated his message through Abraham and then Jesus. For him, a world without God is a world without meaning. When God dies in a society, this is the end of freedom; certainly in present-day Australia, religious freedom is threatened and constricted for people like Folau[3] as irreligion spreads.

---

[2] Benedict XVI, "The Church and the Scandal of Sexual Abuse", 10 April 2019.

[3] Israel Folau, a Christian Australian rugby star, was dismissed from his team in May 2019 for a post on social media about hell and homosexuals. He sued his league, Rugby Australia, arguing that the termination of his contract was a case of religious discrimination. In December 2019, he and the league reached a settlement, and in January 2020 Folau signed with another league.

I remember my atheist friend Paddy McGuinness,[4] one of the most formidable intellectuals Australia has produced, who was completely opposed to the idea of natural law. He recognized that if moral activity had to be governed by inherent moral truths, like the laws of hygiene, then God must follow as the Cause. And the opposite is also true for most. When God goes, natural law dissolves.

Paedophilia will never be abolished completely, another consequence of original sin, the wound in the human heart. But Benedict XVI asked, "Why did paedophilia reach such proportions?" Ultimately, the reason is the absence of God. In Europe probably more than in Australia, even good people took God for granted. For ourselves, too, as believers and churchgoers, it is not difficult to live our lives as practical agnostics.

We are not masters of the faith we profess, as every baptised person stands under the apostolic tradition. The Catholic Church, too, is a God-given Mystery, not just an external shell to be remodelled. Benedict is quite clear: "We do not need another Church of our own design."

Hope is not found in this direction. Jesus Christ has succeeded Job, and just as certainly as in Job's time, the spirit of evil, the great deceiver, the devil is at work characterizing the Church as entirely bad. But for Benedict, expressing the Catholic tradition, "The Church is not just made up of bad fish and weeds [but remains] the very instrument through which God saves us."

Thomas More died because he had come to accept that John Fisher was right in his claim that the pope as the successor of Peter did not simply represent a remarkable and successful example of social evolution, but expressed one essential element of Christ's teaching, the good God's plan. This is equally true of the bishops as successors of the apostles, although it is not established in the New Testament as clearly as the position of Peter, "the rock man". Hamming it up a bit, I used to tell the confirmation candidates that Our Lord renamed Simon as Rocky!

---

[4] Padraic Pearse "Paddy" McGuinness (1938–2008). In 1973–1974, he was an economic advisor to the minister for social security in the Labor government of Prime Minister Gough Whitlam. During the course of his writing career, he contributed to the *Australian Financial Review*, the *Sydney Morning Herald*, *The Age*, *The Australian*, and *Quadrant*.

For Benedict, Jesus Christ was the first martyr, and today there are martyrs and witnesses more than ever, "especially among ordinary people, but also in the high ranks of the Church".

The author of Psalm 106 anticipates our sad situation.

> *Some were sick on account of their sins*
> *and afflicted on account of their guilt.*
> *They had a loathing for every food;*
> *they came close to the gates of death.*
> *Then they cried to the Lord in their need,*
> *and he rescued them from their distress.*
> *He sent forth his word to heal them*
> *and saved their life from the grave.*

Tuesday, 14 May 2019

A few odds and ends today. The weather was beautiful this morning for my exercise: fresh, clear sky, about 18°C [64° F], and no shouting next door.

This month is the five hundredth anniversary of the death of Leonardo da Vinci, the Italian polymath and genius whose portrait the *Mona Lisa* is the most famous painting in the world. He was illegitimate and an autodidact, whose notebooks reveal the extraordinary range of his interests, from the design of a silk mill, still functioning in Florence, to a viola that can be played on a keyboard. I knew his portraits of the Madonna and Child were unusually beautiful, but did not know that they revolutionised the composition of portraiture.

However, according to the *Economist* article which sparked my interest,[5] fewer than twenty of his works survive, major commissions were not completed, and, e.g., his experiment with painting materials has damaged the *Last Supper* in Milan. Until the nineteenth century, he was ranked behind the incomparable Michelangelo, sculptor, painter, and poet (I have used Paul Stenhouse's translation of his religious sonnets for meditation), and Raphael.

---

[5] "Was Leonardo the Supreme Genius, or Just Our Kind of Guy?", *Economist*, 20 April 2019.

The recent *Economist* article pointed out it was anticlerical French historians who created the cult of Leonardo in their fight against the obscurantism of religion. Professor Jonathan Nelson from Syracuse University in Florence says, "I think these shows tell us more about us than about him." Now I understand better why the airport at Fiumicino, Rome, is dedicated to da Vinci, who spent much of his artistic life in Milan and in Paris and was born in Tuscany.

It had clouded over for my afternoon exercise session, where I was granted an hour outside. While it had clouded over, the sun shone once or twice, and it was still pleasant and peaceful; no shouting or loud phone calls next door. Paul and Kartya, the solicitors, called and we talked over recent developments, all good. Paul thought it particularly useful that the judges have asked for the transcript of the committal.

The letters continue to arrive; ten or a dozen on one day, twenty or twenty-five the next. Only one has been confronting (I presume hostile letters are censored out); all the others encouraging, from many countries and different types of persons and messages.

A second person wrote to say she had become a Catholic after my visit to her Uniting Church congregation. Depending on one's point of view, ecumenical activity is hazardous or a blessing! A couple of beautiful cards came from the homeschoolers' retreat. Kathy Chubb, who had been arrested for breaching an abortion-facility exclusion-zone in 2016, and whose appeal to the High Court was turned down on 10 April wrote, "I have offered all the inconveniences, humiliations, and stresses of my Magistrate's Court appearances for your intentions." A Benedictine priest from England quoted St John of the Cross: "The purest suffering bears and carries in its train the purest understanding."

Another English priest, a hospital chaplain in London, is asking St John Fisher to pray for me, adding that the Sydney World Youth Day was an amazing experience for him.

An Australian priest and bishop, both good friends, wrote to assure me of widespread support but that "others are delighting in your predicament and think that they finally have the Church where they want her." One also claimed some priests are delighting in my predicament; not a good sign and something of a surprise to me.

Fr Dermot Fenlon of Newman College, Ireland, sent a prayer, composed by the historian of the White Rose movement,[6] asking for the intercession of Cardinal Mindszenty for "my acquittal and total exoneration", while the Australian writer Gerard Windsor[7] wrote to express his support "in this terrible time of trial" despite our "ideological and political differences". He concluded, "Perhaps when the angel delivers you, you can tell us all what words in all your reading gave you especial comfort and hope."

Yesterday, Archbishop Peter Comensoli[8] visited for a pleasant and informative hour. I was reassured by the strategy he was proposing to reform the pastoral and religious education areas and nonplussed to hear Melbourne was under some financial pressures. This is a little bit like my surprise at the Sydney Anglican Diocese's nine-figure loss after the great financial crisis.

A Protestant pastor from South Australia sent me this hymn verse composed by another Protestant pastor, Dietrich Bonhoeffer, in prison for his opposition to the Nazis.

> *And when the cup you give is filled to brimming*
> *With bitter suffering, hard to understand,*
> *We take it gladly, trusting though with trembling,*
> *Out of so good and so beloved a hand.*

Wednesday, 15 May 2019

The sky was overcast when I took my morning exercise, but it wasn't cold. Swept my small cell, and it took nearly as long to get the dirt off the broom as it did to sweep, which is a regular part of the ritual.

---

[6] The White Rose was a German nonviolent anti-Nazi movement formed in 1942 by a group of students at the University of Munich.

[7] Gerard Windsor (b. 1944) is the author of ten books of fiction, essays, and memoirs. He attended a Jesuit secondary school and trained as a Jesuit from the ages of eighteen to twenty-four.

[8] Peter Comensoli (b. 1964) was named archbishop of Melbourne in 2018, having been bishop of Broken Bay, New South Wales, from December 2014 and auxiliary bishop of Sydney from 2011 to 2014.

Three *Spectators* arrived with Paul Stenhouse's biography of his great grandfather John Farrell, poet, journalist, and social reformer who died in 1904. I have promised Paul a review for *Annals*. This small flood of new literature was a result of Kartya's dialogue with the jail property department. Had to return to give more blood as the specimen recently taken was insufficient. I wondered whether this was someone in pathology wanting to be difficult, but the retake today was performed swiftly and easily, despite my aged, hidden veins.

Pat Power was auxiliary bishop in Canberra-Goulburn from 1986 to 2012 and never in charge of a diocese. I think his background is Irish Lebanese, and if it isn't, it could well be. He is a kind man, who has written to support me in these troubles on three occasions, and he is also a person of Christian compassion. Unfortunately, as he wrote, we were "fairly regularly on the opposite side of the argument". He sometimes went public with his ideas, but I cannot remember writing a public response. As a general rule, which allowed for exceptions, it is not good for bishops to be disagreeing in public, and I did not want to give oxygen to his ideas by rebutting them. In his last letter, he sent me his Ash Wednesday reflection, which he wanted me to see "at first hand", rather than through inaccurate reports. His message merits analysis, because he is not alone.

As members of the same Catholic Church, it is not surprising that I find much that is acceptable, but other ideas are unclear and ambiguous. In a short manifesto, we can find it difficult to know whether an omission was an oversight or intended, either because the idea is unacceptable or is common ground which might not need to be mentioned. Some ideas are misleading or impossible, and I fear the main thread of the reflection distracts us away from the centre of genuine revival and growth.

We have to agree happily that God is with us, that we all need a change of heart, need repentance and conversion, because the Church has certainly failed and hurt many people. More humility and less clericalism are both desirable, and authoritarianism, which implies disrespect of persons and procedures, a refusal to explain, and unpredictability, is always unacceptable. However, authoritarianism ranges across ideological boundaries as some of the most ruthless authoritarians are left of centre. Lenin is the classical example, but one does not need to be like Lenin to be an autocrat. And, of course, we accept Pope Francis' call to renew our hearts and faces through repentance, conversion, and forgiveness.

The bishop lists his eight hopes for the Church, and the last is "a church which reflects the person and values of Jesus". This is not good enough. Christ Our Lord redeemed us, and he and his Church teach truths of faith and morals, not just reflected "values", whatever that means. The first commandment is to love the one true God, and his Son is at the centre of all Catholic life, our Redeemer and Teacher, who is remembered and worshipped especially in the sacraments.

Does a human church mean there should be less emphasis on the supernatural, a quiet downplaying of the vertical dimension of life?

What constitutes unity, and in what type of diversity? Do the Scriptures, the councils, creeds, Magisterium have the last word, or is modernity the final arbiter, changing with every generation?

Does a less clerical Church mean that bishops and parish priests relinquish their leadership roles? Peter Tannock, the first and foremost lay leader in Australian Catholic education, wrote to me in Rome a few years ago outlining his proposal for lay people to take over the parishes as they have already assumed leadership of our schools. What a religious prospect!

The ordination of women to the priesthood is a theological problem, a doctrinal impossibility, while the mandatory celibacy of the clergy in the Latin Church is a matter of discipline, able to be changed. The point at issue is whether changing the discipline would increase the apostolic vitality of our communities. The performance of the Orthodox, Anglican, and Protestant married clergy does not provide conclusive proof of more vitality and fidelity.

It is simply not true to state there "has been a total failure in the mentality and structures of the Catholic Church". The decline in numbers and regular worship continues, but both these factors vary substantially from diocese to diocese, heavily influenced by the presence or absence of recent migrants and by the level of Catholicity and energy of the bishop and clergy.

The religious education in our schools and parishes and the vitality of the university apostolate are prime indicators of the quality of Catholic life. And across Australia, our schools, hospitals, retirement homes, welfare centres, and two universities continue to expand in absolute terms. They have not collapsed.

So the call for "branch and root reform to be fearlessly under-taken" needs, in turn, to be taken with a grain of salt. Christ is the vine, and we are the branches, and only by abiding in the Lord will we bear much fruit. Branches need to be pruned, but if they separate from the vine, they wither and are burned (Jn 15:1–8).

What does a call for a more open and inclusive Church mean in practice? What is required to follow Christ? Surely we need to accept and practise his teachings or try to do so. We have no warrant to pick and choose and discard. And on the Last Day, Christ the Judge will not be inclusive as he separates the sheep from the goats (Mt 25:31–46).

We do have much to learn from the same-sex debate. It is regret-table that so many clergy and laity did not battle more strongly against the same-sex marriage legislation, which is tolerable in itself, but will now be used as a springboard to try to prevent us from teaching as the New Testament teaches.

I know as well as any Australian the imperfections in the Vatican, but the Vatican is not "a large part of the problem", as the bishop claims. As the successor of Peter, as the bishop of Rome, the pope is part of Christ's plan and sociologically essential if the Church is to be one, rather than a collection of national churches, like the Anglicans and Orthodox. The true Church is one, holy, universal, and apos-tolic, and each note is essential.

I think it was T. S. Eliot who said we are always looking for a new system so we do not need to be good.[9] He (if it was he) would have expressed the idea more elegantly, but rejuvenation goes far beyond even essential administrative reforms.

To try to legitimise homosexual activity, ordain women as priests, radically reduce the authority and reserve powers of the papacy, eliminate the prophetic and kingly roles of bishops and priests while allowing them to celebrate the sacraments are all dead ends, incapa-ble of realisation. And fighting over these issues takes up time and energy, as we saw with the decade of struggle over women's ordina-tion in the Anglican Church.

The emeritus pope Benedict summed it up: "We do not need another Church of our own design", but we do need to repent and

---

[9] People try to escape "by dreaming of systems so perfect that no one will need to be good". T. S. Eliot, "The Rock", VI.

believe in the one true and transcendent God of love and his only Son, our Redeemer.

Excerpts from Psalm 93 are particularly helpful.

> *The Lord will not abandon his people*
> *nor forsake those who are his own.*
>
> *When I think: "I have lost my foothold";*
> *your mercy, Lord, holds me up.*
> *When cares increase in my heart,*
> *your consolation calms my soul.*
>
> *As for me, the Lord will be a stronghold;*
> *my God will be the rock where I take refuge.*

Thursday, 16 May 2019

On reading Cardinal Thuan's meditation on the Eucharist, I solved a problem which had perplexed me. At some stage during his thirteen years in prison, including nine years in a harsh form of isolation, he had confessed he was unable to pray. I could not understand this, although I understood only too well that one can feel reluctant to pray, dry, or get nothing out of prayer, receive no consolation. But I was mystified that a man I regard as a saint could not pray.

He was misleading us, setting too high a standard. He explained that when his physical and moral miseries prevented him from praying, he "repeated the Hail Mary hundreds of times". By any standards, that is prayer enough.

Our shouter, or one of them, has changed his technique so that he punctuates his abuse with periods of loud banging. Most of the guards have left after 4:30 pm lockdown, and a close neighbour has briefly joined in the banging. It lasted some minutes, so that now we have only a shouted desultory conversation at the far end of the unit. Mostly all is quiet because both procedures are tiring.

The day was quiet with my two customary exercise breaks, punctuated by an unusually long one-hour visit through the glass from Fr Michael Mason, CSsR, my oldest friend, as we came together at St

Pat's, Ballarat, in the early fifties. He is a sociologist of religion, who studied with Peter Berger at Columbia University in New York. We spoke for a long time about the case, and to my surprise he did not know of the articles by Windschuttle and Friel, but was keen to read them. The Redemptorists have seventeen seminarians in Kew, all of them from Asia.

Peter Berger was a conspicuous opponent of the theory of inevitable secularisation in the modern world, and I wondered to Michael what he would say today. He died four or five years ago. Michael himself, like many of my correspondents, is rather pessimistic.

By coincidence, on my return to my cell after the visit I opened a letter from a Protestant in Brisbane who had worked close to "the cutting edge of Christian witness in our society". There, he claimed, he had encountered the hostile "powers of this dark age" so that he gained a deeper awareness of the impact of the ideologies replacing Christianity. He listed four basic propositions.

1. Once a society rejects the concept of "love your enemies", then it is acceptable to hate, denigrate, and demonize anybody who you ideologically oppose.
2. Once society rejects the concept of sin, then it is easy to divide society into "in" and "out" groups according to their ideological purity or membership in a group.
3. If a society rejects existential Truth, then it will hold and promote any appealing lie.
4. If a society rejects individuals as sons and daughters of a Sovereign Creator, then it has lost its fount of human dignity, purpose, and goodness.

After his list, he also claimed that there "is no lack of examples" of all this in the Scriptures and in secular history.

We have here a Christian vision, or a Christian explanation of identity politics, and it explains why freedom of speech is under threat when an increasing number believe there are no truths to be arrived at, to be discovered by debate and discussion.

More than twenty years ago, the retired High Court judge whom we have quoted had warned that "some modern epistemologies seriously challenge the rule of law in so far as they strive to make the enquiry into truth meaningless."[10] Identity politics is a new and different example of one such modern epistemology.

This is a new threat to the capacity of juries to arrive at the truth, because one does not need to accept such a theory explicitly, or even to be aware of its existence as a theory, to be caught up into its way of thinking about those who are politically incorrect or those who have been demonised by the old and new media.

Dr Tim O'Donnell is the president of Christendom College in Front Royal, Virginia, a strongly Catholic liberal arts college. When he was appointed president, an old, holy Irish missionary priest (his words) gave him this prayer, which I have changed into the first person plural.

> *May the God of strength be with us,*
> *holding us in strong-fingered hands;*
> *and may we be a sacrament of his strength*
> *to those whose hands we hold.*
> *May the blessing of strength be upon us. Amen.*

Friday, 17 May 2019

Bob Hawke, prime minister of Australia, 1983–1991, died yesterday. Born in South Australia, the son of a Protestant minister, he became a Rhodes scholar, studied at Oxford University, and created the world record for the speed with which he sculled a huge glass of beer. He returned to union work in Australia, then became president of the Australian Council of Trade Unions. After entering the Federal Parliament, he was prime minister after only three years in the House.

He was our most loved prime minister, with John Howard calling him Labor's best prime minister. Tony Abbott summed it up, saying Bob had a Labor heart and a Liberal head, referring to the free market

[10] Susan Crennan, review of *Talk of the Devil: Repressed Memory and the Ritual Abuse Witch-Hunt*, by Richard Guilliatt, *Australian Law Journal* 71 (1997): 1001–1004.

reforms he introduced with Paul Keating[11] as treasurer. They were essential to our prosperity today.

Most Australians knew him as a larrikin, highly educated with the common touch, who loved to wallow in his vulgarity. Almost to the end, he was swilling his beer for the TV cameras at international cricket matches, and a year or so ago during an interview, he excused himself to go to the toilet off the patio where he was being filmed.

Unfortunately, he left his religious convictions behind him, although he was not anti-Christian or anti-Catholic, and left his wife of thirty-nine years, Hazel, for his biographer. One reporter described him as fabulously flawed, but he also had outstanding gifts. I remember his eloquence when he was one of about twenty or so speakers at the Centenary of Federation celebration in the Exhibition Building in Melbourne. I was to have one of the full-time slots, but finished up sharing the time happily with the female head of the Salvation Army, General Eva Burrows. Everyone recognized that "Hawkie" loved Australia, and we all know that those who have loved much can be forgiven much. We pray that this is so.

Outside it was clear and cool for my two outings in the pen. Unfortunately, my right knee has blown up, quite swollen, and now difficult for walking and rising from a chair. Originally, I thought I had strained some ligaments above the knee but am not sure now that the situation is so simple. It might be a bit better this evening as I write this during a break in the AFL Eagles versus the Demons. I informed the doctor at the medical centre, where the care is meticulous, but nothing happens quickly.

The letters continue to arrive: from a German history professor who believed my accuser, judge, and jury should be jailed (not a view I share), and another from a slightly anticlerical atheist, an Aussie, who is opposed to "witch hunts and baying lynch mobs". Tomorrow I will give a few more beautiful and various examples.

However, I spent most of today studying Chris Friel's latest contribution: "Walkabout".[12] I repeat that I regard his series of articles,

---

[11] Paul Keating (b. 1944) was prime minister of Australia and leader of the Labor Party from 1991 to 1996. He had previously served as treasurer from 1982 to 1991, when Bob Hawke was prime minister.

[12] Chris S. Friel, "Walkabout", https://chrisfriel.academia.edu/research#drafts.

completely unexpected, as providential, as are the somewhat less unexpected articles of Keith Windschuttle, who probably would not object to being described as acting as an agent of the Good God, although I don't know him as a religious man.

Friel continues to examine the truthfulness, motivation, attitudes, and activities of, as well as the level and type of cooperation between, the agents in this drama. My best defence is truth, and I am interested especially in the way this fantasy was created, because there was no rudimentary activity, e.g., no chance encounter in a sacristy to be developed and expanded.

Two examples merit being mentioned. Why did the police wait two years after J's complaint in 2015 before they started to interview other choristers? The delay includes nine months' inactivity after my Rome interview. Friel suggests it might have been because Sheridan and Reed[13] did not think the case would go forward, but were overruled. My jaundiced and cynical hypothesis had been that they desisted because they feared they would receive no corroboration. In my case, they didn't; no other witness corroborated the complainant.

My information sheet for the Rome interview and Louise Milligan's first book in 2017[14] did not mention the Mass before the alleged incidents. What is the reason for this? Was it a wilful omission to provoke confusion or a false step? Or was it from ignorance? Or was the narrative constructed in stages and by whom?

At this time, I don't know the answers.

God our Father, your Son and our Lord told us in the Beatitudes listed in Matthew's Gospel: Blessed are those who hunger and thirst for righteousness, for they will be filled.

Fill my family, friends, and supporters with your peace, and reward all those who, unsolicited, are working so hard for justice and righteousness in my case.

---

[13] Superintendent Paul Sheridan and Sergeant Christopher Reed are Victoria Police detectives. Both had traveled to the Vatican to question Pell about the allegations that had been made against him.

[14] Louise Milligan, an investigative reporter for ABC TV, authored the 2017 book *Cardinal: The Rise and Fall of George Pell*.

Saturday, 18 May 2019

I have not long returned from my morning exercise; another beautiful morning, cool and clear, with no clouds visible. My knee is still swollen, but better than yesterday. This suggests that it was my enthusiastic exercising which did the damage; I was kicking up my heels too much, trying to get extra bending into my knee. I am sure the Voltaren[15] helped, but my tube is almost finished. Have requested another.

I regard the pasties which are sometimes served at Saturday lunch, with tomato sauce, as the best meal available here. An added and unusual bonus today was that it was warm; not hot, but warm food is still something special. *Deo gratias*.

I believe the prayer and support I have received from hundreds of people in Australia and overseas help explain my spiritual and psychological equilibrium. Of course, I have my ups and downs as everyone does, and on last Thursday night, when I received a particularly beautiful group of letters, my spirits rose.

All this reminds me to digress about my first, much-loved bishop, Sir James Patrick O'Collins, who certainly wasn't a depressive. He told me that he knew how terrible depression was as he had once suffered an attack. So, he went to bed, had a good night's sleep, and was OK next morning.

A second digression about when I learnt a valuable lesson. When I was director of Aquinas Campus in Ballarat, now part of Australian Catholic University, a young woman undergraduate, with a strong personality and strong faith, came to tell me that she had just been to a doctor who had prescribed for her antidepressants. I reacted promptly against this, giving my usual advice that everyone's spirits rose and fell and that the best way forward was to struggle on with prayer, exercise, regular sleep and food, and not too much alcohol. Generally, then, the hills become a bit lower and the valleys less deep, and we progress toward equilibrium. In those days, some doctors, too, promptly offered young women patients an antidepressant or the contraceptive pill rather than giving them extra time. I thought the young woman would take my words with a pinch of salt.

To my surprise she returned about a week later to tell me she had taken my advice, gone home and flushed the antidepressants down

---

[15] Voltaren is a gel applied to the skin that works to relieve arthritis pain.

the toilet! She had a couple of hard days, she went on, but now she was coming back to normal, and she accepted my thesis. After that, I was much more circumspect in my advice in similar situations, although I have no recollection at all of suggesting she flush the tablets away, and I never backed away from recommending a good walk.

Back to the letters and as a connection to the Friel material, a good friend, a senior academic and lawyer, wrote that he was "no more than an average enthusiast for conspiracy theories, but these are truly chilling. As a book story they are unnervingly convincing and if even partially true, quite evil."

Perhaps the strangest letter came from someone in South Melbourne, who described himself as "barely an agnostic" and was jailed for seven years for selling oral contraceptives over the Internet without a prescription. He was "worried about over-population". He wrote from jail to "many famous people, but only you and Amanda Vanstone[16] replied". Now, he returned the kindness, "concerned that the baying of the green-left wolf packs seem to be overpowering justice in your case".

The letters give evidence of the divisions my case continues to provoke. A friend travelled overnight by train from country New South Wales [NSW] to be present at the sentencing and found at the court a "carnival atmosphere" that was "excited, salivating, giddy with delight". All that was missing, she felt, was the hotdog stand.

Another writer, also from NSW, compared me to a "21st-century Dreyfus", because of the anti-Catholicism of the West's elites. She felt the Catholic Church is "reviled among these 'useful idiots' as the last bastion standing against their godless globalist dystopia".

A younger religious priest made a similar point more pacifically, writing that I was "victimised by dark forces" as "part of a campaign to destroy the moral authority of the Church. Non praevalebunt." They will not prevail.

However, the divisions do not strictly follow denominational lines. Some radically liberal Christians delight in my predicament, and quite a few atheists with a passion for justice have spoken up for me.

With all this talk of culture wars and confrontation, we should conclude with one verse from a prayer of St Thomas More.

---

[16] Amanda Vanstone (b. 1952) is a former Liberal Party senator for South Australia (1982–2007) and former ambassador to Italy, a friend and supporter of Cardinal Pell.

O Lord,
Give us a mind that is humble, quiet, peaceable,
Patient and charitable,
And a taste of your Holy Spirit
In all our thoughts, words, and deeds.

Daughter of Time

19 May–25 May 2019

Sunday, 19 May 2019

Managed to be awake for the 6:00 am *Mass for You at Home* without the non-functioning alarm. It was celebrated by Fr John Corrigan of the Ballarat Diocese in exemplary fashion, and his short sermon had one unusual consequence, because it made me stop and think at length about his message.

He told the story of a young woman who was physically attacked. Her assailants were charged but escaped a guilty verdict and punishment on a legal technicality. She was aggrieved by the attack, and the not-guilty verdict was a further blow, so that her faith weakened and almost collapsed, and she was unable and unwilling to forgive.

This impasse was broken one Holy Week by hearing Jesus' words from the Cross: "Father, forgive them, for they know not what they do." In response to this, she prayed, "Dear Lord, I am unable to forgive. You forgive my assailants for me."

The parallels with my own situation were clear, and I am well aware that forgiveness can come and go, that a decision to forgive can be threatened, even submerged, by a surge of emotion or some new blow.

I have no high opinion of my accuser, but no enormous difficulty in forgiving him, recognizing his own sufferings. It is more of a challenge to forgive those around him and those who destroyed my good name in the media.

Fr Corrigan's sermon prompted me to realise that my decision to forgive, with varying degrees of ease, must be helped by the prayers of many thousands around the world. As George Weigel from the Ethics and Public Policy Center in Washington wrote, "I expect that you have a sense of the global spiritual solidarity that envelops you." I have also taken Jesus' teaching about the necessity of forgiveness seriously since I was a teenager and preached on it regularly. Sometimes I quoted a saying of Bishop O'Collins: "If you have hate in your heart, you won't do any good; you won't be at peace, until you get rid of it." After one such occasion, a woman came to me after Mass saying she had heard the bishop give that injunction; she realised that was her situation, forgave, and felt much better afterward.

Can you forgive a person while you take legal action against him? It depends on the motive for the decision, presuming the legal activity is moral in itself. Issues which are wider than my personal reputation are in play, such as the good name of the Church and the principle that the person is innocent until found guilty and has a right to defend his good name against calumny.

Songs of Praise came from Hereford Cathedral in the UK. All good.

Yesterday, the nation voted in the federal election. I was eventually given a form to apply for a posted vote but discovered the length of my sentence precluded me from voting.

The Liberal government was returned despite the polls, the predictions, and the bookmakers' odds. In fact, the Labor Party received 5 to 6 percent fewer votes than anticipated. What does it all mean?

Why are the polls so wrong so often? I believe there is a margin for error in every poll, up to 3 to 4 percent, if my memory serves me. But the large number of polls should obviate this.

Given the rising intolerance of any expression of support for politically incorrect positions, it seems more people are unwilling to express their true views to pollsters, particularly if they are suspicious of the sponsors or agents of the polling company. I remember an English Jesuit telling me that he was staying in a French religious house in the countryside when there was a referendum vote on [Charles] de Gaulle. Nobody had a good word to say for the general in the religious house, but when the voting result for the whole village was announced, only one person had voted against de Gaulle.

I don't know whether the mistaken polls in Australia regularly underestimate the conservative vote, and I wonder whether the green-left attitudes of many pollsters colour the nature of the questions and the evaluation of the responses. It is strange.

Voting patterns now differ immensely across Australia. Victoria is another country, like Massachusetts in the US. Queensland is a bit like the Deep South.

I suspect history will judge the emphasis on the threat of climate change as bizarre. The climate is always changing, and, despite the bluster, we don't know what raises global temperatures. As political commentator Alan Jones[1] said last night, carbon dioxide constitutes .04 percent of the atmosphere, and human activity contributes 3 percent of the carbon dioxide, while Australia contributes less than 2 percent (one fiftieth) of the 3 percent. Australia couldn't make a difference even if it knew how to do so.

In a middle-class suburb like Warringah, it is political suicide to be sceptical of or hostile to the climate-change movement. But someone will cry out eventually that the emperor has no clothes.

Tony Abbott[2] was defeated in his middle-class electorate, evidence of the collapse of Christianity and social conservatism in those ambiences. It was ugly, and I wonder who paid for the immense anti-Abbott campaign, especially by GetUp.[3] Tony's defeat is a loss for Australian political life; he leaves as a fighter, not a quitter, but it is probably better for him personally than spending years on the backbench like Ted Heath.[4]

God our Father, we thank you for the many blessings we enjoy in Australia. We ask that these continue in our democracy and that we continue to enjoy freedom of speech, freedom of religion, and civilized public discourse in a prosperous and tolerant society. May God bless Australia.

[1] Alan Jones (b. 1941), a former Australian rugby coach, was a popular morning radio personality from 1985 to 2020. Currently he is a prime-time television commentator for Australia's Sky News.

[2] Anthony John Abbott (b. 1957), a member of the Liberal Party, was prime minister of Australia from 2013 to 2015. Afterward he remained in Parliament. He lost his seat to a Labor candidate in the federal election on 18 May 2019.

[3] GetUp is a political organization in Australia.

[4] Sir Edward Heath (1916–2005) was prime minister of the United Kingdom from 1970 to 1974 and leader of the Conservative Party from 1965 to 1975. He served as a member of Parliament from 1950 to 2001.

Monday, 20 May 2019

Today is the feast of St Bernardine of Siena, a famous Franciscan preacher from fifteenth-century Italy. I adapted and used many times one of his sermons, where he gave seven or eight pieces of advice to university students. One of these was on how to deal with a donkey which was kicking everyone who came nearby. He gave the enquirer a piece of string. To the mystified recipient, he said, "Unroll the string, keep that distance from the donkey, and you will be safe." I usually suggested pornography as today's village donkey.

I found the sermon in a book of letters to different persons in history written by Pope John Paul I, who was pope for thirty-three days only and had been patriarch of Venice.

I stayed in the patriarch's *palazzo* a couple of times, as I am a friend of Cardinal Angelo Scola,[5] the leading "papabile" before the election of Pope Francis. It was an honour to use the apartment of St Pius X[6] and sleep in his bed (diagonally). This pope had introduced the practice of First Communion at the age of eight or nine. It is a beautiful practice for children in church-going families of faith, introducing them earlier to traditions of piety and giving them access to Eucharistic grace.

Here in Australia, we should be asking whether early First Communion is still the best practice, when the families of most of these children are not practising their faith at regular Mass. This makes it difficult to convince them that what is being received is the Body of the Lord, not a symbol of Christ, and difficult also to explain to them that they should be practising their faith and living good lives (in a state of grace) and should have the personal dispositions required by St Paul for a fruitful reception of Communion.

There is no groundswell of opinion even for exploring the possible option of reintroducing the ancient Western practice of First Communion after confirmation (while leaving confirmation at about the age of twelve). It would mean fewer taking Communion. The danger is that receiving Communion once in a while comes to be seen as

---

[5] Angelo Scola (b. 1941) is an Italian cardinal, philosopher, and theologian. He served as patriarch of Venice from 2002 to 2011 and archbishop of Milan from 2011 to 2017.
[6] St Pius X was pope from 1903 until 1914.

a formal rite of passage, a routine gesture, something like a low-key wedding reception or Sunday luncheon, rather than a profoundly significant religious occasion. The transcendent, vertical dimension of worship is being obscured and lost.

The necessity of preserving the vertical dimension of community worship is one reason why I also favour the practice of the priest praying to God with his back to the people during the Eucharistic Prayer.[7] This would make it brutally clear that the priest is not the centre of attention, not the centre of the action, which must be found elsewhere.

Anyone coming to Mass should be made aware that the celebration is mysterious, a reaching out to the silent, hidden God, and a commemoration of the suffering, death, and Resurrection of our leader, Jesus Christ, nearly two thousand years ago, which changed the course of human history and still calls us today to conversion, to prayer and repentance.

Bernardine's sermon today in the breviary is a fine piece of work, telling us that the preaching of Jesus gave us "the great, sudden and shining light of faith that filled the world". We are still moving through the Book of Revelation for the first readings: Great Babylon fell some days ago, and today, faithful and true, the Kings of Kings has appeared on a white horse to fight the beast, the kings of the earth, and their armies. One of my fellow prisoners, a man of violence, writes mad letters to me frequently and signs himself "king of kings".

I suspect the second wave of shouters has moved out of Unit 8, although they might simply have quietened down.

Yesterday I had a visit from a senior official, whom I had not met previously, who came to ask how I was and to tell me the director would make a decision on my case this week and then they would begin a transition process to transfer to Unit 10. My approaching appeal on 5–6 June obviously impinges on this, but, he explained, they usually do not prefer to keep prisoners in solitary confinement for three months. We shall see what happens. I was pleased when Mr Harris, often in charge of this section, a just man who had read up on my case, agreed that I had strong grounds for my appeal.

---

[7] This posture involves the priest standing between the people and the altar, with both priest and the people facing in the direction of the altar during the prayers addressed to God.

Paris, a young woman from North Albury, recommended the first verse of Psalm 57, prayed by David when he fled into hiding from Saul.

> Have mercy on me, my God,
> have mercy on me, for in you I take refuge.
> I will take refuge in the shadow of your wings
> until the disaster has passed.

Tuesday, 21 May 2019

I should begin by catching up on day-to-day life. Received only one letter yesterday, which frees up the day. I will be surprised if the supply has dried up so suddenly.

Yesterday was visiting day, and Claudio Veliz and Philip Ayres were in the contact room when I arrived. To my surprise, Maria Isabel[8] was not there, but in Cabrini Hospital with severe pneumonia. Claudio had been disconcerted that the doctor had asked in her presence whether she wished to be resuscitated. She is ninety-three years old and sent me a lovely note of apology. Am confident of her recovery.

Ayres is a historian, who wrote the biographies of Malcolm Fraser[9] and Cardinal Moran,[10] among others, and Claudio is a Renaissance man, a "philosophe", an author, and the instigator of the Conversazione series of speakers, dinner, and dialogue, then questions, which continues and was based in Melbourne, Boston, and Oxford.

When I told them I was reading *War and Peace*, Claudio launched into a discussion of Tolstoy, whom he regarded as a fox, with remarkable insight and awareness of detail, who wanted to be a hedgehog, i.e., someone with an overarching theory or explanation.

This led to Tolstoy's theories on war, where he downplays the importance of individual leaders in wartime in favour of an "ebb and

---

[8] Maria Isabel is the wife of Claudio Veliz.

[9] Malcolm Fraser (1930–2015) was prime minister of Australia from 1975 to 1983.

[10] Patrick Francis Moran (1830–1911) was archbishop of Sydney and the first cardinal appointed from Australia.

flow in the affairs of men" theory. Tolstoy knows much more about war than I do, but leaders like Napoleon and Wellington inspired tens of thousands of people, soldiers included. Tolstoy's theory probably faces greater difficulties in today's conventional warfare, but the religious situation in the Western world is fertile soil for him. One metaphor might be indicative: the tide of Christian religion is going out in the West, and we work to resist this so that a tsunami does not return to damage us further.

Following this line of thought, Claudio believed that Morrison's[11] victory and his vindication of miracles might signify a change, that the high point of anti-Christian, anti-"deplorables" political correctness might have peaked. I am sceptical because the social media remain, even if they become better controlled and censored, and so do all the other media remain, which are regularly un-Christian in their attitudes.

At the weekend, I also abandoned, for the time being, my plans for a haircut. After recovering from the blow of hearing that we have no visiting barber, I requested a pair of scissors to trim the edges. A grim red box arrived, with an electric shaver and implements covered by a red check cloth. Lifting the cloth revealed two or three large, dark, spade-shaped plastic combs. I decided I would wait when the final condition was revealed: that I had to perform outside in the exercise pen. At some stage, action will be necessary, but I might last out until a successful appeal hearing; or I could try to obtain a ribbon.

Met with Ruth, Paul, and Kartya on my list of queries on the Friel material.

As a preliminary, Ruth reported that Justice [Peter] Kidd from the trials will not present a report to the appeal, but the judges would know already of his scepticism on the jury verdict.

My hope that we might be able to discover evidence on how the set of accusations was constructed was clarified by the fact that in the June 2015 statement, J claimed the first attack occurred in my early months as archbishop "after church". Therefore, the reference to "after choir" in the document sent to me in Rome is strange, but possibly only the result of muddle and incompetence. However, at

---

[11] Scott Morrison, elected prime minister of Australia in 2019, a social conservative and devout Christian, hailed the unexpected win of his ruling coalition as a "miracle victory".

that early stage, J had the choir returning internally, so that when Reed came back to court after an absence from the committal, he was surprised to find the choir returning externally! J had changed his mind.

We still don't know why the police waited two years before interviewing the other choristers. In fact, they only did so when directed by the prosecution. Ruth does not believe Reed's claim that they did not regard the choristers' evidence as relevant!

J spoke to Barrett[12] of Broken Rites before he made a statement to police in June 2015, but after he had spoken with his mother three times. The mother had been speaking with Barrett earlier but only about Fr G's abuse of J. My recollection is that Barrett claimed at the committal that my name was not mentioned to him by J at the first meeting.

Ruth felt a day's work would be needed to answer all my questions on Friel's material, and they did not have this time available with only a fortnight remaining. At the moment, they are assembling evidence to put a stake through every shonky prosecution claim.

I agreed sadly with Ruth's view that there was no new Friel evidence able to be used in the appeal.

Almighty and eternal God, look down, we pray, upon your servants who are appointed to minister justice according to the law, convicting the guilty and restoring the innocent. May they diligently, impartially, and compassionately fulfil their lawful duties, to the good of your people and the glory of your Holy Name.

Wednesday, 22 May 2019

First of all, a confession. I read *War and Peace* until well past midnight last night. Napoleon has entered an empty Moscow, and the Rostovs have left with their carts full of wounded Russian soldiers, after emptying them of their valuable possessions; Prince Andrei is dying, and Pierre has gone walkabout. And during all this narrative, Tolstoy returns again and again to the nature of victory and defeat, the reasons

---

[12] Dr Bernard Barrett is from Broken Rites, an organization that supports complainants.

for advancing and retreating, while outlining the chaos and emerging lawlessness in Moscow.

After the lean years come years of plenty. I am not sure that "years" is the best word, but we have today two excellent readings in the breviary. In the Book of Revelation, after so many woes, the Holy City, the New Jerusalem, has come down from heaven dressed like a bride, with Jesus, the Alpha and the Omega, at its centre, drying all tears, so there is "no more grief, crying or pain" (21:1–8).

Disconcertingly, the New Jerusalem is not inclusive, excluding cowards, traitors, perverts, murderers, the immoral, magicians, worshippers of idols, and all liars, who will be plunged into the second death, the lake burning with fire and sulphur. Those excluded are, of course, only those who are unrepentant, not those who might have fallen, even many times, and then turned back to the light and to love. In our era of identity politics, the list is explosive, although it has been around, read, and revered for at least 1,900 years.

Wrongdoers who believe in sin, in categories of right and wrong, know the risks they are running, the consequences of their choices, and hope for the chance to repent or at least, like the good thief on Calvary, to throw themselves on the mercy of God.

Those who reject the notion of sin, of an offence against God, and also reject the categories of right and wrong, of moral truths for whole areas of life, e.g., marriage, family, life issues, and sexuality, often assert their right to espouse any variant of doctrine and practice, while also asserting that those advocating the traditional (for us) Judaeo-Christian ethic have no right to state publicly that some choices are intrinsically wrong. They are condemned as bigots, blind and narrow-minded, who (for the moment) can hold these views in the privacy of their homes. Normally, advocates of moral autonomy, the social Darwinians, do not believe in any life after death, rejecting such claims as religious nonsense, while still taking deep offence at any claim that their moral positions will merit godly punishment after death.

Some of the debate runs at cross purposes. No one goes to hell, in the Christian dispensation, simply because he is a member of some group, e.g., Muslim, homosexual, atheist. No one goes to hell by chance or because of ignorance. No one is condemned because he has a strong libido or is instinctively mean or has a capacity to invent and tell lies. What is significant is how we use our capacities, control our aberrant inclinations. While the individual conscience does not have primacy, because some blind ignorance is culpable (other sins have blinded us in some point, hardened our hearts, stifled our inclinations to good), ignorance and moral confusion are often real and not culpable.

The advocates of personal moral autonomy can change their minds, their moral views on an issue, but they cannot repent, acknowledge a culpable mistake, without accepting some norm beyond their personal judgement.

Izzy Folau, who is not a Catholic, would have benefited (like most Catholics today) from reading the old "penny Catechism" for young people, which set out what was necessary to commit a "mortal" sin, i.e., a death-bearing sin which separates us radically from God and bars us from heaven: full consent, full knowledge, and serious matter. The Book of Revelation and St Paul are probably the most specific in the New Testament about what is "serious matter", but only God can judge the human heart, the extent of understanding, and the level of freedom and consent.

The second-century letter of Diognetus is a description of the small Church of saints, the exemplary and tiny Christian community living quietly in the hostile, pagan empire of Rome. They are like the soul of the community (body); they return good for evil; they do not expose their infants (infanticide).

Being a Christian then was unpopular, sometimes dangerous, and converts were self-selecting. The weak and sinful were not too visible, because conversion only came at a high social price. It is now fashionable to decry the arrival of Constantine, the first Christian Roman emperor, who issued the Edict of Milan in 313 granting religious freedom, because ordinary, weak people found it easier to enter the Church. I favour sociological currents which help people in the Christian life, rather than currents which are anti-Christian, making it harder to live well. Young Christians today face stronger hostile forces than I did fifty years ago, through marriage breakdown, lower church-going rates, drugs, pornography, and the dubious blessing of social media.

Our world today is different from that of second-century Rome. We Catholics live in a democracy where we can help decide our own fate; we constitute nearly one-quarter of the population and have multiple institutions which can continue to be life-giving or degenerate into religious façades, even when doing good work. We should be visible, and we need sociological markers to strengthen identity and loyalty.

To conclude—a short adaptation of the blessing from the Book of Numbers 6:24–26.

> *May the Lord bless us and keep us.*
> *May the Lord let his face shine on us and be gracious to us.*
> *May the Lord look upon us kindly and give us peace.*

Thursday, 23 May 2019

The physio called this morning at my cell and briskly worked on my left arm and upper back. He has helped a lot, as I can do more now with the arm, which has wasted considerably around the shoulder and the biceps. I suggested he try to come again next Thursday as my appeal will be running on Thursday week.

Anne McFarlane also visited, but without Tim, who had a root-canal procedure on one of his teeth this morning. Unfortunately, they will be away during the appeal, as Tim is giving a lecture at a conference in Salzburg. Anne was pleased with the Liberal victory at the weekend federal elections, while lamenting Tony Abbott's loss. All the extended family are well, although Dave is disconsolate about Melbourne's poor AFL form. Arranged for my black suit, small white plastic collar, and braces to be readied for my trial. I need to clear with the authorities here on how it all can be brought in and kept uncreased.

Had two outings in the exercise pen in beautiful weather; the morning outing went for nearly an hour. The building next door has gone up by at least three stories in the last few weeks.

Assessment committee of four persons came to see me after three months in solitary. Mr Harris' report on my behaviour was read out, and I received a good pass. Some discussion about moving to Unit 10 and of the advantages of being able to use the gymnasium. They noted the appeal was in a fortnight and Harris' comment that the appeal is strong.

We have just been locked down for the evening at 4:30 pm, preceded by a hectic shouted row at the other end of the unit and some loud banging. It passed quickly, and all is quiet now.

Spent some hours last night and part of this morning studying Friel's "The Kid, the Choirboy and the Conjunction" and putting my thoughts in order to send to Tim O'Leary. I managed to speak with him by telephone this morning, and he informed me he had only received my letter yesterday. Friel has written three more articles, and George Weigel has gone into print again in *First Things*; Tim will send me copies.

The mysterious ways of providence continue to play out strangely. It is no surprise that George Weigel is defending me from New York, but to have a champion in Wales, a country with few Catholics, who is prepared to devote so much quality time to my defence is a small miracle.

For a couple of days, only one or two letters were passed to me, but the flow of twenty or thirty a day recommenced yesterday.

To return to Friel. Much remains opaque in the pretrial, precommittal period, and Friel is slowly deconstructing [Louise] Milligan, like peeling layer upon layer from an onion.

He has claimed previously that Milligan's account is opaque; now he claims that this is intended, not the fruit of incompetence, and is attempting to identify the principles underneath the deception. He has begun to suspect a crucial connecting role for John, the father of the dead choirboy, and has already shown how hugely implausible their accounts of their interactions are; no less implausible are some of their denials, i.e., of the group around J.

J himself told Milligan he was frightened, under pressure, that more was going on and that he wanted her to continue her investigations. And then he refused to give her any information about the alleged incidents. As Friel keeps repeating, quoting Kant,[13] "Truth is the daughter of time"; and time is passing.

As always, the letters bring consolation. One friend, something of a poet, sent me a few useful lines from Mary Ward, founder of the Loreto Sisters, who started my education and was herself imprisoned,

---

[13] Immanuel Kant (1724–1804) was a German philosopher and Enlightenment thinker.

I think by the Inquisition. "Remember, wherever you find yourself, not the place, but the practices sanctify."

A regular correspondent from the United States wrote of a difficult family situation, where, she insists, she has forgiven, although she sometimes calls her daughter-in-law Herodias and her poor son Herod. She doesn't know whether this is evidence of lack of forgiveness or of biblical wit. She hopes the latter. Who am I to judge?

Let me conclude with a short and beautiful prayer sent to me from France by a woman convert from Islam. She writes that Jesus gave her the lines "for the time of tribulation".

May the divine light be lit in my heart constantly, so that Jesus can walk there at his convenience.

Friday, 24 May 2019

A dreary day weather-wise, grey and overcast. It was raining slightly as I took my morning exercise, so I was constrained to walk under cover in half the pen. One good consequence is that the rain cleans up the pens—to a degree. Cooler also, so I swapped my blue cardigan, very much the worse for wear, for a green prison top over my shirt. Have begun negotiations to bring in my suit for my court appearance and leave it in my cell to prevent bad creasing.

David Foster, the liaison officer, called to inform me that the director, a woman, was still examining my situation, so I would stay in solitary until my appeal. If this was unsuccessful, I would certainly be moved. I was asked a couple of times and said I had no complaint. I might say, when they return early next week, that I hope they were genuinely undecided over the last six weeks and not just stringing me on with palaver to keep me quiet. Nothing I might have said would have made any difference, so I will mull over what I might or might not say next week.

I tend to use the word "beautiful" too often when I am writing. This I discovered when I was proofreading my sermons for publication. At any rate, the most beautiful letter recently was from a young Melbourne man, now living in London with a French-born wife, whose son was about to make his First Communion. The parents found it useful for their faith and enjoyable to be involved in the parish preparation program. The father had lived for a year in a L'Arche community and informed me of the death of Jean Vanier,[14] a great man, and also how his brother-in-law Jeremy, with Down Syndrome, has a full and reverent understanding of the Eucharist. Jeremy will serve the First Communion Mass.

My correspondent filled out some important facts about the Notre Dame Cathedral fire. The priest-chaplain Fr Jean-Marc Fournier had indeed returned into the burning cathedral and brought out the crown of thorns from Our Lord's passion, but his prime concern was to save the consecrated Hosts from destruction, which he did. The secular media could not cope with such a piece of news. My friend used this story to explain to his young son what we believed about the Real Presence and why the chaplain risked his life.

I myself experienced a similar example of secular media incomprehension. During a lecture one summer to the Comunione e Liberazione festival for youth at Rimini (tens of thousands attend the different sessions), I explained that it was more difficult to convert a person than it was to reform the Vatican finances. Press reports had me saying exactly the opposite, despite the fact that I put out an immediate correction of the misreport.

But to return to Notre Dame. In an interview on the morning after the fire, beamed across the world, the archbishop of Paris, Michel Aupetit, explained the nature and purpose of the cathedral. "Why was this beauty built? What jewel was this case meant to contain? Not the crown of thorns. It was built for a piece of bread, the bread that we believe is the Body of Christ."

It was fine and overcast for my afternoon exercise session.

Fr Tom McGovern in Dublin wrote that after his successful campaign to enlist the Irish convents of contemplative nuns to pray for my cause, he has now written to all the similar Catholic convents in Britain and was surprised to find seventeen in England. The UK still has a powerful cultural influence in all the English-speaking world and in the spread of secularism, but the Catholic Church, with a

---

[14]Jean Vanier (1928–2019) was a Canadian Catholic philosopher and theologian who founded L'Arche, a worldwide organization supporting adults with various disabilities.

much smaller percentage of population than our 23 percent, has hidden strengths. The contemplative convents are one example, and, before the First Synod on the Family some years ago in Rome, five hundred UK priests signed a petition in support of the scriptural basis for marriage and the proper reception of Communion. I have received a good number of letters from English priests promising prayers and sometimes fasting and penance. One fine young man and ex-student of Redfield College in North Sydney, who tragically died from cancer, told his priest (his brother) that he was offering his suffering, his death agonies for my cause. I suppose this is one example of a high mountain, too high to cross, which impedes the clouds and produces torrents of rain.

I have only received a few messages from the Czech Republic, but one family from there reminded me that Resurrection Sunday always follows Good Friday and sent me a short prayer of the fifth-century pope St Leo the Great, which we can apply without presumption to our departed friend.

The age-old night of sin has given place to the true light.

Saturday, 25 May 2019

Weather was fine and pleasant for my exercise session this morning. Tried unsuccessfully twice to phone Michael and Ruth[15]; they were probably out at Mass. Spoke for ten minutes about the Friel material with Terry [Tobin], who seemed to have read an article which was not of enormous interest to me, not least because I had not read it. He quoted Bret Walker's explanation that the High Court does not allow new material to be introduced in an appeal.

Unexpectedly, I had a visit from Kartya, our junior solicitor, committed 100 percent personally as well as professionally to my cause. She was quite excited and showed me a letter they had sent to the court.

Evidence demonstrated that the only occasions on which I celebrated Sunday Mass in 1996 in Melbourne cathedral were on 15th and 22nd of December, which is an insuperable difficulty for J's claim

---

[15] Michael Casey is a former secretary to Cardinal Pell, 1997–2014. Ruth is his wife.

that the two offences were about one month apart. To obviate this difficulty, the prosecution suggested a 23 February 1997 date for the second incident, which was totally unsupported by any evidence and contrary to what J himself said in court. They also alleged, as an alternative possibility, congruent partially with J's claim that the first incident was in the spring, in my first months as archbishop – they alleged a 3 November 1996 date, when I was not present but celebrating at St Francis' Church and the Mass was held in the Knox Hall. The breakthrough was that we presented evidence that the choirboy (R) was in hospital on that weekend. With both bookend dates excluded, we are dangerously close to game, set, and match. The prosecution withdrew that 3rd of November possibility.

I propose this afternoon to reread all of Friel's articles, as, following Friel, I am coming closer to a coherent hypothesis about how the accusations were concocted.

Today the breviary readings from the Book of Revelation came to a triumphant conclusion, after wading through days of bloody strife. John warns that all those who add anything to the book will be stricken by plague, while those who take anything away from it will lose their share of the fruit from the tree of life (22:18–19).

For decades, I have taught publicly that we have to accept, not literally, all the content of the Bible, especially the New Testament, most of which is easily accepted and understood. We are not free to discard whole sections because the teaching is uncongenial to us. I repeat that we all stand under the Word of God as its servants, not its masters.

The water of life is flowing through the New Jerusalem, where the throne of God and of the Lamb has been established, the tree of life is bearing fruit, and the words of the prophetic book are to be obeyed. Jesus, the first and the last, is coming to separate the good from the evil (Rev 22:1–7).

Two initial considerations come to mind. The succession of disasters and the avenging angels remind us of how serious the battle is between good and evil. In a prosperous and free democracy like Australia, most of us can insulate ourselves, separate ourselves from the worst and obvious evils. We do not live under a popular tyrant, as in the Philippines; not in war-torn Syria; not under the threat of violence as in India or Pakistan; not under surveillance as in China.

But drug abuse, domestic violence, and especially the scourge of paedophilia demonstrate the dark and satanic currents under the surface.

My second thought is that, at my age especially, I should be spending more time contemplating heaven, life after death with Christ, rather than wondering what I shall do when I am released from prison, how I will cope with my advancing years.

In my youth, we were encouraged to pray for a happy death, to ask Jesus, Mary, and Joseph to assist us in our last agony. I remember sixty years ago visiting my uncle Tom dying in hospital with cancer and loudly repeating the prayer aspirations he learnt as a child.

All of us, no matter the age, should "ponder our last end", try to be glad that we will be with Christ in glory, try to remove any large obstacle blocking God's love, and evaluate again, in our heart of hearts, whether our goals and activities are worth all our striving, directed in faith and hope to love.

To conclude, from a prayer of St Francis de Sales (1567–1622).

My God, I thank you now for the moment and circumstances of my death. I want to offer this moment to you with the hope that I will be departing this world in your peace. At death may I have no grudges or resentments. May I have forgiven all my enemies and have sought and received your forgiveness.

I want to affirm now the gift of faith, hope, and love you have given me through the Holy Spirit, to renew my baptismal promises, and to thank you for the eternal life promised by Jesus for those who eat his Body and drink his Blood.

P.S. pie for lunch—almost hot. Bravo.

WEEK 14

Looking Ahead

26 May–1 June 2019

Sunday, 26 May 2019

Winter is coming, because it was cold outside this morning. But it hasn't arrived, as the maximum temperature was about 13°C [55°F], and it was warmer in the afternoon.

Last night, Richmond had a solid win over Essendon in an AFL game which was preceded by a ceremony celebrating Australia's aboriginal heritage. The best man on the ground was Bachar Houli of Richmond, a Muslim. Interviewed afterward about the Ramadan fast he was following, he spoke honestly and without embarrassment of his heritage, the Prophet Muhammad, and how contemporary studies demonstrated the benefits of fasting. In every way, it was impressive and good for our society, which desperately needs courageous leadership from the Islamic moderates. When I was archbishop of Melbourne, we used to have a "football" Mass each Sunday before the Grand Final, which always received a lot of publicity, especially in the Murdoch press, and was well attended by fans, officials, coaches, and retired players. However, it was very hard work to ensure that players attended. Pious grandmothers had to be conscripted to do some persuading. I never achieved big player numbers, and after the Royal Commission and all the paedophilia scandals, the problem could be greater. However, there is no AFL football Mass now, and I salute the courage of Houli in speaking up for his faith.

Fr John Corrigan was again celebrant for the televised Mass and spoke well on confession. Jesus was mentioned in the ten-minute segment I watched of Hillsong [Church], while *Songs of Praise* came from Harrowgate in London. As always, the music was good, and the content edifying.

However, the news of the day which most struck me was the opening of a multi-billion-dollar suburban railway line from Rouse Hill in the northwest to Chatswood in greater Sydney. The stations and trains are stylish and will double the daily capacity for travel. There was universal rejoicing. However, the trains are without drivers. This disturbs me.

Jean Hughes Monier is a Frenchman, resident in New York, and a senior executive of McKinseys, who advised on the Vatican financial reforms we initiated. McKinseys seconded about twenty or so "young guns" who alternated working with us every six months or so. An outstanding group, who could regularly work ten hours a day plus, their contribution was invaluable. I was frightened that they would be scandalised and their faith weakened (many were Catholics) by what they encountered. The opposite proved to be the case, as they were proud to be part of this historic attempt at reform.

At Christmas, Jean Hughes, who is a devout Catholic and a friend, sent me a book by Kai-Fu Lee called *AI Superpowers*, which I completed reading here in prison. It deals with artificial intelligence, automation, robots, about the tidal wave of change which is approaching.

Monier had also arranged for a delegation to come from Silicon Valley to the Vatican about three years ago to discuss the future and what was essential to being human. The delegation was led by a couple of young men from London, a Catholic and a Muslim, from the group Deep Mind, which had developed computers with the capacity for deep learning, which it was explained to me meant that a computer could learn from its mistakes. Deep Mind produced the computer which first defeated the world chess champion after playing one million practice games against itself.

The Chinese were the first to develop a civil service, before the Romans, around two centuries before Christ. These mandarins dominated Chinese public life for a couple of millennia, and they were obliged to learn to play Go, a much more sophisticated and difficult game than chess. In 2017, another computer, AlphaGo, defeated Ke Jie, the world champion at Go, in three matches which were watched on livestream by 60 million viewers.

We are entering a period of change comparable to the Industrial Revolution, which will come upon us more quickly and where the US and China will be dominant and probably divide the world's markets between them. Sydney's driverless trains are one taste of what is to come.

The AI revolution is more like atomic power than the atomic bomb, because it will produce fabulous wealth (for a minority) and enormous gains in productivity as well as job losses, which will vary in different areas of life. Computers are much better with their "brains", e.g., processing immense amounts of data, than with their "hands", e.g., doing housework.

So important differences from the Industrial Revolution will become apparent. In the Industrial Revolution, displaced workers generally needed fewer skills in their new jobs. Work in a factory was usually simpler than subsistence farming.

Another difference will be that as many or more job losses will occur among white-collar workers than among blue-collar labourers, and generally all categories of displaced workers will need higher and different skills for new jobs.

Already, the middle class is being squeezed, perhaps more in the US than in Australia, as the link between gains in productivity and wage growth has been broken. The danger is that the emerging inequality of incomes will increase dramatically within societies and between countries.

Estimates vary about how many jobs will be eliminated by automation and how much human activity can be enhanced by automation, as it is already in, e.g., car manufacturing.

Opinions also vary about what we can do to prevent this "Brave New World" from descending upon us and about what we can do to mitigate its effects through, e.g., retraining, reducing working hours, and redistributing incomes.

Public discussion in Australia on these changes needs to increase, so that governments, businesses, and unions can examine what is coming. We need time to muddle through, for governments to realise their responsibilities, and for individuals to take an interest and generate discussion.

The free-market economy, more than anything else, is the foundation of our prosperity, but for the market to sustain societies like that of Australia, a moral framework is needed, with vigilant, forward-looking governments, strong and enlightened unions and businesses, international and local, aware of the social consequences of their activities, of the fact that a profit is essential, but not at any price.

Another Sister from Granmain sent me a copy of James McAuley's poem "Nocturnal", which I had forgotten.

> *The Swan was flying*
> *Seaward, as if to quit the shore*
> *That heeded its design no more.*
> *I cried: Do not depart. . . .*
>
> *It seemed that it replied:*
> *Do not complain if absence rules the season;*
> *The works of men are freighted on a tide*
> *Whose secret reason*
> *Moves also the bright signs above:*
> *Turn back and fight the wars of love.*

Monday, 27 May 2019

Only one letter arrived today, not the usual twenty or thirty, from the Miracle Prayers group in West Australia. I had mentioned that not many letters had come from the far West, but this one compensated, being too generous in their praise but promising Masses, prayers, and fasting, including Holy Hours and rosaries. They insisted Our Lord was fighting for me and that he would bring victory.

The First Epistle of John has replaced the Book of Revelation in the breviary. I have often remarked that most parts of John's writing are better food for meditation than source material for regular Sunday sermons. However, I have to concede that when John is not theologizing, he is a splendid storyteller, e.g., when the man born blind is cured by Jesus and then deals with the Jewish authorities.

The first epistle is a masterpiece, elegant and profound. What an opening:

Something that has existed since the beginning,
That we have heard
and we have seen with our own eyes; . . .
The Word, who is life—
this is our subject.

John goes on to tell us that God is light and that we are in some sense living in darkness because we are sinners.

Unfortunately, the Church is not short of sin. I read today an article in the April issue of *The New Yorker* on the paedophilia crisis in the United States. Although there are perhaps seventy million Catholics in the US, the scale of the crisis and scandal, the number of sins and crimes (and both nominatives are needed for a Catholic understanding) is enormous. The standing of the bishops has been damaged by multiple factors, and I receive a dishonourable mention in the rogues' gallery.[1]

It is no real consolation to anyone to observe that our situation might not be much worse than that of the US, especially if I can win my appeal. The only way forward is to face the truth, especially when it is grim, and to continue to do what we can to avoid the worst in the future and do better.

The New Yorker article is inclined to condemn the US bishops if they do and if they don't. Cardinal Dolan[2] has set up an independent compensation panel of lay people (in 2016) and is accused of dodging and shifting away responsibility from the bishops.

The Australian situation is different because no Australian state has a statute of limitations, as exists in some states in the US. The US has no national equivalent to the Royal Commission, although grand jury enquiries are running in some American states, and Melbourne set up its compensation scheme for victims in 1996. In both countries, the number of offences has dropped significantly since the 1990s, although we do not have the range of services and expertise which they can mobilise in the US.

No Copernican revolution is possible or desirable in Catholic structures. The truth requires that the progress already achieved since the 1990s be acknowledged, and care must be taken to ensure the

---

[1] Paul Elie, "What Do the Church's Victims Deserve?", *New Yorker*, April 15, 2019.

[2] Timothy Cardinal Dolan (b. 1950) is the current archbishop of New York, appointed by Pope Benedict XVI in 2009.

pendulum does not swing too far so that employees, priests, and religious do not have to live in a climate of fear from frivolous and sometimes false accusations, inadequately protected.

I also reread Chris Friel's articles on my situation, although I am still waiting for three more which he has already published. Not much, if anything, of his work will be admissible in the appeal, but it is immensely valuable in attempting to know how the accusations came to be.

He introduces possibilities, which I had not seriously considered. Was the hostile press campaign and the slow progress of my case designed to distract attention from the police at the Royal Commission? I hadn't realised that Milligan's ambiguities and inconsistencies might have been intentional, rather than inadvertent. Friel lists the prolific tweeting activity of the mysterious Lyndsay Farlow on the *Rolling Stone* magazine and with Broken Rites and wonders about the role of Broken Rites in composing Farlow's messages. All in all, his work is a bonus and blessing beyond any expectations.

I continue to pray each day for all the victims of sexual abuse, and this prayer was sent to me.

God our Father, may all those who have been abused physically, emotionally, and sexually by your ministers be respected and accompanied by tangible gestures of justice and reparation so that they may feel healed with the balm of your compassion. We ask this through Jesus Christ Our Lord.

Tuesday, 28 May 2019

Not long after my breakfast, David from the management team came to my cell, suggested I sit down, and then said that the director had cancelled plans to transfer me and that he would come to see me next week if I were still here after the appeal. I explained that this was likely as they would need perhaps a couple of weeks to complete the written verdict, even if the appeal is successful. I made no comment or complaint. Sr Mary, who came to bring me Communion after lunch, said that this was typical of the way things were done.

I am coping, perhaps better than expected, with the help of my breviary, rosary, the many letters, good visits, and support—and my TV set and kettle. God works through everyday events. I am sure the tsu-nami of prayers and sacrifices underpins my whole situation, the quality of my appeal, with its most recent development; and the investigative work of Windschuttle, Friel, George Weigel, and *First Things*.

The faith gives me purpose and direction, and the Christian teaching on suffering is the key. I think Kiko Arguello, cofounder of the Neocatechumenal Way, is correct in his claim that our doctrine on suffering is a major point of contrast with modern secularism. So is our teaching on forgiveness.

During the Communion service, Sr Mary prayed for my accuser, and I added a prayer for all his entourage. And a special prayer for at least the Melbourne members of my legal team, who are good, very good, but godless. Naturally, I don't believe God is not with them (I am sure he is), but they don't know he is there and probably don't miss his presence. I don't know anything one way or the other about the religious convictions of my Sydney QC, Bret Walker, although I was told he is a son of the manse.

My brother David, Judy, and their daughter Rebecca came for the Monday visit, and it was a lovely meeting. Apparently Sonny is proving to be a great talker for someone not yet three years of age. As we used to say, his mother's family at least has "the gift of the gab". Margaret has another ulcer on her leg, unfortunately, but I spoke to her by phone this afternoon, and she is due to return from hospital to Mirridong on Friday.

I am wondering whether the man who murdered the young woman in Royal Park will come to our unit. Almost certainly I won't know until after the event. We have a new shouter, not so loud, who carries on like a child. But he is mercifully brief. A lot of sadness and suffering in this block. One warder and one of my prison correspondents explained that prisoners are treated the way they treat the guards. I think we do somewhat better than this in our unit, given the nature of some of the prisoners, occasionally violent, unreasonable, sometimes damaging and dirtying their cells.

My reading continues as I am well into Fr Paul Stenhouse's biography of his great grandfather John Farrell.[3] On the *War and Peace* front, Prince Andrei has finally died, Pierre is imprisoned by the French,

---

[3] *John Farrell: Poet, Journalist and Social Reformer, 1851–1904*, by Fr Paul Stenhouse, MSC (1935–2019), who was a distinguished Australian scholar and writer.

barefoot with a head full of lice, and Moscow has been burnt so that Napoleon and the French troops are about to begin their inglorious retreat across Europe, which I first learnt about in the Victor Hugo poem set for the secondary school Alliance Française competitions: "Après la plaine blanche, une autre plaine blanche", etc.

Tolstoy is carrying on more than ever on his theory of history. He is not simply giving the Russian version of Murphy's law (that what can go wrong, will go wrong), but saying that there are mysterious tides in human events more powerful than all leaders, whose abilities are regularly overestimated. Put like this, one could hardly disagree, but Moscow did not ignite through spontaneous combustion. The burning was ordered and encouraged, although it is easy to accept that the massive looting of the empty properties by the French soldiers and even the Imperial Guard fatally damaged their discipline and morale. By any account, the author of such a magnificent sprawling novel is entitled to his self-indulgent theorizing. (Isn't every writer, at least sometimes?)

I am not sure whether the flow of letters is diminishing or the censor is the holdup. Perhaps both. Only one letter yesterday and nine today. More on the letters tomorrow.

John Milton ranks as a writer only after Shakespeare; a devout Christian, Protestant, and antipapal, he is best known for his epic *Paradise Lost*. "At a Solemn Music" is his work.

> O may we soon again renew that Song
> And keep in tune with Heav'n, till God ere long
> To his celestial consort us unite,
> To live with him, and sing in endless morn of light.

Wednesday, 29 May 2019

All archbishops over a period of time receive strange letters. Most, of course, refer to Church business, some express gratitude and praise, a regular percentage are complaints about the clergy, and some are downright hostile. One gentleman denounced me for my indifference to the poor as I slept in silk sheets in Cathedral House, Sydney! Usually my replies were models of reticence, but on this occasion I lapsed and replied directly, but courteously, pointing out that there were about eight hundred beds in the CBD[4] near the cathedral for the poor, and the Catholics offered four hundred of these, as well as a couple of food-distribution vans on nights during the week. I concluded by asking, "What does your mob offer?" I never received a reply.

I also used to receive occasional messages from God. Or so their authors claimed. A couple wrote regularly, and I didn't even bother to reply after a time.

I was careful, because, like our Prime Minister "Scomo",[5] I believe in miracles, in the reality of the supernatural, and the possibility that God might intervene in an unusual way. This has been rare in my experience. Once when I was in New Zealand, Catholic school authorities in a city were wildly alarmed because one of the children was claiming to have seen a vision. They were concerned that the word would get out. I wasn't sure which alternative would be worse for them: that the claim was a sham or that there was truth in the story. In any event, the approach of the supernatural, real or imagined, was unwelcome.

Most letters of divine messengers show signs of mental instability, but I have received a couple while in prison which do not fit the pattern. The writer from New South Wales claims to have a good track record of seeing the future in his dreams. Small examples of this are not unknown.

I decided to record what this gentleman is now claiming in order to compare it in the future with what happens. He believes God is watching me closely, that I will be released around the time of my appeal, as his dreams indicate my innocence. He adds that my accuser will end up in trouble, that his supporters will desert him, and that my story will trouble a lot of people. All this betokens a turning point which will help the Church and heralds change.

Much of this could be intelligent human conjecture by a person who has taken an interest and informed himself on the case; and this has spilled into his dreams. I don't know of any legal mechanism which would allow me to be released at the time of the appeal. He has informed the police, and heaven only knows what they might

---

[4] CBD is the "central business district" of Melbourne.
[5] Scott Morrison (b. 1968) became leader of Australia's governing Liberal Party in August 2018 and is currently prime minister.

think, as many irreligious people are quite superstitious and even less sceptical than believers. And at a nonrational level, I instinctively take consolation that his dreams are running in the right direction!

I have just returned from my afternoon exercise session. It was clear this morning but raining this afternoon, so I walked in the covered half of the pen. Snow on the Victorian Alps, heavy winds which don't penetrate my area, and quite cold, but not like the worst of the Ballarat weather in the fifties.

The charts show about four vacant cells; the shouter was distressed and vocal a few moments ago, but he has lapsed into silence now.

Over twenty-five letters arrived today, so the delay is obviously with the censor or another example of the "go slow" policy for prisoners.

Kartya called this morning, bringing a couple of pairs of socks, to update me on the state of preparations and to tell me a parcel of clothes, my suit, had arrived at her office. She feels the prosecution is somewhat sulky and not particularly cooperative, although they have agreed that the folders detailing both sets of evidence be sent to the judges, probably this afternoon.

The court wishes to provide all the basic documents to the media before the court sitting in the interests of transparency and accuracy. Naturally we support this, and the court has asked the prosecution to give reasons for their opposition to this measure. We wonder whether there is some tension in their ranks. Citing their concerns about my mobility and security in the Supreme Court [of Victoria] building, the court wondered whether I would prefer to watch via live streaming. Kartya had been sure what my reply would be.

I consented to Bret Walker showing his material to Tom Hughes, a friend, distinguished barrister, and formerly John Gorton's[6] federal attorney general. He had offered to defend me earlier on and is still formidable.

One verse of a long prayer St Thomas More wrote in the Tower of London is apposite.

To think my most enemies my best friends; for the brethren of Joseph could never have done him so much good with their love and favour as they did him with their malice and hatred.

[6] John Gorton (1911–2002) was prime minister of Australia from 1968 to 1971 and led the Liberal Party.

Ascension Thursday, 30 May 2019

At about 6:30 am, a voice over the intercom asked me whether I was going to court today, as they had been told to bring me there. I explained that my appeal was to be heard on 5 June and not today. "OK", he replied, and seemed satisfied.

About 7:00 am, while I was still in bed, the cell light went on, the door opened, and a dark, middle-sized guard announced they were taking me to court. I explained why I believed that was not the situation and recounted my earlier conversation with his boss. Even if my information was correct, they would still have to bring me to the court if those were the orders, he insisted, and said he would go off to check the situation and then let me know. I made the obvious point that if I had to go to court, obviously I would do so. He never returned. Only afterward I realised that I did not have any court clothes, as I had passed out my summer gear and was still waiting for my suit to come up to me. It would be interesting to discover the reason for the confusion. One reason for muddle is that the staff are rotated through different sections of the jail to relieve the tedium and prevent them from becoming too friendly with particular prisoners. As a consequence, the right hand does not know what the left hand has done (sometimes).

It is about 10:00 am, and I noticed big raindrops running down the opaque glass or plastic of my narrow window. Heavy snow has fallen on the Victorian Alps, and the news showed some snow in Ballarat.

Have just returned from my morning exercise, where it was cold and drizzly. I put on my old battered blue cardigan over the prison top and shirt for protection. Spoke with Kartya to learn that I would have no visitor today, and Monday looks dubious. I suggested she contact Steve Lawrence.[7] Ruth has forwarded some legal documents to be delivered as soon as possible. We shall see what ASAP means.

I have had an insight on the Friel material, only an intuition, no direct evidence. One mystery is that J urged Milligan to continue with three or four activities, but refused to give details of the incident.

[7] Steve Lawrence, friend, convenor of university chaplaincy services in Sydney Archdiocese from 2001 to 2008, and director of catechesis and evangelization for World Youth Day in 2008.

My hypothesis is that he did describe it, she realised that the story did not stack up, was not coherent, and she forgot he spoke on the issue. I will be interested to learn if Friel has a view on such a possibility, which he was probably considering, with others, weeks ago.

Last night while reading my mail, I realised what a difference it made to my morale. Naturally, the letters vary in eloquence, insight, and areas of concern, but they nearly always give evidence of deep faith and of prayer and sacrifice for my poor cause. One refrain is that I would be surprised how many people are praying for me in many countries. Many letters come from the US.

Another common, but not universal, theme is the current weakened situation of the Church and increased hostility from the world around us. A Sydney woman quoted Hilaire Belloc, a prolific Catholic author from England early in the twentieth century, who was an outspoken opponent of George Bernard Shaw and an ally of G. K. Chesterton. He famously proclaimed that "the faith is Europe and Europe is the faith" and would be doubly wrong now, with a majority of Catholics in South and Central America and a rampant secularism in Western Europe.

I will always be grateful to Fr Jim McInerney, SJ, the Jesuit rector at Corpus Christi College seminary in Werribee, who introduced me to the authors of the English Catholic literary revival beginning in the later nineteenth century such as Cardinal Newman; then Chesterton, Belloc, Ronnie Knox, Graham Greene, Evelyn Waugh, and earlier the incomparable Gerard Manley Hopkins. I remember talking to my old French teacher, years after school, who said that all subsequent "modern" English poetry was an anticlimax for her after Hopkins.

Belloc got it right this time, when he wrote, "The Church is a perpetually defeated thing that always outlives her conquerors", provided we go back to the sources. We can only emerge from our present weakened state by a moral renewal and a deepening of faith to fuel and power any sociological changes we might make. Perhaps the most important achievement of the Second Vatican Council was the empowerment of the laity for mission, as we see in the Neocatechumenal Way and in Opus Dei, founded before the council, but influential in the preparation of the conciliar document on the laity.

For this moment, Hopkins should have the last word.

> *Flesh fade, and mortal trash*
> *Fall to the residuary worm;*
> *world's wildfire, leave but ash:*
> *In a flash, at a trumpet crash,*
> *I am all at once what Christ is,*
> *since he was what I am, and*
> *This Jack, joke, poor potsherd,*
> *patch, matchwood, immortal diamond,*
> *Is immortal diamond.*[8]

Visitation of Our Lady, Friday, 31 May 2019

Not as cold as yesterday and managed to avoid the rain showers during my two exercise sessions. Nicholas O'Bryan[9] and Patrick Santamaria[10] called to discuss my civil case.

In today's breviary, Pope Leo the Great, from the fifth century, has a most informative sermon on the significance of yesterday's feast of the Ascension.

Through Christ, human nature is placed above the angels close to the throne of God the Father. Today, angels are not given special prominence, indeed, no prominence on occasion, as though they had been banished to Limbo. However, when the awareness of the supernatural was higher, as in the first century, it was regarded as significant as well as proper that the Lord should outrank the angels.

A priest friend of mine who was dying said to me, "Well, soon I will know the truth about the angels." I don't have any problem with the teaching, because it is clearly in the Scriptures and accepted by Jesus. Moreover, if the good God could (and did) create a universe so unbelievably immense and mysterious, I have no problem accommodating another rank of supernatural beings. I am not suggesting the angels are hiding in some corner of the Milky Way, because they are not in our order of creation, but they are not the only mystery or

---

[8] Gerard Manley Hopkins, SJ (1844–1889), "That Nature Is a Heraclitean Fire and of the Comfort of the Resurrection".

[9] Nicholas O'Bryan, solicitor, Galbally & O'Bryan.

[10] Patrick Santamaria, solicitor, Galbally & O'Bryan.

enigma. As one famous scientist commented, "Life is stranger than we can suppose."

St Leo explained that salvation through faith cannot be achieved by believing what we can see; therefore, the Redeemer's presence is now mediated through the sacraments. The apostles had been so devastated by the Lord's Passion that they had difficulty accepting the Resurrection, and they were still fearful. With the Ascension, their fear started to turn to joy. It was as though the Son of Man was seen more clearly in his divinity as the Son of God when his humanity was not visible. They no longer wanted to touch the risen Christ's body, as they understood more deeply through the Spirit that the only begotten Son was the equal of the Father.

I came from a family which said the rosary each evening and went to two schools where devotion to Mary, Our Lady, was strong. At St Pat's in Ballarat, we had a Marian altar with masses of flowers (obviously arranged by men) and candles, where we gathered for devotions in May, at the end of the corridor flanking the original wooden chapel, which was used as a classroom for the ninety of us who made up year seven in 1953.

In those years, Monsignor Fiscalini led the Wednesday night novena to Our Lady of Perpetual Succour every week, and for years the cathedral was packed full of people of all ages. We went as a family, except for my non-Catholic father, regularly writing our petitions and thanks and placing them in a large box at the front of the church. The format we followed was that of the Redemptorist devotion, which still flourishes in Singapore, I believe.

The Visitation is a happy feast, not like remembering Mary at the foot of the Cross. While there were no adolescents in these days, only a brutal transition from childhood to adult life, about the age of fifteen or sixteen for boys and a few years younger for the girls, it is encouraging to read of the pregnant teenager Mary walking from Nazareth to the hill country of Judah to assist her older cousin Elizabeth, who was carrying the baby we know as John the Baptist.

We are pleased to hear of people we admire who did the right thing. A contemporary of mine, active in the pro-life movement, told me that her family once lived in Ballarat, the home town of the Burkes, my mother's people, and that when her mother suffered postnatal depression, it was my grandmother who helped her through it.

Nothing spectacular. Nothing too remarkable, but I was well pleased. So too with the Visitation.

My favourite Marian prayer is the Memorare, somewhat florid in its medieval piety, which I prayed entering and leaving the cathedral for Mass and when I am under pressure. Usually when people asked for my prayers, I would offer to say Mass for them. As this is not possible in Australian jails, I immediately pray a Memorare on receiving such requests and add them to my overburdened prayer list. *Ecclesia supplet*, the Church will come to the rescue.

Let me conclude with some verse I wrote when I was a young teenager. Plainly, it was not written by James McAuley, but it is evidence of the Catholic world I came from.

> *Star of hope and happiness*
> *Kindly, bright and fair,*
> *Show us the path of virtue*
> *When we are in despair.*
>
> *Take us by the hand,*
> *Guide us through the night*
> *And when the morning dawns,*
> *Then lead us to the Light.*

Saturday, 1 June 2019

The day began with a surprise. Before the siren sounded to get out of bed, loud Middle Eastern music blared from a nearby cell. At least I think it was Arabic, as it wasn't Western or Chinese, and neither was it like the Islamic prayer chants of the two would-be terrorists who were here weeks ago. After twenty minutes, it faded and then disappeared. We might have a newcomer, or one of the old hands might have been bored.

About the same time, the shouter gave half a dozen almighty bangs on his door (no novelty) and then fell silent until 9:20 am, when he gave about a dozen more, somewhat quieter bangs. No shouting this time.

After morning exercise and lunch of a couple of sausage rolls with tomato sauce, always a culinary high point for the week, the senior official with a crown on his epaulettes, someone called him the governor, came to see whether all was well. He was aware of my appeal, which he thought could be successful, and this was the reason I had not already been transferred to Unit 10. I asked whether I could have my braces returned to wear to court. They cannot be with me overnight, but I should be able to obtain them on Wednesday morning.

Prison is a place of punishment, and one part of the punishing is to be denied easy access to newspapers and magazines. The *Herald Sun* is available three times a week and has to be ordered separately for each copy. Despite my best efforts, it took me two months to obtain five or six copies of *The Spectator*, which I recently swapped out to obtain three more and still be below the limit of six magazines.

Some days ago, I received three April numbers of *The Spectator*, and on 20 April, Christopher Akehurst had written on "Compensating Abuse". From this courageous and honest article, one point he made about the Ballarat Diocese was important and typical of most of Australia. Bishop Peter Connors, who was in charge from 1997 to 2012, did not receive one single reported allegation from that period. My friend Danny Casey asked a question about the situation in the last twenty years in the Broken Bay Diocese, north of Sydney, of the local bishop at a parish meeting. Not one allegation in that diocese, either, and Danny told me the Catholics present were astonished.

It is in nobody's long-term interests to have the general awful situation portrayed as worse than it is, as though nothing had been done until the start of the Royal Commission. The commission certainly broke new ground unearthing shameful crimes, but some incidents were covered for a third or fourth time, and the commission dealt with very few crimes committed after the middle 1990s and possibly earlier. In other words, the central core of the problem, its back, had been broken. Much needed to be done to bring crimes to justice, to organize counselling, and to provide compensation, but the evidence is that the worst of the institutional wrongdoing in the Catholic community was radically curtailed, where it was not eliminated, over twenty years ago.

Akehurst also reported that there was a rally of about one hundred victims and supporters in Melbourne in early April to protest the inadequacies of the commission's National Redress Scheme, which caps compensation at $150,000. As the years pass, it will be interesting to chart the criticisms and commendations of the commission's work and learn whether the rapturous endorsement of the prime minister and leader of the opposition last year is endorsed or tempered.

Ruth's footnote analysis of the prosecution's written case and schedule of evidence, which she deposited on Thursday, arrived this afternoon. An exhilarating read, as it is so rigorous and detailed, exposing the sophistry of the prosecution. I have a few minor points, one or two things I don't understand, and one major issue. Is the crucial role of Msgr Charlie Portelli covered sufficiently? He gave the most important alibi for me with three others. How many alibis are needed?

A couple of pieces by Christopher Friel arrived some days ago from Tim O'Leary. The most important is "Milligan and the Kid". I was correct in my estimate that Friel would be miles ahead of me in his analysis, as he now proposes that Milligan's main objective was to support the choirboy's father in his quest for justice and damages for his deceased son, and that this second group, unknown to Milligan, was pressuring J.

In my not completely limited experience, the paedophilia crisis is the most vexed area I have encountered, where it is often difficult to identify the truth. Neither do I know of any other area of life with an equal capacity to warp and damage individual judgement, whether the persons are good, bad, or indifferent. And of course, the prospect of financial gain can be distorting, especially when individual memories are sorely burdened with trauma, family deprivation, drug and alcohol abuse, and the passage of decades.

False accusations are made, as my own personal history and the falsities alleged of some prominent persons in Britain demonstrate.

I have been surprised by the quality and number of prayers by St Thomas More which have been sent to me. Here is an abridged version of "For Resistance to Temptation".

Almighty God, by Your tender pity of that Passion that was paid for our redemption, assist me with Your gracious help so that to the subtle suggestions of the serpent I never incline the ears of my heart, but that my reason may resist them and master my sensuality and keep me from them.

WEEK 15

Appealing the Conviction

2 June–8 June 2019

Sunday, 2 June 2019

Managed to be awake for the 6:00 am *Mass for You at Home* on Channel 10, again celebrated by Fr John Corrigan. Another excellent homily which demonstrated why he is asked to celebrate these Masses. It is a mystery that he is appointed to a couple of small parishes on the periphery of his country diocese; or perhaps it isn't.

Decided to give Hillsong ten minutes and finished up watching the full half hour. Brian Houston was not preaching to his congregation but conducted an interview with a US pastor and author, Robert Morris, on tithing. As the first-born animal was offered to God in Old Testament times, so the first tenth of our income should be given to the Church. He claimed that sixteen out of thirty-eight parables of Our Lord mention money. I flicked through Luke's Gospel, and the pastor could be right. Jesus was explicitly mentioned and acknowledged, but, as usual, most of the references were to Old Testament passages. One reason why the New Testament is mentioned less frequently, I suspect, is that Our Lord is insufficiently prescriptive on our day-to-day activities.

Songs of Praise came from Preston in northern England with a variety of church music and more about social work with the homeless in London. The hymns weren't inspiring, but it was excellent as always.

A couple of warders wished me well for the appeal, and I have received two large bundles of letters yesterday and today.

After reflecting on the documents of Ruth and Friel I believe two conclusions are justified:

1. The accusations against me changed and evolved in the period before I was charged and afterward. In court, J changed his story twenty-four times.
2. Only the evil one, Satan, can prevent us from winning this appeal; such is the clarity of the evidence.

As always, it is good to be busy, rather than looking for something to do, so that I am not too displeased that I have a surplus of letters which I would like to mention. The first of these tells of Fr Jim Esler, a Marist priest, ninety-six years old, who was a lawyer and is a distinguished member of that tradition of priest-scholars which has enriched humanity (this is not an exaggeration). He is a relative of a relative of mine by marriage, in a Catholic aged-care facility where he suffers a lot from, e.g., cracked ribs and finds it difficult to sleep. When Mary Clare Meney told him of my conviction, he asked her to tell me that he was "offering up my sufferings for him from now on".

One young girl explained that every morning on the way to school in the car, her family prayed for "George", although she wasn't sure who he was. Mary Clare believes my misfortunes have proved to be a "wake-up" call for many Catholics, but a schoolmate who wrote to express support explained that because of the scandal, and not just my part in it, his wife no longer felt able to go to Mass. Another felt my conviction was "not a personal thing, but an attack against the Catholic Church", expressing a hatred of God.

More happily, a Melbourne mother of ten children wrote that this Lent she felt closer to Our Lord than ever through watching my suffering.

Some recall happier experiences from years ago, remembering when I gave a talk to university students on heaven and hell, which I entitled "Turn or Burn". I had to coin this title because I had been upstaged by an eloquent student who gave an excellent lecture on the Resurrection: "The Rolling Stone".

Quite a number have taken it on themselves to work hard to spread accurate information on my case to their friends and on their blogs, and I am in favour of this as the truth is my best long-term defence, despite the fact that the alleged actions are disgraceful.

One lady from Doncaster set up a Facebook page on my trial, which, she explained, has a good number of followers not only in Australia, but in the US, several European countries, Singapore, and New Zealand. I, too, have received letters from all those distant places, a comfort for me and a sign of the essential universalism, catholicity, of the Church. She mentioned that there were two or three other Facebook pages which focused on prayer, that her own prayer had over a thousand users in two days, and, to my delight, she commended the work Chris Friel was doing.

She concluded by accepting that God's ways are not our ways and claimed there "is huge movement in our Church and in the faith of many as a result of your imprisonment". My prayer is that I don't impede any good work which is being done. At this moment, I remember that G. K. Chesterton wrote, "Angels can fly because they can take themselves lightly."

I commend myself to the protection of Mary our Mother in the opening words of the Memorare.

Remember, O most gracious Virgin Mary, that never was it known that anyone who fled to your protection or sought your help was left unaided.

This does give me confidence.

Monday, 3 June 2019

Before talking about today, which turned out to be quite busy, I was delighted yesterday when one of the warders asked me to pray for his two children. He was also good-humoured, friendly, and, as we used to say, had "kissed the Blarney Stone" (in Ireland), suggesting to me I was about sixty-five years of age. I replied proudly that I will be seventy-eight in a few days' time.

Paul and Kartya, the two solicitors, came to brief me on progress, which continues to be good. I informed Kartya that, according to the governor of the jail, she had the braces in the material she collected, and so it proved to be, as they arrived to me in the afternoon.

I had closely examined the legal documents Ruth had prepared for Bret Walker, the senior barrister, and offered some comments and questions. The quality and level of detail were first-rate. Paul confirmed that it will not be possible to use the Windschuttle and Friel material in the trial.

I informed them that I was surprised by the limited references to Msgr Portelli, who vouched for my innocence, explaining he was always with me. I am insisting the defence acknowledge his crucial role, because the guilty verdict implied he was a liar or a complete fool. He is neither. Both solicitors completely agreed with my approach.

I am also keen that Walker makes it clear what the prosecution was doing, especially at the second trial, which was to create uncertainty, confusion: not working toward clarity. Their documents for the appeal still speak of possibilities, feasible alternatives, which are not sufficient for a prosecution which has to prove guilt beyond reasonable doubt. One crucial point they have misconstrued or misunderstood is the five or six minutes which Potter, the sacristan, said that he waited before going to the sacristy, thus allowing time for the crimes in the sacristy in their theory.

There are two problems for them in this hypothesis. Potter was waiting for the procession to exit down the cathedral aisle and return along the outside of the cathedral (a necessary preliminary before the two complainants could enter through the south transept). During this time, the sacristy was locked until Potter opened the doors when the procession came near and the servers entered.

Paul stated that my case could not be in better hands, as Walker is a lawyer who comes once in a generation.

Steve Lawrence came to visit me for the hour-long contact visit. I impolitely began by greeting him, then telling him I thought I had lost more weight than he had! He laughed—not too enthusiastically—but he is used to me and tolerant.

One of the better things I did in Sydney was to reform the university chaplaincies, and Steve was the first coordinator. Instead of an isolated priest at each university (and I didn't then have many priests suitable or available for this work), we set up small teams of young men and women graduates at each university, with a priest or priests available to work with them and for the sacraments. The Dominicans helped a lot by providing a regular supply of priests. We modelled the operation on what the Sydney Evangelical Anglicans were doing with their graduate volunteers at Sydney University, and it was a young Anthony McCarthy who suggested the idea to me. The FOCUS[1] groups at the secular universities in the US are another

---

[1] Fellowship of Catholic University Students

rough parallel. The work has been blessed, and at least forty vocations since 2002, men and women, have spent some time in these communities. Many more good lay men and women have also graduated. University campuses are now a vital battleground.

I also gave Steve responsibility for the spiritual dimension of Sydney's 2008 World Youth Day. My fear was that while the WYD would be well organized, and it was, we might struggle to make the days spiritually effective, as a call to prayer, worship, confession; in a word, to conversion. Steve had not studied at the Harvard Business School, or any business school, and his style contrasted with that of our executives. But we were successful on both fronts. The faith was not just a façade. I remember hearing the birds singing in the silence after Communion at Pope Benedict's final Mass and will never forget the Way of the Cross. Steve delivered. He and his wife, Annie, are now conducting retreats courses and giving lectures, and he is still leader of the Emmanuel Community in Melbourne.

He brought me greetings from his friend Michael O'Brien in Canada, the best Catholic novelist writing in English today. Steve reminded me that I put him onto O'Brien by giving him a copy of *Father Elijah*, a great read, prophetic in its insight. I had been so impressed with it that I bought six or ten copies and gave them to friends and young leaders. God has been good to us on many occasions, and we must be grateful.

The friar I revered from a distance as Padre Pio is now known as St Pio of Pietrelcina. This is the beginning of one of his prayers.

Teach us, we ask you, humility of heart so we may be counted among the little ones of the Gospel, to whom the Father promised to reveal the mysteries of his Kingdom. Help us to pray without ceasing, certain that God knows what we need even before we ask him

Tuesday, 4 June 2019

Have just returned from my morning exercise. While it had been raining and there is snow up the east coast even into southern Queensland, the weather was not too cold and overcast. I noticed that the large building next door under construction had gone up four stories (one more than my last report?). According to one of the warders, it will become the new police headquarters.

It seems a bit unreal that we are on the eve of the appeal. Three months is nothing, or very little in any scheme of things, except when you are impatient, in less than pleasant surroundings, and keen to be vindicated. I had never expected to be found guilty by a jury of the cathedral offences, following all the legal advice and my own judgement. So, I am now wary, but clear which way the appeal should go. A not-guilty verdict is important for the Church, but also for the standing of the Australian justice system among Australians and overseas, especially in the United States, where George Weigel in his magnificent series of articles has been blunt, but truthful.

This reminds me that I received yesterday, forwarded from Rome by my secretary there, Fr Anthony Robbie, a small card, covered with tiny illegible writing from Ted McCarrick.[2] Despite repeated efforts, I could not read 80 or 90 percent of it, so that I could not even recognize his main message to me. He is eighty-nine years of age and signed himself "Ted McCarrick, Catholicus, olim cardinalis", Latin for "Catholic, formerly a cardinal". He was always courteous toward me and was a gifted networker and fundraiser, well connected across the board and especially with the Democrats. Sadly, he caused a lot of harm in more ways than one.

Fr Tom McGovern from Dublin is still writing to me regularly, and in one letter he quoted Fr Brendan Purcell's statement that I pray regularly for the priests who have sinned in this area and the bishops who did not meet their obligations. I was always concerned that guilty priests, laicised or otherwise, should hang on to their faith and repent, and I remember visiting one such priest on his deathbed to make sure of this. He told me, and I believed him, that he had made his peace with God, and I was much relieved.

While I pray explicitly each day for the victims, I have not had a category on my prayer list for offending priests and delinquent bishops. I should remedy that, and I have prayed for Ted McCarrick, olim cardinalis.

---

[2] Theodore McCarrick is a former American Catholic cardinal who was laicized in 2019 for having sexually abused adults and minors.

I have just returned from a half-hour video conference with my legal team. Walker did not have a great deal to say, except that he was very keen to start and dangerously close to being overprepared. At Paul's invitation to speak, I repeated the two points made yesterday on Mgsr Portelli and the failings of the prosecution. I was pleased when Walker endorsed the view that the prosecution's case had been very shoddy. I wished them all "God speed", acknowledging that for three of them that would not mean much. Ruth interjected, "You chose us", and I replied happily, "And I did good."

Sr Mary brought me Communion after lunch and wished me well for tomorrow. She had hoped to visit me on Saturday for my birthday, but that was not possible. The sky was clear and the sun shining for my afternoon walk when I phoned Bernadette [Tobin]. She was a bit anxious, so I suggested she burden herself with some distracting task—as I do! She was heartened by my response.

Yesterday, Steve made a point, which had already been made to me in a letter from Deacon Joe Murphy, a clever young man who wrote his master's thesis on Aristotle. Both suggested that [Prime Minister] Morrison's success was influenced by fear of the Labor policy limiting religious freedom. I am not sure whether the Catholic bishops did or did not issue a statement. But I was pleased the Protestants did speak up, including, I think, an auxiliary bishop of the Anglican Archdiocese of Sydney. It remains to be seen whether the prime minister will have insight enough, and sufficient numbers in the party room, to ensure continuing religious freedom, a task no one was willing to attempt in the Parliament before the election. It is fascinating to wonder about the political gains the deplorables have made in the US, the UK, certainly in Italy and France, perhaps in Australia, but not in Ireland or the Qantas boardroom.

While remembering Catholic sins, crimes, and woes and before turning to Psalm 84, I recall that I heard on the grapevine that Gerry Ridsdale, probably the most infamous clerical offender, has truly repented of his crimes, while he remains in jail, probably for life. His health now is very poor.

> *O Lord, . . .*
> *You forgave the guilt of your people*
> *and covered all their sins.*

Revive us now, God, our Helper!
Put an end to your grievances against us.

Let us see, O Lord, your mercy,
and give us your saving help.

Appeal Day, Wednesday, 5 June 2019

The day of my appeal hearing has finally arrived. Not surprisingly, I had my worst sleep for years and certainly since I came to jail. I woke about 2:30 am and dozed and slept fitfully after this.

I had been told to expect a wake-up call on the intercom before 6:00 am and that we would start to move toward the court at 7:15. The wake-up call came at 6:15, and we started the move away at 6:45 am. I had to ask leave to clean my teeth and had no time for my breviary morning prayer.

The routine is that you are taken downstairs, dressed in court dress (of black suit, Roman collar, for me), complete with my specially negotiated belt and braces! Near the exit, I was confined, following the normal procedures, in a small bare cell with a toilet, where I was given cereal and a coffee. Generally, I only drink tea here as the coffee is ordinary, no cappuccino or espresso!

The two most unpleasant activities are the strip search and handcuffing to a belt around the waist, very useful in my case because belt and braces are removed, and the waist of my trousers is now far too large.

Warders were decent and helpful, and I was placed into a type of paddy wagon to go to the court, with an armoured door outside the small window. I was left in the dark for a few minutes, then the light was turned on in a somewhat grotty cell area, where some enterprising and angry prisoner had scratched obscenities on the steel walls with his handcuffs.

At the Supreme Court building in Lonsdale Street, the photographers were about forty metres [forty-four yards] away from the entrance at the end of the lane but were able to obtain partial photos.

As I was tense, I passed the time with prayers, meditation in the John Main style, repeating the prayer "Jesus, Son of the Living God, pray for us."

A pleasant surprise awaited me, as I was asked to wait in the jury room, complete with en suite, which was also used by the warders.

The court commenced promptly at 9:30 am, with me coming in last after the judges. The chief justice of the Supreme Court, Anne Ferguson, presided, hearing the case with Court of Appeal President Chris Maxwell and Justice Mark Weinberg. The chief justice was a taller woman, who did not intervene regularly. Justice Weinberg looked like a wise senior judge should look, reminding me of my friend and canon lawyer Fr Frank Harman or Peter O'Callaghan.[3] Justice Maxwell intervened regularly, good-humoured, but to the point. Lawyers have called him the smiling assassin.

My senior counsel, Bret Walker from Sydney, reputed to be among the best, if not the best, barrister of his generation, led off on a formidable exposition of the reasons for the appeal. He spoke throughout the day, taking questions and comments from the judges and, not surprisingly, looking exhausted at day's end.

Even at an appeal, my team does not have to prove my innocence but only establish that the jury decision convicting me beyond reasonable doubt was not established and was unsafe.

Walker restated the basics of the case clearly and comprehensively, pointing out that if the first alleged offence did not occur on the 15th or 22nd of December, 1996, then the Crown case fails; that the prosecution's assigning of the second offence to February 23rd, 1997, went against the complainant's allegation of both events in the choral year of 1996. Other issues pursued were the complainant's reliability, McGlone's and Connor's evidence, and the fact that if Fr Portelli was always with me and not lying and if I remained on the front steps after both December Masses, then the Crown case fails again. He emphasised the fact that the alb could not be parted to allow the awful attacks; all in all, a multiplicity of factors demonstrate that a guilty verdict beyond reasonable doubts was not logical.

---

[3] Peter O'Callaghan was the founding independent commissioner for the Melbourne Response to the paedophile crisis.

David, Judy, and Sarah were in court with the usual band of loyal followers.

The return trip followed the same procedures as in the morning, except for the fact that I barked at a friendly guard, "Don't be bloody silly", when he asked if I was contemplating self-harm or suicide.

They had reserved spaghetti carbonara for my evening meal, which wasn't too bad except for the fact it was almost cold.

In my cell, I suddenly felt tired and was tempted to abbreviate my breviary daily prayer. I wanted to pray in thanks for a good day and decided on this occasion not to be like the nine cured lepers who did not come back to thank the Lord. So I carried out my duties.

I unwound by watching the State of Origin rugby league match between New South Wales and a victorious Queensland team.

I had neither the time nor the energy to open the thirty or so letters which had arrived.

Today's Psalm 69 captures the moment.

> Let there be rejoicing and gladness
> for all who seek you.
> Let them say forever: "God is good",
> who love your saving help.
>
> As for me, wretched and poor,
> come to me, O God.
> You are my rescuer, my help,
> O Lord, do not delay.

God our Father, I ask you to bless my legal team, all those who have defended me publicly, often at some cost, and the thousands who have been praying for me, including those who prayed the daily vigil outside the jail.

Appeal Day Two, Thursday, 6 June 2019

The basic procedure to court and in the court was the same as Day One. One small difference was that S, a Unit 8 warder who accompanied me to court on both days, called me not long after 5:30 am, and we did not leave for the cell until about 7:15 am. I had been given special permission to obtain my razor and mirror (both cannot be kept in the cell) and shave yesterday evening when I came back from court. I used the interval to pray my breviary morning prayers, which is a much easier procedure than having to start with morning prayer and move through the hours when you are tired in the evening.

One big difference was that I knew the procedure, had been buoyed up by Day One, and was much less tense, although not exactly relaxed! I also enjoyed the change of being in the civilised surroundings of the jury room when not in court.

Chris Boyce, the senior counsel representing the prosecution and speaking for most of the day, is no Demosthenes. My frequent critic David Marr wrote on Friday that the prosecution case was a train wreck and that Boyce showed he was under pressure, with his nose and cheeks twitching convulsively for some little time.

One warder said my barrister's performance had been outstanding yesterday. I agreed wholeheartedly but pointed out he had a good hand of cards: the evidence in the case was with him overwhelmingly.

Conversely, Boyce had no cards at all. This was almost literally true, because not one of the twenty-two witnesses the prosecution called corroborated the complainant's allegations.

Boyce began with the bald assertion that J was a compelling witness, not a liar and not a fantasist. Justice Maxwell quickly intervened to point out this was a conclusion, which needs to be examined by the judges. What indicia could Boyce provide to assist the judges? he asked.

This proved to be a continuing problem for the prosecution, who clutched repeatedly at straws to claim that it was the role of the jury to decide what were the facts of the case.

The Crown basically tried to continue the tactic used in the trials to muddy the waters, be scarce with direct answers, and denigrate the witnesses. However, persistent questioning by the judges exposed the fact there was little or no evidence to support many of its assertions.

The Crown worked to damage the credibility of Portelli, McGlone, and Potter, so that their evidence could be set aside. The extraordinary claim was made that no one was clear what anyone was doing on the days in question, citing the lack of specific recollections and ignoring the evidence of unvaried practice, supported by particular witnesses.

Boyce was reduced to long periods of silence on a number of occasions, once explaining his silence by his unwillingness to use platitudes. He could not explain what advantages in judging the evidence were enjoyed by the jury and not available to the judges. Theirs Honours did not seem to be much taken with his suggestion that they might try on an alb, rather than have one inspected.

Walker summed up magnificently in just over an hour, being particularly good at responding to the judges' comments on points of law and precedents from the High Court. I was pleased with his demonstration of the reliability of Msgr Portelli's evidence and the impossibility of setting it aside in any valid way. Walker's case had been to demonstrate on multiple grounds and at many levels that the whole body of evidence demonstrated the impossibility of the charges being true, although he pointed out that this impossibility was more than was needed for the application to be successful.

The proceedings ended quickly without fanfare, and it was announced that the trio of judges reserved their decision, to be announced at some date in the future.

I was only able to spend five or ten minutes with the legal team, as Bret had to catch a plane, I had to return to prison, and Ruth was leaving on the next day for a five-week holiday. Our mood was optimistic, and I expressed the hope to Ruth that I would be out of jail by her return. She hoped so, too.

Despite family and friends being in the court, I was unable to meet with them, and I deeply missed being able to sit around and discuss the proceedings over a meal and a drink.

The prison guard who was obliged to ask me about my intentions proved to be a Catholic, very friendly, of Italian background, and keen to talk about the Vatican, mentioning Dan Brown's *The Da Vinci Code*. I jokingly preempted his question on my mental health by explaining I had no intention of self-harm. A few of the warders have asked about the Vatican, the underground passages and cellars, and the conclave!

Had a brief and pleasant chat with the counsellor I had to visit, whose parents are the rare mixture of Serbian and Croatian.

I was again given some spaghetti carbonara, and, rather than lament my isolation, I wrote up the Day One diary and then celebrated with a camomile tea and my customary two rows of Cadbury chocolate.

Lord Jesus, I believe in the providence of God our Father, who has no hands except ours but has to cope with our sins and successes, with the mighty currents of events, and with blind chance. I thank you for bringing me to this point.

Friday, 7 June 2019

I was tired when I struggled out of bed this morning a bit late and physically flat during the morning. I wasn't depressed, as I was heartened by my understanding of the two days in court. I hadn't exercised for a couple of days, and this increases lethargy, although I was able to take both my sessions outside today. It was cool, not cold, and the sun was out.

Managed to speak with Margaret, my sister, missed David, but did contact Chris Meney and Bernadette Tobin. Terry was home with Bernadette and was able to report that he and his senior legal friends were quite confident, believing the decision will be 3-0 in my favour.

I seemed to have bungled my attempt to place $50 into my phone account, as I am almost out of credit and keen to phone around at the weekend. At this stage, I am still not sure I have remedied the situation, although S promised to do what he could to fix it up.

Four burly senior guards came and asked to perform the routine monthly check on my cell. When asked abruptly if I had any forbidden substances in my cell, I replied a little cantankerously "not much". But I received the all clear. You leave the cell during the examination, so I took my second exercise session.

Life has changed now that it is useless to be pondering aspects of the case, looking for insight and angles. It is a bit like retiring as archbishop of a diocese, where there is not much point any longer in wondering what else can be done, half hoping for a breakthrough, some new channel for the Spirit to follow.

Yesterday, when I was passing through the smaller second court en route to the jury room, I noticed Jim Gobbo's portrait on the wall. He was governor of Victoria when I was archbishop of Melbourne, is a strong Catholic, as is his wife, Shirley, and was a judge of the Supreme Court. He unveiled Nigel Boonham's fine statute of Archbishop Daniel Mannix in the St Patrick's Cathedral grounds during my time, most appropriately, as he was a migrant schoolboy in Catholic schools in Mannix's time. He is a wonderful example of the success of our post–World War II migration program and of the social mobility possible in Australian life, fostered by Catholic schools. He worked tirelessly for many causes, for the Order of Malta, and for the elderly Italians. He did not want to see them forced into Irish-Australian nursing homes, compelled to eat potatoes and sing "Danny Boy"!

I should say a word on the contrasting styles of the two senior barristers who defended me. Richter's style is aimed at convincing a jury, proceeding logically, but often swirling off in unexpected and interesting ways. He is a blessing for journalists, often providing good and provocative copy in his court addresses. I got to know him quite well over the months and realised how surprised and hurt he was when the second jury found against me. I am not surprised he has a large chair which once belonged to Dr Johnson[4] in his man's cave of an office.

Bret Walker does most of his work in the High Court and Courts of Appeal and proceeds with remorseless logic, keen insight, making no concession to humour or quirkiness for the media. He knows his judges and plans accordingly. Judges have captive audiences, especially when they are delivering a verdict, and don't have to work much at all to capture the interest of their audience. This is not the lot of politicians or priests. Richter could win over mixed groups in any social setting, while Walker is a lawyer's lawyer used to convincing judges.

I watched Geelong destroy Richmond tonight in the AFL by around seventy points. I feared we would be well beaten, but not by this much. Access to Aussie Rules football news is one advantage of being in Melbourne, but when I went to Sydney in 2001, I estimate I gained at least an hour a winter week's reading time because Aussie Rules news and gossip are limited there.

---

[4] Samuel Johnson (1709–1784) was a British writer who made a lasting contribution to the English language, especially through his famous *Dictionary of the English Language*.

Was called to the infirmary for a blood test. Not for the first time, the first two attempts did not draw blood. I informed the senior nurse who had tried on the second occasion that if the third attempt was not successful, then no more tests. Three strikes and you are out, I explained. She called the doctor, who successfully completed the test. I suggested that they switch to the pin prick test I use at home, with the doctor concurring that it would also be cheaper. The nurse congratulated me on my birthday tomorrow, with one warder suggesting I would be ninety-one!

I restate my belief that my appeal is in a good position and am grateful for the high-quality work of my legal team. I pray today's [Saturday's] Psalm 106.

> *Let them thank the Lord for the goodness,*
> *for the wonders he does for men:*
> *for he bursts the gates of bronze*
> *and shatters the iron bars.*

Saturday, 8 June 2019

Rose promptly at the siren and was not as tired as yesterday. Unusually, I was offered a half hour for exercise at 8:30 am, which I accepted. The weather was cold, but the skies weren't too dark. After my twenty-minute circuit with rosary, I checked my phone credit, and only $1.20 remained. I used it to phone my brother, David, who sang "Happy Birthday"—or at least the start, until I explained my limited time. He and Judy are coming with Chris Meney on Monday.

Not for the first time, Mr Harris, in charge of the unit, was helpful and able to add $50 phone credit for the afternoon. The other warder conveyed the request to Harris, who was then out of the unit, as a special favour because it was my birthday.

Was able to speak to the McFarlanes in Salzburg, Austria, where Tim is to give a paper next week. He had watched the entire proceedings on the internet. Naturally, they were well pleased. Did not manage to speak to Tim O'Leary, but spoke again to Margaret and to the Tobins. Terry was out but had discussed the matter with Joseph. Apparently, friend David Marr had approached Fr Frank Brennan, SJ, in the court and lamented that it was "a f ... train wreck". No, replied Frank, it was a victory for justice and transparency. Danny Casey was delighted, reporting that Ed Pentin's account in the *National Catholic Register* had been strongly supportive, that John Ferguson in *The Australian* was on the right side of the argument, and conveying best wishes from Pablo Elton[5] in Hong Kong. Pablo had been an indispensable help when we were purchasing and then renovating Domus Australia[6] in Rome.

Spent most of the day going through four days of mail, of which about one-third remains to be opened. I will return to some of them at some length later, but a few merit a brief and immediate mention. All letters to and from the prison are censored, so one lady from Kingaroy in Queensland had added a PS to her script: "To the person who reads these letters first, thank you for your time and take yourself off to Mass on Sunday." An Opus Dei numerary from Sydney wrote that many people had said that my conviction would be catastrophic for the Church in Australia. "Well that is not what I have experienced", he continued, as Mass attendances have not dropped, and for the young men following formation courses, "your situation has led them to be more prayerful and determined in following Christ and building the Church." This is only part of the overall picture, but it is consoling.

Best of all was the text of the speech a young man from year eight at a New South Wales high school gave to his class. His second Christian name is Chrysostom, after St John "with the golden mouth", a late-fourth-century archbishop of Constantinople, a famous writer and preacher. There might be something in this lad's name. The school is a government school, nonreligious.

"Pride and Prejudice: The Character Assassination of Cardinal Pell" was a splendid piece of work intellectually, which would have scored well in year twelve. An honest and competent teacher gave him full marks: 20/20. What encouraged me, and humbled me, was his courage, in front of his peers, even more than the quality of his logic and expression. I intend to write to him this weekend to thank and congratulate him.

[5] Pablo Elton is a friend and advisor.
[6] Domus Australia is a pilgrim house in Rome owned by the Australian Catholic Church.

Otherwise, life continues following the daily pattern I adopted early on. The only change came from the pleasant necessity to read the flood of letters, which I had not anticipated.

I finished the narrative section of *War and Peace* on the night of the first day of the appeal, leaving only Tolstoy's three short epilogues and an introduction by Richard Pevear, one of the two translators, which I decided to read when my reading was finished, so that my reactions were not patterned by a secondary source. It is the finest novel I have read, and I am struggling to nominate a serious rival.

On most days, I try to complete at least one Sudoku puzzle, usually two, and I nearly always manage to solve the easier version, which is becoming harder as I move through the book.

John's First Epistle concluded in the breviary a few days ago and remains one of my favourite pieces of Scripture. I have asked Chris Meney to bring the next volume of my breviary, which begins on Monday, after the great feast of Pentecost.

Edith Stein was from Germany, a Jew and a philosopher, who converted to Catholicism, joined the Carmelites, an order of contemplative nuns, and died in the Nazi concentration camp at Auschwitz. She had fled to Holland, and all the Catholic converts from Judaism were arrested when the Dutch bishops protested against the Nazis' atrocities. It is one thing to be criticised or punished for public objections, another worse stage when family members are also punished (as, e.g., Henry VIII had Cardinal Pole's mother, the blessed Margaret, Countess of Salisbury, executed), and yet a further atrocity when a large wider group who had nothing to do with the alleged offences is imprisoned and killed. This is the background for those who criticise Pope Pius XII's "silence" on the Nazi extermination program of the Jews, and this is the background for this prayer of Sr Teresa Benedicta of the Cross (Edith Stein), one of my favourite saints. I lobbied to have her nominated as one of the patrons of Australian Catholic University, without success.

We know not, and we should not ask before the time, where our earthly way will lead us. We know only this, that to those who love the Lord, all things will work together to the good, and further, that the ways by which our Saviour leads us point beyond this earth.

WEEK 16

Descent of the Holy Spirit

9 June–15 June 2019

Pentecost Sunday, 9 June 2019

Today is the feast of the Holy Spirit, the go-between God who is in our hearts and whose providence allows me to be in jail, but confident of soon being released. Thanks be to God.

The mystery of the Trinity—Father, Son, and Holy Spirit, one God in the three Persons—is peculiar to Christianity and not shared by the other two major monotheist religions, Judaism and Islam.

Tradition tells us, without any certainty, that it was St Patrick himself in the fifth century who used the imagery of the three-leafed shamrock to explain the scriptural evidence of the one true God; others appeal to the different physical forms taken by water: liquid, ice, steam.

St Irenaeus, bishop of Lyon in France in the second half of the second century, a disciple of St Polycarp of Smyrna, was crucial to the clarification and development of the Catholic form of Christianity. I believe he was the most frequently cited theologian, outside the New Testament authors, at the Second Vatican Council.

Irenaeus explained, as we read in today's breviary excerpt from his work *Against Heresies*, that at Pentecost, "the Spirit came down upon the disciples with power to grant all nations entry into life and to open the new testament." He explained that "we need God's dew, so as not to be burnt up and made unfruitful, but rather to have a Counsellor when we have an accuser." We are like dry wood, which "can never bear the fruit of life unless the rain from heaven falls upon our wills".

The Spirit has to be with the Church so that the body of the faithful through their leaders, the successor of St Peter and the successors of the apostles, can answer the questions that emerge and meet new developments. As the apostolic generation passed into history, the early Christians wanted to be sure that they were being taught what Christ himself taught, and they consulted particularly the churches founded by the apostles and especially the church in Rome founded by St Peter and St Paul.

St Irenaeus was the first Christian writer to speak of the apostolic succession of bishops, returning to the apostles themselves, where the bishops are agents of the Holy Spirit, the guarantors of the truth of the tradition. For this they don't have to be fine theologians or preachers, although these qualities help; much less are they called to provoke or disturb their congregations. Their role, inspired by the Spirit, is to identify what is true and sometimes to exclude certain understandings. They do this through their individual teaching, but more usually on major issues through the gathering of the bishops in ecumenical councils, under the pope.

We know that Our Lord left no writings and that no angel decreed what writings should be recognized as inspired by the Holy Spirit and so included in what we now call the canon or list of New Testament writings. The early churches, inspired by the Holy Spirit, ruled on these matters, often by their regular practice, constituting the apostolic tradition from the Scriptures, as articulated in the questions asked of the catechumens at baptism, which were later clarified and expanded through the solemn teachings of the councils, beginning with Nicaea in 325, and, in turn, synthesised in the creeds.

St Irenaeus was crucial in the development of this web of understanding, because he, too, was an outstanding agent of the Holy Spirit at a time when "spirituality" was all the vogue and the bizarre confusions of the Gnostic movements threatened to drown the teaching of the Gospels and St Paul.

The basic elements of the Catholic package can be recognized in the teaching of Irenaeus. There is no secret knowledge concealed from ordinary believers, as the apostolic tradition open to all the baptised, which gives us Jesus' teaching, is guaranteed by the bishops, as guardians and not masters of that same tradition. Today, we too, like St Irenaeus, must "make the coin entrusted to us bear fruit and multiply for the Lord".

Naturally these lofty considerations are far from the daily life of Unit 8 in the Melbourne Assessment Prison, where we prisoners condemned to solitary confinement are confined.

No Christian celebration of any kind was held in this jail today, and, in any case, I would not have been allowed to attend, for my own safety. I believe Sr Mary will bring me Holy Communion tomorrow.

I missed the first part of *Mass for You at Home* at 6:00 am, since I am still without an alarm, but continued on to watch Hillsong, which made no mention of Pentecost. Pastor Houston's address was genuinely God-centred, based on a text from Isaiah, with no New Testament quotes and a short singing endorsement of Jesus as Lord. The huge congregation was more animated than in previous weeks, and a lively music section was included.

For the first time, I persevered with watching the Protestant evangelist Joseph Prince from New Creation,[1] an American production (I think) in an immense multi-layered auditorium. The preacher is a small, handsome man, Chinese perhaps, nattily dressed and much closer to my idea of a Protestant evangelist. His text was from Ephesians, emphatically centred on Christ. He mentioned sin, sexual sin, and pornography, not at inordinate length, but effectively. I enjoyed it and had no theological objections.

However, the highlight of my morning of Protestant devotions (apart from my prayer of the Church and meditation) was *Songs of Praise* from the Gothic chapel at Windsor Castle, decorated by Henry VII. In this wonderful setting, with a mixed choir of adult men, boys, and girls, the congregation sang old favourites, such as "Jerusalem" and "Ancient of Days", with faith, enthusiasm, and style. I love the Catholic polyphonic tradition which I fostered both in Sydney and in Melbourne, but the Anglican choral tradition, aided by great hymns and a congregation who knows how to sing, is one of the most precious inheritances in the English-speaking world. *Floreat*. Long may it thrive.

---

[1] The evangelist Joseph Prince was the senior pastor of New Creation Church, which he helped to found in Singapore. He heads Joseph Prince Ministries, Inc., which in 2014 founded Grace Revolution Church in Dallas, Texas.

I passed most of the day opening and reading my beautiful letters and managed to take both my exercise periods. Food-wise, Sunday is the highlight with roast chicken for lunch and cold chicken in the evening with a sweet of jelly and fruit.

I conclude with a short Pentecost prayer sent by a regular correspondent from the United States.

Lord, I pray that like the dewfall the Holy Spirit descends on us and gives us his peace ... and, with sufficient frequency, reasons to laugh.

Monday, 10 June 2019

The wake-up siren sounded five minutes early today, but I recovered from this blow. The weather was cold and overcast for my first exercise session—early once again around 9:00 am—somewhat warmer, clear, and sunny between 3:00 and 4:00 pm. I managed extra time outside, which is always pleasant, provided it hasn't been raining, when the steel bench is too wet to sit on.

David and Judy came for a contact visit with Chris Meney today. All had been in court, Chris for the Tuesday only, and David, Judy, and Sarah had been harassed by photographers, appearing on some television news. They informed me Gian Pietro[2] and Caterina Pagani[3] had also been in court, although I didn't see them, while my legal friend Joseph[4] suggested I have a haircut as soon as I am released. They shared the common view that the appeal went well.

No new mail arrived today on this Queen's birthday holiday, and no newspaper came with my Cadburys chocolate purchase. Still wasn't able to contact Michael Casey; as Tim O'Leary said, he is difficult to catch.

The *Scripture Diary* published by the Carmelite Monastery in Kew listed today as the feast of Mary, Mother of the Church, although there was no trace of it in my 1974 breviary.

The feast was announced by Pope Paul VI at the end of the Second Vatican Council in 1965, when I was a student at Propaganda

---

[2] Gian Pietro Pagani, a friend from the Neocatechumenal Way
[3] Caterina Pagani, a friend and wife of Gian Pietro.
[4] Joseph Santamaria, friend, retired judge of the Court of Appeals, Victoria

Fide College on the Janiculum Hill, next to St Peter's in Rome. We were about three hundred seminarians from sixty-three nationalities with a group of thirty Australians, which increased in number each year until I left in 1967. It was a happy time and broadening for a Ballarat lad.

The progressive forces persuaded the majority of bishops not to publish a special conciliar document on Our Lady, and so she received an excellent section in the Decree on the Church, *Lumen Gentium* (Light of the Nations). The two driving themes of the council, often in tension, were *ressourcement* (back to the sources) and *aggiornamento* (modernising), and both were at work in the conciliar teaching on Our Lady.

John XXIII had called the council to help the Church cope with the unbelief driving both Nazism and Communism and in post-war France, where he was nuncio for some time under de Gaulle's leadership. The council proved to be more sensitive to the Protestant world than to the Eastern Orthodox. Medieval Church devotions such as Benediction, prayer before the Blessed Sacrament and to the saints, and the rosary were downplayed, when they weren't denigrated, and the ancient devotion to Mary, the Mother of God (*Theotokos*, God-bearer in Greek), was also wound back in too many quarters. Even as recently as about twenty-five years ago, when I was a young bishop, I remember a nun, a theologian, who gave a talk to our bishops' conference meeting on "women in Scripture" and never mentioned Our Lady. At question time, I enquired about the reason for the silence, and she replied that Our Lady wasn't in the literature.

Most of this still lay before us in 1965. However, Pope Paul VI had a strong devotion to Our Lady and was already aware of the minimalist forces at work when he, as pope, without consulting the Council Fathers, created the feast of Mother of the Church. Some objected because Mary is obviously a member of the Church, as the chapter in *Lumen Gentium* correctly demonstrated, and therefore shouldn't be venerated as her mother; while others objected to unilateral papal rather than conciliar teaching. Pope Paul was correctly making the point that the role of Peter is not subordinate to that of the successors of the apostles, which is why there can be no valid council without papal leadership and approval. I am not sure how much popular devotion exists in the Church to Our Lady under this title.

WEEK 16: DESCENT OF THE HOLY SPIRIT

I don't want to suggest for one moment that I have enjoyed my time in jail and that an unexpected rejection of my appeal would not be a blow, but I have received many blessings. One of these is the book *Jesus and the Jewish Roots of Mary* by the North American layman scholar Brant Pitre, sent to me by the Abraham family.

I learnt a lot from this high-quality book. Scott Hahn, the convert scholar, wrote that it is "the best biblical study of Mary I have ever read". High praise.

Pitre explained that worship is always accompanied by sacrifice, which is why the honour we give to Our Lady is not worship; that the devotion to the queen mother, the mother of the king, was traditional in Jewish times and readily understandable because the kings had so many wives and concubines.

Over the decades, I had referred in my sermons to "the brothers and sisters of the Lord", usually adopting the Western tradition, taught by St Jerome, that these were in fact cousins. More recently, I also mentioned the Eastern tradition that St Joseph had been married earlier, was a widower, and these were the children of his first marriage. Pitre also shows that in those times and later there was a practice where husband and wife abstained from lovemaking for religious reasons, so that Our Lady's perpetual virginity belongs to a tradition.

I had realised that there could not be two Marys as blood sisters in the one family, but Pitre validated the Western theory by pointing out that Mary the mother of James and Joseph, Simon and Jude, was still alive (the widower hypothesis for Joseph collapses) and that she was probably the wife of Clopas (Jn 19:25), the brother of Joseph. To complete the picture, we should note that James and then his brother Simon were the first two bishops of Jerusalem. This information comes from Eusebius' *History of the Church*, quoting the second-century historian Hegesippus. After all this, and more, I am better prepared for my future sermons on Our Lady.

Mother Mary, Mother of your divine Son, Jesus, our brother, we ask you to intercede with him on our behalf and on behalf of all those who have asked for our prayers.

Mother of Mercy, help us in Jesus' name to live more deeply, forgive more readily, and so follow that narrow way and enter that narrow gate which leads to eternal life.

Tuesday, 11 June 2019

Sr Mary brought me Holy Communion, and we used the Pentecost Sunday readings for our little paraliturgy at the table in the common area, complete with a small candle and a red cloth to symbolize the Holy Spirit.

Life proceeded as usual around us and in the cells. We have a new-comer who is more of a banger than a shouter. During our prayer time, he made a tremendous racket. I was mystified how they managed to create such a loud sound repeatedly, although it was clear that only the door in the cell was capable of producing any significant sound. I surmised that they used their forearms, which obviously would be bruised from repeated use. But a warder, in response to my question, explained that they turned their backs to the door and kicked like a horse. Although everyone has to wear prison gym shoes, rather than heavy boots, the noise generated is still quite significant.

The sky was beautifully clear this morning, and the weather almost warmish; in the afternoon, a light veil of cloud returned with the cold.

I swept and mopped my small cell this morning and had my laundry done yesterday. I am rather pleased we are not trusted with the washing machines, as I am no expert or experienced laundryman.

Naturally, I explained to Sr Mary how we believed the appeal had gone. She had seen something about it in the media. Typically, she had wanted to visit me on my birthday last Saturday, outside her routine time, but was denied permission because Saturday is a visitors' day for most prisoners and something or other would not be possible. Small frustrations like this are not rare, although I suppose it is in everyone's interest that I am not given special privileges.

I wrote half a dozen letters, four of them to prisoners, the only category of writer who certainly receives a reply at this stage. I will send replies to everyone after my release—a huge task.

My legal friend Joseph is not only a generous and kind man, a good husband and successful father both in religious and human terms, but a great letter writer and at considerable length. It would not be true to claim he sent me four pamphlets, but they were more than letters, like missives which ran in total to about sixty-five pages. He obviously felt I needed some intellectual sharpening up and an activity to help pass the time and was correct on both counts.

The topics ranged from the life of Daniel Fitzpatrick, a left-wing thinker and activist in the Melbourne of Archbishop Daniel Mannix, to the Greek Cardinal Bessarion in the first half of the fifteenth century, who was excluded from Constantinople and came within a whisker of becoming pope (or so it is alleged); from a discussion on the notion of equity in common law and how this relates to our debates on conscience to the manifold contributions of John Finnis[5] and the difficulties with Brexit; from the beautiful letter of a former member of MI6[6] to his godson only to be opened when the lad turns twenty-one, to a sympathetic treatment of Cardinal Wolsey,[7] an acknowledgement of the ability of that rogue Thomas Cromwell,[8] and the martyrdom of Thomas More all of them brought down in different ways by the notorious Henry VIII.

Joseph also sent me a couple of reviews by a mutual friend, the Chicago-born Jesuit Fr Paul Mankowski. Paul has enjoyed a difficult relationship with his Jesuit superiors for decades. One of my correspondents wrote explaining that my problems were "mainly" not my fault; Paul, too, can be direct, zealous for his Father's house, for the Lord and Catholic truth.

Paul is Polish-American, a member of the Church militant, with an unusual range of interests and abilities. While not a tall man, he is built like a Sherman tank and, as secretary of the Boxing Club at Oxford University, he recruited the young Aussie Tony Abbott[9] to fight in the heavyweight division for Oxford against Cambridge. On two succession years, "Abbo", as the Oxford paper dubbed him,

[5] John Finnis (b. 1940) is an Australian law professor and scholar at Oxford, known for his work in moral, political, and legal theory.

[6] MI6, which stands for Military Intelligence, Section 6, was the designation of the United Kingdom's foreign intelligence service during World War II and is still commonly used today.

[7] Thomas Cardinal Wolsey (1473–1530) was an English statesman and chancellor during the reign of Henry VIII. He was an important political figure in England until he failed to secure from the pope an annulment of the King's marriage to Catherine of Aragon. He died of natural causes shortly after being accused of treason.

[8] Thomas Cromwell (1485–1540) was an English lawyer and chief minister to Henry VIII. He helped to engineer a new Church of England so that the King, as its head, could annul his own marriage. He oversaw the dissolution of the monasteries. Yet he was later executed for treason.

[9] Anthony Abbott (b. 1957), prime minister of Australia from 2013 to 2015, attended Queen's College, Oxford University, as a Rhodes Scholar in the 1980s.

disposed of his opponent in a couple of minutes. "Mate, I can't box; I had to finish him off."

I met Paul for the first time in the 1990s when I was a member of the bishops' group from the Congregation for the Doctrine of the Faith in Rome, meeting with a group of North American bishops on the topic of biblical translation. Paul provided the ammunition for us, far superior to anything we received in the return fire. Actually, it was an amicable meeting, and our most formidable interlocutor was Francis George, later cardinal and archbishop of Chicago, who shared most of our views. I was to work closely with him on the Vox Clara Committee, advising on the English translation of the Roman Missal, one of my most significant and pleasant achievements.

Not every specialist scholar can write well outside his specialised area, but Paul can. He doesn't write much, to my knowledge, on the Church today, but he would rank with George Weigel and Ross Douthat[10] for his insight and grasp of the situation. He is also a first-rate satirist, too insightful for his own good. Years ago, one of his anonymous pieces circulated through the House of Representatives provoking mirth and admiration.

Friend Joseph had sent me Paul's review of a new translation (Robert Alter, *The Hebrew Bible: A Translation with Commentary* [W. W. Norton & Co, 2019], 3,500 pages).[11] The role of the translator is difficult and contested, so that the Italians speak of the *traduttore* as a *traditore*, i.e., the translator who is a traitor, a distorter of the original. The debate continues between the schools favouring dynamic equivalence or formal equivalence, which is not the same as a literal translation. All the committees involved wrestled with this problem in the translation of the Roman Missal, where I became a strong opponent of dynamic equivalence, at least for liturgical texts. This theory can be used to explain the text, as Mankowski objects, but it can also be used to change and "improve" the text, as it was used in some postconciliar translations to downplay merit, sacrifice, even redemption, the "perpetual" virginity of Our Lady, and to depersonalize the angels.

---

[10] Ross Douthat (b. 1979) is an American conservative political analyst, author, and *New York Times* columnist.

[11] A version of this book review by Paul V. Mankowski was published as "Word for Word" in *First Things*, August 2019.

Dynamic equivalence can throw up too many translations which are not equivalent and too few which are dynamic. The review endorsed the work of Robert Alter, the author.

Paul's second article charts the religious decline of a set of institutions which were one of the glories of the second Christian millennium, the nearly three hundred tertiary Catholic colleges and universities in the US, a number of teaching communities which has never been equalled in any country since the universities developed in Europe in the thirteenth century, sponsored by the Church. The first university in Asia was the Catholic University of St Thomas, founded in Manila by the Dominicans in the 1620s. The Catholic universities are now more heavily endowed, with highly qualified lay staff, committed to excellence, and often with splendid facilities; but many no longer even call themselves Catholic. They prefer to proclaim they adhere to or derive their ethos from the Christian or Jesuit tradition. Not many priests and religious, even in Jesuit universities, are on the academic staff, and the specifically Catholic and spiritual dimension is attenuated, when it hasn't disappeared.

The book reviewed is Fr Bill Miscamble's *American Priest: The Ambitious Life and Conflicted Legacy of Notre Dame's Father Ted Hesburgh* (New York: Image, 2017).[12] Fr Bill is Australian born, a priest of the Holy Cross Congregation which owns Notre Dame, an accomplished historian, and de facto leader of the "Catholic" party at the university.

Paul begins the review by quoting Hesburgh, who has "no problem with females or married people as priests", so conflating doctrine and discipline, an example of his "debonair self-confidence" and his attachment to "the imperatives of liberal sentimentalism".

I met Hesburgh on a couple of occasions in the seventies at Catholic tertiary education gatherings. By any standards, he was a good priest, an outstanding educator, who was charming and politically astute. He celebrated Mass every day and lamented that he had not meditated daily (he explained to me), but I recall what is now seen as his "debonair self-confidence". I was talking with him and the Jesuit theologian Avery Dulles, not yet a cardinal, about moral principles.

[12] A version of this book review by Paul V. Mankowski was published as "His Excellency", *First Things*, April 2019.

At that time, I was writing a thesis on moral autonomy and had become explicitly committed to moral realism, the moral tradition of Aristotle and St Thomas Aquinas. Hesburgh quickly pronounced that this type of thinking was finished, prompting Dulles to reply quietly that this was not true and that the tradition would come again to have its day. Even then I considered the put-down to be slick and superficial, which is why I remember it.

By his own criteria, and in the public mind, Hesburgh was a spectacular success. During his reign at Notre Dame as president from 1952 to 1987, the annual budget went from $10 million to $176 million, and the endowment from $9 million to $350 million.

In 1967, he convened a meeting of carefully chosen Catholic educators at the Land O'Lakes villa in Wisconsin, where they issued a formal declaration of Catholic university autonomy and academic freedom: freedom from all external authority, lay or clerical. Oxford and Cambridge, Harvard and Yale had all originated as Christian institutions which secularised, and most of the US Catholic universities launched themselves enthusiastically onto this trajectory.

According to Miscamble, Hesburgh was central to this program, substituting the pursuit of truth with the pursuit of excellence, so that Catholicism no longer remained in the academic heart of the university, and "he neither completely recognized nor ever really admitted" this disaster.

With their optimism and managerial self-confidence, Hesburgh and his allies were not well placed to recognize the profound changes wrought by the sexual revolution of the '60s sparked by the invention of the contraceptive pill.

Mankowski quotes Christopher Caldwell, who wrote that after 1968 "the Left split into a 'socialist' political wing and a 'Woodstock' lifestyle wing ... the Woodstock limb survived, and the socialist tree collapsed."[13]

Hesburgh had been on the board of directors of the Rockefeller Foundation since 1961, always objecting to their abortion programs, but after he was hissed into silence at Yale in 1973 because of a few sentences denouncing abortion, he spoke little or never on the topic afterward. Not surprisingly, he was not an enthusiast for Pope John Paul II.

[13] Christopher Caldwell, "1968", *Weekly Standard*, 6 September 1998.

The Woodstock life-style victory meant that it has become almost impossible for pro-life and pro-family candidates to be nominated for the Democratic Party in the US. I warned a succession of [Australian Labor Party] ALP leaders and prime ministers about the danger of a similar development here in Australia. We are not at that stage now. Ironically, Turnbull[14] tried to get rid of the social conservatives before Shorten[15] could be tempted.

Who was it who said, "Hell is truth seen too late"?

Wednesday, 12 June 2019

A quiet day, with heavy rain crossing the state—up to 20 ml. I think that is nearly one inch, because I still pass instinctively to imperial measure. My mother, after Australia had switched to decimal currency and dollars, would sometimes ask, "How much is that in real money?" I remember a friend of my age explaining that a family was seriously wealthy: "They were pound millionaires."

Spent some time finishing off yesterday's lengthy diary entry. Much shorter today. Took both exercise sessions in the drizzle, but the puddles showed heavy rain during the day.

Only two birthday cards yesterday, and a good letter from my niece Rebecca today.

Kartya, who had recovered from a migraine attack, came for a visit, and we discussed the trial. She is cautious but optimistic. We both sympathized with [Christopher] Boyce (for the prosecution) who had been saddled with such a weak case. Apparently, we will receive one or two days' notice before the verdict is delivered.

Rebecca, my niece, who is a good letter writer, usually concludes with one or two quotations. This is the one she chose today from Pope Francis.

It is no easy task to overcome the bitter legacy of injustices, hostility, and mistrust left by conflict. It can only be done by overcoming evil with good.

---

[14] Malcolm Turnbull (b. 1954) was prime minister of Australia from 2015 to 2018 and served twice as leader of the Liberal Party.

[15] William Richard Shorten (b. 1967) was leader of the Australian Labor Party from 2013 to 2019.

Thursday, 13 June 2019

Being in jail means a prisoner is not in charge. This does not result from ill will, with some exceptions, but from the design of the system. It cannot and should not be otherwise.

On Tuesday, June 6th, the day before my appeal commenced, I realised that my volume 2 of the breviary ceased on Pentecost Sunday, so I phoned Chris Meney, who I knew to be driving down on the 5th, to ask him to obtain my breviary from the seminary and bring it with him. He did so and left the book of prayers with the lawyers. I phoned and urged haste, but Kartya was ill and did not bring the missing item yesterday. Here's hoping it will at least be in the prison today to come up at some stage.

When I was consecrated as an auxiliary bishop in 1987, Fr Peter Cross, who was on the staff of Corpus Christi College seminary with me, commented, "This means you will spend the rest of your life doing as you are told." He was right—in part. A couple of years younger than I, he gained a first-class honours degree in Oxford and was learned and astute. He didn't publish much, but was good-humoured and a gentleman. He was mortally offended when, at a staff meeting, I denounced the philosophy the seminarians had to study as "Existentialist flimflam". While he differed from me on what he thought best for the Church, he normally coped with a wry smile when I erred. I had not intended to offend him, but he thought I had gone one step too far. Actually, the exchange reflected an important difference between us on the type of philosophy priests-to-be need. One major reason why priests are able to contribute so much to society derives from their philosophy studies, which develop their capacity to think, to analyse and synthesize. And I think priests should have more than a nodding acquaintance with the thought of Thomas Aquinas.

At public events, you are always told what to do, and I followed instructions. Once I literally brought the house down, at the opening of the refurbished Cathedral Hall on the Melbourne Campus of Australian Catholic University, when the ten-metre-high scaffolding hidden by the curtains collapsed slowly on the stage as I was speaking. Thank God no one was hurt. At public events, the bishop is never alone and follows instructions.

At a deeper level, too, priests, bureaucrats, and lay faithful are often clear about what they want the bishop to do, and a bishop needs strength and imagination to choose correctly. The second, and equally important, part of the paedophilia crisis is the folly of the bishops, which was not universal. Few bishops, if any, suspected the enormity of the crisis; few, even among the experts, recognized the extent of personal damage done to many victims, but it was easier to deal with the problem as the whole of society was coping with it and follow inherited patterns. Sometimes the bishops need to refuse to do what they are told, and the Australian bishops faced up to the paedophilia crisis in the mid-1990s and changed course. The results were not perfect, but it was a sea change.

Bureaucrats in Catholic education, health, welfare, aged care, etc., will want to have the last word in their areas, but that belongs to the bishops. The pressure for all those agencies to secularize is innate and powerful, and one of the bishops' tasks is to ensure God is not sidelined. Pope Benedict and Cardinal Sarah[16] are correct in asserting that the absence of God is at the heart of our problems, and if a bishop has to reject advice or public opinion to return God to centre stage or keep him there, so be it.

The sky was clear and the weather crisp as I took my two exercise sessions. I managed to contact my sister on the second call, spoke to Bernadette [Tobin] as she flew to Canada, and had a good half-hour visit with [friend] Peter Tellefson.

Just as it was important for me not to become preoccupied by the months ahead of me, so when I entered jail, I needed to focus on my daily routine rather than wondering when the verdict might be delivered. Still using a Lectio Divina style of meditation with Matthew's Gospel, but meditated more easily under the clear sky of the exercise pen.

We might be near, but it is certainly not yet. A verse from Bishop Lancelot Andrewes'[17] hymn to God the Father ["The Dial"] captures something of my situation.

---

[16] Robert Cardinal Sarah (b. 1945) was appointed prefect of the Congregation for Divine Worship and the Discipline of the Sacraments by Pope Francis in 2014.

[17] Lancelot Andrewes (1555–1626) was a scholar and a bishop in the Church of England during the reigns of Elizabeth I and James I, greatly admired by St John Henry Newman.

Thou who has willed the ninth hour to be an
    hour of prayer:
Hear us while we pray in the hour of prayer and
Make us to obtain our prayer and our desires
    and save us.

Friday, 14 June 2019

Richmond were beaten by Adelaide last night by three points, but they struggled well, led for half the game with (we claim) nine out of their best thirteen players injured. Dusty Martin is again playing well, but I still don't think he has the magic he displayed in 2017, when the team was close to its peak.

Unusually the birds were chirping merrily when I took my morning exercise, although I couldn't see them. The day was cool, the sky clear, and with extra time I managed fifteen minutes of meditation as well as my rosary while I was walking.

During my three months as a guest of Her Majesty, about half a dozen people have sent me copies of the Surrender Prayer composed by Fr Dolindo Ruotolo, a Neapolitan priest, who died in 1970. In my ignorance, I had not heard of either the prayer or its author.

Born into a miserably poor family, living in a hovel with a father who was physically and psychologically violent, Fr Ruotolo only escaped at the age of fourteen into a Catholic boarding school. It was here that his vocation developed so that he became a seminarian and was ordained priest (in some unnamed religious order) in 1906.

After working in Naples, he was transferred to the Taranto seminary, where things started to go wrong when he objected to moral depravity among some seminarians. I only have access to one article, which was sent to me, and so have limited information on precisely why he had twenty years of trouble with Church authorities. His faculties to celebrate Mass were removed, and he could not even receive Communion. During his banishment to the Diocese of Rossano, he received apparitions from the Lord and Our Lady and the gifts of prophecy and reading souls. In 1910, he surrendered himself completely to the will of God, and later that year the Vatican declared his innocence and restored his priestly faculties. On a second occasion, he was suspended by Rome and even spent a few weeks in a priests' prison. He was suspended a third time, cleared in 1921, but only had his faculties to celebrate Mass and the sacraments restored in 1937. He remained a priest and did not criticise the authorities.

He has near perfect credentials to talk to us about accepting God's will. The response, in the prayer's English version, is "O Jesus, I surrender myself to you, take care of everything." I have no problem with this prayer for accepting God's will, although this may be difficult; no difficulty in believing in God's providence.

However, I discontinued the novena after a few days because the prayers stated that accepting God's will requires us to close our eyes and rest, not be active for any particular solution. I was busy working to establish my innocence, believing that God has no hands but ours—while fully accepting that God works through others, sometimes in unexpected ways. This is true in my case.

Part of the problem might be in the English translation "Jesus ... take care of everything." The Italian is "Gesù, pensaci tu", which literally means "You, Jesus, think of us", which might be expanded to "You, Jesus, look after us." The Italian in that phrase doesn't ask God to take care of everything![18]

It is always best to accept God's will and, when everything has been done, not to lament or complain, whatever the outcome. So I am not sure of the extent of my problem with the Surrender Prayer.

A very different approach to suffering was expressed in one of the first letters of support I received from a Melbourne doctor, who had been a couple of years ahead of me at St Pat's in Ballarat and who also supported me with daily prayer. He learnt from his mother the verse chiselled in stone beneath the statue of Adam Lindsay Gordon,[19] next to the Victorian Parliament. Unfortunately, Gordon took his own life, which adds poignancy to his lines.

> *Life is mostly froth and bubble,*
> *Some things stand like stone,*
> *Friendship in another's trouble,*
> *Courage in your own.*

---

[18] The cardinal is translating literally, but in colloquial Italian, "Pensaci tu" means "You take care of it."

[19] Adam Lindsay Gordon (1833–1870) was an Australian poet (the first to be recognized internationally), horseman, police officer, and politician.

Saturday, 15 June 2019

Yesterday's memorial service for Bob Hawke[20] depressed me, but only for one reason. Everything was well done and not repetitive, which is unusual for funeral eulogies; the music included Handel's "Hallelujah Chorus", the Sydney Opera House was full, and 1,500 people were outside. But there was not one word spoken about God or Christ or life after death, if we leave to one side the chorus.

Bob was the son of a Protestant church minister, and his loss of faith is typical of many of his generation. And unfortunately, this trend has gathered force with the years. It is not universal, e.g., many of our recent prime ministers are Christians with faith. Nonetheless, I found it sad and offered up my rosary for him when I was called out for exercise immediately after the celebration.

Today is or was my deceased father's birthday. I owe him and my mother a lot. I only realised how good they were when I began to encounter many other parents as a young priest.

I always realised that Mum and Dad would do any good thing in their power to help us. Dad did not complete his secondary education, was a champion swimmer and boxer (ranked the second-best heavyweight in Australia and the British Empire), and no good at Aussie Rules and cricket (according to his brother). He inherited no money, made a lot of money, and then lost it (when the mining shares collapsed), and he successfully ran a small hotel for twenty-five years. He had a short fuse and was a master of the English-Australian language as it was spoken by Anglos in the first half of the twentieth century: terse, to the point, and colourful. He insisted on a good education for all of us, including my sister, because he said that his lack of university qualifications had barred him from senior positions. He was nominally an Anglican, tone deaf religiously, and my mother felt he never became a Catholic (although he called all of us for early morning Mass) out of loyalty to his mother, who was a genuine anti-Catholic. One of Dad's sisters announced that my studying for the priesthood was a disgrace to the Pell family, so he wrote to all his siblings dissociating himself from those views. His genes have helped

[20] Robert Hawke (1929–2019) was prime minister of Australia and leader of the Labor Party from 1983 to 1991.

me survive my few months in jail, but, more than that, I am sustained and inspired by his strength and persistence. I hope and expect he is resting in peace.

By coincidence I received a welcome letter today from Paul, one of my Pell cousins. Margaret had mentioned recently that we had not heard from them, and Paul explained he had only just learnt my address from Fr Michael Moore, rector of the Redemptoris Mater Seminary in Perth.

A few of the letters I have received are sad, but not many, not even among those from my fellow prisoners. I have received around thirty such letters, but, to my surprise when I counted, from only ten or so prisoners. Writing is useful therapy in a prison, and one prisoner has written thirteen letters, full of goodwill and containing good advice.

A couple of days ago, I heard of a Catholic fellow in Spain condemned to eleven years in prison on uncorroborated sex charges against minors. He is protesting his innocence and is on probation under house arrest until his appeal is heard around the end of the year. A couple of letters from the US listed similar cases there, where one priest is jailed for twenty-five years, while claiming he is innocent. And we have the infamous Billy Doe scam in Philadelphia.

My time in jail is no picnic, but it pales into holiday time when compared with some other jail experiences. My good friend Jude Chen, originally from Shanghai and now living in Canada, wrote of his family's imprisonment under the Chinese Communists.

In 1958, Jude's brother, Paul, a seminarian, and sister, Sophie, at high school, were jailed for their Catholicism, and spent thirty years in two different jails, Sophie's being in the cold of northern China. The family was allowed a monthly fifteen-minute visit when they were in a Shanghai jail and a letter of a hundred words per month for the three decades.

Jude's grandfather Simon, who had been a wealthy man, building a parish church dedicated to the Holy Trinity, had all his property confiscated. Jude loved him, and they lived in the same house for nine years until the old man died. Jude recounts that when asked about his confiscated property, he replied, "Everything was from God and shall be returned to God."

After the Cultural Revolution began in the spring of 1966, the Red Guards raided their house and were disappointed to find Grandfather

Simon dead. So, they destroyed his grave, ransacked the house, forcing Jude's mother to burn all their religious objects. Jude's father was sacked as a teacher, reduced to janitor.

Aged eleven and in primary school, Jude was forced to confess to his forty classmates that he was a criminal from a criminal family. He can still remember his teacher telling his fellow students to give him a wide berth.

At seventeen years of age, Jude himself was sent to a labour camp for eight years in a Shanghai suburb. As he was leaving, his parents instructed him, "Jude, keep no hatred in your heart but only love." This is the holy fuel which powers the Church.

My new breviary has just arrived (at about 2:20 pm) and was exchanged for my volume 2.

Jude's grandfather Simon used to pray for small troubles to come along, so that he would not become proud, so that his heart would not harden, so that he did not become insensitive to the transcendent and unable to recognize God at work. And if these small challenges did not emerge, he was afraid great problems might come to sweep him away. His misfortunes could scarcely have been greater, but his faith and love endured.

WEEK 17

Mystery of the Trinity

16 June–22 June 2019

Trinity Sunday, 16 June 2019

> Firmly I believe and truly
> God is three and God is one;
> And I next acknowledge duly
> Manhood taken by the Son.

My mother was pleased that I was born on Trinity Sunday, insisting it was a great feast, subordinate of course to Christmas, Easter, and Pentecost. I was not short of parental love, especially because my parents had lost twins the year before my birth, one stillborn, the other dying after a few days.

Mum was ambitious for us, for our education and for our music. Her family had some good musicians, and we grew up singing Irish and some Scottish songs around the piano. My sister, who played for thirty years in the first-violin section of the Melbourne Symphony Orchestra, cleaned up nearly all the musical talent (although I have sung Pooh-Bah from *The Mikado* on two continents!). However, my mother's proudest achievement was handing on the Irish faith of her fathers to her three children. One of seven sisters, formidable women all of them, they did not need the feminist movement to boost their self-confidence. She was a woman of faith and prayer, deeply Catholic.

As a young priest, I found it difficult to preach on the Trinitarian aspects of the one true God, although I realised early on that God was slipping in the rankings. I would say now we were becoming too anthropocentric, too centred on one another, too horizontal and not vertical enough. So, I mentioned God and his love frequently, while the mystery of the Trinity left me short of insight and ideas for my sermons and articles.

I remember claiming in an article in *Light*, the monthly magazine of the Ballarat Diocese, that there was more devotion to the Little Flower than there was to the Holy Spirit. This was not true in many places, because the charismatic movement had sprung up unbidden after the Second Vatican Council, but it was not strong in our country diocese.

I was baffled by the claim of the Australian theologian and apologist Frank Sheed, who spent his adult life in England, married Maisie Ward, an author in her own right, and founded Sheed and Ward, the Catholic publishing house. Sheed claimed that people were always deeply interested when he spoke to them about the Trinity, and he was a regular outdoor speaker in Hyde Park, London, for many years. His *Theology and Sanity* is still a good book.

I was always conscious that God was one and have never preached incautiously to imply that somehow there were three gods. The most important point to stress is that God is a mystery of love beyond all telling, who sent his Son to take on a human nature and live with us and who is present among us as the Spirit of Love.

Eventually, in trying to explain the transcendent mystery of love, which God is, beyond all creation, I used to begin with the reality of a good father's love for his children—that powerful, invisible force, which is so needed by children.

I don't like those Trinitarian images where the Father is a powerful, broad-shouldered, elderly man with a beard, and the Spirit is represented by the traditional dove. The human image of the Father is distracting and distorting, especially for us materialist Australians, taking us away from the spiritual, the supernatural, the transcendent. For God, I prefer the icons of the Eastern Christians, and the Maronites have good catechetical material on the Trinity to cope with the objections of the Muslims.

A couple of days ago, I received a beautiful photo of a two-year-old child gazing upward through the slanted light and shadows from a forest of towering and slender redwood trees in Rotorua, New Zealand. The sender was an Australian scientist, and he called the photo a science Christmas card.

He quoted Albert Einstein (or Eugene Wigner, also a Nobel Prize winner) to the effect that creation consists of two miracles. The first is "that the universe exists", and the second is "that we know it exists". The redwood forest represents the universe, and the unseen photographer represents God the Father Almighty. My correspondent sees the young child as "the dawning of human consciousness", which for present purposes I see as also representing the Christ Child, while the Spirit is symbolized by the beautiful light (my interpretation).

This imagery helps the scientist affirm his belief as he recites the opening of the Nicene Creed: "I believe in God the Father Almighty, Creator of all things seen and unseen."

There are hymns which men and boys will sing and hymns which they won't sing. One of the most vivid memories of my school chapel at Ballarat is of three hundred young men, boarders, singing "We Stand for God" and "Faith of Our Fathers". It is a moot point how much was a tribal anthem, but the faith was real, too. To be done properly, the hymns have to be sung with sentiment, loudly, slowly, piously, and with a hint of menace. One or two choirmasters with a Protestant background were never able to get their choirs to capture this dimension and used to breeze through them as though they were "Pop Goes the Weasel".

Sixty years later, I experienced the same phenomenon at Sunday-night Mass for the boarders at St Joseph's College, Sydney, as they sang "Ancient Words". When I complimented the headmaster, he replied, "Yes, it's a great hymn for men; the sort of tune you would use to invade Poland." Grace works through human nature.

I thought I had mastered the alarm on my prison watch, but I hadn't and missed *Mass for You at Home*, and I couldn't muster the courage to watch *Hillsong*. My solicitors Paul and Kartya came for a chat, and I missed my second exercise session. No harm done.

I will close with "St Patrick's Breastplate":

> *I bind unto myself the name,*
> *The strong name of the Trinity:*
> *By invocation of the same,*
> *The Three in One and One in Three;*
> *Of whom all nature hath creation,*

Eternal Father, Spirit, Word;
Praise to the Lord of my salvation—
Salvation is of Christ the Lord! Amen.

Monday, 17 June 2019

I discovered that I had mastered the workings of my watch when, this morning, while dozing and half awake, I heard the faintest sound of an alarm. I am not surprised that I slept through it.

The most spectacular development of the day was that Tim O'Leary was turned away from visiting me for the second time. When told that an unauthorised visitor was below, I managed to find the form where I had placed him on the list, but I also discovered another form, from two months earlier, which I had used recently to add Steve Lawrence's name. Unfortunately, a crossed-out, already registered deletion of Tim's name was mistakenly used to cancel him again. I was unaware of this, as they don't give a list of those registered unless it is requested. I huffed and puffed a bit, but later explained to the warder, who was the messenger, that I wasn't blaming him! I should not have used a pre-used form and should have made the situation crystal clear. While this depends somewhat on the personalities involved, the system is not designed to identify and resolve problems; so, difficulties like this are not uncommon and sometimes not unwelcomed. I phoned Tim this afternoon, and he was his usual gracious self both to me and earlier with the prison staff.

I had two longer sessions in the exercise pen, under a clear sky. But in the morning, it felt the coldest I have experienced in jail.

As my volume 3 of the breviary has arrived, I am now moving through week eleven of Ordinary Time. The first reading was from the Book of Judges (4:1–24), where Jael, the wife of Heber the Kenite, used her hammer to put a tent peg through the temple of the sleeping Sisera, the commander of the army of Jabin, King of Canaan, who had unwisely fled to her for refuge after his defeat by the Jewish troops under Barak, who had been induced to join battle by Deborah the prophetess. Two formidable women.

The second reading is from St Cyprian's treatise on the Lord's Prayer, which will run through this week. The finest theologians in the Western world in the patristic period came from the prosperous and fertile Roman province in North Africa, the granary for Rome. The first of these was Tertullian, who straddled the turn of the second and third centuries, then St Cyprian, bishop of Carthage, who was martyred in 258, and the finest of them all, St Augustine, who died in Hippo in 430 as the Vandals were besieging North Africa.

The world was coming out of a warm period, with temperatures similar to our own and hotter than the medieval warming to come; Britain was a Roman frontier province, not distinguished in any way, on the edge of the known world, while Ireland was not in the Roman Empire and was unusual because it didn't have any cities. In the East, Alexandria was the leading theological centre of the Catholic world rivalled only by Antioch.

The emperor lived in Constantinople after 330, and the papacy was asserting itself more and more in the ancient capital of Rome without an emperor. By a quirk of fate, I know as much, or more, about Cyprian, and from the primary sources, than I know about any other saint or writer; but, apart from the few years when I lectured in early Church history, I have rarely written or spoken publicly about him. I am not regretting this, merely noting it, because in the Catholic Church, particularly in a smallish Australian Church, many finish up working in unexpected areas, different from their first area of expertise. I thank God for the opportunities I had to serve in a variety of ways. It suited my temperament and my abilities.

The letters continue to come, various and thought-provoking. One regular correspondent from Dallas told of her love for hymn singing, so she feels "part of the worldwide community of Christians, centuries of believers who remind me God is faithful".

She also recounted the story of a Harvard neuroscientist and surgeon who had a near-death experience for which he could find no scientific explanation. A parishioner and friend of mine had one such experience, which he told me about, and after it he had not the slightest fear of dying.

The retired physicist from New Zealand who sent the science-parable photo wrote that he hopes that when released I "will continue to speak and write with clarity in appropriate forums on the case for belief in God", which he considers "every bit as crucial to the survival of civilization as the current physical threat global warming poses".

Francis Thompson's "In No Strange Land" beckons our "benumb'd conceiving".

> O world invisible, we view thee,
> O world intangible, we touch thee,
> O world unknowable, we know thee,
> Inapprehensible, we clutch thee!
>
> The angels keep their ancient places;—
> Turn but a stone, and start a wing!
> 'Tis ye, 'tis your estranged faces,
> That miss the many-splendour'd thing.

Tuesday, 18 June 2019

The sky was overcast during my morning exercise, and cold, but not bitterly cold, despite 20cm [8 in] of new snow at Mt Hotham. No better in the afternoon.

Swept out my cell, a weekly exercise, and dusted the surrounds. Was even offered Harpic, a disinfectant for the toilet, an extra that I never knew was available.

Letters and articles continue to arrive, provoking thought from a number of different directions. One good woman, who wrote on the feast of St Germanus (28 May) expressed her belief that "Jesus has allowed this injustice ... to bring about the salvation of your accuser." If that is God's will, I have no problem with the proposition, and even if it isn't, I still have no problem with my participation. Certainly, the accuser is not describing anything that happened with me, but while he is troubled, I don't know his state of mind and soul, don't know the percentages of fantasy and fiction. And we all need to be saved. I don't even know the country this woman is from.

Mary, probably from Australia, emailed me with the following message, promising me prayers and Masses, as "the lucky ones get a greater share in Our Lord's Passion." She then added, "There is a thinking among those who attend church that you are innocent, but it is only right that you should suffer for the guilty." We have no suggestion from her that this thinking is compatible with justice in the courts, and it is an extension of the proposition that "we are not sure if he is guilty, but some leader from the 'old church' needs to be punished." I would not volunteer for such a role, but I am keen for my sad misadventure to make a bad situation better, and not make things worse. And for this I need exoneration.

Bernadette sent an article on religion in Australia from Henry Ergas, writing as wisely as ever in his column in *The Australian*. He claims, presumably as a non-believer (but I am not sure of this), that "we increasingly struggle both to understand faith and to respect it."[1] The problem with Israel Folau, sacked from playing for any rugby union team, is not that he is an evangelist, but that he won't keep his mouth shut!

The origins of the prohibitions on offensive speech are traced to the medieval world in Germany and France as well as England. Ergas quotes the philosopher of toleration John Locke (1632–1706), who initially favoured laws prohibiting dissident sects, but then dramatically reversed course because the laws were abused, provoking animosity and encouraging hypocrisy.

Tertullian wrote eighteen hundred years ago that the blood of martyrs is the seed of the Church, while Ergas is more restrained, limiting himself to "Time and again, however, faith has proved a tough nut to crack." He is absolutely correct.

The deplorables have enjoyed some victories lately and not just with Trump and Brexit, but here in Australia. The new development is that being a serious Christian, not just a card carrier, is now enough to list you among the deplorables. Our present and coming adversity will revitalize the Catholic Church by forcing many to consider just what is at stake in the Christian message and whether this is worth preserving. The number of people without faith, ex-Catholics and nonpractising Catholics, who have become active defenders of my cause is considerable. One doctor from Pymble wrote that perhaps my travesty "will reignite the hearts of Catholics who until now have been complacent and mute".

A welcome two-page letter arrived a few days ago from Fr Paul Mankowski in Chicago quoting a 1989 talk of Professor John Finnis from Oxford University on St Thomas More's condemnation in Westminster Hall on 1 July 1535. Paul explained that this excerpt

[1] Henry Ergas, "Evangelising Is Any Good Christian's Calling", *Australian*, 7 June 2019.

speaks more profoundly than he could "about the realities of your predicament and about the deeper meaning of the witness you have been called to give". After he was condemned, More told his judges that he prayed that, like St Paul and St Stephen, all of them "may yet here after in heaven merrily all meet together, to our everlasting salvation". Left unspoken was any reference to the necessity of St Paul's conversion.

Finnis concluded his reflections by quoting from More's *Dialogue of Comfort against Tribulation*, which shows that he knows atheists are not rare and how "even the faithful recoil with revulsion from reflecting on the prospect of hell." Four and a half centuries later, atheism is much stronger, and the revulsion deepened. I myself have written on how many reject a God who judges. Finnis insists that this part of the Gospel must be taken seriously and that "the failure to take this responsibility seriously . . . is the heart of the crisis of faith and morals. Only if we do take it seriously can we experience a hope, which goes beyond words, to meet St Thomas More, merrily, in heaven."

In the margin of his Latin prayer book, More penned this prayer:

> *Give me thy grace, good Lord . . .*
> *To walk the narrow way that leadeth to life,*
> *To bear the cross with Christ;*
> *To have the last thing in remembrance,*
> *To have ever afore mine eye my death, that is ever*
>   *at hand;*
> *To make death no stranger to me,*
> *To foresee and consider the everlasting fire of hell;*
> *To pray for pardon before the judge come. . . .*

Wednesday, 19 June 2019

Sr Mary, the prison chaplain, came yesterday for our weekly Communion service, which I so appreciate. I suspect she is less mobile than she was a couple of months ago, but she strongly rejects any such suggestion. She has done this good work for more than twenty-five years and told me she learnt something on every day of dealing with the prisoners.

We were only disturbed once during her hour-long visit, when I had to return to my cell while another inmate was transferred. "Solitary" means no contact with any other prisoner, and I have not seen one of my fellows in Unit 8. As usual, life went on noisily around us during our paraliturgy, perhaps louder than ever.

Sr Mary always brings me a couple of sermons on the previous Sunday's readings which we use each Tuesday. The better of the two is usually Sr Mary McGlone's, taken, as I subsequently discovered, from the *National Catholic Reporter*, which I have not read regularly for nearly fifty years. Its rival in the United States, the *National Catholic Register*, on the other hand, has been a regular champion of my cause and generally of the causes I support. However, by every standard, her sermons are excellent.

However, on this Trinity Sunday, I awarded the prize to the anonymous author from the Marists. He had a number of useful and appropriate images hinting at, and illuminating, the mystery of the Trinity.

One such image, which I had never used myself, was to compare the Trinity to three different notes sounded together to produce a harmonious chord.

I had on a number of occasions urged my listeners not to be like dogs at a concert, who, when confronted by the spiritual and transcendental, hear all the sounds and none of the music.

Not all music leads to God or comes from God, as Wagner shows in his own compositions. The "Pilgrims' Chorus" from *Tannhäuser*, which the choir of my college in Rome, Propaganda Fide, sang at the dinner immediately after our priestly ordination in Rome on 16 December 1966 and which the St Mary's Choir sang at my last Mass as archbishop in Sydney (a surprise which moved me deeply), is very different from the music of Venusberg.[2]

But some music is godly, such as the two *Passions* (Matthew and John) of J. S. Bach or Mozart's "Ave Verum Corpus" or Elgar's *The Dream of Gerontius*.

What chord would best express, give the best hint about, the nature of the one true God, Creator of the universe, who loves each person so much that he sent his Son to suffer for us?

---

[2] Richard Wagner's opera *Tannhäuser* (1845) tells the story of a legendary knight who dwells for a time in Venusberg, the land of the goddess of love, and then seeks forgiveness for his sins through a pilgrimage to Rome.

It is a legitimate question, but for someone else to answer. I don't know enough about musical theory, and I am not sure what exactly I would be listening for, how to define the question more fully. The right music does help us lift our hearts and minds to God, and Albert Einstein, among the greatest scientists but an indifferent musician, famously exclaimed after hearing a beautiful piece of music: "Now I know there is a God."

Getting a little toey as I wait for the verdict to be handed down, but I take my mind back to my daily routine of prayer, exercise, writing, reading, Sudoku. One of the senior officers, H, a fellow Richmond supporter, called to see how I was and whether I had any complaints. None. I explained truthfully that I was well but would want to shift out of solitary confinement if, by some disaster, my appeal was unsuccessful. He thought that would not be necessary and was optimistic about the appeal.

The canteen had no Cadbury's chocolate, so a little involuntary penance is needed until stocks are replenished. The weather is cold, but there were bursts of sunshine and light clouds during my morning exercise.

Worked to clarify my visitors' lists. Apparently, mishaps, like Tim O'Leary's, are not rare. Kartya called; no news about when the verdict might be handed down. She will not be in the office for the next couple of days.

I have just heard from Kartya that Jaidyn Stephenson, a young, fair-haired Aussie Rules football star from Collingwood, has been stood down for ten games and fined $20,000 with another twelve games out as a suspended sentence for gambling on the football. A small number of bets for small amounts have been mentioned. The punishment seems extraordinary and excessive. The Irish-Australian women used to say that it was preferable to be married to an alcoholic rather than a gambler, as you were less likely to lose the house with a drunkard. We certainly don't want the game damaged by gambling, as international cricket has been, but ... Life is full of surprises. While I have never met the man, I would have thought him to be among the least likely culprits. If he has a habit, I hope he can best it.

As for myself, I need to continue with my daily routine in calm and patience. St Thomas More's last prayer before his execution will help.

Lord, give me patience in tribulation, and grace in everything to conform my will to thine, that I may truly say: "Thy will be done on earth as it is in heaven." The things, good Lord, that I pray for, give me thy grace to labour for. Amen.

Thursday, 20 June 2019

The unit is unusually quiet today, so our banger might have been transferred elsewhere. I saw from the board that two out of the twelve cells are vacant and another one is "reserved".

Received about thirty letters today after a couple of quiet days. At least twice a week, according to one of the warders, a couple are outside the prison praying during the daylight hours. Apparently, they travel by train for three hours each way, according to my informant. I don't deserve such support or the prayers from all over Australia and many other countries, especially the US, England, and then Ireland. Many of the letter writers perceive an increasing hostility against the Church.

The dreamer who foresaw a dramatic release for me around my trial date has written again as things, on that particular point, did not turn out as he predicted.

He still predicts that I will be freed and that the complainant will run into serious trouble after the trial. He also expanded at much greater length on how he saw his own role. This disturbed me, because it was unusual in every sense and no inducement to judge him as reliable. I am not doubting that he dreams, but predictions from dreams are a different matter. His predictions could even be the provisional theories of someone who has studied the scene at some depth. And J will be in some sort of trouble if my exoneration is clear-cut.

Another woman who only gave her Christian name and did not even name the district she comes from, asked my prayers for herself and her children and her husband, whom she described as a good man. He has been captured by pornography and so far cannot break the habit.

He is not alone, because internet porn is a new scourge and another destroyer of marriages and families. It is no longer just a male weakness, and young addicts can be turned off human sexual activity as an imperfect, insufficient second best. I miss not being able to offer Mass for such requests at this moment, and I certainly added that man and his family to my prayer list.

I spent most of the day, apart from my routine activities, dealing with the mail and preparing some thoughts on Fr Alexander Sherbrooke's[3] analysis of Church life, starting in Soho Square, London. I will probably pen a few thoughts tomorrow.

Tim and Anne McFarlane visited, after arriving back from Salzburg on Tuesday. Tim's talk on mediation went well, and he believes that Victoria leads the world in the number of disputes it successfully mediates. One judge from the US, who does mediations, explained that in his practice the two sides never come face to face. "Well," replied Tim "you wouldn't get a job in Victoria!" Apparently, it was my old Melbourne friend Chief Justice John Phillips who introduced this mediation system to cope with a huge backlog of cases through a spring and then an autumn offensive. Both were successful and continue today in the mediation system.

A regular correspondent from Swanston Street, Melbourne, thinks that some of my opposition is demonic, and so do I, while she wondered if I would think it odd if she claimed that at the appeal the "the Holy Spirit was with you and his presence was made known through all the courtroom." I totally agree. She was thankful "that this time, the proceedings were open and transparent, and people were able to assess for themselves what this was all about." Once again, I agree completely and feel both my short- and long-term interests are best served by making the facts available and accessible. She was also pleased I wore my priestly collar.

Anne McFarlane informed me that [Nathan] Buckley, the Collingwood coach, has defended his young star Stephenson against the severity of the sentence for gambling on his matches. I phoned Paul Galbally, my solicitor from a traditional Collingwood family, urging him also to give some public support for the lad. I fear the AFL leadership has been infected with political correctness, forgetting that many of its followers are "deplorables" or worse.

---

[3] Fr Alexander Sherbrooke is a priest of the Westminster Diocese who has served St Patrick's Church in Soho Square since 2001, guiding a remarkable renovation of both the church itself and the life of its parish.

I have always admired St Joseph, being quite sure that many of Our Lord's best masculine qualities have come to him, not through nature, but through the nurture of his foster father Joseph. But I have prayed to him or through him rarely. These lines are offered in reparation.

O St Joseph, assist me by your powerful intercession, and obtain for me from your Divine Son all spiritual blessings, through Jesus Christ Our Lord, so that having engaged here below your heavenly power, I may offer my thanksgiving and homage to the most loving of Fathers.

Friday, 21 June 2019

Today is the feast of St Aloysius Gonzaga, a young Jesuit seminarian who died at the age of twenty-three in 1591, after being stricken with the plague while working with the sick. From the noble Castiglione family, he was born near Mantua in Italy.

Today's breviary reading is an excerpt from a letter to his mother while he was dying, which is formal, but loving, and with some remarkable teaching on heaven. While we should pray for our faith to be strong at the time of death, and therefore, in the traditional terms, for a happy death, the joys and, indeed, the reality of heaven constitute a better topic for meditation than the "passing over" experience itself.

Aloysius tells his mother that he is overwhelmed by the divine goodness, "which is as deep as the sea and as boundless" and which is summoning him to eternal rest for so "short and trifling a service". He asks for his mother's blessing "as I cross this sea toward that shore where all my hopes are centred".

The recognition of the dignity and role of the laity, the overwhelming majority of the baptised, is one of the finest fruits of the Second Vatican Council, but the decline and, indeed, death of many religious orders in the Western world is one of the saddest developments in the postconciliar Church. The Jesuits are a front-runner in this decline.

I have often said that I would like to see the swathe Ignatius of Loyola would cut if he were to return for a time. However, we know from the New Testament that no one would listen to him; they would just psychologize away his message as coming from an earlier, more ignorant age.

I knew Pope Francis, a Jesuit, had his own problems with the Jesuits, and I had spoken with him about the need for reform. So far we have, or at least I have, no evidence of progress. However, renewal is always possible, especially for a tradition as valid as that of Ignatius. If enough good young Jesuits can survive the formation process, God will certainly bless them and might reward them by allowing more pockets of Gospel vitality to flourish.

The sky is almost clear, the light is bright, it is cold, and showers are about. Twenty or so letters were delivered, and I sought permission to phone Tim Fischer,[4] who is probably not far from eternity, due to cancer. Paul Galbally cut short my exercise session after I had said my rosary, and we discussed the severity of the Stephenson penalty (the young footballer) and the time line for my verdict. Paul conjectured this would be long enough to produce a water-tight document, mindful that an innocent man is in prison. I don't think we can conjecture more reasonably than this.

I have mentioned Fr Alexander Sherbrooke's reflections after sixty years of life and thirty as a priest. Perhaps the best way to demonstrate what I think of their quality is to say that I intend to send a copy of them to special friends, a few archbishops, some key priests who would be open to his message. I don't agree with every one of the many points he makes, but it is a prophetic document, with a whiff of Savonarola, not so much about the future (where I hope he is somewhat pessimistic), but through its insights into our present situation and the only way forward.

Karen (from somewhere, with no surname) wrote that her husband was a supporter of mine, because he had "read that you took the Church back to the original teachings of the Bible, and he understands and agrees with you why you did it." I did try to do what Christ taught as this had come to us through the Church's Magisterium and practice.

Fr Alexander is working on the same basic lines in Soho, one of the centres for homosexuality in London, where life can be very raw and the poor and wounded are not in short supply.

---

[4] Tim Fischer was the Australian deputy prime minister from 1996 to 1999 and the Australian ambassador to the Holy See from 2009 to 2012. He died of leukaemia on 22 August 2019.

Pope Benedict has repeated that we don't need a new Church, and we don't need a new set of teachings. Fr Alexander points out that there is no easy answer, no magic bullet for renewal, and he is more pessimistic than I am about programs and strategies. World Youth Days still provoke conversions.

But he is absolutely right that we must contemplate Christ in prayer and in the sacraments, that the difficult business of striving for holiness has to be at the centre of any attempt at renewal. He speaks of Satan, of the need to repent of our sins, of the collapse of sexual discipline, of our distance from the poor, of the damage from the crisis of paedophilia and homosexuality, of our introspection, on "the unbridled and effective attack on the Church" weakened by scandals and poor morals, and on the grim reality that many outside the Church are no longer interested in what we say. I don't believe this is the whole truth, because if the hostile world believed that our teaching was not a provocation and that our forces are spent, they would leave us alone.

The Church is in decline but is still the Body of Christ, not the "old curiosity shop". Priests remain central to Church life, and the nine characteristics of priestly life are spelt out. A beautiful and dignified liturgical life is essential, and Alexander has a huge enthusiasm for prayer before the Blessed Sacrament, for silent adoration and its fruitfulness. All lovers of Christ and his Gospel will find much to ponder in these reflections.

Since the French Revolution in 1789, many European countries in many periods have been ruled by governments hostile to religion, anticlerical and sometimes persecutors. The Nazis and the Communists are not alone, and the religious peace in England since the Gordon Riots in 1780 (which coincided with considerable anti-Catholic prejudice)[5] is not typical of all the Continent. We are not sure whether the religious peace in Western Europe since the Second World War, when the West was remade by Catholic politicians like Charles de Gaulle, Konrad Adenauer, and Alcide de Gaspari[6] is going

---

[5] A London protest of the Papists Act of 1778, which was intended to reduce official discrimination against British Catholics, turned into several days of rioting.

[6] Charles de Gaulle led the Free French Forces in the Second World War and the French government afterward; Konrad Adenauer was the chancellor of West Germany from 1949 to 1963; and Alcide de Gaspari was prime minister of Italy from 1945 to 1953.

to be a precedent for the future or an aberration, an island of stability followed by steady hostile pressure or worse.

Some lines from T. S. Eliot's "Ash Wednesday" speak of our situation.

> *Where shall the word be found, where will the word*
> *Resound? Not here, there is not enough silence*
> *Not on the sea or on the islands, not*
> *On the mainland, in the desert or the rain land,*
> *For those who walk in darkness*
> *Both in the day time and in the night time*
> *The right time and the right place are not here*
> *No place of grace for those who avoid the face*
> *No time to rejoice for those who walk among noise*
>   *and deny the voice.*

Saturday, 22 June 2019

Seventy-eight years ago today, a fortnight after the day of my birth, Operation Barbarossa started. It was a Sunday when the Nazi troops, across a front that eventually stretched for 2,900 kilometres [1,800 miles], invaded Russia.

This unusual piece of information was sent to me by a prisoner in New Zealand, a professional man, who either had an interest in history or knew that I had.

The Allied landings in Normandy three years later involved about 155,000 men, but the battles on the eastern front involved more personnel than any other war in history.

Four million Axis soldiers invaded the western Soviet Union, supported by 600,000 motor vehicles, between 600,000 to 700,000 horses for non-military operations, and 3,000 planes.

The hatred and ferocity, the tenacity and heroism on both sides are beyond our pedestrian, day-to-day imagination. Stalin and Hitler had signed a nonaggression pact (which our Communist union leaders in Australia used to disrupt the war effort), so that Stalin refused to accept warnings of the invasion and went into psychological meltdown for some days after it occurred.

I have read Antony Beevor's history of the Battle of Stalingrad, ferocious beyond belief, and a Russian victory which was a turning point, and I have a framed copy of the Stalingrad Madonna, drawn on a wall in Stalingrad by a German Christian soldier, depicting Mary and the Christ Child surrounded by the words *Licht, Leben, Liebe* (Light, Life, Love), a poignant expression of faith. So terrible was the danger that Stalin had to wind back for a time his persecution of the Russian Orthodox Church to enlist its help in saving the Motherland.

The Nazi armies captured 5,000,000 Red Army troops, about 3,300,000 of whom died, and put in place a Hunger Plan to eliminate the Slavic population and replace them with German settlers. Their death squads also killed one million Soviet Jews. Hitler, as at the battles of Normandy, was a considerable help to the Allies because his orders to the German army to stand and fight caused unnecessary casualties in the German retreat.

Why mention such a tragedy and evil in a diary written in a humane prison in distant Australia? There are a few reasons. It reminds us of the blessings we enjoy in Australia, of a peace and prosperity most people in history have not enjoyed. It reminds us, not of the banality of evil, but of its sheer awfulness, of the death and destruction when the spirit of evil, Satan, is rampaging and triumphant. The Book of Revelation, heaven and hell, are seen in a new perspective on the Eastern Front. One young German told me that about a hundred young men from his village went into Russia, and three returned.

It reminds us, too, of the advantages we have in Australia from being so far away from the centres of power and from being surrounded by so much ocean. This provides no ultimate guarantee, but it is a big help.

St John Paul II visited Australia in 1973, before he was elevated to the papacy. He came from Poland, a country which was written out of history for decades, caught between Russia, Germany, and the Austro-Hungarian Empire. He was asked what he thought of Australia. He replied that he was amazed by our prosperity, and, secondly, he wondered how long we would be able to hang on, to remain in control.

We have a new banger and shouter in the unit, some poor fellow who only performs episodically but sometimes sounds very distressed.

It was drizzling when I exercised this morning, but fine in the mid-afternoon. A pie for lunch, warm and almost hot, once again a culinary high point for the week. Still no chocolates, so the penance continues.

A Josephite Sister from Lochinvar, elderly I suspect, sent me this prayer, which I did not know, written by Fr Julian Tenison-Woods, cofounder with St Mary of the Cross of the Josephite Sisters, a country priest, and an accomplished scholar and scientist. One of the two large buildings on the north Sydney campus of the Australian Catholic University is fittingly named after him.

We pray his simple prayer, remembering the millions who have died in awful suffering.

> *Follow me*
> *Onward to the open side*
> *All who to themselves have died.*
> *Hear the Lover crucified*
> *Calling "Follow me."*
>
> *Follow me, despising pain,*
> *Follow, sharing all my shame,*
> *Heeding not the world's hard blame,*
> *Seeing only me.*

WEEK 18

Real Presence

23 June–29 June 2019

Corpus Christi, Sunday, 23 June 2019

I once asked an altar server in Ballarat East in the 1970s what "Corpus Christi" meant. He replied that it had something to do with the Christian Brothers! It is, of course, the Latin term for the Body of Christ, and the medieval feast highlights the ancient traditional Catholic belief in the Real Presence, that Jesus is truly present, body and blood, soul and divinity, in the consecrated Eucharistic bread, and that his presence is not merely symbolic. This is called the doctrine of transubstantiation and is a major point of difference between us and most Protestants. The classical Lutheran belief is in consubstantiation, that the substance of the bread remains with the substance of Christ's Body, rather than being replaced. Transubstantiation is a favourite point of attack for Richard Dawkins.

Eucharistic adoration, the celebration of Benediction, and the doctrine of transubstantiation all slipped into the shadows, when they were not explicitly rejected, in progressive circles for decades after the Second Vatican Council. They were not scriptural, and they emphasized our differences with the Protestant world.

The late Bishop Bill Brennan of Wagga Wagga, who in November 2001 retired after a massive stroke, was very sharp and learned. He was one of the first leaders of the Gospel fightback in Catholic Australia, with Archbishop Barry Hickey of Perth, and a formidable debater. In catechetical circles, the prevailing line was that "transubstantiation" was too long and formal a word to be used with young people. "Nonsense," said the good bishop, "it has the same number of syllables as reconciliation", which was the new preferred term for confession, the sacrament of penance, which is still a casualty of the postconciliar world.

Today, when devout young Catholics, even in the Western world, are enthusiastic about the celebration of Benediction and silent prayer before the Blessed Sacrament, while the Corpus Christi processions have recommenced here and there, it is salutary to recall that when I was rector of Corpus Christi seminary in Clayton from 1985 to 1987, with a body of seminarians and staff who did not share all my views, I only achieved one celebration of Benediction. I did somewhat better with Our Lady when I managed, after considerable resistance, to have her image placed on the chapel's front wall, but not too close to the altar or tabernacle.

The Corpus Christi feast was introduced into the universal Church from Belgium in 1264 after a number of theologians, such as Berengarius, had denied the Real Presence. The classical Latin hymns for Corpus Christi, "O Salutaris", "Tantum Ergo", and "Adoro Te Devote", are masterpieces whose words were written by St Thomas Aquinas, after, so the legend tells us, a contest between him and St Bonaventure to produce the better prayers.

Fr Thang Vu, of Corpus Christi seminary, celebrated the *Mass for You at Home*, which I watched, although my watch alarm did not function despite my following the instructions punctiliously. I lasted out the *Hillsong* half hour, which included a section on Jesus, from chapter 15 of John's Gospel. Still mostly Old Testament.

Songs of Praise had an unusual format as the narrator went on a pilgrimage on the Llyn Peninsula in Wales from one sixth-century pilgrimage site to another, with very small ancient churches, finishing at the island of Bardsey, the Island of the Resurrection. This was punctuated by singing from two splendid choirs, one all male, of traditional Protestant hymns, such as "Abide with Me".

The sky was clear, but the temperature low during my two exercise sessions. My niece celebrated her thirty-first birthday in Bendigo, and her two-year-old son delighted my sister, Margaret, by giving her a big hug and a kiss.

I cannot think of a better conclusion than one verse of the Latin hymn "Pange Lingua".

Tantum ergo Sacramentum
Veneremur cernui: et antiquum documentum
Novo cedat ritui:
Praestat fides supplementum
Sensuum defectui.

Monday, 24 June 2019

Enjoyed a happy hour with my brother, David, his wife, Judy, and niece Sarah, although there was confusion over the time, which meant we met in a box, rather than together in the guest area. People are keen to know what I plan to do when released, but I reply: First of all, I have to be released, and then we will see. I propose to stay in Melbourne for some days to visit some people such as Msgr Portelli and Bob Burke, after the death of his wife, Yvonne.

David had a marvellous (true) story of some Catholic who had not been to Mass for thirty years, who saw a hostile poster or photo of me on a church fence, pulled it down, and decided to return to Sunday Mass.

Fr Brendan Purcell, my Irish friend from St Mary's in Sydney, sent me a card after attending a retreat on the theme of the Trinity. He recounted a beautiful insight into Our Lady, who was so loved by the Trinitarian God that she became through the Incarnation the Container of the Uncontainable. Apparently, the Chora Church in Istanbul has an image on this theme, so that Mary is more like the sky, which contains the Son of God, than like the moon reflecting his light.

Brendan then went on about my problems, acknowledging that a sword is now going through me. He went on, "Surely (God) the Father saw that without a sacrifice like yours, being punished with the same 'justice' as so many of your brother bishops in China, the East, and elsewhere, Mary cannot give rebirth to the Church in our times." This is a hard truth which I have been slow to accept and understand but is now a consolation.

I never anticipated being convicted, not simply because I was innocent, but because of the absence of evidence (apart from the poor plaintiff) and what my legal team and other lawyers were saying to me. As I like to repeat, the magistrate who committed me for trial on the cathedral allegations said that if the evidence of the master of ceremonies and the sacristan was accepted, no jury could convict. My being charged caused scandal around the world, and my conviction was a further blow, especially in Melbourne. I lamented the damage to the Church, not only among the Church's enemies, but among the moderately interested fair-minded and the churchgoers.

Because I didn't believe I would be convicted, I didn't think at all, until the last few days, about what time in jail would be like or about the effect my incarceration would have on different groups. I knew many would be delighted, if for different reasons, and hoped that not too much damage would be done to the hearts and minds of good people.

Naturally I realised, and was intensely grateful for, the hard core of support from family, my team, and well-wishers. But I did not antic-ipate receiving many hundreds of beautiful messages from around the world, the reports of so much praying, groups fasting and doing penance. I did not dare hope that there would be spiritual fruit from my misfortune and was also frightened that so many good prayers, so much penance, was somewhat "wasted" on a person like myself. Of course, I realised that prayer is never wasted but was slow to acknowledge that spiritual fruit was possible and that in some ways, here and there, the Kingdom was being repaired.

Sometimes the letters to me went in entirely unexpected directions. One Australian woman, a supporter, wrote, "I believe God was in the courtroom the day (the prosecutor) spoke. I believe God struck him dumb, unable to speak properly or get his words out.

"To watch it live was an incredible experience. . . . I thought he might have a seizure." The writer's friends, on the phone that eve-ning, "were incredulous of the display put on by him". All of this is true, but the first problem of the prosecutor was the absence of sup-porting evidence, and he was an honest man.

Last Saturday was the optional memorial feast day for St Thomas More and St John Fisher from the England of Henry VIII. I admire both as models of holiness and scholarship, while contributing through their public positions in church and state. They were men of courage, and this is infrequent in every age. Among their peers, they were almost completely alone because of their theological views on Catholic truth and especially on the papacy. I feel more of an affinity with them now after spending some time in prison.

An unknown correspondent from Germany wrote to me to apologise for believing me guilty before he studied the evidence. He headed his letter with the following quotation from St Paul's Second Letter to the Church in Corinth (2 Cor 12:10), and I pray that I will come to understand better its message and live it out more fully: "For the sake of Christ, then, I am content with weaknesses, insults, hardship, persecutions, and calamities. For when I am weak, then I am strong."

Tuesday, 25 June 2019

This morning I had almost finished the exercise section of my time outside (twenty minutes) when I was interrupted by the news that Paul and Kartya were downstairs to see me. They presented a text from Katrina Lee[1] of a statement to be put out on my release, which I amended by spelling out the identity of the different groups I will thank. I mentioned to Paul that I might deliver it orally, rather than put out a statement. Paul reluctantly consented to this possibility, provided I did not answer any questions.

Paul then spent some time preparing me (indirectly) for the possibility that I might still be in jail, even if my appeal is successful, until at least the second half of July. On Monday the 1st, the Supreme Court goes into recess for two weeks, and we are not sure when the chief justice will return from her longer holidays or whether she will want to be present in person. The delay is not necessarily a bad sign for us.

The whole possibility of delay was more irritating than disappointing. And, of course, we might still be pleasantly surprised. Undoubtedly those more closely attuned to coping with and accepting the developments allowed by God's permissive will would be more serene than I manage to be with these changing prospects. Generally,

[1] Katrina Lee, press officer for Cardinal Pell from the Archdiocese of Sydney.

however, unless the news is catastrophically bad, I can cope pretty well with the passing of some time. A few weeks more in jail means very little, and it is an opportunity for some much-needed penance!

Sr Mary the chaplain called after lunch to bring me Communion and for her customary chat. She looked a bit fresher today as she gave me news that Sr Anne Derwin died on Sunday after a longish illness. She was the religious superior of the Josephite Sisters. When St Mary of the Cross MacKillop[2] was canonised in Rome, eight thousand Australian pilgrims came for the ceremonies. It was a wonderful time, and the [organizing] committee under Sr Anne worked very well with all of us in the Sydney Archdiocese. May she rest in peace and be rewarded for all her good work.

I mentioned to Sr Mary that it is not possible to get hold of tissues in jail. You have to use toilet paper as a handkerchief, which is not too hard on the nose, but it disintegrates quickly in your pocket. This prompted Sr Mary to recount an incident from a meal she shared recently with some prisoners. When they sat down to eat at the table, a prisoner produced a roll of toilet paper and placed it on the table to help anyone who wanted to use a serviette.

As always, Sr Mary brought me two sermons from the readings of the feast of the previous Sunday, Corpus Christi. As usual, both were excellent, but the anonymous priest when writing of how we are absorbed more deeply into the Christian community, the Body of Christ, through receiving Communion, gave two splendid quotations.

The first was from Mother Teresa of Calcutta urging people not to come to help in Calcutta but to spend the money on the local poor. She added that the "worst disease today is not leprosy or tuberculosis; it's being unwanted, it's being left out, it's being forgotten."

The other quotation was from St Teresa of Avila, which the author used to explain the profound implications which follow from "our being joined and bonded to Christ and one another". Most of his quotation follows below. It makes me feel a little easier about my setting aside the "Surrender Prayer" of Fr Dolindo Ruotolo as not suitable in my situation.

---

[2] St Mary of the Cross MacKillop (1842–1909), founder of the Sisters of St Joseph of the Sacred Heart (the Josephites), was the first Australian to be canonized and is the patron saint of the country.

Christ has no body now but yours,
No hands, no feet on earth but yours.
Yours are the eyes through which he looks
    with compassion on the world.
Yours are the feet with which he walks to do good.
Yours are the hands with which he blesses the world.
Yes, Christ has no body now on earth but yours.

Wednesday, 26 June 2019

When I went out for my exercise soon after breakfast, the air was crisp and cold, the sky was clear, with not a cloud in sight, or at least not one visible through the skylights in the two neighbouring pens. When the sun comes up and the sky is clear, my spirits rise. So it was this morning.

After trying for two days to obtain a broom, I pushed again this morning, urging that I be given a broom "now", before my walk, rather than losing the opportunity afterward. I was successful. It is not that the cell is particularly dusty, but dust and fluff collect relentlessly, probably spurred on by the air conditioning.

The *Quadrant* issues for March, May, and June arrived with three excellent articles by the editor, Keith Windschuttle, and one by Christopher Friel on my case. I had seen the online versions, but it was good to see them in the printed magazine. I remain very definitely a print man. The more recent online articles of Friel still have not arrived. By a coincidence, the J Mullins who alerted Windschuttle to the Billy Doe case in Philadelphia and the 2011 *Rolling Stone* account of this scam is a brother of Andy Mullins, the former principal of Redfield College in Sydney.

The Israel Folau funding saga continues to roll on. When his collection agency GoFundMe bowed to pressure and removed his legal funding campaign, the Australian Christian Lobby set up another fund, contributing $100,000 themselves, so that by news time this morning about $1,500,000 had been collected. This case will set important precedents in the struggle for religious freedom, and the Australian Christian Lobby has shown good judgement in backing Folau.

While I am not in favour of condemning people to hell (this is God's business), Folau is simply restating the teachings of the New Testament, listing activities not compatible with the membership of the Kingdom of heaven. What is strange is that there is no complaint from the idolators, adulterers, liars, fornicators, etc., protesting their exclusion. I wonder how many of those hostile to Folau are Christians and how may believe in heaven and hell. People who are secure in their beliefs are not too much concerned by the expression of different or opposing views, especially if they are regarded as nonsensical. The increasingly uncouth forces of political correctness are not satisfied that all persons are treated with respect and love, but are demanding in the name of tolerance, not only that homosexual activity be legal as well as same-sex marriages, but that everyone must approve these activities, at least publicly; and that everybody should be prevented from espousing Christian teachings on marriage and sexuality in any public forum. This would be the end of religious freedom.

Folau's wife, a professional athlete, and Gary Ablett, the Geelong AFL star, have also been subjected to public pressure and hostility because of their support for Christian teaching. It is interesting to note how quickly and easily much of big business has capitulated and is now prepared to use its power, generally money for advertising, to impose the new world view of marriage and sexuality. Their demands will change and expand with the years unless they are checked. The universities need to show they will defend free speech on campuses, and here too we find many ominous signs to the contrary.

We are entering a new world of ideas with the collapse of monotheism, especially in the middle and upper classes. The WASPs have morphed into the WASSs, the secularists. Human beings no longer have an innate dignity because they are made in God's image; men and women are no longer made for one another, by any divine providence, because there is no such thing as human nature and therefore no moral laws to enhance human flourishing, despite the fact that many unbelievers adhere fiercely to the laws and truths that must be followed to enhance human physical health, personally and publicly, and to protect the environment.

Western civilization has made us what we are, and one reason for its achievements is the creative tension between Athens and Jerusalem. Both cities are under attack. Jerusalem and Rome (her ally) bear the brunt of this assault, the frontal assaults, but her weakness makes it hard to defend Athens. When God is lost in the fog, whether it is the fog of lust or of possessions or of power, the defences of reason and truth are breached. Only now, at least in the English-speaking world, are we coming to terms with the second reality, the changes to public life which follow from the dissolution of Christian convictions.

A recent poem in the May *Quadrant* by Peach Klimkiewicz captures this.

> *Don't talk of gender*
> *or of sex.*
> *Don't talk of science*
> *at all events.*
>
> *Don't talk of him.*
> *Don't talk of me.*
> *Don't stand for*
> *masculinity.*
>
> *Don't talk ideas,*
> *Don't ask for proof.*
> *Don't be so brash*
> *to ask for truth. . . .*
>
> *Don't think it through.*
> *Don't be that chump.*
> *Just sing along*
> *to "I hate Trump".*
>
> *There is no God.*
> *There was no Fall.*
> *In fact, you'd best*
> *not talk at all.*

Thursday, 27 June 2019

Before I forget once more, Chris Meney informed me a couple of days ago that Pope Francis, when he was speaking to all the Australian bishops during their *ad limina* visit to Rome this week, warmly commended me as a personal friend, implicitly endorsed my cause, and explained that he had not asked for my resignation. I haven't seen the text, but am very grateful. Apparently the visit generally is going well.

Anne McFarlane visited me today for forty minutes. Tim couldn't come as he was working. We discussed the weekend article in *The Australian* by John Ferguson, which mentioned my anonymous friends' concern about my safety and accommodation after my anticipated release. Once again, I haven't seen the article, but I won't be spending my time dodging the press, much less avoiding imaginary attacks. I asked her to purchase a copy of Thomas Hobbes' *Leviathan* (I think that is the name of his principal work), which I have wanted to read for decades. If I am to be in jail for another month or so, it would be good to get this done. He is one major British philosopher whom I have not read.

Next on the list would be something substantial from Bishop Berkeley of Cork, whose ideas Dr Johnson refuted by proposing to kick a stone.[3] Despite some sporadic efforts, I failed to establish a connection between him and my great, great grandfather, the medico Dr David John Berkeley from Skibbereen in Cork. I was unable to discover his grave, or much about him, except that he did attend a public meeting in Skibbereen in the early days of the famine to decide how best to help. Halfway through reading an account of the meeting, I realised that nothing practical or useful would eventuate. And so it was.

Once again the skies were bright and clear during my two outings. However, just as every silver lining has a cloud, rain is on the way.

It was my friend Daniel Hill, convenor of the Catholic Chaplaincy at Sydney University, who introduced me to Dr Howard Brady, a senior scientist, whose book on climate change *Mirrors and Mazes: A Guide through the Climate Change Debate*, 2nd ed. (2017), was reviewed by me in the *Annals*. Knowing my interest in this vexed and fascinating area of history and science, and to help me pass the time in

---

[3] George Berkeley was an Irish mathematician and philosopher whose theories of human perception were misunderstood to mean that he believed objects only exist as ideas in the mind, hence Dr Johnson's quip about kicking a stone to prove him wrong. From 1734 to 1752, Berkeley was the (Protestant) Church of Ireland bishop of Cloyne in County Cork. The city of Berkeley, California, was named for him.

jail usefully, Howard sent me a 2017 piece, "The Positive Impact of Human CO_2 Emissions on the Survival of Life on Earth", written by the Canadian scientist Dr Patrick Moore, who was a cofounder of Greenpeace. After fifteen years with them, he published *Confessions of a Greenpeace Dropout*, leaving them as their interests turned to environmental issues not based on sound science.

Moore is, of course, committed to working for a sustainable future for the planet and is a cofounder of the CO_2 Coalition Group, which works out of Princeton University.

One of the major messages from the group is that our earth is currently in a CO_2 drought, that carbon dioxide levels have generally been higher during the planet's history, a benefit to life on earth, and that the human emissions of CO_2 have fostered a considerable increase in the growth rate and biomass of plants, including crops and trees.

This growth is not disputed, as CO_2 is used regularly in hot houses, and three photos in the article show different heights for three similar bushes grown in atmospheres with different levels of carbon dioxide.

Most people do not know that planet earth has been covered with immense sheets of ice for most of its four to six billion years of existence. These ice ages generally last for around 100,000 years, and the warmer interglacial periods for upward of ten thousand years.

We are in the Holocene interglacial, which is somewhat cooler than previous interglacials and has already lasted longer than some previous interglacial periods. We might be overdue for a cold snap.

These trends work out over thousands of years and not millions. The Holocene Thermal Optimum was between five thousand to nine thousand years ago, and since then the warming peaks have been diminishing and the cool periods have been colder. The Little Ice Age of about three hundred years ago was the coldest since the Holocene Optimum.

Are we facing catastrophe or salvation from an increase in CO_2 emissions? James Lovelock wrote his book on the Gaia hypothesis in 1979, proclaiming that humans had become a rogue species, violating the earth, so that by the year 2000, billions would die. They didn't. This caused a rethink. In 2010, at the London Science Museum, Lovelock recanted, claiming that CO_2 emissions are now our salvation, stopping "the onset of a new Ice Age".

I am a sceptic, not a denier, and I am sceptical of Lovelock's new thesis, but it is certain that carbon dioxide is essential and that more is beneficial for plant life. The relationship between an increase in CO_2 emissions and rising temperatures has not been identified. The science is not settled as no computer predictions have proved to be accurate, and over millions of years we do not find a correlation between levels of CO_2 and temperature levels; indeed, during the last 50,000 years, CO_2 levels tend to lag behind changes in temperature. To quote Moore: "The Earth's climate is a chaotic, non-linear, multi-variant system with many unpredictable feedbacks, both positive and negative."

Irreligious people, especially first-generation unbelievers, who are prosperous, who have been educated to abandon many of their inherited beliefs, and who have had their common-sense understandings deconstructed seem to need to fear some great danger, some looming catastrophe, more than they need a noble cause to espouse. Religious people who are not monotheist also often have ugly, frightening religious imagery. Human life presents a choice between "fearing" a loving God or fearing the unknown, cruel, and capricious.

God our Father, we love your evolving creation, which reflects your beauty.

> *The world is charged with the grandeur of God,*
> *It will flame out, like shining from shook foil.*

We acknowledge the consequences of the Fall: pain, evil, natural disasters. We give thanks that your Son suffered with us, demonstrating that the mass of suffering can be converted into the energy of the Spirit, loss into gain through love. We know that your Son will come again to establish the new heaven and the new earth. We pray to become, not pessimists, not optimists, but brothers and sisters in Christian hope.

> *Oh, morning, at the brown brink eastward, springs—*
> *Because the Holy Ghost over the bent*
> *World broods with warm breast and with ah! bright wings.*
>   "God's Grandeur", Gerard Manley Hopkins

Feast of the Sacred Heart, Friday, 28 June 2019

We have some new shouters in the unit, one predominantly, and at least one other. I was woken at 3:00 am by a loud argument, probably one telling the other to be quiet, but they didn't persist.

Another beautiful clear day, like a Sydney winter, but cooler. Went to the doctor, and my blood pressure was 130/70, but I wasn't feeling weak or dizzy and my weight (clothed) had dropped another kilogram—7 or 8 kgs [15 or 18 lbs] loss in all. Prison has been good for my health.

A couple of days ago in Singleton, New South Wales, two twin six-year-old girls and their eleven-year-old brother were killed in a house fire. The neighbours saved the mother and another daughter. No foul play is suspected in this tragedy. Why does God allow these mishaps? I can understand that when men and women have free will, they will sometimes choose evil and inflict cruelty beyond the capacity of the most ferocious animal. Freedom can only come at a price, and sometimes the price is terrible, which merits inexorable condemnation, and if the sinner is unrepentant, then damnation.

But when death comes to children through no human evil, not even significant carelessness, through sheer bad luck, we have a different reason for sadness.

The problem of innocent suffering is the strongest argument against the existence of God. It is not sufficient to disprove God's existence, because of all the outweighing goodness in men and women and because Jesus suffered with us to show that good can come from evil and pain. Even with the answer, a question remains. And I would like to be able to ask the good God, "Why is there so much evil and pain?"

A godless universe provides no balm whatsoever. Blind chance is heartless and remorseless. We need God in the next life to set those things right, to balance the scales of justice, and to look after all the victims, especially the innocent victims.

From the life and teachings of Jesus, God's only Son, we know that God will look after in a special way all those who missed out in this life, that God is and acts as we want him to be and to act.

All this is part of the reason for the popularity of the devotion to the Sacred Heart. The heart is the symbol of love, and the image of Jesus' heart, topped with the crown of thorns and burning with fire, has brought consolation to imperfect, often poor people for generations. I grew up under an image of the Sacred Heart in the house, which had belonged to my maternal grandparents, proudly Irish Catholic. The devotion today in Australia, especially among the Anglos, is not as strong as it was, although it runs in parallel with the new enthusiasm for the Divine Mercy.

Some depictions of the Sacred Heart have been unfortunate, with the Sacred Heart looking soft and effeminate. Sometimes it even seemed that Jesus' hair had been permed.

On a visit to Paray-le-Monial in south-central France more than twenty years ago, I found a number of sketches of the Sacred Heart, which had been drawn not long after the apparitions, following the instructions of St Margaret Mary Alacoque (1647–1690), who had received the visions. I was relieved and not surprised that the images of Christ did not depict an emotionally flabby, soft, and sentimental person, but one who was serene, strong, and compassionate. In other words, drawings of a man capable of loving, helping, and forgiving us, the Son of the Father, who rejoices more over the repentance of one sinner than over ninety-nine righteous persons who do not need to repent.

We pray today's prayer from the Divine Office.

Almighty God and Father, we glory in the Sacred Heart of Jesus, your beloved Son as we call to mind the great things his love has done for us. Fill us with the grace that flows in abundance from the heart of Jesus, the source of heaven's gift.

Feast of Sts Peter and Paul, Saturday, 29 June 2019

The clouds have arrived, but not much of the promised rain. Once a day or so, someone, perhaps the shouter, groans and laments obscenely and piteously. It doesn't last for too long. Recently I adverted to the fact that I haven't heard any cursing or blasphemy. It is probably another sign of the advancing irreligion, just as an ex-jail chaplain lamented that the disproportionally high percentage of Catholics among the juvenile delinquents in prison up to thirty years ago has also disappeared. Certainly, there is more blasphemy in Italy than in Australia.

No sooner have I proposed a tentative reason for unheard curses than I feel constrained to acknowledge that I might be mistaken, too cynical. Certainly, for many prisoners, jail enhances personal honesty and sincerity, a grappling with the realities of goodness and evil. And it is equally certain that solitary confinement is no place to get to know fellow prisoners, even when you allow for their letters.

I have just returned from my afternoon exercise, where I discovered it had rained quite heavily, although a slight drizzle was all I received during my circling or walking diagonally in the small pen. Managed to phone Tim Fischer and wish him well, promising my prayers. He was in good spirits and still fighting.

The feast of St Peter and St Paul is an important feast, not so much for the liturgical year, but for the patterns of life in our universal, or Catholic, now worldwide Church. It reminds us of the ancient Church in the city of Rome, then capital of the world, founded by the two martyrs, and of the continuing presence there of the pope, the successor of St Peter and bishop of Rome. Even when the popes lived in Avignon, in southern France, in the fourteenth century, they were there as bishops of Rome. Following the general Church pattern, today we celebrate the martyrdom of the two apostles, not their birthdays.

The office of the papacy was founded by Christ himself, when he renamed Simon as Peter, which means the man of rock. While it was Peter's faith which prompted the appointment, when he correctly responded to the question on the identity of the Son of Man, it is Peter himself, not his faith, which is to be the foundation for the Church, and Peter and his successors who have the keys and the power to bind and to loose. It is this entire Church of the apostles, strengthened now by Peter's role, over which the gates of hell will not prevail. This is no guarantee that Christianity will survive in every country, as, for instance, Egypt, North Africa, and Turkey were once Catholic, but the Church will survive.

The ways in which the popes have led the Church have changed immensely over two thousand years. An underground, illegal, and often persecuted community for three hundred years under the pagan Roman Empire offers radically different possibilities for leadership from the situation today of 1.2 billion Catholics, linked by modern means of travel and communication. Surprisingly, more Catholics around the world today are being persecuted than at any time in the Church's history, although, thank God, we in Western countries enjoy religious freedom.

At least since the Industrial Revolution, our world has looked forward to a better future, although this might be changing as many young people today are no longer confident they will be richer than their parents. Whatever of this, for most of human history, people have looked backward to some Golden Age, real or imagined. Therefore, the ancients found it more congenial than we do to accept that what Christ and the apostles taught determined the rule of faith. Christians wanted to know that they were being taught what Christ taught, and they went to the churches founded by the apostles to ascertain this. And the Church of Rome, founded by Peter and Paul, home of the successor of Peter, was more important than any other centre in authorising compatibility of doctrine with the apostolic tradition. The defence of this ancient tradition was the purpose behind the definition of papal infallibility by the First Vatican Council in 1870.

Immense changes occurred in the Church in the twentieth century. The majority of Catholics are in Central and South America, where nominal Catholics are being swept up by Evangelical communities. Dramatic Catholic expansion in Africa is running neck and neck with Islamic expansion there. The picture is mixed in Asia; the brief period of optimism for Catholics in China has already waned, and Europe has seen a spectacular weakening in many countries. The last three popes have not been Italians, and Pope Benedict resigned, the first such resignation since that of Pope Celestine V in 1294. All of these developments make the maintenance of Catholic unity more difficult.

The Church exists to praise God, to encourage her members to live well, and to preach the Gospel.

Within this context, the special role of the pope and his curia is to ensure teaching conforms to the apostolic tradition and to maintain Church unity. The present situation of the Orthodox, Anglican, and Protestant communities demonstrates that worldwide unity is a blessing, something of a miracle, never to be taken as a given.

I favour the millennial tradition that the popes do not resign, that they continue until their death, because this helps maintain the unity of the Church. Improvements in modern medicine have complicated the situation, ensuring that the popes of today and tomorrow are likely to live longer than their predecessors, even when their health has been much weakened. My first bishop, James Patrick O'Collins, who was head prefect at Propaganda Fide College in Rome in the 1920s, told me the story of an Italian cardinal he much admired who did not allow his name to go forward as "papabile" because of dementia in his family. As always, whether the pope is well and especially when his capacities are diminished, much depends on the quality of his senior executives, such as the secretary of state and the *sostituto*, etc.

However, the protocols on the situation of a pope who has resigned need to be clarified, to strengthen the forces for unity. While the retired pope could retain the title of "pope emeritus", he should be renominated to the College of Cardinals so that he is known as "Cardinal X, Pope Emeritus", he should not wear the white papal soutane and should not teach publicly. Because of reverence and love for the pope, many will feel reluctant to impose such restrictions on someone who once held the See of Peter. Probably the measures would be best introduced by a pope who had no surviving predecessor.

The papacy is like the episcopate, the role of the pope like the role of the bishops; both offices were instituted by Christ himself and are essential to God's plan for the Church. The papacy distinguishes the Catholic Church from all other Christian churches and communities. It is difficult to overstate its strategic importance, so that the Jesuit priest-scientist Pierre Teilhard de Chardin spoke of the axis of hominization passing through Rome. He was right.

The papacy is robust. We have seen in the past bad popes, mediocre popes, as well as great leaders, saints, and scholars. We have every reason to be confident about the popes, but we should not be careless.

Let me conclude with the prayer we prayed regularly when I was a schoolboy.

May the Lord preserve Pope Francis and give him life. Make him blessed upon the earth, and deliver him not into the hands of his enemies.

WEEK 19

Web of Deceit

30 June–6 July 2019

Sunday, 30 June 2019

After two big feasts, we return to the liturgical year program of Sundays, where I followed my usual TV religious schedule.

Managed to wake up for *Mass for You at Home*, which was celebrated by Fr Thang. A reverent and prayerful celebration, which was entirely unremarkable except for the celebrant praying for the bishop of Rome, rather than using the term "Pope Francis". I am not sure what this signifies, if anything.

Pastor Houston of Hillsong broke new ground in my limited experience by giving an excellent New Testament sermon on "Knowing God", although he started, as he did last week, with chapter 11 of Daniel. I noticed that the congregation was the same one shown last Sunday (a vacancy in the front row and three young fellows at the back, with baseball caps and mobile phones). Probably he records a number of addresses with the same congregation, which would help to explain his tired gravelly voice and the somewhat inert congregation.

As always, Joseph Prince's style was different. He was celebrating Resurrection Day, although I don't know whether this had been recorded at Easter. Jesus was raised for our righteousness, he explained, giving an exegesis on the Greek word *dikaios*. Therefore, we should be too blessed to be stressed. Like the royal family, Joseph has a different and expensive set of clothes for each performance. I was tempted to say that set liturgical vestments for each season have sociological advantages, like school uniforms, in preventing

competition, ostentation, and expense. However, even in the prescribed Catholic tradition, some vestments can be beautiful and
elaborate. Pope Francis is not of such a mind. In a sacramental celebration where the priest should not be central (hence my sympathy
for the priest praying the Canon of the Mass with his back to the
people), we have a different situation from a prayer or teaching session. The Curé of Ars, St John Vianney, was renowned for his simple food (cold boiled potatoes) and simple clothes, but he believed
that money spent on beautiful Mass vestments was right and just. I
am in the Curé's line of thinking.

Songs of Praise featured the top ten hymns chosen by thousands of
voters in the UK. My top three were "How Great Thou Art" (no 1),
which Aled Jones uses to finish his hymn festivals at the Albert Hall
[London]. Then the Welsh "Guide Me, O Thou Great Redeemer",
which was a favourite in the trenches in World War I (no 8), and "Be
Thou My Vision" (no 4), the Irish hymn commemorating St Patrick
lighting the first Easter fire at Tara in 431, despite the prohibition of
the Irish kings. Greg Craven, the Australian Catholic University vice
chancellor, has commissioned a fine bronze of Patrick lighting the
fire for the St Patrick's Campus of the university in Melbourne.

The Gospel passage in today's Mass tells of the unsuccessful visit
of Jesus and his team to a Samaritan village and the remarkable
request from the sons of thunder, James and John, to our Lord, asking
whether he wanted them to call down fire from heaven to destroy
the indifferent or hostile wretches.

The question is not only reprehensible, contrary to the core of
Jesus' moral teaching, but also ridiculous and disproportionate. Because it is so unworthy of an apostle, its preservation in the record
has the ring of truth. Were the apostles really so uncouth and morally
blind? Was it an attempt at humour? Was it a brain snap because of
their outrage? Whatever the explanation, Jesus rebuked them.

I am well aware that our instincts and impulses are not always
reasonable or moral. In the last few days, I have had to work harder
than at any other time in my period in jail not to be cross and dis-
gruntled because the judges are so slow in delivering their verdict.
There are many others who would be higher in any logical order of
merit for my displeasure in this sad business. The judges are moving
slowly but are likely to do the right thing. They have not earned any

disproportionate petulance. I have to get back to my routine and count my blessings. So I pray.

For everything I have received in a happy, full life and for all I am about to receive, may I be truly grateful.

Monday, 1 July 2019

Last night I watched a program on the sad, tumultuous life of Mary, Queen of Scots, and the barbarous society in which she lived; then a documentary on the Allied landings in Normandy from D-day, 6 June 1944. The sufferings and courage of hundreds of thousands of combatants on both sides of the conflict were a useful corrective, enabling me to see my own small difficulties in proper perspective.

Yesterday evening when I was in the exercise pen, I couldn't see any birds, but I could hear a Victorian bird song which I recognized. It didn't come from a magpie or a crow, or from a sparrow or a gull, but it might have been the two-note cooing of a dove. Whatever it came from, it was welcome.

During my time outside in the early morning, H, my fellow Richmond supporter, came to discuss the Tigers' good win over St Kilda. When he asked how I was going, I replied that I had hoped to be outside by this time, but I was "going all right". I was a bit surprised when he said they had noticed I was quieter than previously, although I should not have been surprised as they would have seen hundreds in situations similar to mine. He then asked whether I would like an hour in the gym every other day or perhaps some time in the garden area. I would still be alone in both places, but I explained I would be delighted with the change of scene and the possibility of stretching my legs.

From 11:00 am to midday, I had my first spell in the internal gymnasium, which is larger than a basketball court, with a few table tennis tables and many machines for walking, stretching, lifting, and rowing. I walked for twenty minutes, then had some time on a treadmill-type apparatus. The bicycles did not fit, but I did a few exercises to strengthen my thighs. I went very carefully, as I did not want to cripple myself prematurely. Thoroughly enjoyed the change of scenery and realised how far I am from fitness. My arms and shoulders need particular work, although my left arm has strengthened a lot with my daily exercise.

On this third attempt, Tim O'Leary managed to gain entry, and we spent an hour in the lawyers' box, as the visitors' area had already been booked. His family had been down at Aireys Inlet for the school holidays. His son Joe had enjoyed a good school term, and all the children were going well. Georgia will be back from Exeter University in the UK in a fortnight. As I already knew, Friel is continuing to write and now has about 250 followers as he goes chapter by chapter through Milligan's book. Tim also promised to sort through recent articles by John Allen and Sandro Magister on the Rome scene[1]; he also informed me that Wilton Gregory had been named archbishop of Washington and that Pope Francis had written to the German bishops on the eve of their national meeting.

No letters arrived today, unlike the previous four or five days. One Australian priest informed me that he had just received six Muslims into the Catholic Church, baptising and confirming them, and that two had been ostracised by their family. He enquired of one why she was willing to take this step, and she replied simply that "she wanted to love Jesus, whatever the cost." He himself then commented, "I suppose that for all of us that should be our only motive and goal." These are part of a steady subterranean stream of Muslim converts.

Received a letter from my Australian-born friend Sam Gregg, who works with the Acton Institute in the US. An accomplished writer and thinker, he promised to send me his new book, *Reason, Faith, and the Struggle for Western Civilization*. It is good to see so many continuing to answer the basic challenges we are confronting.

St Thomas More wrote beautiful prayers. This is part of one written when he was a prisoner in the Tower of London.

> *To know mine own vility and wretchedness,*
> *To humble and meeken myself under the mighty hand*
> *of God;*

[1] John Allen is the American editor of the Catholic news website *Crux*. Sandro Magister is the editor of the Catholic blog Settimo Cielo on the website of *L'Espresso*, an Italian weekly news magazine.

To bewail my sins past,
For the purging of them patiently to suffer adversity;
Gladly to bear my purgatory here,
To be joyful of tribulations;
To walk the narrow way that leadeth to life,
To bear the cross with Christ.

Tuesday, 2 July 2019

We have a couple of domestic developments in our small twelve-prisoner family in Unit 8, where we never see one another. Gargasoulas and I exchange letters, but I don't even know who else is here, now that the Muslim duo have gone.

For the last couple of nights around midnight, a prisoner from the other end of the unit has been making merry, not very loudly, but shouting "yippee" and enjoying himself. My guess is that he is sleeping too much during the day and unable to sleep at night. On the last two mornings, before we rose, he was again making merry. He wasn't anguished at all.

We also have a newcomer at our end of the unit. I was not sure whether he was a newcomer or one of the old hands who had "flipped". After a discreet enquiry as I returned after my exercise, the warder confirmed he was a newcomer and they were hoping he would move on quickly. He is poorly spoken, claims to be sick (and probably is), and alternates between loudly lamenting his lot and denouncing the authorities. He also did some banging. He has been silent for a couple of hours, but if he performs tonight, I shall be close to the action, with a ringside seat, so to speak. The warders dealt well with him, ignoring most of his performance. We fellow prisoners, locked in our cells, cannot help him in any way, except perhaps through a prayer.

Fasted from midnight, as I had a series of blood tests preparatory to my meeting with the heart specialist by video link. I was due to be seen at 9:00 am, but they took me twenty minutes early, so I wouldn't have to wait too long for breakfast. The blood was obtained from the first needle, which had to be repositioned. The doctor was called, but he was on the toilet, and the situation was retrieved without him.

Like everything else in prison, medical help arrives slowly, but the services are excellent and comprehensive.

Sr Mary called for my weekly Communion, and we received extra time. She remarked that I would never have prayed in noisier circumstances, and she was right, because the warders' activity continues unabated around us. Sr McGlone has been replaced as *National Catholic Reporter* sermon writer by another Scripture graduate who will not continue on my list if her second offering is similar to her first.

The newcomer is noisy again, with a few denunciations and a ritual banging. Please God he will run out of steam early in the night.

Managed to write three letters, two of them to prisoners who had written to me. These replies have been my priority so far, but I will do more by way of replying, which will lessen the task on my hoped-for release.

Another correspondent, a Catholic woman from Mandurah in West Australia, wrote to say that she and her friends had been praying for me and felt that Our Lady the Undoer of Knots had been busy during my appeal, unravelling the prosecutor's speech. She wasn't impressed with his performance, but I believe the truth was set free and exposed in the court, so that all my friends and many foes saw through the confusion, and the prosecutor did not attempt to prevent this in any reprehensible way. I wonder if he knew the truth was not on his side.

About ten or twenty years ago, I managed to read the *Consolation of Philosophy* by Boethius. I was initially disappointed because too much of it was known to me. A few moments reflection reminded me of the extent of his achievement. His thinking was now so embedded in the tradition of philosophy I was taught and then followed with my own reading. You cannot do much better than have many of your insights become commonplace.

An unknown supporter from New York wrote to me about Boethius, also known as St Severinus,[2] and his book. "I believe that he wrote that wonderful book while imprisoned for false accusations. I have heard that you are writing in prison." He continued:

[2] Anicius Manlius Severinus Boethius (ca 477–524) was a Roman senator, philosopher, and theologian. He is considered a martyr for the Catholic faith and was canonized under the name of St Severinus.

I hope that your writings will prove helpful to the Church now and in the future. I hope that this letter and others you receive will encourage you. Finally, I hope you are inspired by the examples of saints and martyrs throughout Church history. May their prayers strengthen you.

I say: *Amen to all that.*

Wednesday, 3 July 2019

Today is the feast of St Thomas, the doubter, who was a suitable patron for the age we are just leaving in the Western world. Doubts are good, because usually doubters are searching for the truth. But when there is only my truth and your truth, when truth is the product of power and can be imposed on others by the more powerful, the search for evidence becomes superfluous, even annoying. St Thomas is no patron of the thought world which is rearing its head in a number of places.

My quiet life continues on its usual patterns. I am well into the third epilogue of *War and Peace*, but I probably won't finish it as I don't think much of the level of argumentation. Tolstoy seems to create too many straw men and is too hostile to the influence of human leadership. Great men are rare, cannot walk on water, but leaders are mightily important.

Tolstoy hasn't heard of Murphy's Law—What can go wrong will go wrong—and in fact never mentions Britain's contribution in the Napoleonic Wars. The most we learn is that English Clubs existed in Moscow and St Petersburg. But Tolstoy did know about human muddle and the mysterious tides in human affairs.

In every sphere of life, good or inefficient leadership counts for a lot. Good leaders are aware of Murphy's Law and are able to limit, direct, or surmount the succession of difficulties which emerge. Businesses rise and fall, religious orders and dioceses wax and wane, and whole countries can be damaged by inept leadership, as Cameron and May have demonstrated with Brexit; or, although much more rarely, they can be saved by inspired leadership, e.g., by Churchill. The Church in the Western world, and not just the ex-Communist world, would have been different without St John Paul the Great.

I am moving slowly through St Matthew's Gospel for my meditation, now at about chapter 15. The three *Quadrant*s I have received have been read, and I do one or two exercises of Sudoku each day. Today I failed to resolve both the easier alternative in the *Herald Sun* and the next one in my book. A useful antidote to overweening pride.

Apart from his healthy independence of mind, we know next to nothing of the post-Pentecost labours of St Thomas. I have visited his tomb, or perhaps it is only an official memorial, in Madras, now Chennai. The Indian priest who brought me to the shrine pointed proudly to a statement by an earlier Anglican bishop, who claimed that Thomas' presence in India was better evidenced than Peter's presence in Rome. As the quotation came from pre-ecumenical times, I feared it was faint praise indeed, but I kept my suspicions to myself.

The second reading in the breviary is taken from a wonderful homily by the late-sixth-century pope, St Gregory the Great. Gregory understood the twists and turns of human nature and possessed wonderful insight. According to the pope, Jesus showed Thomas his hands and scars and so healed the wound of Thomas' disbelief. Gregory wonders whether Thomas chose to be absent at the time of the earlier apparition. But God's mercy worked wonderfully because when the doubting disciple touched Our Lord's wounds, "he cured the wound of our disbelief."

"What (Thomas) saw was one thing," continued Gregory, "what he believed another. A mortal man could not have seen God. Thomas saw a man, but by his words 'my Lord and my God', he acknowledged his divinity."

I was fond of the Irish practice of praying "My Lord and my God" as a post-Consecration popular acclamation and lobbied for its inclusion in the new English translation of the Mass. The liturgists were solid in their opposition as it was too much of a novelty, out of keeping with the Roman rite. More's the pity.

The unit enjoyed a peaceful night. Our friend at the far end yelped happily a few times between 11:00 pm and midnight and again before we rose in the morning. My neighbour lapsed into silence and has been quiet all through today. A half hour ago, the yelper had been crying out in anguish, but he too has now gone silent. It would be sad and fascinating to know the stories, often tragic I fear, of my unknown cohabitants.

*God the Father, in our world today, when the pressures for conformity
are so fierce and intolerant, we pray you to send us men and women
like St Thomas: strong, sceptical searchers for truth. Bring them to
know your Son Jesus, the Son of Man, and open their hearts in faith
to the mystery of your transcendent Love. We pray this though the
same Christ Our Lord.*

Thursday, 4 July 2019

Today is their great national holiday Independence Day in the US
and time to acknowledge Australia's debt to the United States in
the last world war, our enduring national friendship, and our debt
to the American Church. Australian seminarians have studied at the
North American College in Rome for more than fifteen years and
been well formed. Despite their present problems, the best elements
in the American Church show how Gospel Christians can confront
modernity. And President Trump has done better than any opponent
of his ever expected, has nominated two good judges to the Supreme
Court, and is not working to damage the Christian forces, as his predecessor was.

We have all heard of unintended consequences. Life is strange. I
was called unexpectedly to Dr Mahomet once again, who gave me
the results of my blood tests. My blood pressure was 120/70, choles-
terol 2.00, and iron level at 2.5. No sign of diabetes. In the doctor's
words, "results don't come any better"—presumably for someone
seventy-eight years of age. Weight loss, regular prayer and exercise,
no alcohol, and a quiet routine have worked wonders. I cannot help
thinking that all the prayers from around the world and the letters
have helped produce these physical and psychological fruits.

Toto and Rita Piccolo, the lay leaders of the Neocatechumenal
Way in Australia, called to see me today, bringing prayers and greetings from members of the Way across the world. Unfortunately,
neither the Turchis nor the Paganis, two families in Sydney who
have been particularly good to me, have received my letters, written
probably ten to fourteen days ago. I enquired a couple of times on
my return and was told that if the letters were not sent, I would be
told and reasons given. The censorship office is under considerable

pressure, they explained, and, I added, not least from the letters I am receiving.

The Piccolos provided a new twist to the saga of the unfortunate prosecutor. One Melbourne priest at the hearing had apparently told some of my supporters that he was praying for the prosecutor to mess up his presentation. As his performance deteriorated, the priest murmured to his companions, "See, my prayers are working!" I would have preferred, and been well satisfied, if he had prayed for justice to be done, which, I am sure, was his underlying prayer.

About fifty letters came in last night after a couple of quiet days, which reminded me once again how much these letters have changed my time in jail, my daily program, my thinking and my praying, my peace of mind.

Tim O'Leary sent me the long-promised five articles by Christopher Friel which deal systematically with Louise Milligan's book. While there might be no knockout blow, Friel is scoring points in every round, pointing to truths and showing that conspiracies cannot be excluded. His chapter on Operation Plangere is significant.

Detective Sgt [Kevin] Carson was a Ballarat policeman who produced a report indicating that Catholic [clerical] sex abuse in Victoria was responsible for forty-three suicides. The story was leaked in *The Age* on 13 April 2012. Soon afterward, the premier announced a parliamentary enquiry into the Church's handling of sex abuse.

The police themselves set up a review of Carson's work in July 2012, Operation Plangere, the Latin term for "lament". They were only able to identify twenty-five of the forty-three persons Carson named, and sixteen of these had suicided. Four were victims of childhood sexual assault, and one of those, who had suicided, had been assaulted by a member of the clergy. Instead of forty-three suicides from clergy abuse, Operation Plangere found one. One is one too many, but it is not forty-three.

Equally disgraceful is the fact that the report was hidden away for two years and only revealed to the Royal Commission in 2015 and then made public. At the risk of repeating myself, who would have imagined that a scholar in Wales, with remarkable energy and the intuition of Sherlock Holmes, would have been able to throw so much light on this web of deceit and smears, which is one further dimension beyond the abuse itself and the cover-up?

We might still discover more, following the words from Kant, which Friel delights in quoting.

Truth is the child of time, erelong she shall appear to vindicate thee.

Friday, 5 July 2019

The siren did not sound this morning, so I slept or dozed until 8 minutes to 8, when the trap door, a small opening for a hand, was opened by the warders taking the morning roll call.

The day was fine, no rain with a bright sun and light cloud. I managed to speak with my sister in the afternoon after getting my brother to inform her that I would be phoning. She was well, and, contrary to my last report, her legs were improving.

The gymnasium is closed on Fridays and Sundays, but I should be able to go down between 11:00 and 12:00 midday tomorrow. The prisoner with whom I am supposed to alternate does not always take up his option.

One of the warders and D, the placement or welfare officer, were asking about the date for my verdict to be delivered. I repeated the two pieces of information, i.e., that the court is in recess for a fortnight, that the chief justice is supposed to be returning within the next week after that, and so the best bet is for a verdict in the last week of July. But, I emphasized, this is a guess.

The bangers and the shouters seem to have moved on, because all is quiet, and I notice on the board that four of the twelve cells are vacant.

Another smaller batch of letters arrived today, most of them unopened as yet. However, by way of distraction, I did allow myself to open one card, which came, I discovered, from a mother and daughter who had both drifted away from theism. Seven years ago, the daughter became a deist, while the mother went farther, falling into atheism.

The daughter explained that "seeing the ugliness and injustice of what had been done to you", she has now come closer to God, "praying for the first time in years and have even gone to Mass". The mother also was upset by the media smear campaign against me and told her daughter, "I'm praying for Cardinal Pell, and I hope God exists so he will have true justice one day." *Deo gratias.*

Reading my letters is a bit like a day in the parish or diocesan centre, because you can never be sure what will come next, and "next" brings a lot of variety.

A prisoner who has spent decades in prison is now fully repentant but still somewhat concerned about God's forgiveness and wondering whether he would be obliged to undergo every medical procedure if his illness is incurable. Catholic doctrine provides reassurance on both points.

Another letter came from an anguished and somewhat cross mother with younger children, whose older child has moved in to cohabit with an opposite-sex partner. Could I give any advice?

Not knowing the family or the situation places you at a disadvantage, but I urged the mother to continue to pray for both of them, to make it clear, calmly and charitably, what her position was, not to harp on the subject to anyone, to continue to treat her child with courtesy and charity, not to break communion but maintain social contact. I suggested that many people today are genuinely confused, and this makes giving reasons for the Christian position even more important. I urged the mother to remember that siblings love one another as well as their parents and that the challenge is not to hurt the child unnecessarily, rather than focussing too much on the hurts received. I did not explain that if the adult child in the relationship was urging the neo-pagan approach on partners to the youngsters, then more distance might be required. My conclusion was that we needed to be kind in our person-to-person dealings, so the couple cannot claim that Christians are cold and uncaring. Moreover, this is the only Christian approach.

Loving God, you are our strength. Support us in our weakness, give us insight and wisdom, peace of heart and patience. Take us under your care, give us your love so that we will have the strength to embrace our weakness and confront our challenges.

We make this prayer through Christ Our Lord.

Saturday, 6 July 2019

The day was entirely predictable, even to the anticipated arrival of the meat pie with tomato sauce for lunch. I returned from exercise in the gymnasium, so the pie was cold but still good.

Had my third spell in the gymnasium and discovered anew what I cannot do at seventy-eight. After discovering a basketball, I continued my walking, bouncing the ball with my right hand and then my left. Very rusty and uncoordinated when I began, especially with my left hand, I had improved by the end of the session. I managed to change the length of the extension used to strengthen thigh muscles and did a small number of exercises. I am cautious, perhaps too cautious, but experience has taught me that sometimes I can manage exercise quite well at the time and still become either tired or sore afterward.

Also climbed onto the rowing machine and rowed a bit, not much at all, with a low resistance rate. The difficulty came when I wanted to rise from the very low seat, as I needed to pull myself up, and my weight moved the whole machine when I pulled on it. Eventually, I slid the rowing machine to the device used to strengthen arms, which had a whole pile of weights. This was secure, so I pulled myself to my feet without the embarrassment of having to call for help.

Usually I write my daily entry on the same day. However, I am writing this on Sunday, as I spent yesterday reading, before watching an excellent program on Windsor Castle, and then Footscray unexpectedly beat Geelong, the top team in the AFL. My legs were a bit stiff at the end of the day, but I had done myself no damage. I also managed to complete reading all the big pile of letters and enclosures which had come in over the last couple of days.

My friend the dreamer has written for a third time, as his latest dream had me still behind a barrier and weeping; so my appeal might not be successful. Nonetheless, everything will turn out well for me. He now seems to have covered both possibilities in his dreams, which will no doubt help him maintain his claim to accurate "prophecy". Every bishop, and more probably each public person, is used to receiving strange letters, and I should not be surprised this continues while I am a prisoner.

A couple of days ago, I received word that Dr Joe Santamaria, the medico brother of Bob, had died, aged ninety-five. They were a brilliant immigrant family, with Bob claiming that his sister, Josie, who gained a couple of exhibitions at Melbourne University, was the brightest of them all. Joe was truly a good man of faith, who worked with addicts for most of his professional life and did fine work as a pro-life and pro-family campaigner. I owe an enormous debt to the Santamaria tribe for their decades of friendship and support. B. A. Santamaria (Bob) was, of course, one of the great Australians, whom I admired since I was a teenager and consulted as a friend and admirer when I was a bishop. He was the best sounding board and strategist I spoke with, and I have been blessed with first-rate friends.

Another fine mentor of mine was Sir Bernard Callinan, a hero in East Timor in the Second World War, a professional engineer, chairman of the committees which built the new Parliament House in Canberra and La Trobe University in Melbourne, and the only chairman of the Institute of Catholic Education, which is now the two Victorian campuses of the Australian Catholic University. I learnt more about leadership from him than from any other person and remember two examples of good advice. Never push people into a corner, because they have no alternative but to fight. The second was to remember that once you get your foot in a doorway, no one can shut the door. It is not rocket science, but they are good, shrewd rules.

I think the antiphon for the introductory psalm in today's Office strikes a good note on which to conclude.

Let us listen for the voice of the Lord and enter into his peace.

WEEK 20

Hopes and Dreams

7 July–13 July 2019

Sunday, 7 July 2019

Woke up at 5:00 am and settled down to wait until 10 to 6. The next thing I knew was the nurse leaving my tablets at 6:15. So I only saw the last ten minutes of the Mass, celebrated by Melbourne priest Fr Michael Kalka, whose grandfather was a brave Labor politician, Johnnie Mullins, who went with the Democratic Labor Party in the Labor Split in 1955. I remember as a young teenager listening to the election results and being astonished when the DLP was wiped out, although their second preferences kept the Federal Liberals in power for seventeen years.

Pastor Houston preached on the Roman centurion who asked Our Lord to cure his daughter. It was another New Testament sermon, and a good one, to the same congregation as last week. Although he had a new sports coat and backdrop for this session, he is stylishly dressed like Joseph Prince.

It struck me that I have never heard the pastor call his large congregation to repent or discuss sexuality or fidelity in marriage. My experience is limited, and in Catholic circles, in reaction to the severity when I was young, many priests go more softly on these issues, and some even avoid them. We have the saving grace of the opening Penitential Rite at Mass, the Confiteor and Kyrie, although even here, blander or most positive alternatives are often used. The secular drive for autonomy and the erroneous Catholic claim to primacy of conscience have pushed the call to repentance out of the spotlight, and many are loathe to concede that an individual decision, as a mortal, or death-bearing, sin, can destroy our relationship with God.

Part of the outcry with Folau's teaching is the widespread feeling that people have a (near) universal right to happiness in heaven. The difficulty is that this assumed and unthinking right degenerates in a generation or two into disbelief in life after death. For an increasing number, the prospect of annihilation after death is better than the prospect of a God who judges. But our estimate of what lies beyond death does not change the situation one whit, whatever our opinion.

As always, Joseph Prince's sermon from the US was much bigger, brighter, and more Christ-centred. Most but not all the congregation are Asian, and I am not surprised it is popular. He preached on Christ's bloodline of protection, which delivers life from death, just as Rahab's red cord hanging from the window saved her family from Joshua's troops capturing Jericho. Prince described Jericho as a notorious pagan city and claimed its walls were fifteen feet across, wide enough for a chariot. I would be interested to see his evidence for this.

He mentioned the importance of families protecting their children from exposure to pornography and violence through the different forms of media, although he didn't develop this subtheme or offer practical suggestions on how to resist these bad habits. Another oddity for me was that I didn't notice many young children or, indeed, teenagers present in either congregation (US or Australia), although Prince's congregation probably had a majority of young adults.

As Catholics, we should be pleased with the successful efforts of any group which teaches Christ's basic teachings. It is no consolation that the radically liberal wing of Protestantism is melting away into secularism faster than we are. In fact, the Gospel Christians, and I believe Catholics are Gospel Christians, in every denomination should support one another. I thank God for the Sydney Anglicans, with their preaching of Christ, of the necessity of faith and repentance for salvation, of the need for worship, prayer, and good works. I concede that they do not have a developed or appropriate theology of the sacraments or of the Church, but we can stand together for the Trinitarian God and his Son. And we shall need to do more of this if neo-paganism continues to expand. Protestant-Catholic antagonism is not Christian, and sociologically it is a distraction in the culture wars between Judaeo-Christianity and the different brands of secularism, e.g., identity politics.

Paul Galbally and Kartya Gracer, my solicitors, called to inform me that they will meet with the registrar of the Appeals Court tomorrow at his invitation. (Naturally, the prosecution solicitors will be present.) They also informed me they have seen written evidence that J, the complainant, did not want the second trial to go ahead and informed the authorities of this. I am not entirely surprised.

Another excerpt from St Thomas More's "Last Prayer", written just before his execution.

Almighty God, "teach me to do your will.... Take hold of my right hand, and lead me on the straight path.... Draw me after You. Bind my jaws with bit and bridle when I am not drawing near to you" [Ps 143:10; Ps 73:23, 273; Ps 32:9].

Monday, 8 July 2019

Songs of Praise yesterday came from Lindisfarne, the site of a former Benedictine monastery founded 1,300 years ago, and now a site for pilgrimages and retreats. The ancient church was filled for the enthusiastic hymn singing. A contemporary religious music group also sang a couple of numbers, less successfully, in my partisan judgement.

The second Sunday reading in the breviary was from sermon 19 of St Augustine, and it contains some favourite sentences, which I have quoted publicly a number of times.

"Let a man's life be praised insofar as he asks for pardon. But as for men without hope, the less attentive they are to their own sins, the more they pry into those of others. They see, not what they can correct, but what they can criticize."

It was these lines which prompted my observations on an apparent gap in Hillsong's preaching. I would hope that my limited knowledge is misleading, but others have also made the point to me.

Augustine's claim is still true regularly today and is a typical way for the spirit of evil to lead disaffected men and women from bad to worse. They want to rejoice in the misfortune and sins of others.

God loves sinners, while still rejecting sin, which is always damaging, sometimes less obviously than at other times. Love the sinner and hate the sin is irritating, sometimes offensive, to those who want to redefine this or that sin out of existence. But all people of faith are consoled to know that God loves us, despite our imperfections, great or less.

When the proud Pharisee, who was heavily into self-affirmation, went into the Temple to pray, to tell God he was not a sinner, that he fasted, prayed, and gave regularly to the Planned Giving program, he was not justified before God.

Rather, it was the tax collector, too embarrassed to raise his eyes to heaven, at the back of the Temple, as he prayed simply, "God, have mercy on me who is a sinner", who, Jesus said explicitly, "went home justified before God".

Until sin makes a comeback, the Church cannot go forward.

The sky was clear and bright for my first exercise session, and the pen was dry. In the afternoon, it was not raining, but the first pen had its customary large puddle, and the sky was overcast. It had been raining. I had another hour in the gymnasium, walking, using light weights for my arms, and performing more exercises for my thighs. Unfortunately, the basketballs were not out, so I could not do anything to improve my coordination by bouncing the ball as I circled the court area.

Paul and Kartya arrived just as I finished in the gymnasium, to recount the different procedures to be followed with different verdicts. Fr Peter Joseph[1] called to visit as expected for 1:00 pm, but I had omitted to put him on the list of approved visitors. On discovering this, I remedied the gap and also placed Michael and Ruth Casey on the same list. I hope to see all three on Thursday.

Pope Clement, the third successor of St Peter, wrote to the Church in Corinth to dampen their feuding and encourage unity. He urged them "to take the innocent and upright as (their) companions, for it is they who are God's chosen ones". I am blessed with my family and friends, who are caring for me in a wonderfully human and godly way. I owe them an enormous debt, as I also express my thanks to the thousands in many countries who are still praying for me, fasting, and interceding and the 1,500 or so who have written to me and continue to do so. They are all "God's chosen ones".

Brother Andrew was a holy Australian priest who worked closely for many years with St Teresa of Calcutta. He returned to Australia,

---

[1] Fr Peter Joseph, parish priest (pastor) at St Dominic's, Flemington, is a close friend of Cardinal Pell.

and it was my privilege to visit him in Fitzroy and pray with him as he lay dying. This is one of his prayers.

Most of us can't do much about our governments, and they seem to be able to do even less. But what you and I can do, and are called to do, is to live our lives with light, truth, and beauty. To be a little oasis of life with our family and for our neighbour. And that is possible for us, not if we try it alone, but if we sit still in solitude for a moment and turn to God with simple hope and trust.

P.S. only one vacancy in Unit 8 tonight.

Tuesday, 9 July 2019

A quiet day where the highlight was the visit of Sr Mary, the chaplain, to give me Holy Communion and remain for a chat.

I had an unexpected brief video link with Paul and Kartya. When called, I suspected there was some important news, but such was not the case. They had met the excluded Fr Joseph yesterday and wanted to set the score right for my next visits. They were happy when I explained that he was coming with the Caseys on Thursday. I mentioned that I had been pondering J's unusual request to forego a second trial. Paul's only response was that J's statements after the verdict were not typical.

No rain during my two exercise periods, although the sky was somewhat overcast.

Wrote a letter to one of my nieces and to a long-term prisoner who has written regularly and whom I regard as a friend, although we have never met. He has undergone surgery and feels unwell and a bit anxious. I outlined a couple of basic Catholic theological principles for him and then gave my advice on what were the strengths of the different English versions of the Bible. I urged him to obtain a Catholic version, or at least a version with the extra Old Testament Deuterocanonical books, explaining that "nasty" Catholics claim Luther excluded them because they were inconvenient for Protestant doctrine, e.g., Maccabees on praying for the dead.

Naturally, I am aware of the obligation to forgive those who wronged me with false allegations, be they fantasy or fiction. And I have done so and continue to do so. This was not difficult for the complainant, but takes more of an effort for anyone I suspect of shaping his recollections, or worse. I therefore prayed my rosary for one such suspect. It is not good to spend too much time considering these issues, but the decision to forgive is a bit like the gift of faith, which needs regular nourishment.

Sr Mary brought me the usual couple of sermons on the Sunday readings, and both were excellent. Thank heavens Sr Mary McGlone was back, so I did not have to take any exclusionary action with her replacement sermon writer!

Today she began by comparing John Lennon and Isaiah, with their two different versions of human flourishing.[2] My friend Katrina Lee, who lectured in media studies and deals with the media for me, explained to me years ago how influential the Beatles and the Rolling Stones were in spreading the norms of the sexual revolution of the sixties around the world.

I think Lennon had a Catholic background in his Liverpool youth, but he described his famous song "Imagine" as "anti-religious, anti-nationalistic, anti-conventional, anti-capitalistic", explaining his belief that if the world were not bound by heaven or hell, not looking for the transcendent and living for today, the world would be at peace, living as one. This version of socialist anarchy is dangerous nonsense. We are living with its consequences. Isaiah spelt out the importance of God's love, as his loving power works to satisfy all human hunger.

McGlone continues on to talk of the importance of vocations as the Gospel describes Jesus sending out seventy-two disciples to evangelize. She proposed the following caption for a vocations poster: "Enjoy the excitement and challenge of being lambs among the wolves!"

Our anonymous Marist preached on peace, the peace the disciples must offer to each house they visit. He explained the Jewish concept of *shalom*, a gift from God, being at one with God and with one another.

[2] Mary M. McGlone, "Imagine", *National Catholic Reporter*, 28 June–11 July 2019.

He explained in Australian terms that being at peace means wishing and working so our fellow Australians get "a fair go". While it isn't exact Gospel teaching, "a fair go for all" and "have a go" sum up much of what is good in Australia. He quoted Indira Gandhi, herself prime minister and daughter of Pandit Nehru, the first prime minister of the newly independent India. "You cannot shake hands with a clenched fist."

We finish, as our preacher did, with a section of the peace prayer ascribed to St Francis of Assisi.

> *Lord, make me an instrument of your peace;*
> *where there is hatred, let me sow love;*
> *where there is injury, pardon;*
> *where there is doubt, faith;*
> *where there is despair, hope;*
> *where there is darkness, light;*
> *where there is sadness, joy.*

Wednesday, 10 July 2019

Perhaps the most unexpected part of my day was to learn that I wasn't to have my hour in the gymnasium. My next turn was tomorrow, which would also enable me to go on Saturday, after the regular Friday gym closure for staff in-service training. I had no problem with this.

Had my two exercise periods outside under the 6 metres × 6 metres [20 ft × 20 ft] barred skylight. The morning was beautiful, clear and cool, while my almost an hour outside in the afternoon was under a cloud-covered sky. Sometimes I can hear the prisoners outside below me, sounding like a happy, noisy group of adult schoolboys. But not today. I had remarked yesterday to Sr Mary on the courtesy of the guards. She concurred willingly, saying that this represented a significant change of style from the old Pentridge days.[3] She added that there were always a "few snakes in the grass", with three in jail at the moment. It is not a pleasant job, and quite a number take stress leave. Until a correspondent from another jail suggested I use my DX

---

[3] Her Majesty's Prison Pentridge was an Australian jail first established in 1851 in Victoria and closed in May 1997.

number rather than my CRN number,[4] I hadn't much looked at it. It is 210666, i.e., concluding with the numerical symbol of the devil. Hard to think this was a coincidence.

Received a letter from another dreamer, but this man is very different from my earlier correspondent, who boasted of his power to predict the future, revealed in his second letter his delusions about his own role, and then changed his tune when his predictions did not eventuate.

The second writer is a regular correspondent, an inmate of a Victorian jail, and a serious and well-informed Catholic. He was upset by his dream.

The dream opened in a dark room with a well-dressed group drinking red wine, which included his mother. This scene changed as the space became full of light, which he realized was a windowless church of red bricks.

Jesus was on the large cross, when I appeared with the writer's mother and a monk whose face was obscured. The dialogue was in Italian.

He went and hugged his mother and me, asking what was going on. I replied in Italian that we were rejoicing because I had been freed from prison. "When?" he asked, and I replied, "On August 1st." He was pleased and tried unsuccessfully to speak to the monk, who disappeared.

Then he said to his mother that Padre Pio (St Pio of Pietrelcina) had heard his prayer. I smiled a kindly smile, and the vision ended. Naturally, he awoke agitated and confused at 3:11 am on June 29th, the feast of Sts Peter and Paul.

In real life, my friend was not pleased by the date, as he would like me "to go home yesterday and not on August 1st".

Far from making any extravagant claims, the letter listed seven problem questions, such as "Why did the monk have no face?" and "Was he my guardian angel?" He didn't suggest it might have been Padre Pio.

I have mentioned that my correspondent is a serious and well-informed Catholic, and I think he summed up the situation well:

[4] CRN is the number each prisoner announces at the regular roll calls. The cardinal's number was 218968. The DX number is used for mail. He avoided using this '666' number.

"August 1st and my dream probably have no meaning. Maybe it is my mind or the Evil One playing tricks on me. But I thought to let you know of my dream anyway." With my inexpert eye, I can see no sign of the devil at work.

It is best he has the last word. "Caro padre, August 1st is four weeks away. I just need to wait and see if it is just a silly dream or a premonition."

Some kind person, not the dreamer, had sent me a prayer to St Pio written by St John Paul the Great.

Teach us, we ask you, humility of heart so we may be counted among the little ones of the Gospel, to whom the Father promised to reveal the mysteries of his Kingdom.

Help us to pray without ceasing, certain that God knows what we need even before we ask him....

Accompany us on our earthly pilgrimage toward the blessed homeland, where we hope to arrive in order to contemplate forever the glory of the Father, the Son and the Holy Spirit. Amen.[5]

Thursday, 11 July 2019

Today is the feast of St Benedict, who was born in Norcia, central Italy, in 480. It is a small Italian town which I know well, before it was destroyed by two devastating earthquakes in 2016.

A Benedictine monastery was built over the tombs of Benedict and his sister Scholastica, which was quite unusual because it was on the town's main square, unlike the typical monastery built in rural isolation. The buildings had been vacant for decades until about twenty years ago, when a charismatic North American monk, Fr Cassian, who had been lecturing at San Anselmo in Rome, founded an international community there, following the old Rule of Benedict and

---

[5]John Paul II, homily for the canonization of St Pio of Pietrelcina (16 June 2012), no. 5, http://www.vatican.va/content/john-paul-ii/en/homilies/2002/documents/hf_jp-ii _hom_20020616_padre-pio.html.

WEEK 20: HOPES AND DREAMS

the old Tridentine Latin rite. It grew steadily over the years to about fifteen to twenty members, was much loved in the town, and many tourists drifted into the large church as the monks sang the Office in Latin.

The monks had set up a successful brewery, which I had blessed at its opening. This survived the first earthquake, as did a substantial part of the complex, which the monks were restoring. They had not long moved into a restored refectory, which I had also blessed, and were decorating the vaulted ceilings and walls with beautiful murals, the work of a gifted Italian artist. More than half the library survived the first shock with many of the books, which had been donated from Pope Benedict's personal library. Everything went down in the second quake, leaving only the façade of the church standing; the rest was otherwise completely demolished.

The town is surrounded by medieval walls and was the birthplace of the Emperor Vespasian, who with his son Titus completely destroyed Jerusalem in AD 70. It was evacuated and cordoned off, although I managed to get permission to enter and see the damage firsthand about three years ago. I am not sure what the situation is now, but restoration work is notoriously slow and difficult in financially embattled Italy.

The monks had been unable to obtain the freehold title to the monastery from the diocese and had purchased a good site, with a disused church and building in the nearby hills, to which they moved. When I called, they were living in a long simple hut, which held their chapel, eating, cooking space, and dormitory. Under the new prior, Fr Benedict, also from the United States, a convert from Judaism, I am confident they will continue going forward. As young priests after the Second Vatican Council, few of us envisioned, fifty years in the future, the development of a thriving new monastery, with highly educated monks, many from the United States, celebrating the Mass in Latin in the old rite and following the earlier Benedictine Rule, all in central Italy.

Monasticism developed toward the end of the third century in Egypt, when hermits came together for mutual support. Egypt became a Christian powerhouse, so that the patriarch of Alexandria sometimes strived to rival the papacy, and their theological school was rivalled only by Antioch. The monastic movement then spread to the West, where Benedict's Rule was originally one among many Western variations.

Because of its moderation, its emphasis on work and prayer, and brilliant leadership, the Benedictine movement eventually became a dominant feature of Western Catholicism for more than a thousand years. The monasteries were special targets of the Protestants and Henry VIII in the sixteenth century. Henry closed the English monasteries, confiscated their wealth, which was considerable, and, in a brilliant move which locked in their self-interested support, gave the local aristocracy a significant part of the loot. Recent scholarship has shown that the Catholic Church in England was not dead on her feet at the time of the Reformation and retained much popular support for generations. One consequence of the closure of the monasteries, often unremarked, was that the only sources of social welfare in England were closed. Thousands of the poor died.

Unlike the situation in Australia, the monasteries in England flourished once again there after Catholic Emancipation in 1829, and the first two archbishops of Sydney, Polding and Vaughan, were English Benedictines from Downside.

The early colony of New South Wales was a wild place, a bit like the medieval Dark Ages in Europe, but in both ambiences, the monks planted and conserved faith and learning. They did not long flourish in the Australian colonies, where they were replaced by Irish clergy who led their Irish-Australian congregations religiously and socially through parishes and schools. It was only under the Pope Pius XI, from the 1920s to 1930s, that Australians were appointed as bishops here.

One feature in many Benedictine monasteries is that excerpts from the Rule are put up in the corridors to prompt reflection. Sydney now has a retreat centre dedicated to Pope Benedict, known as B16, where the complex follows a monastic pattern and there is a splendid statue of St Benedict, Builder of Civilization, by the English sculptor Nigel Boonham. This centre also has its quotations from the Rule. Perhaps the most striking is as follows.

Run while you have the light of life lest the darkness of death overtake you.

Friday, 12 July 2019

Last night, England thrashed Australia in the semi-final of the one-day cricket World Cup at Edgbaston Stadium in Birmingham. Steve Smith batted well; not many others did, and our genuinely classy bowling attack only managed to capture two wickets. I am tempted to send a message to my English friend Fr Alexander offering congratulations and explaining that the shame of being in jail was less than the shame of such an annihilation at the hands of the "old enemy".

A much happier Thursday highlight was the visit of Ruth and Michael Casey with Fr Peter Joseph. We managed some good laughs, and the guards kindly gave us an hour, double the usual time. Peter was at the annual conference of the Australian Confraternity of Catholic Clergy held at Keilor Downs with Msgr Portelli.

Had my usual two outings yesterday in the small exercise yard, under an overcast sky. Still no gymnasium, but I was informed that the area was being used otherwise for a couple of days. I should be able to take my hour on Saturday.

Today I have just returned from an hour outside. It had been raining, but was still overcast; the sky cleared, and the sun made a welcome breakthrough at one stage, and we had a single burst of bird song, but I did not manage to sight any of them. Strangely, I was not allowed a second spell of exercise, although I had more than thirty minutes first up. I will explain tomorrow my preference for two outings a day.

I have taken to using my time outside, after I've done my twenty minutes' exercise, for my daily meditations. Outside under a section of sky in the fresh air seems no less a sacred space than my small cell. I usually take one of two aspirations for repetition. The first is commonly used for meditation: "Jesus, Son of the Living God, have mercy on us", while the second is of my own devising, once again turned toward Christ: "My Lord, my God, my Creator, Redeemer, Brother, and Friend." When I first began using this simple prayer nearly twenty years ago, I had not included "Creator". However, as my thoroughly amateur knowledge of science and evolution increased through reading over the years, I became more and more impressed by the beauty and complexity of the universe and by the extraordinary improbability, the beyond human calculation (almost), of a successful evolution. To go simply from amino acid to life requires one path in $10^{40,000}$ options. The mystery of the universe has helped to strengthen my faith. To believe the Supreme Intelligence is good, loving, and interested in us requires another step, of course.

From my early years, I knew and accepted that God loved me, but even as an adult I found it hard to nominate Christ as a friend. Strangely, I had no problem with nominating him as a brother. Perhaps "friend" seemed a bit too informal for someone educated in the 1950s as an Australian Catholic to describe his relationship with the Second Person of the Trinity. The fear of God takes many forms, and only perfect love drives out fear. I now find it easier to acknowledge that a person can be imperfect and still remain God's friend and a friend of his Son.

I believe all beginners need some structure as they start to meditate, and I still do. What is important is to keep praying and not to worry too much about whether our prayer form is higher or firmly on a plateau.

The supply of letters has slowed, but they are still arriving at about six to ten a day.

Yesterday, the Indian physio turned up unexpectedly and worked on my shoulder.

Today, we have a distressed shouter at the other end, after some days of comparative quiet. He is claiming loudly and colourfully that something is not fair. We have a couple of warders on duty whom I have not seen previously.

Paul and Kartya called for a good chat, without any legal news, reporting that they have still been prevented from leaving new magazines for me.

The classic Christian "mantra" is a good conclusion.

Jesus, Son of the Living God, have mercy on us.

Saturday, 13 July 2019

Yesterday we had a replay of last year's AFL grand final between Collingwood and West Coast, with a different result, after a terrific and close game. Although a long-time anti-Collingwood fan (until their supporters took up collections to help Richmond remain in

Victoria when we were threatened with banishment to Queensland), I supported them in both matches against the "foreigners" from the West, and their win last night by one point was memorable. A wealth of sport on the TV with the final week of the tennis at Wimbledon and the first week of the Tour de France, which I watch a bit during the day, marvelling at the beauties of the French countryside.

Today was a pleasant day, although it was overcast, when I managed to regain my two regular outings. Every Friday is used for in-service training, so the warders were "fill-ins" who did not know my routine and didn't even collect the rubbish. As an old hand now in solitary confinement (the maximum is usually no more than three months), I am attached to the regular program, although I am certain any suggestions along these lines would not be welcome!

Had nearly an hour in the gymnasium, doing some circuits bouncing the basketball first with one hand and then with the other. I was pleased to find my coordination improved a lot with practice, and I increased the number of exercises with the weights for my arms and thighs. Progress is steady, although my sense of balance still needs to improve. I managed to climb the fifteen steps out of the gymnasium without hanging onto the bannister, although I only risked the last six steps on my descent without the bannister. As yet, when climbing stairs by myself, I am more than usually awkward and ungainly. I suppose that sitting in a chair nearly all the day, every day is not conducive to improving one's balance.

The gymnasium is a boon to myself both physically and psychologically, and I am sure this is true for the other prisoners. A plaque proclaims that it was opened in 1989. A good move. One long-term prisoner, who helped to set up the altar when I celebrated the last Christmas Mass at Pentridge in 1996, wrote that he himself "can remember a time when there was not even power in the cells in which citizens were placed, with everyone required to shower in an outside shower area with even a bucket parade for bodily waste, with no toilet in the cell". I hope and presume not all sections were like this, more than ten years after the Victorian Council of Churches report on the prisons, in which I then participated as a young bishop from the other side of the fence!

The July-August issue of the *Quadrant* arrived. In this prison section, we are allowed six books and six magazines which can be changed over, but to obtain clarity on what the property section believes is on your lists, and sometimes to obtain new copies of magazines like *The Spectator* and *Quadrant*, is often like trying to post a package in an Italian post office; it cannot be achieved in under three attempts. Staff are rotated through the different jail sections and offer different levels of cooperation, regularly refusing to accept new books or magazines to be kept in the office until items can be signed out by the prisoner. It took a week's work to obtain this *Quadrant*, and a cooperative local warder has asked for a comprehensive statement of what I am supposed to have in my cells, so I can respond appropriately. He explained that things move slowly in jail, and I agreed.

This is the third issue of *Quadrant* which has contained at least one article strongly supporting my innocence and lamenting the whole sorry procedure. The editor, Keith Windschuttle, has done me a great service.

The editor's column was headed "The Majesty of the Law" and concluded with these words: "Those of us who still believe the traditional notion of the law's majesty remains an essential social pillar that helps preserve us from barbarism can only hope that the B-grade spectacle we have witnessed at so many places in the persecution of George Pell is an aberration and not a portent of some squalid, unwatchable future."

I pray that Windschuttle's hope is realised just as I pray that my appeal is successful and that my friends and support group, with myself, will have the wisdom to move forward in the most effective way to ensure that what happened to me does not happen to another innocent Australian for a long time.